LADIES, UPSTAIRS!

LADIES,
Upstairs!

My Life in Politics and After

MONIQUE BÉGIN

McGill-Queen's University Press
Montreal & Kingston • London • Chicago

ISBN 978-0-7735-5522-8 (cloth)
ISBN 978-0-7735-5583-9 (ePDF)
ISBN 978-0-7735-5584-6 (ePUB)

Legal deposit first quarter 2019
Bibliothèque nationale du Québec

Printed in Canada on acid-free paper that is 100% ancient forest free
(100% post-consumer recycled), processed chlorine free

Funded by the   Financé par le
Government   gouvernement   Canada Council   Conseil des arts
of Canada   du Canada   for the Arts   du Canada

We acknowledge the support of the Canada Council for the Arts,
which last year invested $153 million to bring the arts to Canadians
throughout the country.

Nous remercions le Conseil des arts du Canada de son soutien. L'an
dernier, le Conseil a investi 153 millions de dollars pour mettre de
l'art dans la vie des Canadiennes et des Canadiens de tout le pays.

Library and Archives Canada Cataloguing in Publication

Bégin, Monique, 1936–, author
Ladies, upstairs! : my life in politics and after / Monique Bégin.

Includes index.
Issued in print and electronic formats.
ISBN 978-0-7735-5522-8 (hardcover).
–ISBN 978-0-7735-5583-9 (ePDF).
–ISBN 978-0-7735-5584-6 (ePUB)

1. Bégin, Monique, 1936–. 2. Canada – Politics and government –
1963–1984. 3. Cabinet ministers – Canada – Biography. 4. Women
cabinet ministers – Canada – Biography. 5. Politicians – Canada –
Biography. 6. Women politicians – Canada – Biography. 7. College
teachers – Canada – Biography. 8. Autobiographies. I. Title.

FC626.B42A3 2019   971.064'4092   C2018-904255-9
                                        C2018-904256-7

Tout passe et tout reste
Mais notre destin est de passer
Passer en faisant des chemins
Des chemins sur la mer
~Antonio Machado

Every journey has a secret destination
of which the traveler is not aware.
~Martin Buber

Two roads diverged in a wood, and I –
I took the one less traveled by,
And that has made all the difference.
~Robert Frost

Contents

Foreword

BOB RAE

Politics is known as a harsh business, full of unprincipled people more interested in themselves and their own ambitions than anything else. It is said to be a ruthless game, where friendship and loyalty count for little and ideas and talent mean even less.

Having had the immense pleasure of working with Monique Bégin for nearly forty years, I can only say that none of the above applies in even the remotest sense to her. Hers has been a life dedicated to public policies that have directly improved the lives of millions of Canadians. She is interested in ideas but not ideologies. She is deeply principled but is also pragmatic and practical. She has made friends in all parties that have lasted for decades. Her word is her bond. Anyone interested in a life in politics would do well to learn from what she has done and how she's done it.

I knew her first when she was a minister and I was a rookie NDP member of Parliament. She was changing a universal benefit into a more focused program that would do more for those who needed it most. What impressed me was her willingness to go beyond the partisan battle and engage in a real discussion. This was not a game to her, it was something she thought made sense. She heard the arguments against, weighed them, and then sent notes suggesting a further dialogue. She was charming, disarming, funny, and above all, engaged. She won the vote, but she also won the argument.

Her stature grew with her appointment as minister of health, and here again she took problems and criticisms seriously. When New Democratic members of Parliament brought forward cases in question period of individuals and families being charged extra for surgeries that were already covered by medicare, a debate began in the country that concluded with the passage of the Canada Health Act in 1984 and the subsequent decision of most provinces to ban the practice. Her passion for social justice never wavered, nor did her gift for public administration.

When I became premier of Ontario, I asked Monique to take on the task of reforming Ontario's public education system. With her fellow commissioners she did an outstanding job and produced a report that became the blueprint for changes and improvements that have stood the test of time and many changes of government.

These great public achievements are matched by her style: she is fiercely pragmatic, insists on facts and evidence, is never afraid to do battle for what she is convinced needs to happen, and does it all with a huge smile and a great laugh. She has won hearts as well as minds.

A deeply progressive liberal, a passionate federalist, a feminist, and a dear friend, I count Monique as a guide and an inspiration. Long may she continue to make her outstanding contribution to our public life and happiness as a country.

The Hon. Bob Rae, PC, CC, OOnt, QC

Top: My mother, Marie-Louise Vanhavre, as a young woman in Brussels, 1929.

Bottom: My father, J.L.O. (Lucien) Bégin, in Paris, 1925.

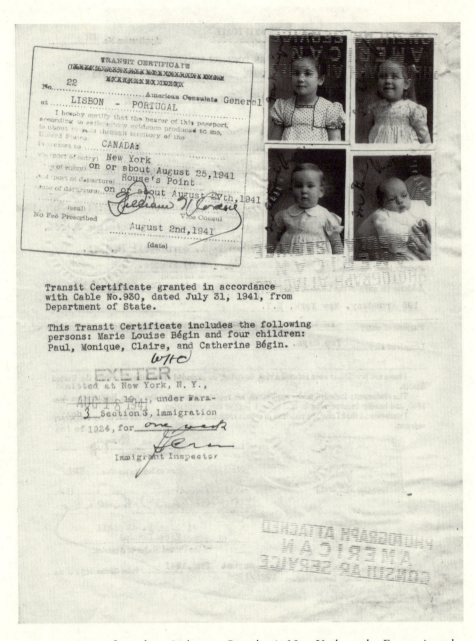

TRANSIT CERTIFICATE

No. 22
at LISBON - PORTUGAL American Consulate General
I hereby certify that the bearer of this passport,
according to satisfactory evidence produced to me,
is about to pass through territory of the
United States

Premises to CANADA

(port of entry) New York
of entry on or about August 25, 1941
and (port of departure) Rouse's Point
(date of departure) on or about August 27th, 1941

(seal)
No Fee Prescribed
Vice Consul
August 2nd, 1941
(date)

Transit Certificate granted in accordance
with Cable No.930, dated July 31, 1941, from
Department of State.

This Transit Certificate includes the following
persons: Marie Louise Bégin and four children:
Paul, Monique, Claire, and Catherine Bégin.

EXETER
Admitted at New York, N.Y.,
AUG 18 1941, under Para-
3 Section 3, Immigration
of 1924, for one week

Immigrant Inspector

Our transit certificate from Lisbon to Canada via New York on the *Exeter*, issued
in Lisbon by the US Department of State, 31 July 1941. We landed in New York
on 25 August 1941.

Mme Bégin mit au monde dans un fossé un enfant qui fut tué par les nazis

Catane attaqué

ROME, 19, (P.A.) — Le communiqué du haut commandement fasciste rapporte que, le matin du 18 août, un appareil ennemi a jeté plusieurs bombes près de Catane, en Sicile. L'attaque n'aurait pas causé de dommages ou de victimes. Les raids aériens des 15 et 16 août ont fait 25 morts et 37 blessés.

Prisonniers libérés

CHALONS-SUR-MARNE, 19.—(P. C.) — Les autorités occupantes ont résolu de libérer les derniers officiers français qu'on ont fait la grande-guerre de 1914 qu'ils demeurent encore dans des camps de concentration.

NEW-YORK, 19. — Le transatlantique américain "Exeter" est arrivé hier de Lisbonne à Jersey-City.

Parmi les 195 passagers il y avait des Américains qui rentrent d'un séjour en Europe; il y a aussi des Européens qui viennent chercher ici un abri et la paix.

Un Canadien, M. Joseph Bégin, ingénieur minier, qui a demeuré en France pendant plusieurs années est rentré avec sa femme et ses quatre enfants. Il rapporte une histoire des plus poignantes sur la façon dont il s'échappa de Seine.

Lors de l'invasion allemande, il suivit l'armée qui s'éloigna de Paris pour retraiter vers le sud. Pendant cette fuite tragique, Mme Bégin donna naissance à un enfant. Elle n'eut d'autre refuge que le fossé de la grand'route. Comme les Messerschmitts faisaient pleuvoir les bombes de toutes parts, le nouveau-né fut tué. Le père donna la sépulture la plus convenable possible à son enfant, dans le champ voisin, tandis que la mère resta étendue 72 heures dans le fossé, ne mangeant que des croûtes de pain et ne buvant que de l'eau.

Quand on parvint enfin à se libérer il dépasse sur le moment et se mit à manger et à boire le produit que M. Bégin avait pu obtenir. La semaine de la dernière ville rejoignait sa famille à Dayton où il tient l'hôtel Biltmore.

M. René Montérand est un autre passager de l'Exeter. Il se rend à Dayton où il tient l'hôtel Biltmore.

La plupart des passagers de l'Exeter appartient de l'Europe en plaide-er général pour de la nourriture.

Prévenir

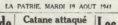

Echappés à la terreur nazie

A peine deux jours avant l'entrée des Allemands à Paris, CLAIRE, MONIQUE, CATHERINE et bébé PAUL furent emportés par leurs parents vers le sud. Leur père, JOSEPH L. BEGIN, ingénieur minier canadien-français, les ramène tous de France à Montréal.

Les Soviets recourent à la stratégie de Napoléon pour

Les conseillers veulent l'abolition des repas avec les liqueurs

Les représentants de l'élément ouvrier, au conseil municipal, ont l'intention de soumettre, à la prochaine réunion du conseil municipal, certains projets d'amendements qu'ils croient nécessaires à la loi des liqueurs qui a été adoptée à la dernière session de la Législature provinciale.

Lors du congrès de la Fédération provinciale du travail, qui eut lieu à St-Jean, en fin de semaine, les délégués ont appuyé une résolution de l'Union des maristes, qui réclame la discontinuation des repas de 40 sous, lorsqu'une personne se présente dans un restaurant pour y prendre une consommation quelconque.

Le conseiller J.E. Gauvin, l'un des délégués du conseil des métiers et du travail, a déclaré qu'il était fortement en faveur d'un amendement à la loi des liqueurs en ce sens, parce que cette loi selon lui, entraîne la perte d'une forte quantité d'aliments.

"Je suis en faveur de tel amendement, et je suis assuré que la majorité des conseillers se sont de mon avis" a déclaré M. Gauvin.

Le conseiller Hugh Graham, autre délégué du conseil des métiers et du travail, a l'intention d'étudier l'affaire avec ses collègues, avant la reprise du 2 septembre.

Le conseiller J.E. Foucault, l'un des représentants de ce conseil catholiques, a déclaré que la chose l'intéressait qu'il allait en faire une étude approfondie afin de pouvoir en discuter lors de la reprise du mois de septembre. Les conseillers Arthur Landry, F. Hooley, Victor Lévesque et Camille Côté sont en faveur de l'amendement.

Double accusation contre M. Deyglun

M. Henri Deyglun, de Montréal,

Having settled in Montreal, very European Sundays for Mother and the seven children; here we are at the Botanical Garden, 1947.

Getting permission to enter the NDG Girl Guides opened up a world
of camaraderie and escape into nature. I am eleven years old at my
first summer camp, Lac L'Achigan, in the Laurentians, August 1947.

Classroom teacher at Collège Cardinal-Léger, in Rosemont, my last year as a teacher before starting my full-time graduate degree in sociology at Université de Montréal. Montreal, 1957–58.

Co-founding the Quebec Federation of Women in 1966 under Thérèse Casgrain's leadership would somehow change my life. After her too-short tenure as a senator, she came back in my ministerial life, helping me time and again.

Top: Judge Doris Ogilvy and Dr Jacques Henripin discussing the family law and services chapter of the report (1967–70).

Bottom: Chair Florence Bird and myself reviewing the report of the Royal Commission on the Status of Women in Canada.

The Globe and Mail

TORONTO, THURSDAY, APRIL 12, 1973

—Studio Impact

The women of the House

hese five women participate in the business of Parliament facing Olym-   of Flora MacDonald, Grace MacInnis, Jeanne Sauvé, Albanie Morin,
an odds. They are outnumbered in the House by 259 men. The story   and Monique Bégin, uncommon women in Ottawa, is told on Page W1.

The iconic *Globe and Mail* picture of the five women elected to the House of Commons on 30 October 1972, including the first three from Quebec. We were outnumbered by 259 men! Credit: Studio Impact.

As the new parliamentary secretary for Allan J. MacEachen, minister of external affairs, I represent Canada at the twenty-fifth anniversary of the Colombo Plan, Colombo, Sri Lanka, 2–5 December 1975. Prime Minister Sirima Bandaranaike receives me most graciously. Credit: Joe Perera, Colombo.

Having joined Pierre Trudeau's Cabinet in September 1976, as minister of national revenue, my first official task is the sod-turning for the new Shawinigan Taxation building in Jean Chrétien's riding, October 1976.

I was a new minister when, in awe and honoured, I received a first doctorate *honoris causa* from St Thomas University in Fredericton for my work for human rights. May 1977.

Prologue

How did a young French-Canadian woman, a person who distrusted politics, become one of the most powerful ministers in Ottawa and then abandon politics and go on to establish a high-profile academic public career, not just in Canada but internationally, after leaving the political fray? How was she able to do this despite starting with few advantages, suffering from crippling shyness, and frequently finding herself in circles unwelcoming to women?

These memoirs are my attempt to answer these questions, both for myself and for all those interested in the issues that have driven me throughout my life: inequality, health care, poverty, feminism, human rights, and federalism.

But first I must acknowledge the larger changes in Canada and in the world around me throughout my public life. My own trajectory did not occur in a vacuum; we all respond to the context in which we live.

In June 1963 Canada was a country full of hopes and contradictions. Fresh from Paris, where I had pursued my doctoral studies, I came home to find Canadians enjoying the benefits of what economist Galbraith had called the "affluent society," while Prime Minister Lester B. Pearson headed a minority Liberal government and John Diefenbaker led the Opposition. But I could feel the winds of change. Quebec was in the grip of the Quiet Revolution. The counterculture, spawned in California, was sweeping across the continent, bringing with it student uprisings, rock concerts, and demands for sexual freedom. The second wave of feminism had begun.

I was then given the opportunity to prove myself as the executive secretary of the Royal Commission on the Status of Women in Canada (1967–70). At thirty-one I had an on-the-job crash course to organize and run a national royal commission on time and on budget. The commission's report was a huge success, with women across the country ensuring action on its recommendations. A defining moment for feminism.

It was now the 1970s. I stayed in Ottawa, accepting an invitation to become a civil servant at the Canadian Radio-television and Telecommunications Commission (CRTC) because of the wonderful leadership of Pierre Juneau. That decade turned into an unanticipated and challenging economic and political time that should have been the great years of Pierre Trudeau's "Just Society" and "participatory democracy." Circumstances rapidly derailed these aspirations: the FLQ crisis, the War Measures Act, divisive regionalism, the first Quebec separatist government, the oil crisis.

Once more my life then went in an unplanned direction. I joined the Liberal Party of Canada, ran for office in the October 1972 general election, and won a Montreal riding. I served as an MP in Trudeau's minority government. In his majority return in 1974, I went from backbencher to parliamentary secretary and then to minister of national revenue. I joined Trudeau's Cabinet after the dreams had faded, the test of time already wearing heavily on the PM and his government.

Moving to the position of minister of national health and welfare a year later, in September 1977, my policy objectives were almost crushed by the first wave of neo-conservative economic theories springing from the work of 1976 Nobel Prize–winning economist Milton Friedman: monetarist theory and the all-powerful ideology of the free market. The Liberal government was defeated in May 1979; the decade, however, ended with the Liberals, who had convinced Trudeau to come back as leader, defeating in turn Joe Clark's short-lived Conservative government.

"Welcome to the 1980s!" Pierre Trudeau had said on his extraordinary comeback on 18 February. I was fortunate to be reappointed to lead the biggest department, National Health and Welfare. However, the welfare state built over time in the West following the Second World War was under duress, helped by the very serious economic recession in a number of countries, with "stagflation" in 1982 at home. Trudeau announced his retirement in February 1984 (but stayed until the end of June), and I had long since also decided to leave politics but could not tell anyone. In September 1984 Brian Mulroney became prime minister. At that time, in my prime at forty-eight, I changed careers, embracing life after politics as an academic, teaching – quite a new challenge.

The 1990s saw me in a newly created academic senior management role, dean of the Faculty of Health Sciences (separate from the Faculty of Medicine), at the University of Ottawa. I truly lived the 1990s discovering Ontario politics. At Premier Bob Rae's pressing request, I agreed to co-chair on a full-time basis the Ontario Royal Commission on Learning, while continuing to serve as dean. I was also invited to join my first international commission: the Independent Commission on Population and Quality of Life.

In July 1997, despite my university president's request to remain as dean until the new millennium, I decided to retire. At sixty-one I needed a break; I spent some time travelling in Europe. Back home, I participated in key research initiatives, steering committees, and task forces, mostly on our health care system. After repeated invitations by the dean of administration to join the University of Ottawa's master of health administration program as a regular visiting professor, I accepted in the fall of 1998.

As we entered the year 2000, the Rio World Summit on Sustainable Development adopted the Millennium Goals. The social equity agenda, which had been in full retreat for more than two decades, was back on track. But international terrorism derailed these dreams: the 9/11 attacks, the Iraq and Afghanistan wars. The last straw was the 2008 world financial crisis.

I spent that decade actively participating in developing the master of health administration program. In 2005 I was appointed a member of my second international commission, the World Health Organization Commission on Social Determinants of Health – an extraordinary experience.

Finally, in 2011, I truly retired: from the university, from boards, from committees; I also resolved to no longer accept speaking engagements. Then, in the summer of 2014, I totally surprised myself and started writing these memoirs, wanting to tell my story of extraordinary adventures that very few men – and even fewer women – have lived through.

My following story unfolds in chronological order except for Part III – the five chapters describing my years in National Health and Welfare, thematic, but lived concurrently.

PART ONE

Beginnings

From Europe to Canada:
Life as a Refugee

As far back as I can recall, I have always felt different: belonging to two worlds, constantly finding myself at odds with my surroundings.

I was born in Rome on a Sunday afternoon, 1 March 1936, at the Clinica Sant' Anna on Via Garigliano, christened on 5 March in the clinic's chapel, and registered in due form at the British Consulate as a "British subject by birth" five days later. My father, Lucien Bégin, then forty-one years old, was an electrical and sound engineer. He was designing and installing the Fono-Roma Studios at Cinecittà (Rome) and the Picorno Studios at Tirrenia (Pisa) – an assignment from his Paris employer, the Société de Matériel Acoustique (SMA). Mother, who was born Marie-Louise Vanhavre, was a thirty-year-old Flemish accountant from Brussels who had eloped with Dad in February 1935. (They had met in Brussels, where he had been sent to reorganize the Belgian branch of SMA, where she worked.) I was their first child.

They both relished living in Rome. They spoke fluent Italian and enjoyed the people, the food, the places, the cultural life. I have a few photos of the two of them, radiant and in love, and of Dad enjoying life with his technical team at an outdoor production site at Cinecittà. There is no photograph of their wedding, which took place in the parish church of Saint Gioacchino in downtown Rome, with a few local people serving as witnesses. I like to fantasize about what Mom wore that day. I know it was not the now-customary long white dress. Rather, this slim young woman of medium height wore a long-sleeved printed silk dress in a darker colour ... very 1930s. She who had always loved custom-made hats from a milliner must have sported a small hat, turned up on one side, revealing the low chignon she wore all her life. Their honey-moon was in Capri – how romantic we, their children, found that! Through years of peace and war, Mother wore her wedding ring, a classic round, clear, quality diamond in a platinum setting.

I was barely two months old when Dad was called back to Paris. After living for six weeks in a hotel, our little family settled in an apartment in the Fifteenth Arrondissement for a year before moving to a larger apartment in Bois-Colombes, a nearby northwestern Paris suburb. There my two sisters were born: Claire in November 1937, and Catherine in April 1939.

It had been a long and fascinating journey for both my parents to this point. Born in 1895 in Saint-Henri-de-Lévis, across from Quebec City, Father was the third of eight children who had survived. His parents were Marie Fontaine and Jean-Baptiste Bégin, the eighth generation of Bégins who had settled in New France. Too poor to own a farm, Jean-Baptiste was a railroad worker for the Quebec Central in Lévis who moved the family to Mégantic when Dad was young; his father's employer was building rail lines to carry asbestos and other natural resources from there to the state of Maine. Curious and bright, the young Lucien finished high school in Lac-Mégantic at sixteen and got his first job with the Canadian Pacific Railway, working there for five years as a certified telegraph operator until June 1916.

Now twenty-one years old, and having graduated from the Marconi School in Montreal as a radio-telegrapher and taken evening courses in mathematics and chemistry, he registered with the Canadian Department of the Naval Service (his studies had been interrupted by the First World War and his voluntary enrolment on OHMS warships). Then it was back to Marconi as instructor-in-chief. After taking charge of the Louisbourg transatlantic station for five months, he was posted to Montreal as chief engineer responsible for the design, testing, and production of the first experimental broadcasting station in Canada. Nineteen months later he left for London, England, to study electricity; shortly afterwards, on 16 March 1921, he took a train from St Pancras Station to Gare Saint-Lazare in Paris. (A few years ago, I found his original train ticket in a box of documents we had never opened!)

At long last, real life had begun for this young French-Canadian adventurer. The Roaring Twenties had just started, and he was exploring the Old World, discovering fine wines and gourmet food, joining in passionate discussions on art and literature. As a handsome bachelor, he was the life of the party. He found a job right away as senior technician in high frequency, pursued studies in electricity, discovered and studied philosophy, had several inventions patented – by himself or with his great friend from Montreal, the architect Émile Venne, who was also living in Paris – and setting up his own engineering research company. In 1929, he got a job with SMA.

Mother, the only child of Jean-Baptiste Vanhavre and Angèle Crispeyn, was born in Brussels in 1906. Like many Belgians during the First World War, the eight-year-old Maria Ludovica (Marie-Louise) and her mother had to escape to England – in their case, alone on a small boat with a smuggler. Her father would join them later. By the end of the war in 1918 Mother had completed elementary school (Grade 6) at the Ursuline convent in Bexleyheath, in southeast London. She went to high school back in Brussels, then took the three-year commercial course at École Couvreur, which still exists. Mom lost her father in January 1926, when she was twenty. Her mother then married a retired police officer, Jean-Baptiste Essemaeker – we called him *Bon papa*, as Mom did.

Mother had natural class; she was pleasant company and level-headed. She had a British sense of humour and didn't fail to notice the absurdities around her. A rather quiet person, the too rare photographs of her as a young woman portray her beautiful oval face in a melancholy pose. She did not like showy things but rather chose old European quality in everything – textiles, perfume, appearances, clothing, language, and so on – and she passed these tastes on to me. She loved photography and played the violin. She also had a fine voice and loved singing lighter tunes, operettas and lyrical works, as well as Wagner. Before her marriage in Rome, she had been an assistant accountant, shorthand typist, and translator (English to French, and vice versa), for various employers, starting with the Neuhaus Chocolate Company. When she was angry, we knew it was not too serious if she reprimanded us in Flemish, of which we knew only one or two words. (It was even less serious if we were lectured in *brusseleir*, the Brussels patois.)

We lived in Paris because my dad loved that international city: the City of Light, the door to Europe. He was a true European even before Jean Monnet's European Union, with its roots of nurturing peace and solidarity among citizens of many neighbouring countries sharing an old civilization. It was a part of the world where art, culture, ideas, and the best of human values were recognized in a way he could make his own. As a senior sound and electricity engineer who specialized in the movie industry, his expertise was in demand. While he knew the United States and Canada, his country of origin, he felt that they had already become overly materialistic and that brutal capitalism was their common credo. As for the Quebec Catholic Church, he loathed its narrow-mindedness and ignorance. In the months before war was declared in 1939, it seems he had applied for French citizenship.

In that spring of 1939, despite the fact that the Third Reich had already annexed Austria the previous March (and soon Czechoslovakia as well), the first public opinion poll from IFOP (the French Gallup) showed that in May 1939, 67 per cent of the respondents did not believe France would inevitably be led into war. It would be only in July that that figure dropped to 34 per cent of respondents, when Germany's invasion of Poland seemed inescapable. In June of that year, like everyone around him, Dad had received a formal notice from the municipality of Bois-Colombes to send the measurements of his and Mother's faces and to pick up their gas masks at once (for 140 francs), which he did. (Earlier, on 12 May, General Georges Vanier, the "minister of Canada" at our Paris Legation, had sent all registered Canadians a letter asking them to get a gas mask and follow all future instructions from the French authorities regarding evacuation.)

On 31 August, three days before the declaration of war, Dad had written a letter to his seventy-two-year-old mother, who was living in Farnham, Quebec. (While our Belgian family, Mother's family, knew us – I have pictures of me as a baby in the arms of my Flemish grandparents – our Canadian family did not. So Dad had included with the letter photos of his three daughters.) The letter still distresses me today, nearly eighty years later, for it shows how many in France believed there would have to be a negotiated solution instead of a war:

> Depuis plusieurs jours déjà l'on évacue les femmes, les enfants et les vieillards vers la province. Il est malheureusement probable que Marie-Louise et les enfants devront en faire autant d'ici un ou deux jours car la situation politique internationale n'a pas l'air de s'améliorer – bien au contraire. Nous ignorons encore dans quelle direction il vaudrait mieux aller; dans la famille de Marie-Louise, à Bruxelles, ou quelque part en Normandie. Quant à moi, je devrais prendre mes trois semaines de vacances à partir de lundi, mais, vu les nombreux rappels parmi nos employés, il n'est pas impossible que j'aie à reporter mes vacances à une date ultérieure afin de combler une partie du vide. D'autre part, je me propose de mettre mes vacances à profit afin de rechercher un nouvel emploi où je serais mieux rétribué. Il n'est d'ailleurs pas impossible que j'aille faire quelques sondages en Espagne, du côté de Barcelone; tout dépend du résultat de la demande de visa de mon passeport que j'ai présentée au Consulat espagnol et à laquelle je compte avoir une réponse dès après-demain.*

Sending us to Belgium or Normandy ... Wanting to go to Spain, which was just emerging from a terrible civil war ... He speaks with

---

*A few days ago they started evacuating women, children, and the elderly to the countryside. Unfortunately, Marie-Louise and the children will probably have to be evacuated in the next couple of days, as the international political situation does not seem to be improving – quite the contrary. We don't know yet which is the best place to go: to Marie-Louise's family in Brussels or somewhere in Normandy. I am supposed to take my three weeks of holidays starting Monday, but given that many of our employees have been called up, I might have to postpone my holidays to help fill the gap. On another note, I would like to use my holidays to look for a new job where I will be better paid. It's possible that I will go and make a few inquiries in Spain, in Barcelona; it all depends on what happens with my request for a visa that I submitted to the Spanish consulate and to which I hope to have an answer by the day after tomorrow.

optimism of his request for a visa and dreams of better employment opportunities in Barcelona. This is three days before France is at war!

Poland was invaded by Hitler's armies on 1 September 1939. France and Great Britain declared war on Germany two days later. The evening of that same day, a Sunday – carrying luggage filled with basic necessities and clothing, and bringing the massive baby carriage with us – Dad, Mom, and their three daughters hastily left Bois-Colombes by train. The next day, we stopped in Buzançais (Indre), a tiny village of the Berri some 300 kilometres south of Paris. Why Buzançais, I wonder? How would Dad have heard of it? We knew no one there. Was it one of the suggested places for evacuation? This village of only 4,000 people was not even on the main train route from Paris to Toulouse and the south of France. We had had to change trains at Châteauroux, as Buzançais was 25 kilometres west of that city.

After a few days at the local hotel, Dad found a tiny, empty, very modest house with a garden just outside the village. He settled us there before going back to work in Paris. Dad would come to stay with us more or less regularly on weekends, as trains, although no longer on schedule, were still operating. In the two dozen photographs I have that Mom and Dad took of our time in Buzançais, we are outside: sitting on the dusty ground playing with two rubber dolls (mine was Princess Charlotte, a young girl dressed for the outdoors in 1930s fashions), or eating outside – with baby Catherine, always smiling, in her carriage. Everything was stored in cardboard boxes, as there was not much furniture. For Mother there was a reclining beach chair, but no radio, no telephone, not a book, nothing to read, no newspaper, not even a welcoming village. The toilet was in a cement-block outhouse in the garden. Catherine, four months, Claire, almost two years, and I, the responsible eldest at four, are always smiling and relaxed in the photos. Claire and I wear crowns of flowers made by Mom: daisies for the blonde Claire and buttercups for my thick brown curls. As children, we didn't hear anything about a war.

My earliest memories are from Buzançais. When we arrived, I was three and a half; I celebrated my fourth birthday there before we returned home to Paris. I recall going with Mom to wash clothing, bedsheets, and more, beating them on the stones in the river, with the local women chatting to each other a little further down. The washed clothes were then laid out in the meadows to dry. I also have memories of running down fields filled with flowers. On Easter Sunday in 1940, Dad took Claire and me to Pellevoisin, twelve kilometres away, to pray at the shrine to the Virgin Mary that honoured Our Lady's appearances to a poor, sick servant.

We stayed in Buzançais from 4 September 1939 to 11 April 1940: in fact, for most of *la drôle de guerre* – the British "Funny War" or American "Phoney War" – when the Germans, after having settled in part of Alsace and Lorraine, remained inactive and invisible on French soil. Convinced, like many others, that there would definitely be a negotiated solution to avoid a war, Father decided to take us all back to Paris. As we were now a family of five, he had rented a sunny and comfortable new two-storey house with a garden and several fruit trees at 29 rue de la Marée (now rue Gabriel-Péri), in Taverny, near Pontoise, northwest of Paris. We were to live there for less than two months.

I loved that house! The first thing I noticed were the French doors opening onto the garden, so different and more joyful than our earlier serious and dark Parisian windows. I recall to this day the elegant Art Deco furniture Father had designed then had made by the Catalucci Studio in Rome. Lacquered in light sage green and light pink, the cabinets, dressers, a dining table and chairs, and bookcases remained the epitome of luxury for the child I was. The same is true of the warm, pale brown patterned textile covering the elegant and comfortable sofas, armchairs, and ottomans in the living room, which I would probably still recognize. I will always love the Italian Lenci porcelain *Mother and Child* that Father brought from Rome to Paris and which he recovered in 1948 and shipped back to Canada. With SMA closing up shop in Europe, Father had started working for Metro-Goldwyn-Mayer in the Ninth Arrondissement in Paris.

April came and went. France was still in the *drôle de guerre*, with no German divisions around. Suddenly, early on 10 May, German bombers dropped bombs six kilometres from our house. At the same time, German troops invaded Luxembourg, the Netherlands, and Belgium. From that day on, Father organized some basic supplies and stored them in the basement (I recall the candles and boxes covered in

burlap), blacked out the house windows as requested by the municipality, and explained to us how to go downstairs and sit quietly as soon as
we heard the air-raid sirens. In mid-May and afterwards, German panz-
ers invaded France from the northeast to the north Atlantic coast. Mom
was always careful to maintain an atmosphere of calm and love – as
she would do all through the war. My memory of myself down in the
Taverny basement is of someone serious and curious following all that
was going on. My sister Claire was always a nervous, anxious child
(and, later, adult), afraid of everything and of nature: spiders, flies,
worms, storms, and more. She did not eat everything, as I did. Catherine, who had a baby face so round that I can still hear Dad calling her
"*Ma grosse pomme rouge du Canada,*" was always smiling and placid.

Attacks on the region of Paris started suddenly with Operation Paula
on 3 June, as 300 Luftwaffe planes carried out a massive bombing campaign. Paris emptied over the next five days; German occupation would
start on 14 June. On 11 June, Taverny's mayor forced our family to
leave at once: Catherine was just over a year old, Claire was two and a
half, and I was almost four and a half. Although we were born in Europe, we had automatically become British subjects through Dad (we
wouldn't become Canadian citizens until 1947), and we were therefore
at war with the Germans, too. We left quickly on the evening of Tuesday, 11 June, under heavy bombing, taking the train to Paris–Gare du
Nord; our luggage and the baby carriage had disappeared by the time
the train reached Paris. After crossing Paris from north to south, we arrived at the Porte d'Orléans. No more trains were leaving the city, and
no other means of transportation was available.

Discouraged, Dad sat down on the sidewalk, exhausted from carrying baby Catherine. Meanwhile, Mom, optimistic and positive as always, started hitchhiking, convincing a man driving a small van to take
us with him. The driver left us further along a road outside Paris. As
my little sisters could not walk for long, Father was holding Claire while
Mother carried Catherine; I walked, like a big girl. We joined thousands
of civilians and defeated French soldiers. I recall very well jumping in
the ditches when the ground-attack aircrafts, the Stukas, and their scary
"Trumpet of Jericho" sirens were heard – to this day, I remember that

sound. We had to find milk and bread to eat at friendly farms, and we slept outdoors. Dead horses and other animals lay along the roads. After a bombing three days after our exodus from Paris, Mother, who was five months pregnant, miscarried on a side road. Her life was saved thanks to a military doctor who passed nearby as he accompanied a truck of retreating soldiers. She was taken to the Puiseaux Hospice, where she was looked after and then released to join us three days later, on 16 June.

That day we managed to cover fifty kilometres, walking and being picked up by trucks or cars. I vividly recall crossing the Loire River at Châteauneuf-sur-Loire in the early evening of 16 June in a small car with my mother and sisters. We were under intense bombing – the Loire still a magical division between war and peace. I remember it clearly for three reasons: the bridge was bombed immediately after we crossed it, and destroyed; when I looked behind me, I saw the tall Romanesque church bell tower in flames, which made a deep impression on me; and we couldn't find Dad. Mother had lost her handbag, which contained all our papers and her passport, never to be recovered. Although she was still weak from the miscarriage, she had to carry Catherine while I held Claire's hand, helping her to walk. We found Dad several days later, on the steps of a church – or was it a city hall, and in what village? His dark brown hair had turned completely grey.

Eight days later, around 24 June, we finally reached Périgueux, just after all territory north of it had been declared an occupied zone, complete with border crossings, or *Demarkationslinie*, further to Marshall Pétain's deplorable Armistice signature with Hitler on 22 June. Périgueux is about 500 kilometres southwest of Paris by today's highway and 140 kilometres northeast of Bordeaux – almost two-thirds of the way down from the north of France. The city had already welcomed 15,000 refugees from Alsace and Lorraine and was well organized to receive more. Volunteers sent us to an impressive address, a manor-like property where we stayed as refugees for eight months. We lived in the small double attic above the garage and former stable, at the end of the large garden: we had no running water, no electricity, no toilet, nothing. The first few nights we all slept close to each other on straw on the floor; I was terrified by the tiny mice running around and over me. Later Mother would rail against the daily bedbugs on our nightgowns. The bites made us itch and scratch.

The owners, the Gaston Archambeaud family, were nice. They already had individual refugees living with them, and their house was full. The father owned an insurance company. Dad, handy in practical matters, repaired things for them, accompanying the owner downtown in the mornings to do all the paperwork required for registering us as refugees, and to allow us to return to Taverny or leave France. We lived off private donations, the charity of citizens' community groups, and a modest municipal biweekly allowance for refugees. From the Municipal Office for Refugees, Father obtained four narrow mattresses and bed frames, three sleeping bags for us children, two bedsheets and one blanket for himself and Mom, an Alsatian traditional *kachelofen* (like a small Franklin stove) and a coal shovel. (He faithfully returned all of these items to the municipal office, with his thanks, when we would leave Périgueux.) He had also built a table, three small stools, and two chairs. (In 2010, while in France, I had occasion to visit the owners of the place where we had lived as refugees. They were gracious enough to have located the only surviving member of the Archambeaud family: Paul-Henry, then eighty-three years old. He remembered my dad very well and had brought a picture of one of the wooden stools Dad made for us, which Paul-Henry still had in his garden! I reminded Paul-Henry that he was the cause of my lifelong fear of dogs. He had taken pleasure in scaring me stiff with the story of their manor's basement being full of police dogs, ready to run after me in their large garden.)

That is when I visited the attic over the stables where we had lived. It was exactly as I remembered ... tiny and miserable. The dangerous, narrow, steep indoor staircase, the low, sloping ceilings, and one skylight. Outside, on the ground, a cold-water tap over a stone basin for the horses. Mom and I would carry pails of water upstairs. Each daily activity, usually taken for granted, was a challenge: going downstairs to empty the chamber pots, dispose of the garbage, bring up drinking water; and carrying baby Catherine up and down the stairs. A small addition to the manor at the far end of the garden was our laundry room and toilet. Mom could go to the manor to iron our only clothes and possibly take a bath once in a while.

Three nice local women befriended Mother and took us for walks, to a park or to do the grocery shopping. In the rare few photos I have of Périgueux, Mom and we three girls appear happy, well dressed in one of our two outfits (one for summer and one for winter) and home-made cardigans (Mom made us everything possible so we would look cute), with our hair done and all of us smiling. But one photo shows the three girls seated on a bench, with the three local women smiling and happy standing behind us. We are not smiling. We look like or-phans, with poor clothes and felt shoes, and our hair not done. That is when we had impetigo – my case was quite serious – due to lack of proper food and hygiene. I ended up spending two weeks at the Château de Trélissac, which had been turned into the local hospital annex, where I was alone in a huge ballroom full of empty beds. Nobody could visit me because of the fear of contagion. A nurse would come to care for me, with the only medicine being *eau bleue* (a mixture of violet, gentian, methyl green, and 60 per cent alcohol). She washed my wounds, in which my long curly hair kept getting stuck. It was painful, and I had scars on my arms for decades.

Even though Périgueux was south of the occupied territory, France was still at war with Germany. So in the free zone, ration coupons, a shortage of certain foods, and heavy bureaucracy controlling the move-ment of people were the norm. When Dad applied for a Certificate of Refugee Repatriation, thinking we might go back home to Taverny, the approval document was in both French and German.

Those eight long months in Périgueux were due to Father's discovery that he had to deal with American diplomats based in Marseille, partic-ularly with the American consul general in charge of British interests, Mr Hugh S. Fullerton. This had to do with repatriating us somewhere and obtaining more survival welfare money. About ten years ago, I came across the twenty-eight replies signed by Fullerton – it was a bureaucratic nightmare. Fullerton wanted to send us to England, or back to Taverny, but could not send us to Canada unless we tried getting there by our-selves via Lisbon. Dad's age (he was then forty-six) was making it impossible to leave France, as he was still of military age for the French. In the end, he had to go to Marseille in person to get all the necessary passports and documents. He obtained an exit visa for all of us to get from Périgueux to Lisbon, stamped on 8 February 1941, and valid for one month. By then Mother was six months pregnant.

We were able to leave by train for Carcassonne, changing there for a local train to Cerbère, the French border town with Spain on the Mediterranean, at the foot of the Pyrenees. We had to stay there for two days, our modest luggage having been lost. We finally crossed the border on 27 February 1941 and stayed one day in Portbou, where our parents and I were searched separately by customs officers with guns in hand. (This scared me for life when it came to anything having to do with customs and uniformed officers.)

We then continued by train 160 kilometres south to Barcelona, where we stayed for four days. Dad, with his scrupulous honesty, mailed our remaining refugee free milk tickets back to Périgueux. Why did we stay there a few days? Probably to give Mother some rest and to allow Dad to explore local work opportunities. I imagine we also celebrated my fifth birthday! On 4 March we continued on to Madrid by train. We stayed there only two days, as the country was lacking everything, starting with food – although I do have a vivid memory of green olives the size of eggs.

We left Madrid for Lisbon at the Delicias Station on 6 March at 11 p.m. – travelling some 650 kilometres on a train without sleeping cars or a dining area, and only second- and third-class seats. We left Spain the next day at breakfast time, entering Portugal at the border crossing. At last, some food was distributed to passengers. We reached Lisbon and the Atlantic Ocean that evening.

We first stayed on the top floor of an excellent urban hotel – La Nova Pensao Camoes, in the Bairro Alto area, which was recommended by the Madrid British Consulate. After a few months, I was speaking Portuguese fluently. Dad would take us three girls to visit Lisbon – I have pictures of us playing on Praça do Comercio and in Santa Catarina Park. We were in Lisbon for about six weeks when my brother Paul was born on 18 April 1941. He was immediately registered at Sao Sebastião da Pedreira church, near the current Gulbenkian Museum.

Despite Dad's letter and visits to the Canadian immigration officer insisting that as a Canadian-born person, he wanted himself and his family repatriated to Canada, nothing happened. We did not have enough money to survive indefinitely. The British Repatriation Office in Lisbon pressured Father to buy our tickets on a ship to Britain right away. He refused. They then forced us to move, the six of us, to a one-bedroom suite with shared toilets and kitchen in a boarding house at 128, Avenida Joaô Crisostomo. We lived there for about three months. It must have been horrible for Mother, who was still weak from child-birth and breastfeeding Paul.

As nothing was happening to get us to Canada, Dad finally wrote a letter on 19 July to William Lyon Mackenzie King, who was Canadian secretary of state for external affairs as well as the prime minister. Whether due to good luck or simple coincidence, things started to move forward at once. On the twenty-first Father was called to the Canadian immigration office. Smallpox vaccines were scheduled at the British Hospital, and the official visas for the six of us were produced, duly approved by the American Foreign Service. Father and Mother co-signed a contract with Canada's External Affairs, swearing to reimburse the government for all the living allowances and hospital costs for the five months in Lisbon and for the cost of six places on the ss *Exeter* for New York. Our places on the ship amounted to US$1,069.70, a huge sum in 1941. (Once we were settled in Montreal, as the eldest, I was in charge of buying the monthly CDN$12 money order and mailing it to External Affairs, year after year, until we finished our refugee and repatriation repayments.) We left Lisbon on 8 August 1941. The whole family shared a cabin.

The ss *Exeter* had been built in Camden, New Jersey, in 1931 for American Export Lines and was used to offer cruises in the Mediterranean and to Europe. With the war, the ship was redirected to the Lisbon–New York–Lisbon route, bringing hundreds of refugees to New York and bringing back to Lisbon gold bars, provisions, and arms for European governments. The gold was then delivered to the Bank for International Settlements in Basel, Switzerland. Our ship's manifest listed 193 passengers under Captain Wenzel Habel and his staff of fourteen; several Jewish families; a Princess Olga Kotchoubey; a number of Americans;

the Canadian-born dancer Maud Allen; the internationally known nurse Alice G. Carr; the six members of the Bégin family; and many more. On the morning of 12 August Mother slipped on a banana peel on the boat deck, falling and breaking her left arm. We landed at Jersey City, New Jersey, on the eighteenth, having avoided German submarines. (The ss *Exeter* would be torpedoed by a German U-130 on 12 November 1942. During my first year in Montreal, I would have a recurring nightmare of our ship being torpedoed during the night and the water coming towards me in the dark hallway of our bedroom.)

We could not disembark with the other passengers, because of Mother's fall and the insurance documents and medical certificates required. So Dad had seated us children together on a structure of the main deck, me holding baby Paul, Catherine on one side and Claire on the other, wearing our identical sun hats that Mom had sewed. We were told not to move, so we quietly waited for all the bureaucracy to be concluded. That is when newsmen and photographers rushed aboard for fresh news of the war. I don't know what I said in French, but our picture and story were featured in some American newspapers, including the *New York Times*, as well as the Montreal *Gazette* via the Associated Press, *La Patrie*, and *La Presse*: my first press conference! We stayed less than forty-eight hours in New York, then boarded a train for Montreal, crossing the Canadian border at Rouses Point/ Lacolle on 20 August 1941. Canadian Immigration Services then wanted to send us directly to a western province, as refugees, to settle on farmland. Dad would have none of that: he was adamant that we were going to Quebec.

Upon arrival in Montreal that evening, we were welcomed by Father's friend Émile Venne and his family, who took us to their home for the night. The next morning, a relative of his, Dr Venne, examined Mother's arm and made a new cast for her at his medical office on Parc Lafontaine. Then, summoned by Inspector D. Lalonde, a Canadian immigration agent, Father and Mother had to jointly sign a certificate of indebtedness – an IOU – for US$21 for the cost of the train from New York.

The next stop was Farnham, in the Eastern Townships, again by train. We were welcomed at the train station by the mayor, the city councillors, the municipal band, and a crowd of locals. It seems the parish priest had announced our arrival at Sunday mass. At the home of the Lamoureux – Dad's eldest sister's family – she and her husband (who worked on the trains), their five children (quite a bit older than we were), and our grandmother Bégin welcomed us with open arms. We were quite an attraction for this small town with our language and manners, another aspect of the story of the war, in addition to the local Canadian Forces base and the camp of German prisoners.

We stayed in Farnham for about two months. On 13 October Father wrote to Inspector Lalonde, asking for more time to pay back what we owed the Canadian government. Mother no longer wore a cast but could not yet use her arm, and she had contracted pneumonia. Dad had been searching for work in Montreal and had just been hired as senior engineer at RCA Victor; he was now looking for an apartment for the family, travelling back and forth to see us every weekend. We finally moved to the modest and small four-room apartment he had found on the first floor at 3840 Prud'homme Avenue in October 1941.

I was too late to start school right away, according to the school board rules, so I had to wait until the next September. Although my first name was in fashion for French-Canadian girls of that time, I found it hard to fit in. At home I had to speak perfect French, with the proper word for each object; I was punished if I tried to speak Québécois. Meanwhile, I was not understood at school. I was the first refugee immigrant in the school and in the parish, and my European education and tastes (such as bringing an artichoke to school for lunch), my European accent, my long curly braided hair, my clothes (such as the knee-high heavy wool stockings we wore all winter, knitted by Grandmother Essemaeker) – indeed, everything in our family's lifestyle – distinguished us from everyone else in a way that made me uncomfortable. My family contrasted sharply with the socio-cultural atmosphere of this parish, the old Village of Notre-Dame-de-Grâce, as it was still called in our geography textbook. With Dr Karl Stern, a Jewish German psychiatrist who had fled the Nazi regime and arrived shortly before us, we were "the immigrants," "the refugees" of this small, tightly knit, well-to-do francophone community, an enclave in anglophone Montreal West. I would often see Dr Stern in church where we always went as a family, as he had converted to Catholicism in 1943. People found us original, great practising Catholics, and so European!

2

The Love of Learning

My father had a boundless curiosity – my life has been enriched by that side of him. But in a way the war had broken him. The Shoah and the horrific persecution and extermination of six million Jewish people had particularly marked him, and he spoke of it all his life. He had been wounded in all his beliefs and faith in humankind. He never recognized himself in North America – he simply survived as best he could. So did we, his children, especially I as the eldest, paying a price for his difficulty to adjust.

When we arrived in Montreal in the fall of 1941, Canada's largest metropolis truly was Hugh MacLennan's *Two Solitudes*: an island of clearly defined French and English areas. Notre-Dame-de-Grâce (NDG) was the second-wealthiest bourgeois French-Canadian ward in Montreal, after Outremont on the northern face of the "little mountain." Outremont was where francophone judges, professionals, successful artists, and intellectuals (including Pierre Trudeau's family) lived. The very top Montreal neighbourhood was Westmount, on the southern side of Mount Royal – an anglophone enclave for the wealthiest citizens, like the Molson and Bronfman families. On its western limits, Westmount bordered NDG. The NDG parish, a French-speaking area in the anglophone western part of Montreal, had its own small Anglo community in its midst, with St Augustine's Catholic parish and schools.

Because we arrived in Montreal after the 1941 school year began, I had to wait until September 1942 to start classes. NDG's large, beautiful public school, which included Grades 1 to 9, occupied two connected buildings – one for boys, one for girls – with vast separate playgrounds.

Adjacent to the girls' school, towards Décarie Boulevard, was the massive estate of the Dominican Fathers: their monastery and the Notre-Dame-de-Grâce parish church. Attached to the church was a mysterious campanile with an impressive chapel, separate meeting rooms for Boy Scouts and Girl Guides, and, on the upper floor, a welcoming library staffed by parish volunteers. Up to Décarie Boulevard were the tennis courts/skating rink and a parish hall for social activities. We lived almost opposite the church and its manicured grounds featuring shrubs and established trees. The parish was at the heart of community life.

In September 1942 there were more than twelve Moniques in my class of forty girls in Grade 1. I loved school! I would have gone to school twelve months a year if I could. If Mom gave me permission, I stayed after school to help the Congrégation de Notre Dame (CND) nuns, who taught us. (In Grade 2, we had a lay woman as a teacher, but that was unusual.) Since I was always ahead in my schoolwork, I would often read, hiding my book on my knees as I waited for others to finish the exercise of the moment. My reading choices ran from Homer's *Iliade* and *Odyssée* to Jules Verne's *Michel Strogoff* and other novels or biographies from the parish library.

The first "Canadian" child in our family, Sébastien, was born in June 1943 at the private Maternité Beaulac hospital. Dad had arranged with the nearby Dominican nuns to take in the rest of us children for the week. My sister Marie was born in October 1944. There were now six of us children.

On Tuesday, 8 May 1945, a sunny spring day, early in the morning, all the city bells started ringing. The war was over! It was Victory in Europe (VE) Day! We rushed outside to join our neighbours, following Mom, who started crying with joy. We had never seen her cry before. She spoke of her happiness, knowing that her mother in Brussels would at long last find peace and security.

Dad was not with us to share that joyous moment. In 1944, Montreal RCA Victor had transferred him to RCA International Division in Hollywood as a recording consultant. Life was not easy for Mom, alone in our small apartment with six young and very active children, with no outside help, no family, and very little money. Pregnant once again, she became exhausted and had a miscarriage. In January 1947, she would give birth for the last time – to Thomas. She was forty-one and Dad fifty-two.

That September I received permission from Dad to join the parish Girl Guide company. It was a great opening onto the world, and my sisters and brothers soon became Guides or Scouts too. I am still close to the first friend I made in Guides, Mireille (Richard) Fontaine. In the Montreal of the time, NDG was a rare open-minded parish under the Dominican priests. Our Girl Guide group would take us to classical concerts and plays. In 1949 the Montreal Girl Guides answered Archbishop Joseph Charbonneau's appeal to help the miners and their families who were victims of the brutal labour strike in Asbestos Mines. Assigned to St Antonin Church, I collected money for the miners at every Sunday mass for four months.

Although newspapers, magazines, radio, and the telephone were forbidden at home, to protect us from the mediocrity of the world around us, I had a sense of what was happening. I loved the Girl Guides teamwork and took all the steps to team second, then team leader, assistant leader of the parish group, and group leader of the some thirty NDG Girl Guides by the time I was nineteen or twenty. This experience had made me observe and learn about nature as well as the art and fun of camping in summer and even in winter – unique memories of discovery, initiative, leadership, and friendship. School and Girl Guides were completed by the wonderful parish library, where I was a helper as of age nine or ten. There I listened to the older women volunteers, shelved returned books, and of course did lots of reading. I even learned bookbinding skills from Brother Bernard at the monastery next door, which gave me one more badge for my Girl Guide uniform!

In 1949, at the end of Grade 7 – by then I was thirteen years old – most of my classmates left the public school for one of three nearby private institutions to start their eight-year *baccalauréat ès arts* (BA) program. In Quebec at the time, a baccalaureate was obtained from a classical college, not from a university, and was quite expensive. But one could not enter university without one. In NDG most of my friends registered at Villa Maria or Académie St-Paul for their first four years, the Cours Lettres-Sciences. Then they would go to the prestigious Collège Marguerite-Bourgeoys for the next four years, giving them a BA at the end. At the time, the collège also offered the third and fourth years of Lettres-Sciences. Because money was tight in our family, I had no choice but to stay at the NDG elementary school until the end of Grade 9. As most of my classmates had left after Grade 7 for the Cours Lettres-Sciences, we ended up with a split Grade 8 and 9 class. Our teacher, a CND nun, was overwhelmed by a group of tough teenagers from other areas of Montreal who had no choice but go "up the hill" to NDG to finish elementary school. The rest of the class more or less joined them in a total rebellion against our poor teacher's incompetence.

In September 1951 I entered Grade 10 at the closest Montreal Catholic School Commission public high school. Esther-Blondin High School was down Chemin Glen, near the Lachine Canal, in the working-class neighbourhood of St-Henri, which had been portrayed by Gabrielle Roy in her award-winning novel *Bonheur d'occasion (The Tin Flute)*, published in 1945. Luckily for me, Esther-Blondin had been selected for a pilot project offering Latin and geometry for one group of girls in Grades 10 and 11, for which I registered. For the first time I wore a school uniform: a navy tunic over a long-sleeved white blouse. The classes were not too large (about twenty-four students), my new classmates were as motivated as I was, and the teachers, Sisters of St Anne, excellent.

By age seventeen I had completed a quasi equivalent of the famous Cours Lettres-Sciences. My Girl Guide friends were about to start the last four years of the BA at Collège Marguerite-Bourgeoys, a true elite institution. Mom took me with her to the college, within walking distance of our home, to meet with the mother director. Mom was hoping some financial arrangements could be made to open the doors of the college to me. The mother director said I could be accepted because of my top marks and our family history, as we had lost everything in the war. In lieu of paying registration fees, I would be a kitchen employee, serving meals to students in the elegant dining room. Mom, proper as usual, thanked the nuns and refused. "It would do harm to my daughter," she told them, and we left. I fully understood Mom's reaction. We never spoke of it again.

At home I seized the opportunity and asked Dad for financial help. I knew how much he valued knowledge, learning, and culture. Surprisingly, my self-educated father curtly replied that I just had to do like him: *I am a self-made man and you just have to do the same.* I never understood his logic: I thought a parent who had had a difficult time would want to do everything possible to make it easier for his children.

With my Grade 11 diploma in hand, I obtained the $50 annual scholarship needed to enrol in boarding school at the teachers' college in Rigaud (Quebec), also taught by the Sisters of St Anne. In September 1953 I could legitimately take a break from home at long last. Why would I choose to become a teacher? I had never heard it discussed but observed that if girls were not wealthy enough to go to college and then university, they became nurses, office clerks or secretaries, sales girls, or teachers. For me, teaching was closest to the world of books and learning.

Mom, who was still learning about French Canada, thought that the École Normale (Normal School, which is what teachers' college was called then) was the equivalent of the internationally recognized Paris institution of the same name: École Normale Supérieure. Far from it, of course. She became rapidly disillusioned when she discovered the ineptitude of the essays I had to write and how much our lives were wrapped in *bondieuseries* – pious religious practices. In addition, it was understood that teachers' colleges for girls were hotbeds of religious vocations. Eighteen of my twenty-three classmates entered a religious order at the end of our training (only one remains a nun to this day).

After two years of studies, in June 1955, I obtained my teaching certificate, earning the Quebec Lieutenant-Governor's Gold Medal for the highest marks in the province. Although that gave me my choice of class and school, before I knew it I received a letter from the Montreal School Board assigning me to a Grade 4 class of fifty-two little girls for September. (There was no explanation.) I was nineteen years old. The school was once again in St-Henri – as it turned out, this was its poorest school, Sainte-Élisabeth-du-Portugal. I loved teaching but suffered under the rigidity and stupidity of the program and the system. The ultra-religious mentality (the *Visiteur ecclésiastique* would sit in the class from time to time, quizzing the students to ensure that religion was part of every subject I taught, including math: "Paul said the rosary and Marie said twelve Hail Marys: how many Hail Marys does that make?") My being a lone young lay woman with the nuns and the children's terrible poverty were overwhelming; I resigned at Christmas, very close to being in a depression. Only Mom had seen the state I was in; she covered up the situation, helping me as best she could.

Unfortunately my modest salary was needed at home. After the holidays, in January 1956, I was lucky to be able to finish the school year as a substitute teacher in a small kindergarten class in a French private school within walking distance of home. At the end of that school year, in May, I applied to be a secretary, even though I had no shorthand and no typewriting training. The job was with the Social Work department at the University of Montreal. The director, Father A.M. Guillemette, was a middle-aged Dominican priest with a sense of humour. After interviewing me, he concluded that a bright girl with excellent French and no secretarial skills was possibly a better choice than the usual motherhouse graduate who had great stenography and typing skills but was incapable of writing, spelling, and speaking correctly. I was not to tell a soul that I had never typed a word and did not know shorthand. My famous memory was a great help to me. And I still type rather quickly with two fingers.

My aim had always been to go on to university. To study what exactly? I had no idea: learning was what it was all about. But how would I ever obtain a baccalaureate, at that time the only way to enter university? In fall 1956, while I was working at the University of Montreal and meeting up with my NDG friends, who were already enrolled in different faculties, one of them offered me a way out of my dilemma. The only route free of tuition costs and that did not require registration in an institution was to prepare on one's own and pass the French baccalaureate exam. Finally, a solution! I would get ready for Part I of the BA (equivalent to the Quebec Rhétorique) at the end of May 1957, and do Part II (Philosophie) the next year. Professors from Caen University in Normandy came to Canada in June and September to administer the four written exams of the sections offered, followed by the oral and public exams covering all subjects. I could choose to do the orals in the fall after studying all summer. I chose Lettres (French, English, Italian, and Latin), studying every free evening and weekend. Whenever possible, Mom made me do Italian from 9 p.m. until midnight. I passed with marks high enough to be exempted from the oral in these subjects. But a new rule applied that year: all oral exams had to be taken during the same exam period! I did the best I could and was very lucky: I managed well in history/geography and physics/chemistry, although I failed miserably when it came to algebra and trigonometry, which I had never studied.

Meanwhile, I was still working as a secretary for Father Guillemette. In June, traumatized by these oral exams, non-existent in Quebec, I reluctantly turned to the "Bac D" at the University of Montreal. This program, which had been set up in 1952, was not considered high quality; it was aimed at teachers who wanted to become school principals. Courses were given on weeknights, all day Saturday, and full-time in the summer; the program was designed to be completed over five years. The director, Maurice Potvin, listened to my story and my objective, analyzed my detailed results from the French baccalaureate Part I, and granted me 56 credits against the 100 required for this "Bac D" baccalaureate. (The Quebec-equivalent Rhétorique was worth 60 credits.) In addition, he gave me special permission to take these extra 44 credits during the summer of 1957, every evening and Saturday of the school year, and the summer of 1958 full-time. (He knew I was also working full-time.) I still feel an immense debt of gratitude to Maurice Potvin.

What was Dad doing through these years? We rarely saw him while he was working in Hollywood, as he could come home to visit for only a few days every six months. I believe he stayed two years in Hollywood, was sent to Camden, New Jersey, for a short while, and then went to New York until 1950. From these two last cities, he had to be back in Canada for a weekend after twenty-nine days, for immigration reasons. He would always arrive late in the evening from Dorval Airport; on these nights, we had permission to stay up past our usual bedtime of 9 p.m. He always had some tiny souvenirs for each of us, hidden among his dirty socks. The girls would receive beautiful ribbons for their long braids. After a business trip to Cuba, he brought us persimmons to taste. Once, back from Egypt and the Middle East, he had *loukoum* (Turkish delight) in his luggage, which I loved, and a metal box like a sardine tin, except it contained grilled crickets, which we were supposed to eat. When he was away working, he sent each of us a postcard every Monday morning with our individual marching orders for the week, with his love. Despite his terrible occasional surges of anger, we lived happily.

In 1948, when Dad was working in the States, he went on a mysterious nine-month trip to Europe, according to his cv. His passport showed stops in France, Switzerland, Italy, and Spain between early April and the end of December. We knew he was in Europe for his work but had no details. Even during this time, he would send each of us the usual lovely postcards – a different one for each child, but from the same series: wildflowers, birds, rare butterflies, Hummel figurines – but with no indication of where he was.

It turns out that he spent all of April 1948 in France settling the issues relating to our house in Taverny, which we had hastily left just before the German invasion of Paris in June 1940. He still owed rent for the past eight years, which he paid with interest. The house and the property had to be completely cleaned and repaired before he gave it back to the owner. What soldiers and others had not ransacked – furniture, china, crystal, books, art, and so on – was sold at auction in nearby Enghien-les-Bains. Special items like Mom's violin, the silver, and the Lenci Madonnas were crated and shipped to Montreal. The fact that these objects were returned to us after all Paris had been through is in itself extraordinary. I was only twelve, so it is not surprising that Dad's return and the mysterious crate did not register as being exceptional at the time.

That Dad had held onto a rented house in France, with those costs piling up when we lived in relative poverty in Canada, came as a shock to me and my siblings. I didn't come across this information until 2009, as I researched the book I wrote for the family on our exodus during the war. Paul and Sébastien still had unopened boxes of family papers in their basements, which I went through. We had lost our parents in the 1960s, but they had never spoken to us of the war. What I do recall very well is the day Dad came home from France with Mom's violin, followed by the crate and all that he was bringing back from Taverny. It was a Friday and we did not go to school; it was a celebration! Mom shed tears of joy when she touched her violin. But the nonsensical expenditures over eight years, the auction, and all the stories around these events had never been told to us. It would appear that Dad had hung onto his dream of going back to France, finding work in his field, and hence our needing the Taverny house ... (I recall a day that he tried to convince Mom that we should go to India, where he had a great job offer. Mom replied nicely but firmly, "Lucien, I have escaped two world wars and I am not moving from here!")

Despite these debts and further expenses, taking into account the relatively good results of the auctions, Dad must have come back to Canada with some money, maybe $1,000 or $2,000. Putting two and two together, I have since connected that windfall with the plan to buy a two-storey house that was for sale on Addington, the next street over. Mom had even obtained the promise of a mortgage with our local Caisse populaire, or credit union. The whole family visited the house for sale. It was early spring 1949; I had just turned thirteen. I remember dreaming of some space and of a real house, getting rid of the awful second-hand army surplus metal bunk beds and painted butter crates that had been turned into whatever else was needed as furniture. Moving to that house would have changed our life for the better. But at the last minute, Dad said no. We never learned why.

Around that time, things were deteriorating on the family front. Dad, even though he was often out of the country with his work, was omnipresent – either terribly authoritarian or wonderful and fascinating, in person or from afar. When I was fifteen and in high school, I remember praying for him to die, although I never would have wanted a father like our friends had: too boring. As I privately begged Mom to leave him, she preached me patience and tolerance. I understood later that she considered it financially impossible to leave the marriage. School was a peaceful refuge after the pandemonium of a family of nine strong temperaments living in four rooms under the rule of a patriarchal and unusual father. In any event, school was where our real life happened, as we were not allowed to have friends come over or to go to their homes. Despite the constraints of our daily life in Canada, we were a solidly welded clan and very proud of it. We knew we were not like everybody else, and that suited us perfectly. I never felt that being poor was a socio-economic condition in bourgeois NDG, just that the lack of money stood in the way of my dreams of studies and more.

Dad's CV states that in early 1950, after his work in the United States, he had been "delegated to France by the RCA Victor on a 'goodwill mission' to re-establish liaison with pre-war RCA Licensees." Not a word about the nine months he had spent in Europe in 1948! Then, from March 1950 to March 1951, he was a consultant to the CIMABO studios in Rome. When he returned to Montreal for good, he no longer had a job at RCA Victor and had no unemployment insurance. It was terrible to see him looking for work in Montreal. In May 1951 he was hired by Canadair as senior engineer in the Electronic Design Section, then in the Special Weapons Division. At one point he lived in Valcartier (Quebec City), on loan to the Canadian Armament Research and Development Establishment to design missiles. Back in Montreal, he was assigned to the Test Lab of the Canadair Avionic Department. Reinventing himself from a sound and electrical engineer to an aeronautical engineer when he was over sixty years old is in itself remarkable. He would stay at Canadair until some two years before his death in 1964.

In the closing years of the 1950s, my personal life changed dramatically when, on my twenty-first birthday, 1 March 1957, just before supper, Dad, in a dramatic and violent scene (out of the blue, as far as I was concerned), announced that I had a month to find a new place to live: he was throwing me out of the house for "undermining his paternal authority."

I was still working as a secretary at the University of Montreal, studying for the French baccalaureate exams, which I had applied to that May. Now I had to find a low-cost place to rent, unknown at the time for a young unmarried woman alone, and a new job that would pay me more than being a secretary. Being very family oriented, this situation affected me deeply, but life went on. Mom was always there. She and I found a tiny place for me to rent on the third floor of the Côte St-Luc Bar-B-Q: it had cement floors painted deep red, and no hot water. We did not observe, as it was springtime, that there was no heating system, either. I later learned that I was the first tenant there, as this top floor of the building had been the warehouse for the frozen chickens.

One night around Christmas 1957, I was sleeping in my sleeping bag on a folding bed that my friend Mireille had loaned me – I was wearing flannel pajamas and still freezing. I woke up around 3 a.m. to see a Chinese man in rubber boots standing in my bedroom. The floor was covered by several inches of water. With typical late-December ups and downs in the temperature, the water pipes had burst, inundating the whole building. The man took me downstairs, where a large Chinese family was living in a place as tiny as mine. The building owner sued me for several thousand dollars for the flood, and I had to go to court. Thanks to Monique Coupal, whom I had befriended at the French baccalaureate exams, who was now a law student, the newly licensed Claire Barrette-Joncas helped me pro bono and won the case. McGill University friends told me later that my case was referred to in their courses! I finally moved from the apartment, boarding with three different families until September 1961.

September 1957 to the end of August 1958 was the most hectic period of my life. I worked in the Department of Social Work until the end of June.

In September I started as the regular teacher of Éléments latins (the first of the eight years of the Quebec private-sector baccalaureate) at the new Institut Cardinal-Léger, again with the Sisters of St Anne. This affordable classical college for girls was situated in the then homogenous and highly populated Rosemont, an industrious middle-class neighbourhood in the east end of Montreal. The mother director, Sister Marie-Lydia, who knew me, let me take off two mornings a week to study at the Faculty of Sciences, as requested by Maurice Potvin. I had taken full-time courses at the Bac "D" in the summer of 1957 and would do so again the following summer, in addition to every weeknight and all day Saturdays. I loved that year of teaching thirty-three highly motivated fifteen-year-old girls who were committed to learning. As for the forty-four courses I was taking, I recall only one extraordinary double course on the history and philosophy of science, given by Roland Lamontagne: it was a great opening onto the world for me. On top of my work (including a one-hour bus ride to and from Rosemont) and my studies, I had agreed to be second in command to Monique Coupal, the Akela of the Scout cubs of Collège Stanislas, where I was given the marvellous totem name of Rikki-Tikki-Tavi, the mongoose.

In September 1958 I was finally enrolled full-time in the master's in sociology program in the Faculty of Social Sciences at the University of Montreal, even though I hadn't gone through the first five years of the baccalaureate: Éléments latins, Syntaxe, Méthode, Versification, and Belles-Lettres. My knowledge of history, science, and philosophy would always be fragmented, for I had studied piecemeal. I had, however, accumulated other knowledge and acquired another reading of life in society. I had practised a few trades: kindergarten, elementary, and high school teacher, and secretary. I had tamed diverse social milieus that were very different from NDG, including those of a small town, Rigaud. I had lived alone and I had boarded with unknown families, with wealthy Canadians and with some interesting Europeans. Instead of being an obstacle, such an atypical route became a treasure for me. In fact, this sense of being marginalized, which began in childhood, protected me against many future bad surprises, such as being the first or only woman in places of power that were fundamentally masculine and male chauvinist, or just being different.

Why sociology? At first, I considered studying botany – obviously reminiscent of my Girl Guide camps, my love of trees and nature, and my well-kept plant scrapbooks – or going into medicine. The latter was rapidly abandoned because of the costs involved and my poor scientific background. In any event, I was not crazy about either option. As I had glanced at social science texts I typed as a social work secretary – all department support staff were in a single office and we helped each other when needed – or listened to the discussions between professors speaking in our presence, only sociology piqued my curiosity. It became my goal.

I recall my reasoning at the time: I wanted to understand my NDG community and its different social classes under a finish of equality. I wanted to understand why my high school classmates living in miserable and crowded homes in Saint-Zotique parish in the Saint-Henri district were somehow different from those coming from Côte-Saint-Paul, or Ville-Émard, or even Lachine. And why were my fifty-two low-income Grade 4 pupils in Sainte-Élisabeth-du-Portugal, or later, the teenagers in Grade 7 at Saint-Enfant-Jésus-du-Mile-End, straight out of Michel Tremblay's plays and about to leave school for the St Laurent Street factories, seen as losers from birth? And why the street fighting between francophone kids from the Notre-Dame-de-Grâce school and anglophone kids from the neighbouring St Augustine's, when they were all Catholic? On what was the social organization of my new French-Canadian society grounded? And how does social change occur?

3

Sociology Here and Abroad

The Department of Sociology was very new: it had been set up in 1955. When I started in September 1958, it offered only a full-time three-year master's degree, with thesis. Students would arrive directly with classical college baccalaureates, and my BA was considered equivalent. The University of Montreal president was Monsignor Irénée Lussier, and the director of sociology was Father Norbert Lacoste, a priest who had been chosen by the diocese to attend the Catholic Louvain University in Belgium to get a doctorate in sociology. Shortly after my arrival he explained to me how the scientific relativism of sociology acted in a perverse way against the three great Thomist tenets of transcendentalism: the Beautiful, the True, and the Good. Despite my poor philosophy background, I left his office flabbergasted in the face of such a lack of sensitivity between a director and his students. But Duplessis was Quebec's premier at that time, and we were in what some have named *"La grande noirceur"* (the great darkness) – although Gérard Pelletier's book title *Les années d'impatience* (the impatient years) is a much more realistic depiction of the underlying dynamism and movement forward of the period.

Few of our professors were sociologists. Those who made up the department were Hubert Guindon, Raymond Breton, Maurice Pinard (political sociology; he left after a year or two for McGill), and Father Lacoste; Fernand Cadieux had left the year before I arrived. Our other professors were attached to different disciplines of the social sciences: André Raynault and Roger Dehem (economics), Jacques Henripin (demography), Denis Szabo (criminology), and Guy Dubreuil (social anthropology), as well as Philippe Garigue, the new faculty dean who taught us family sociology. When starting our third and final year in September 1960, we were surprised to learn that Guy Rocher, a Laval University professor, had just been appointed department chair: Father Lacoste had gone back to being a simple professor, Guindon and Pinard had left, and several new professors had just been hired.

The first challenge was for each of us to find a thesis supervisor. We were also informed of some new courses that we would have to take. As class president, I had to negotiate no new courses with Guy Rocher, informing him that our class of a dozen had crammed most courses into our first two years, in addition to having to earn our living, and would be researching and writing our thesis in our third and final year. I explained to our new director that the curriculum under which we had registered was a social contract that could not be breached on a whim. A compromise was reached: we would take Fernand Dumont's full-year course Fondements théoriques de la sociologie systématique one day a week, as he had already organized his schedule for it.

Sociology at Laval University had a great reputation, as it was part of the famous Faculty of Social Sciences created by the Dominican priest Georges-Henri Lévesque in 1938. History considers Father Lévesque, who became a friend of mine when I was in Cabinet, one of the fathers of Quebec's Quiet Revolution. He had been a member of the Royal Commission on National Development in the Arts, Letters and Sciences in Canada and would become vice president of the Canada Council for the Arts in 1957. His graduates would be the core group of the Lesage government's Quiet Revolution senior civil servants and political personnel.

To me, the Laval professors appeared to be classical sociologists, not Socratic youth questioning theories and authors. Sociology at Laval was proud of rising stars like Fernand Dumont and Guy Rocher, but our very young master's program at the University of Montreal, in addition to its interdisciplinary quality, had already achieved an exceptional level of critical thinking and academic discussion. And Quebec City will never be Montreal. Our own class of sociology was rooted in the cosmopolitan, dynamic metropolis of Canada, a Montreal that was open to the world and where things were happening.

As I still had to earn a living and could not get major scholarships for lack of social connections, I decided to contact the ex-chaplain of my Rigaud Teachers' College, Canon Edmour Laberge, whose sister lived on our street in NDG and who liked Mom. Canon Laberge was wealthy, and it was known that he was paying for some young men's studies. He invited me for supper at the Côteau-du-Lac rectory, where he had retired. I told him about my studies after Rigaud and my goal of getting a master's in sociology at the University of Montreal. As I was leaving to take the bus back to Montreal, he said I would soon receive his reply, which I did. I kept his reply card for the longest time. He wrote that women were born to be educators or nurses, or to take up other traditionally female roles in society, and that since what I was aiming for went against God's plans, he could not help me.

I finally obtained a renewable interest-free loan from the Saint Jean-Baptiste Society (which took me years to pay back); I also got an annual $50 Édouard-Montpetit scholarship. So, while doing my courses, I went back to being a substitute teacher for the Montreal Catholic School Board, giving private lessons to rich kids, taking on short-term translation and writing contracts, and doing part-time secretarial work.

My class of 1958–61, more than any other, lived the transition between the ultramontane clerical Quebec of Premier Maurice Duplessis and the Quiet Revolution of Jean Lesage. Duplessis died suddenly on 7 September 1959, at age sixty-nine. The final scandal of his government was that his ministers made millions through the privatization of natural gas. His Union nationale party was defeated by the Jean Lesage Liberals on 22 June 1960, marking the dawn of the Quiet Revolution.

Non-violent demonstrations and a student strike had taken place in March 1958, including at the University of Montreal, McGill, Laval, Sir George Williams (now Concordia), and Bishop's.

Demands were now going beyond scholarships. Students wanted free tuition. I wrote one or two articles in *Vrai* (Jacques Hébert's newspaper) and for the *Quartier Latin* (University of Montreal newspaper) demanding free university education, like in France. We, the students, argued and pushed for accessibility of higher education and democracy in general at "Chez Valère" during the lunchtime public debates with the *Cité Libre* authors, or with the guests of the day: Thérèse Casgrain,

Michel Chartrand, Jean Marchand, even Jean Drapeau, the Montreal mayor who was trying to mobilize us to clean up municipal politics and administration.

There was a dozen of us in my master of sociology class, including two women: Marquita Riel and me. I immediately became friends with Raymundo (Ozanam) de Andrade, who had just landed from Brazil. We often talked with the few students of the two classes ahead of us as well. Personal friends from the humanities and literature, from law or other disciplines joined us for weekend ski trips to the Laurentians, sharing books, discussing movies and documentaries. Discussions included the work of the social anthropologists we were discovering in our courses, from Claude Lévi-Strauss's *Tristes Tropiques* to Margaret Mead, Ruth Benedict, and Oscar Lewis and his *Five Families*. We shared meals, we drank together, we listened to music, we went to the theatre. One of my first good moves was to have my whole class, and our group, read and discuss Simone de Beauvoir's *The Second Sex*: the Quebec Catholic Church Index had lifted the ban on it in 1959, ten years after it was published in France.

During our two first years in sociology we had half a dozen great professors, but Hubert Guindon became an intellectual beacon for us and our model for questioning and applying critical thinking to life in society. He was a disciple of C. Wright Mills, the American public political intellectual and professor of sociology at Columbia University in New York: he had published *White Collar* (1951), *The Power Elite* (1956), and *The Sociological Imagination* (1957), which we read and reread. (When Guindon died in 2002, I realized that he was barely older than we, his students. He looked forty and had the intellectual and moral authority of someone that age, but he was only twenty-nine at the time.) Hubert Guindon incarnated sociological thinking for us. Having studied Mills's work while he was a student at Chicago, as well as that of Everett Hughes, Guindon taught us to observe and listen, to always put things back in their historical context, to question and to doubt.

Early on, Guindon introduced us to Max Weber's *Essays in Sociology*, as well as several great authors or great names – which is not necessarily the same thing. Guindon would scoff, even become sarcastic,

when describing the grand empty theories, preconceived ideas, stereotypes, and platitudes of some of the big names in sociology – Talcott
Parsons being his main scapegoat. He did fieldwork, which could turn
out to be a bar at night or the morning sessions of the Court, or participant observation in a village or a neighbourhood: his goal was to have
its secret meaning revealed. Guindon was anything but a super theorist
or a model empiricist. He shared Mills's view that an abusive researching of theory meant overlooking fundamental issues. Guindon was trying to capture real life in society and was even attempting to predict its
next phases. It could be the Quebec Catholic Church, our two national
solitudes, or the Quiet Revolution as a springboard for a new aspiring
middle class. In the end, as he concluded in the book presenting thirty
years of his essays, "I think ultimately all social sciences are – what did
Lasswell call them? – moral sciences. Let's say that society has concerned me more than sociology."

For a long time I believed, rather naively, that applied sociology was
a tool of social change; then I discovered that it was being used to justify
the status quo. That personal view originated from the sociologists I
had studied: C. Wright Mills, our professors, and my mentors (although
that term was not in use then), such as Guindon and Cadieux. They
were not conformist intellectuals. They knew that their discipline too
often described and analyzed power structures, institutions, and social
dynamics, but without a critical lens – not asking the questions stemming from one's personal values and defining each sociologist, each scientific mind – for science has never been neutral or objective.

Guindon would teach at Concordia University for over twenty-five
years, after being forced to resign from the University of Montreal as
my class was entering its final year. He was beloved by his students, not
yet tenured, but his teachings were considered iconoclastic by the new
dean. I kept in touch with him until his death and was at Notre-Dame
Basilica for his funeral on 18 October 2002. Once in a while, I reread
the beautiful tribute to Hubert Guindon's life that Senator Roch Bolduc
gave in the Senate.

It is thanks to Guindon that I met Fernand Cadieux, his sociologist
friend. I started by stuffing envelopes at Cadieux's Groupe de Recherches
sociales when I was a student; later, at Dyname, I moved on to preparing

TV program background briefs for Gérard Pelletier and *Premier Plan* (which began airing in 1959), among others; then I helped to organize the first Montreal International Film Festival in August 1960, as well as those that followed.

Cadieux (1925–1976) had been national president of the Jeunesse étudiante catholique nationale – the Catholic youth movement – from 1948 to 1954, the last of the great student leaders who were opening windows on the world for generations of young people. He had succeeded Gérard Pelletier, Pierre Juneau, and others, each of whom had usually been president for a year. My friend Raymundo de Andrade, whom I had introduced to Cadieux, told me later how Cadieux, who was just twenty years old at the time, had impressed student leaders in Brazil, awakening their conscience to social concerns in the 1950s through his meetings with the Juventude Universitária Católica. Cadieux's friends Plinio Arruda Sampaio and Francisco (Chico) Whitaker would later become leftist intellectuals, politicians, and, in Whitaker's case, organizer of the first Porto Alegre World Social Forum in 2001; they remained Catholics working for social justice through the years.

What a loss for our collective memory is the lack of a biography of that sociologist and universal thinker that was Fernand Cadieux, an important actor in preparing the Quiet Revolution, a man of great discretion, ideas, and action, a humanist. Through Fernand, from the end of the 1950s to around the end of the sixties – at the office, at his daily lunches, at home with his exceptional wife, Rita (Racette) – I met a generation of remarkable intellectuals, artists, professionals, or businessmen who were already leaders in their sphere of influence. It would be impossible to name them all, but they included Claude Robillard, Pierre Juneau, Harry Suffrin, Marc Lalonde, Michael Pitfield, Roméo LeBlanc, Roy Faibish, and Patrick Watson, as well as personalities from abroad who were passing through Montreal. Pierre Elliott Trudeau would regularly come to see Fernand, but never in a group setting, and I saw him only from afar.

While I was writing these memoirs, Raymundo reminded me of another anecdote that expresses Cadieux's immense culture and unending intellectual curiosity. The year was 1973, and Pierre Trudeau as prime minister would be making his first official visit to the People's Republic

of China after establishing diplomatic relations between our two countries on 13 October 1970. While they were discussing the upcoming
trip, Cadieux suggested to Trudeau to offer Chairman Mao a special
edition of the volumes *Science and Civilization in China* that the great
British biochemist, historian, and sinologist Joseph Needham and his
team of researchers had produced on civilization in ancient China.
Symbolic and unexpected. Years later, I would dedicate my first book,
*L'assurance-santé: Plaidoyer pour le modèle canadien / Medicare:
Canada's Right to Health* (1987), to Fernand Cadieux, a beloved mentor without the name.

By June 1961 I had completed my coursework towards my master's
in sociology, but I had not made much progress on my thesis project:
"Cultural Relations between France and Canada after 1763: A Symbolic Analysis." I was still waiting for approval of my thesis proposal
from Guy Rocher, the department director and my supervisor. Towards
the end of the summer I received wonderful news: I had been granted a
two-year scholarship from the new provincial Department of Youth (the
Department of Education had not yet been created), based on my application for doctoral studies. It was a dream come true: I would spend
two years in Paris as a student at the Sorbonne! This was a once-in-a-
lifetime opportunity, at age twenty-five, to discover the world with eyes
wide open.

I left for Europe in mid-September. My first plane trip! I can still recall the thrill of taking off. The next thing I knew, I was living in Paris.
My friend Monique Coupal, who had graduated with a law degree in
June, was taking a year off before starting to practise law and was already in Paris. She greeted me when I arrived – I can still picture my
first lunch with her at the Brasserie Alsacienne on l'Île Saint-Louis and
the room she had booked for me at the Hôtel de Suède on Quai Saint-
Michel. From my room I could see Notre-Dame-de-Paris, majestic but
still black, soon to be cleaned as per André Malraux's new legislation.
A few days later, Monique introduced me to her cousins who had also
just landed, the painter Denyse Gérin and her husband, Jean-Marie
Tétreault, who had also just graduated from law, but as a notary.
Monique had bumped into them on the Pont de l'Alma. During their
year in Europe, I would see them regularly.

Everything was new to me, but I immediately recognized the smell of the subway from my childhood before the war. I did a lot of observing now that I was far from North America, in another world that was waiting to be discovered. First I had to find a place to live. I got some help from Francine Laurendeau, whom I knew from my past secretarial work for the Co-operative Commonwealth Federation (CCF); she had been studying at Sciences Po University for a year. Through her concierge, one of those powerful Parisian female custodians, I was able to rent a very small second-floor room at 60 rue Hallé in the Fourteenth Arrondissement; we called it the "Yellow Room." It overlooked a tiny enclosed backyard and what remained of the house opposite. Francine's room had large windows looking onto the street. We became friendly neighbours but kept our private lives to ourselves.

Although the Second World War had been over for fifteen years, Parisians were still living in poor conditions and lacked comfort – indeed, many were without basic amenities. In my unheated seven-floor building, there were only two tiny Turkish toilets (a hole in the floor): one on the third floor and one on the seventh, and no bathroom in any of the apartments. My Yellow Room had a cold-water tap over a tiny sink, a one-burner gas cooker, and a dresser. No stove, no fridge. In wintertime, for heat, one had to rent a Butagas, a small butane gas burner that was too dangerous to be left on at night. In February 1963 the cold was so intense that I had to stay with the young Canadian family of Monique and Jacques Boucher, who had recently arrived in Paris. My only treasure was my battery-operated AM/FM Philips radio, a gift from Monique Coupal before she left to travel the Middle East. It gave me access to all the classical music stations of Europe, sustaining and enchanting me through my two years in Paris. I still miss that radio.

I dreamed of getting a room at the comfortable Maison des étudiants canadiens, in the large park of the Cité universitaire internationale nearby, still in the Fourteenth Arrondissement. But to get in, one needed connections, which I did not have. In December, when I first visited the maison and recognized university students playing cards, smoking, and having a drink, I thought I was back at "Chez Valère" at the University of Montreal! It was not what I was looking for in Paris.

On rare occasions when I had a few francs left, I would go to the public baths – not to swim but to fully wash, including my long and luxurious curly hair. People could not afford a telephone in those days; even if they had the money, they were on a waiting list for several years. Family, friends, and businesses usually communicated by *pneus* (pneumatic post): one bought a special small, thin, airmail-type folding letter on which to write, folded and glued it, and left it at the post office; it was delivered within two hours. To wash clothes, you went to the laundry store, which cost very little. Later, you would pick up your things, which had been wrung out so well that you just had to hang them up when you got home.

The difference in social classes in Paris was obvious to me. Behaviour, tone of voice, language level, accent, personal comments, manners, and clothes (especially of women and children) revealed a set social hierarchy and a person's place in it. For us Canadians, it was unpleasant, surprising, and ridiculous – we think of ourselves as so egalitarian. As apprentice sociologists we knew, however, that every society has social classes. We also noticed the importance of any authority and the omnipresent bureaucracy. (It was only on 9 January 1963, sixteen months after my arrival and five months before my final return to Canada, that I received my work permit, residence permit, and student registration.)

It is impossible to describe daily life without referring to the Algerian War, hypocritically called "the Algerian events," then at its worst in Paris. The list was shocking: *plasticages* (bombing of stores and other buildings), labour strikes, indiscriminate terrorist attacks against civilians by the Organisation de l'Armée Secrète (OAS – French individuals opposed to decolonization), corpses found in the Seine and in the Canal Saint-Martin, and the CRS (riot control forces) armed to the teeth. From these two years in Paris I retained an acute sensitivity towards the harm caused by colonialism and the mostly horrific wars of liberation and independence of the second half of the twentieth century.

When I arrived in Paris I first went to hear the sociology pundits at the Sorbonne. One of these large auditoriums (pre-May 1968) was full when the master arrived: Georges Gurvitch, then sixty-seven years old, followed by his slightly younger but also well-established colleague

Georges Friedmann. The other senior academics, obviously following a hierarchical order, sat up front; behind them were young professors, followed by lecturers, researchers, and postgraduate students. We, the newcomers about to start a doctorate, had to sit in the back rows and could not ask questions. I had not yet understood that the prestigious Sorbonne of the time was already highly dysfunctional for the day's higher education needs, hence the proliferation of study centres of all kinds. Gurvitch's magnum opus, *Dialectique et sociologie*, would be published a few months after my arrival. In it he revealed and argued the current trends in German philosophy: Husserl, Heidegger. I was completely lost.

I did not understand what the French called sociology or how their graduate and postgraduate studies were structured. There were no printed programs, no organizational charts, and no information booklets on how French universities functioned and how degrees were to be obtained. I had spent my young life asking questions to understand how things were organized, getting answers quickly, and figuring out how systems worked, but not in Paris. I wonder to this day why I never discussed my difficulties with Renée and Pierre Dandurand, who knew how things worked. Probably misplaced pride on my part.

Pierre had finished a year before me in the master's in sociology at the University of Montreal. When I landed in Paris he had already begun his doctoral project under Professor Viviane Isambert-Jamati, an expert in sociology of education. This would become Pierre's remarkable lifetime academic contribution back in Canada. Some of the seminars he and his wife, Renée, took were given by Chombart de Lauwe, Raymond Aron, Fernand Braudel, Lévi-Strauss, Piaget, and Ricoeur. Amazingly, he had managed to obtain his doctorate from the University of Paris in only twenty-six months, with a new baby and limited financial means, and still found time for friends, regular cultural discoveries, and even short trips.

Our individual professors of sociology at the University of Montreal at the time, as well as our Faculty of Social Sciences and our Department of Sociology, had not yet developed any academic or personal networking with their French colleagues. Pierre's success story exemplifies the role and value of this kind of networking. During his last year in Montreal, his thesis director, Father Lacoste, had asked Pierre to do him a favour. Would he drive Professor Jean Stoetzel, a famous visiting French sociologist who was not yet known to our department, around Montreal? Pierre spent the day with Stoetzel, who questioned him and concluded that upon arrival in Paris, Pierre should contact him. Unknown to Pierre, Stoetzel was already well established and the director of the Centre d'Études sociologiques in the Seventeenth Arrondissement. Upon their arrival, Pierre and Renée found an apartment next door to the centre, and Pierre was introduced to Professor Isambert-Jamati.

Foreign students seeking a doctorate in France had two options: a three-year *Doctorat de 3ème Cycle* (or *d'État*), which was costly and littered with pitfalls for foreigners, or a *doctorat d'université* (supposedly less prestigious) requiring no courses, papers, or seminar presentations – just a thesis, which could be done over two years (usually more). The latter option was the choice of most Canadians. All that was required was for one's thesis to be accepted by a thesis director – a situation I finally understood long after my arrival, and too late.

I made an appointment with Georges Friedmann, the key figure in sociology of work and a humanist whom I had heard at La Sorbonne and met with at his luxurious apartment in the Sixteenth Arrondissement. I did not have a developed thesis plan, but I was thinking of studying the case of Billy Graham, the famous American charismatic evangelist ordained as a minister of the Southern Baptist church, an anti-segregationist whom several US presidents – Dwight Eisenhower, Lyndon Johnson, and Richard Nixon – would consult. The growing number of people choosing his church – and their motivations – had piqued my curiosity. Graham was, at the time, an out-of-the-ordinary personality, with a national, even international leadership role. (One month before my return to Canada, I went to a stadium in Paris to hear him speak: 10,000 people attended, chanting and crying. I was rather shocked by this display and the adulation of the crowd.)

Not much came of that meeting with Friedmann, except that he reoriented me towards the joint sociology seminars of Roland Barthes and Edgar Morin at the brand-new Centre d'Études des Communications de Masse, out of the École Pratique des Hautes Études. This was a more modern and dynamic Study Centre of Mass Communications of which he was the founding director and was the new focus of his personal interest. I attended these seminars and lectures all day every Wednesday (sometimes in the evenings as well) and on Thursdays. I discovered those called "the mythologists," decoders of symbolic behaviours, of myths and demystification, and their new jargon, which was almost opaque at times. Barthes explored semiotics, the study of symbols and signs – a field pioneered by Ferdinand de Saussure – and helped establish the intellectual movements of structuralism and New Criticism. At times the exercises appeared far-fetched to me. Barthes and Morin were considered "structural analysts." I tried to connect one of my theses to this new analytic approach, to no avail. In any case, two months after my arrival in Paris, I still had not heard from Guy Rocher about my thesis proposal.

To help me make ends meet, Fernand Cadieux had given me a small contract on cultural relations between France and Canada from 1763 to our day that happened to feed my data for my thesis. Before leaving Montreal, I had gone to Ottawa for a meeting with Monsieur Weymuller, the cultural attaché of the French Embassy; I explained my project and made notes of his suggestions. A year later, even without any reaction from the Department of Sociology and still unsure about what was required for a master's thesis, I had managed to write ninety-five pages.

In Barthes's and Morin's seminars I befriended two students – older than I and much more learned: Jeanne Léon-Blum, who must have been a young sixty years old, and Évelyne Sullerot, close to forty. Jeanne was a distant cousin of Léon Blum, whom she had married in Buchenwald concentration camp in 1943. (He died in 1950.) Jeanne did not mix with the class in these rather frenzied seminars with Barthes and Morin. She had great presence, as is said in the theatre; calm and serene, she observed the scene rather than taking part. I greatly enjoyed conversing with her and listening to her history. Just before Christmas Jeanne invited me for lunch at a restaurant. She encouraged me to pursue my doctoral project and not give up. Too poor to reciprocate the invitation, and intimidated by her past and the very name of Léon Blum, I did not know how to develop this unique connection, even though I found her to be a very friendly person. I regret it to this day.

Évelyne, who had been a young member of the French resistance during the Second World War, was a mother of four who had gone back to university; her doctoral thesis was on *La presse féminine* (women's magazines). When it was published, it was a feminist first and is considered a model of the genre. (A few years later, in 1967, at the University of Paris X Nanterre, she would create the first-ever women's studies course in France, covering women in political life and women in the workplace.) In February 1962 Évelyne suggested that I pursue a double content analysis: that of French-Canadian women's magazines compared to short stories (novellas) in French magazines. I found the project quite appealing, but she remained distant and we did not develop a personal rapport.

Besides the Barthes-Morin presentations, we benefited from ad hoc academic presentations. As well as the French stars Michel Crozier and Jean Stoetzel, we had the opportunity to hear about the German class-conflict political scientist Ralf Dahrendorf; the Swiss sociologist Alfred Willener; researcher Joachim Marcus-Steiff of the Centre national de recherche scientifique; the University of Edinburgh's original thinker of the sociology of organizations and bureaucracy, Tom Burns; and the sociology of communications studied by Paul Lazarsfeld at Columbia University, to name only a few.

Student life in Paris also meant unending cultural discoveries: cathedrals, museums, castles, parks, and surrounding cities and villages. With Canadian friends I went regularly to the *Cinémathèque* or art-house cinemas where we could see the new classics for twenty-five cents, dining on films that had not yet been released in Montreal. We also went to the theatre – the Odéon and the Comédie française, with its cheap student seats up in the gods of the top balcony. During one long weekend in May 1962, four of us Canadian friends went by car to visit Brussels, Bruges, and Ghent, camping (and freezing!) in a public forest in Uccle. My maternal grandmother Essemaeker had died in October 1954, but I managed to find and surprise Great-Aunt Berthe Vanhavre in her very basic apartment in downtown Brussels. I had not sent her a note to let her know, as I was not sure I would be able to locate her. When she opened the door, she hugged me, saying, *"Oh! mais c'est Moniqueke!"* (*"-ke"* being the Flemish diminutive for "dearest"). She had last seen me when I was two years old. I loved her and wrote to her – a nice student would read letters aloud to her, as her vision was poor – and I was able to go back to see her twice before her death in March 1974. With Great-Aunt Berthe gone, my mother's family, the Vanhavres, was no more.

Besides spending time with Renée and Pierre Dandurand, Denyse and Jean-Marie Tétreault (Monique Coupal's cousins), Monique and Jacques Boucher, and some new French friends, I was also invited to a few parties by Mireille Lafortune and Julien Bigras, who were studying with Jacques Lacan, known as the most controversial psychoanalyst since Freud. I also babysat for some of these young families. For my first Christmas, I managed to spend wonderful holidays in London at the apartment of Chantal Perrault and Claude Germain, where I also saw Louis Bernard, Claude and Monique Forget, Claude Garcia, and others.

The highlight of these European discoveries was the realization of an old dream: a summer of camping in the south of France and in Italy with three close Canadian friends – the ones whom had met me when I first arrived in Paris – before their return to Canada in September 1962. I had just started working as the secretary at Télécinex on the Champs-Élysées, opposite François Truffaut's offices. I owed this wonderful opportunity for financial survival to Fernand Cadieux and Pierre Juneau, who knew many people in Paris. Télécinex was a TV-dubbing production company whose biggest customer was Quebec. Besides letting me take some time off for my seminars, the company president gave me a two-and-a-half-month leave for that summer trip. On 15 June I left by train for Périgueux to meet my friends. Since I didn't need to contribute to the cost of a car (which belonged to Denyse and Jean-Marie) or the two tents (theirs and that of Monique Coupal), those two months cost me only $200, gas included. This trip was a gift from the gods, unique, with constant discoveries – we could never have done

it in our adult working lives. Among other places, we visited the unforgettable Lascaux Caves during the last summer they were open to
the public.

In addition to my struggle to take charge of my two projects – a master's thesis and a doctoral thesis – I was dealing with chronic financial
insecurity. A month after I landed in Paris, the value of the Canadian
dollar fell considerably. It fluctuated over the next six months and finally
was devalued in the spring of 1962. My scholarship payments were
greatly affected; on top of this, they were often a month or two late arriving. Solitude was difficult in my second year. Upon my return from
Italy, my mother wrote to tell me that Dad had had thrombophlebitis
in early August; he spent two weeks in the hospital. Six months later,
in January 1963, he had a severe cerebral hemorrhage that left the right
side of his body paralyzed. I became increasingly upset by these events.

Things went from bad to worse: the building where I was living on
Hallé Street was sold, and my tiny apartment was classified C-2 (very
decrepit), as an official document informed me on 1 May. Two weeks
later, I got an eviction notice from the landlady. That was it. I could
not see myself staying in Paris. In any case, my two-year scholarship
had expired.

After shipping my trunks and modest possessions – mainly books
(and architectural magazines for my brother Thomas) – to Canada by
Holland America Lines, I flew from Orly to Montreal on 26 June on
Trans-Canada Airlines (it became Air Canada in 1965). I was not bringing back a new degree or diploma, but I had had a wonderful adventure
of self-discovery, encountering others and exploring the wider world. I
had realized that I was not French but North American – in fact, Canadian – at last resolving the dilemma of my identity. And I understood
the stifling side of Europe. I saw the fundamental differences of nature
and had a renewed appreciation for our forests, the vastness of our
spaces, and the endless northern skies. In those years it seemed to me
that the French were content to die where they were born and had lived
all their life, as if there were no space to move to, to follow one's
dreams. Here in Canada, everything seemed possible! I had lived with
a profusion of beauty and culture, developing my sense of astonishment
and my capacity for wonder.

Mom and my six siblings were at Dorval Airport to welcome me home. It was a warm, sunny day, and life was beautiful! Mom had set an elegant table and had cooked an entire fresh Atlantic salmon in my honour. Quite a change from my impoverished student's diet of pasta and rice.

4

Working and Getting Involved:
Thérèse Casgrain

Upon arrival in Montreal I was taken by surprise when Guy Rocher phoned me, offering me a start as a lecturer at the Department of Sociology (while I had not yet completed my master's thesis and even less a doctoral one!). Even if I needed a job, I did not hesitate a second, thanked him, and declined his offer, explaining that I could not see myself teaching sociology without having learned on the job, having lived the topic(s) he would want me to teach. That was my thinking, but writing about it now, I realized I must have appeared to him as coming from another planet. I was not conscious of not doing things like everybody around. It should be added that, in those years, my classmates and I knew that there were no or very few job openings in our discipline and that we would have to broaden our jobs search. We did not know that, at least in Quebec, sociology was on the verge of becoming super professionalized, with the consequence that a PhD would be required to teach sociology in universities. Have I ever regretted my candid, however negative, reaction? Never.

Shortly after my return in July 1963, I had accompanied Mom and my sister Marie to visit Dad at Notre-Dame-de-la-Merci Hospital, on Gouin Boulevard, an institution for long-term chronic care. It was pitiful to see him there, with others, seriously incapacitated. It was clear to me that afternoon that he had all his mind but could not say even a few words, which came out deformed. He was visibly suffering, so diminished, so lonely. It was all so sad. I have kept a sinister memory of the place, several in one room, and the male nursing aides completely lacking empathy. I would go back to visit him until his death a little more than a year later, on 11 October 1964.

◆ ❋ ◆

After Paris I went back to work with Fernand Cadieux, slowly becoming a true sociologist. To start, my contracts were from some of his friends. From the beginning of July, my first job was to assist Claude Robillard just appointed the first general manager of the Canadian Corporation for the 1967 World Exhibition (Expo '67). A visionary engineer, Claude Robillard had created the Parks Division and the Planning Division at the City of Montreal. After a few months, he resigned from Expo '67, quite angry by the power struggle that arose when Mayor Jean Drapeau brought his good old friend Pierre Dupuy back from Paris. It might also have been the result of Drapeau's grandiose ideas to create new islands in the St Lawrence River and to enlarge St Helen's Island. Mr Robillard then took me with him to the Corporation Sir Georges-Étienne Cartier (Place des Arts), the first part of the complex (including the concert hall Salle Wilfrid-Pelletier) having just been inaugurated on 21 September 1963. As chair of the board, Claude Robillard needed a management study, which he asked me to take on.

When that was completed, through yet another friend of Fernand, Harry Suffrin, a senior economist and a vice president of the super grocery stores Steinberg's, I started on 4 December 1963, reporting to the personnel vice president, Sidney Caplan. My challenge was to study the very high and costly labour turnover rate of their cashiers and to make recommendations. I was an employee and would work at Steinberg's for close to two years.

The turnover rate of cashiers, then their most important contingent of employees, was at 200 per cent per year. The first research contract to solve this problem had been given to an American firm at the then enormous cost of $50,000. The analysis and the recommendations had infuriated "Mr Sam" – the familiar name of the Steinberg's empire founder, Sam Steinberg. In a nutshell, "the cashiers should be glamourized," look

like and dress in a uniform copying air stewardesses! Cashiers work close
to doors constantly opening on harsh Canadian winter at least six
months of the year.

Keeping in mind the research and participant observation work of
Oscar Lewis, I rejected the idea of announcing my role in the company
through an interview in the employee magazine. I asked to remain
anonymous for a few weeks, becoming a candidate cashier myself and
taking the two-week practical course each trainee had to go through.
My purpose was to learn the trade and the acculturation to which they
were subjected through the older employees training them. I was not
the fastest one on the heavy and bulky NRC register cash invented in
1884, even in its latest version, and at times my fingers seemed too short
to punch the keys without looking! The second training week was in
Steinberg's Store No. 35 in the basement of the Morgan (now the Bay)
department store, on St Catherine and Union Streets. A few snobbish
NDG women commiserated with Mom, who happened to be shopping
there that week, on how her eldest had fallen so low. Mom and I had a
good laugh. I had learned a lot on the tricks of the trade, what to do
when one is mad at the boss, such as not punching in an expensive item
once in a while, the customer looking elsewhere, hence punishing the
company. I knew some of what cashiers like, suffered from, thought
was wrong around them, how they judged those above them, and their
opinion of Steinberg's.

In the new year, 1964, my hiring and responsibility were advertised,
as well as the fact that I would survey what cashiers had to say about
their job and would note their viewpoints and suggestions. I actively
participated in the weekend activities of "Miss Cashier of the Year," developed my questionnaire in both French and English, administered
it to a sample, and interviewed enough employees at random. I had
made a few good friends in Personnel: Beatrice Silcoff (and her husband Maurice, president of the Hatters Union, an old personal friend
of David Lewis) and Monique Machabée, as well as Maurice Poteet, an
American, married to a French-Canadian social worker and in charge
of the company magazine and other publications. I had never worked
in English at the time, and Maurice helped me along the way with my
writings. And once in a while I had lunch in the head office cafeteria

with the already accomplished Thérèse Paquet-Sévigny, whom I had first met at University of Montreal in sociology and who would be the first woman to be permanently appointed undersecretary general in the United Nations, as head of the Department of Public Information. If Bea and Monique were two nicely assertive women, Maurice Poteet was very observant and always ready to see the comic side of situations. These four colleagues were true friends, and I kept in touch with each until they died, and I see Thérèse each time I go to Montreal.

The morning I was ready to table my report and recommendations, I came in very early and, before giving a copy to Sid Caplan, my boss, I went quietly to Mr Sam's office and left a copy on his desk. An hour later he called me in, furious that I made a recommendation about the disgusting state of the female employee toilets and so on. He told me to follow him in his limousine and went directly to some stores. Upon return to the Head Office on Hochelaga Street in east end Montreal, he simply ordered that every single one of my recommendations be put into practice at once. We had developed mutual trust for life. A few jobs were then offered to me in the company, but I had concluded that the super-competitive jungle of a big corporation was not for me and I left Steinberg's. Once more I realized that I was a person of projects, not of ongoing processes. I had the rare satisfaction in applied social sciences to learn, a year after my departure, that the cashiers labour turnover had fallen to 18 per cent. Reflecting on this today, I see I probably owe Michel Crozier, the sociologist of organizations I had met and read in Paris, the knowledge that surely helped me at Steinberg's.

I went back to Dyname, working for Fernand Cadieux. He had just obtained an important and strategic federal research contract from the Agricultural Rehabilitation and Development Act (ARDA). The program had been devised to increase income, employment, or standards of living in rural areas. Cadieux's contract was to assess and make recommendations about the year-round tourism potential of Mount Logan in the Chic-Chocs mountain range, part of the Parc national de la Gaspésie. This contract would be running in parallel with, but separate from, the famous Bureau d'aménagement de l'Est du Québec (BAEQ) initiative in the Bas Saint-Laurent and Gaspésie, also with ARDA funding. The provincial experiment in regional development was based on "social animation," with sixty-five researchers on site and twenty community organizers, most young Laval university graduates, "animating" the local villages. The initiative was considered "a virtual social science laboratory." It went on from 1963 to 1966, when their ten-volume report and recommendations were tabled in Quebec City. After the outsiders had left, the local population did not even have one new dock built or an old one repaired. As the main recommendations were based on relocating villages, even towns, the local population went from euphoria to anger. Finally nothing happened with these recommendations.

On our Mount Logan research project we started analyzing the great work of futuristic research already well developed by Stanford University, whose reports and journals we subscribed to. Applying what research in "futuristic projections" taught us on new leisure trends, emerging technologies, foreseeable changes, and their implications was another knowledge window opened. Today we would call it the forecasting or prospective business. What I recall was Cadieux's observation, leading to our recommendations, that outdoor mountain "rediscovery" was an ascending new trend leading to development of new forms of tourism. In this case it called for important development of downhill and cross-country ski trails and for the spring, summer, and fall, climbing, hiking, mountaineering. It meant building an infrastructure to receive, lodge, and feed the travellers, and more.

Cadieux's Dyname had also been granted a small ARDA federal contract for regional development for which he gave me responsibility and kept me busy all summer. As it concerned three regional development projects in the Acadian northeast of New Brunswick, I moved to Fredericton for the contract duration. The northeast was very poor. The challenge was to bring the local communities to develop blueberry farms, peat land and bogs, and fir tree farms. I travelled back and forth from Fredericton, where I worked with the deputy minister of agriculture, Ray Scovil, and his counterpart in fisheries, Léonce Chenard. My work would take me to Caraquet, Lamèque, Shippagan, or Six Roads, Tracadie, and all the way to Tabusintac. It was the dynamic decade of Premier Louis Robichaud's leadership and his Equal Opportunity Program (Chances égales pour tous). When, years later, I returned to the Acadian northeast peninsula as a federal minister, it was a pleasant surprise to see the freshly painted houses and fences, the well-kept gardens with vegetables and flowers, and great local pride and dynamism despite the vagaries of the fishery.

Back in Montreal I worked on an inventory of Quebec talent that might relate to the movie industry to complement the work of University of Ottawa economist O.J. Firestone, who was covering English Canada. This report would lead to the creation of the Canadian Film Development Corporation (later renamed Telefilm Canada) in 1967 under the chairmanship of Michael Spencer. As far as I was concerned, Quebec always had had enormous potential creative talent.

Dyname's applied social sciences projects were becoming more interdisciplinary, which I found new and fascinating. Cadieux had sent me to the McGill Faculty of Engineering to take the NASA special evening post-doc course in project management planning: "PERT and Critical Path Analysis." As the only woman in the group of engineers, the instructors told me to apply it to preparing morning breakfast, while the men were planning the relocation of eastern Montreal oil refineries! Despite the breakfast training, I got the gist of it and loved this new super-logical technique. Back at the office, I was able to apply it to the relocation and extension project of the Constance-Lethbridge Rehabilitation Centre in Montreal West, working with architects, engineers, technicians, rehab professionals, and managers. That was the time I decided not to specialize in a particular branch of sociology but to remain a generalist. I sensed the world would need people rooted in one discipline but capable of understanding the internal logic of other disciplines, as the future would be in multidisciplinary teamwork.

The new profession of sociologist was starting to interest people, and the media now had a sociologist instead of a priest or a psychologist on their panels! I was invited to contribute a few times, and it was a totally new experience. It was in the same vein that the Montreal Catholic School Commission invited me in 1964 to volunteer on a special committee to survey the needs of married women re-entering the working world. A new labour market trend had emerged: there was a cohort of future workers who might never have been in paid employment before marriage and children, or might need recycling after years of absence, and might have no training except a general basic education. At almost the same time a dynamic team of women involved with the YWCA also asked me to work with them on the same topic. One thing leading to another, I was asked to join the Montreal University Women's Club (Association des femmes diplômées des universités) and participate in the Program Committee. I had never been a member of any group. I had gone to meetings and conferences, listening and observing, but I mistrusted ideologies, crusades, and dogmas. The difference this time and the reason I agreed to join was that we would write the club's brief on girls' education for presentation to the Parent Commission on education reform in Quebec, and that was a project that I liked. I remained an active member of the association, eventually joining the board, then returned to being a member until 1991.

Shortly after, in my spare time, there began the great adventure of the Federation of Quebec Women (Fédération des femmes du Québec – FFQ). It all started on 24–25 April 1965 when Thérèse Casgrain invited all women, individuals, and associations to attend a public weekend conference at the Mount-Royal Hotel on Peel Street to commemorate the twenty-fifth anniversary of Quebec women being granted the right to vote. I was enrolled as a panellist on "Women at Work" with another young academic woman, an economist. At the end of the conference, in the widespread enthusiasm of the audience, following a few spontaneous requests – I can still see Simonne Monet-Chartrand, Marthe Legault of the Union des Familles, Paule Sainte-Marie and Renée Geoffroy, both journalists, jumping up to be heard – all women there "voted" for the establishment of an ad hoc committee to organize the foundation of a new federation. I found myself in that small group of about a dozen women of different generations, elites close to Thérèse Casgrain, and unknowns like me.

I did not know Madame Casgrain personally then. Around 1956, however, when I was twenty and she was sixty, and I was accepting as many secretarial short-term contracts as I could, I spent an entire weekend close to her. The occasion was a convention of the Quebec Co-operative Commonwealth Federation / Parti social-démocrate (CCF/PSD) in Montreal. I was the paid secretary, and I recognized some famous faces, but personally knew only Francine Laurendeau and Michel Forest, who were two or three years older than I. We were gathered in a meeting room at McGill University. Pierre Trudeau was most probably there, as well as Jean Marchand and maybe Gérard Pelletier. I do recall Jacques V. Morin, whom I knew a little, and other Quebec union leaders, and I met Frank Scott and Marian, his wife, Michael Oliver, and Eugene Forsey for the first time. We ended up at the Scotts' residence for a cocktail buffet where I had a glimpse of Marian Scott's paintings. Thérèse Casgrain was the indisputable leader that weekend. Confident, serious, and passionate, she was commenting on the big issues of male politics: economic, constitutional, and international dossiers. I was terribly impressed by this grande dame.

At these frequent FFQ foundation meetings in her elegant Westmount apartment, her upper-class manners irritated me, a feminist of a much younger generation. However, I came to understand her *grande bourgeoise* roots and social class behaviour and what it had taken to be a strong woman and public figure of her generation. Suddenly it was as if I had changed binoculars. Thérèse Casgrain was never a team member, but she had networks. She was connected. Like Florence Bird at the Royal Commission on the Status of Women later, she used the power of important men in her social life to get action on an idea, a project, a cause. She would identify the men she needed for this or that initiative and invited everyone to a meeting. After discussions, she announced structures, distributed responsibilities, then rushed to inform the media. When we were founding the FFQ, her ways of working were already irritating a majority of women.

In no time was I thus put in charge of the Program Committee of the future federation. I convinced Rita Cadieux (who had a PhD in social work and was a senior bureaucrat) as well as Gabrielle Hotte (a leader of the Confédération des syndicats nationaux union) to join me. We started working, attending the regular evening meetings at Madame Casgrain's apartment, as well as meetings of our little committee. Rita, Gabrielle, and I developed a questionnaire that, when approved, was distributed as widely as possible notwithstanding our lack of financial means and even an inventory of Quebec women's associations. On weekends we travelled to towns and cities near Montreal, meeting local groups of women, asking what they wanted achieved and suggesting they join the new federation. In Quebec there had never been a feminist movement that was neutral on religion, language, social class, and ethnic origin. This open-to-all approach of the future federation was a big plus. There had also never been a federation made of both associations and individual members. On this point, we owe the innovative proposed new constitution to Alice Desjardins and to the future FFQ president, Réjane Colas.

The founding event took place during the weekend of 23–24 April 1966, a year to the day after the anniversary of Quebec women being granted the right to vote. Some 400 members participated in the event at the same Sheraton Mount-Royal Hotel, adopting a constitution, regulations and procedures, the broad objectives of the program, and electing a board. Thérèse Casgrain was acclaimed honorary president of the FFQ, while Réjane Laberge-Colas became president and I first vice president.

In those days, practices that were often believed to be institutional regulations and laws – federal, provincial, or municipal – were perceived by more and more women as offensive, if not unacceptable. For example, when I started teaching in elementary public schools in Montreal at the age of nineteen, I would have had to resign immediately upon marriage. A woman could not keep her surname after marriage, a serious problem in business and the professions and more. The shocking rule in Quebec by which a mother could not register her child in a hospital, emergency or not, without her husband's signature had just been abolished by the Quebec National Assembly in 1964, further to Minister Claire Kirkland-Casgrain. Daycare centres or any form of early childhood education did not exist, except for a few examples in the private sector for wealthy people. Sale and advertisement of contraceptives and dissemination of information about them were forbidden by the Criminal Code, as was abortion. In immigration cases, the law defined "head of family" as the husband only. Lack of any equity, let alone equality, in pay for working women was particularly shocking, adding to all other forms of discrimination at work based on the usual sexist stereotypes and ghettos of "women's jobs." I could go on with examples of prejudicial treatment of women offenders, women in small family business, poor women, issues of citizenship and Native women's status, and more.

In Quebec, after the Parent Commission on education reform tabled its report and recommendations in 1964, women's action was now redirected towards influencing the major revision of the Civil Code. An important symposium marking the centennial of the Code civil du Bas Canada was held in 1966, spreading the analyses done and reforms proposed. At the same time, Maître Paul-André Crépeau, president of the newly created Office de révision du Code civil, was multiplying study groups on each section of Quebec Civil Law. The Federation of Quebec Women got involved from day one. At the Sherbrooke Civil Code centennial I was invited as a sociologist to present on *Perspectives d'intégration de la femme dans la société civile* (women's integration in civil society) later published in the Symposium Acts.

At the same time, English-Canadian women, through their long-established associations – the National Council of Women, Business and Professional Women's Clubs, National Council of Jewish Women, Women's Institutes, the Catholic Women's League of Canada, Woman's Christian Temperance Union, the Homemakers' Clubs, B'nai B'rith Women, the Junior League, the Voice of Women, Elizabeth Fry Societies, YWCAs, University Women's Clubs, Zonta Club, Women's Press Club, and more – had been regrouping in a vast coalition under the leadership of Lauria Sabia, then president of the Canadian Federation of University Women Clubs. The coalition of thirty-two national women's organizations, called the Committee for the Equality of Women, had articulated one demand from the Pearson federal government: the setting up of a royal commission of inquiry on the status of women, which was also the wish of the only woman in Cabinet, Judy LaMarsh.

At her request, Thérèse Casgrain and Réjane Laberge-Colas met Laura Sabia early in September 1966 to exchange on the topic and to figure out where we stood, we the Quebec women. We had an emergency FFQ Board meeting where the situation was presented and discussed. The only one impatient for results, not for more palaver, I argued the best I could that women had been sufficiently studied and that what needed to be changed was well known, concluding in good faith that I considered this commission of inquiry a waste of time and money. But the unanimity of the board was clear and, in a twist of irony, because of my writing skills I was asked to immediately write the press release announcing our full support for the English-Canadian women's coalition in favour of a royal commission of inquiry!

To be completely open, I should add that, some time later, I received a call from Marc Lalonde, then Lester B. Pearson's chief of staff, asking me if I would be interested in serving as a commissioner on this future inquiry. I asked him for a rapid description of a commissioner's role and concluded in the negative. Then I inquired about the title or function of the person in charge of the commission on a daily basis, to which he replied: secretary general. I answered that such a function might interest me and I forgot the phone call.

5

Executive Secretary of a
National Royal Commission

On 16 February 1967 Prime Minister Pearson announced the creation of the Royal Commission on the Status of Women in Canada (RCSW) and named the seven commissioners. Florence Bird (known under her CBC pen name of "Anne Francis") was appointed chair. The prime minister and most of his Cabinet did not want to create such a commission. Could the government have ignored the women's request for a commission on this topic, and if so, what would have happened? No, it could not. The Liberal government was a minority one, with the New Democratic Party (NDP) holding the balance of power. It was the much celebrated Centenary of Confederation, culminating with the successful Expo '67. This, plus the culture of the sixties – the Commission on Bilingualism and Biculturalism soul-searching on our national identity and the emerging mobilization around human rights issues – made the decision a logical one in the circumstances, although a potential political nightmare. In addition, women as a constituency were simply not part of the political agenda. It is unlikely that politicians quite understood, nor could they assess exactly what was going on, as is often the case when politicians are confronted with social movements.

It is important to note that after the B&B Commission was created, without the full and equal participation of francophone women, it was politically impossible to appoint a royal commission demanded by English-speaking women only. The women's movements in Quebec and English Canada operated within the context of the "two solitudes." The "second wave" of Canadian feminism in the 1960s developed and organized through two separate entities that followed two distinct dynamics, within the context of distinct histories. The Quebec and English-Canadian women's movements did, however, share a similar agenda, connected later in the decade, and once that was created, the commission was inevitable.

So there was a commission but time was going by, and nobody was hearing a word about it, if not that candidates were being interviewed for the position of executive secretary. It was said that some sixty Canadians, mainly successful male academics, Guy Rocher being one, had been discussed by the chair but rejected by the commissioners. Two months later, in early April, I got another call from Marc Lalonde asking me to be in Ottawa the following morning for an interview at the commission. I was met there by Florence Bird and Jacques Henripin, one of her commissioners. It was a cordial interview. Having no specific plan to offer, I just described the type of work we had undertaken at the FFQ and explained how I enjoyed teamwork in research as well as in community action. I added how I could see facilitating women's participation in the public hearings by eliminating or toning down the legalistic settings of an inquiry. And I insisted on the importance of developing a friendly and simpler approach to presentations and discussions. The commissioners rapidly approved my appointment, and the related Order-in-Council was signed at once.

The membership of the royal commission was as follows: the chair, Florence Bird, was an Ottawa journalist and broadcaster much known and respected in English Canada; Elsie Gregory MacGill, an aeronautical engineer from Toronto; Jeanne Lapointe, a Laval University professor of literature; Jacques Henripin, the director of the Department of Demography at the University of Montreal; Lola Lange, the manager of a large Alberta farm and a director of the Farm Women's Union of her province; Doris Ogilvie, a Juvenile Court judge from Fredericton, New Brunswick; and Donald R. Gordon Jr, a journalist, professor of political science at Waterloo University. He would resign on 1 November 1967 and be replaced on 2 February 1968 by John Humphrey, a McGill law professor who had drafted the UN Universal Declaration of Human Rights. The chair was sixty-six when appointed. Two other commissioners were also in their sixties, while the four others were between forty-one and fifty-two years old. I had just turned thirty-one.

This sudden fabulous new professional challenge meant that I would have to terminate the lease on my large and comfortable duplex main floor in NDG, organize another venue for my youngest sister Marie, who lived with me, and find something in Ottawa. I would be making return trips to Montreal every weekend and would find a place to live there, in the absence of any budget coverage when back home and any travelling expenses while in temporary employment in Ottawa. The chair informed me of my salary, of course better than I had ever earned. I admit knowing nothing about negotiating a salary and what to discuss. I did my best to not leave my work at Dyname unfinished nor let down Fernand Cadieux, who had encouraged me without reserve to accept this unique challenge.

Once I was in Ottawa, the clerk of the Privy Council, Gordon Robertson, invited me to his office and explained the situation regarding royal commissions in general and this one in particular. For example, the chair was coming to the office daily while it was expected she might come a day here or there at the most in between commissioners meetings, and her honoraria were weighing the budget down. Gordon Robertson assured me all the help I would need. He concluded with two conditions I had to respect. The report and the recommendations should be completed within three years. As to the budget, total cost should not exceed $2.5 million, which I promised to respect. Besides the vagaries of politics, another problem for the Pearson government was the famous Commission on Bilingualism and Biculturalism, also known as the Laurendeau-Dunton Commission, set up in 1963, which would publish its final report only in 1969, having gone millions over budget, and the cash cow of academics. The cost of the B&B has been estimated at $9 million. The Privy Council knew that the wide open field of our inquiry could rapidly fit the same bill and wanted to ensure this would not occur again. Our commission took three and a half years including printing the report, and cost less than $3 million.

When I started in my new role, the Privy Council Office had already rented offices for us in downtown Ottawa, and it had provided us with basic support staff. I first worked on developing my small management team, who would be the decision-making core group on all proposals, ideas, and initiatives, to be presented to the commissioners for discussion

and approval. We would be four, two younger women and two of retirement age, two francophones and two anglophones. Besides myself
were Dorothy Caldwell (just retired from a key position in the Public
Service Commission), Grace Menard (a psychologist, from Carleton University) and Monique Coupal (a Montreal lawyer). After I had started
my work as executive secretary, I learned that before I was interviewed,
another sociologist, Dr David Kirk, of Waterloo University, definitely
older than I (who had just turned thirty-one), had been hired by the chair
as director of research in social sciences, which I also was, making for
an unclear situation to say the least. Consequently, he automatically became a member of my small management core group but was interested
only in the research program, which he considered his alone. He seldom
came to our weekly meetings. The beginnings of the commission had
been and until the summer would continue to be rather chaotic, as I was
about to discover.

The management team started preparing the next meeting of the commissioners – "our" first – with a structured agenda, information documents, and a tentative list of proposals both about the research program
and the public hearings. I had concluded from the commissioners' biographies that only one commissioner, Elsie Gregory MacGill, was an
informed feminist, knowledgeable about the problems of the status of
Canadian women. She was active in the Business and Professional
Women's Club. So a group learning process of the seven of them and the
four of us was put on the agenda as a priority of that meeting. We presented and discussed the basic feminist literature of the time: Simone de
Beauvoir ("Women Are Made, Not Born" as in *The Second Sex*), and
Betty Friedan's *Feminine Mystique* (1963), articulating a powerful de-
nunciation of "the housewife's" role – "the problem without a name."
Kate Millett's *Sexual Politics* and Germaine Greer's *Female Eunuch* were
respectively published in 1969 and in 1970, when the work of the commission had already been completed. We also looked through a few texts
from the Women's Bureau of the federal Department of Labour. Created
in 1954 by the indefatigable Marion Royce, it was successively developed under Jessica Findlay and Sylva M. Gelber, the latter being its director at the time of the royal commission. Being the unique federal
source of information on women in matters of public policies, it had

nurtured itself, apart from the annual briefs and recommendations of women's associations on the work of the International Labour Office in Geneva. We also reviewed with the commissioners the US Presidential Commission on the Status of Women final report of October 1963, first chaired by Eleanor Roosevelt, then by her vice president Esther Peterson further to the chair's death in 1962. It had been a twenty-four-member commission of men and women, including elected representatives from both Houses. One key approach of the American report was to replace protective legislation for women by equal rights legislation.

The four women commissioners, Florence Bird, Lola Lange, Jeanne Lapointe, and Doris Ogilvie, quickly became at ease in navigating these feminist intellectual frameworks. It was hard to assess the interest of our two men commissioners, at the time Donald R. Gordon Jr and Jacques Henripin, although the latter involved himself fully in the commission's work from its beginning to its very end. We also started discussing the approach and organization we had in mind for the public hearings and their possible calendar, and we went through the research areas needed to feed our final report and recommendations.

Towards the end of "our" first meeting and without a word to the chair, the commissioners invited me privately for a drink at the Elgin Hotel where they were staying. They wanted to get to know me better, and we chatted. Then they told me that they trusted me and that I would have their full support. And they began to tear up their resignation letters, which they had in their pockets! I was shaken. The importance of having developed a positive mutual trust!

Unfortunately, back in the office, the situation suddenly deteriorated. It started when, out of the blue, David Kirk proposed a visit to China to study their daycare system. Our management rejected it as uninformative and financially impossible. I had always dreamt of visiting China but my solid common sense told me the idea was ill-advised, unrealistic, and expensive, and it would teach us nothing because of the incompatible differences between our social, economic, and political systems. In any event, I had completely excluded travels abroad for commissioners as well as staff because of our financial situation. We were still discussing our general research program with the commissioners, but it was understood that if some research took place in the office by our own staff, the majority of the specific projects needed was to be contract research given to Canadian outside experts.

Decades after the commission was over, through the published work of academic socio-historian Gail G. Campbell, of the University of New Brunswick, I discovered details of the first months of the life of our commission that had been totally unknown to me. Before I was hired as executive secretary, the chair was running the commission on a complete ad hoc basis, going from one idea to another, phoning important male individuals she knew to discuss this idea or another, and so on. She had no administration or management experience and did not know the workings of royal commissions. So, shortly before my time, she had created a subcommittee of the two male commissioners, Gordon and Henripin, in charge of identifying a suitable research director. Donald Gordon then put forward the name of Dr David Kirk, a sociologist from his own University of Waterloo, who was then selected on an idea he had. He proposed, as the centrepiece of the commission's research, the development of a questionnaire, to be distributed to 1,200 women and 600 men in each of Canada's four regions (the West, Ontario, Quebec, and the Atlantic Provinces), for a total of 7,600 potential respondents. When the commissioners learned the estimated cost of administering a survey of the magnitude Kirk proposed – $450,000 – and the time frame required, they began to doubt the viability of the project. After much discussion, and on the advice of the Privy Council Office, the survey was scrapped. I knew none of that during my tenure in office. That the clerk of the Privy Council, Gordon Robertson, did not inform me of that relatively recent and key past while briefing me when I came onboard still shocks me.

Unknown to us, after the four of us of the management team had explained to Kirk that we could not go to China, David, supported by Donald Gordon Jr, simply gave Florence Bird an ultimatum: it was him or me. I had never encountered a problem with Commissioner Gordon; he would argue or oppose strongly, being very much his own person, but that was him. The problem was presented to the commissioners in a secret meeting at the beginning of July. After having heard Kirk, they called me in, asking for my viewpoint and testimony. To their general surprise, and my own, we all discovered that he received the same salary as I did, and that he was fully reimbursed for his weekly hotel and expenses in Ottawa, as well as his air travel each weekend. When they asked the chair to explain these unfair discrepancies and difference in treatment, she replied, "It was because he was a man and he was married." David Kirk was dismissed. But the government, then sued by Kirk for breach of contract (who had a 2.5-year contract, while I was not protected by any contract), had to pay an important sum of money to settle the case, I was told in the six figures. My own travelling expenses home to Montreal and lodging in Ottawa were never covered.

I don't want to leave the impression that Florence Bird's dramatic ways of getting on with her job made my relationship with her difficult. That never was the case. Shortly after my arrival, as her office door was always open and she had quite a good voice, I was flabbergasted when she phoned important men she knew to check if what we were suggesting made sense, but I kept it to myself. Very rapidly, however, I discovered that it was to be expected from her generation (I was half her age), a widely admired CBC female broadcaster and political analyst, a generalist, not an expert. I had had the same negative very first impression of Thérèse Casgrain, until one day, it was as if I had changed glasses and saw the milieu she came from differently. Florence Bird was also definitely a member of the Canadian elite with her husband, John Bird, former editor of the *Winnipeg Tribune* and a respected journalist at the *Financial Post* during the commission. When she invited me, alone, to their cottage to meet her family from Philadelphia, or for supper with her husband, or when describing to me what Bryn Mawr had meant to her, I was discovering another world, which I always loved to do. She could be charmingly old fashioned and elitist, but she could express a wonderful juvenile enthusiasm for causes dear to her heart. As Pierre Trudeau would appoint her to the Senate in 1978, where she would serve until 1983, years during which I was already minister of national health and welfare, we saw each other regularly, at caucus, in the Parliamentary restaurant, and at Liberal conventions. I last visited her in her retirement residence with her friend Margaret Wade Labarge, a renowned medievalist historian to whom we had given our very first research contract.

It was summer and I retreated from the toxic atmosphere created by the David Kirk crisis, going back to Montreal every weekend. At the

end of June Mother was rushed to St Luc Hospital, where she was diagnosed with inoperable terminal cancer and had three months to live.
She came back home and we, her seven children, did everything to make
her life the best possible in the circumstances. Mom was very brave and
never complained. She passed away peacefully, fully conscious, on Tuesday, 26 September 1967, with all of us around her. She was only sixty-
one but had gone through two world wars and never had an easy life
once in Canada.

Back at the commission we had started thinking of how to frame our
research program and, for that, the commissioners felt the need to express the values and basic assumptions they shared, which would un-
derpin our work and recommendations. The basic assumption behind
the commission work appears in the foreword of the report: "Women
and men, having the same rights and freedoms, share the same responsibilities. They should have an equal opportunity to fulfill this obli-
gation. We have, therefore, examined the status of women and made
recommendations in the belief that there should be equality of opportunity to share the responsibilities to society as well as its privileges and
prerogatives." In particular, the commission adopted four principles:
first, that women should be free to choose whether or not to take up
employment outside their homes. The second was that the care of children is a responsibility to be shared by the mother, the father, and society. The third principle specifically recognized the child-bearing function
of women and that society has a responsibility for women because of
pregnancy and child-birth, and special treatment related to maternity
will always be necessary. The fourth principle was that in certain areas
women will require special treatment for an interim period to overcome
the adverse effects of discriminatory practices.

    This exercise followed long discussions on a possible theoretical
framework for the research program in particular. We went back to the
feminist literature of the time and then examined whether a theory of
social change and the conditions for it to succeed would help us. Some
commissioners and staff members, less at ease with either de Beauvoir's

concepts, ambiguities, or lack of pragmatic prescriptions for change, chose to promote an "equal rights and opportunities" approach, especially in economic and educational matters. This choice was made in the absence of a proven theory of social change. The only Canadian planned experience of social change at the time of the RCSW had been in matters of regional development through federal-provincial projects set up further to the 1961 Agricultural Rehabilitation and Development Act (ARDA), more particularly the BAEQ in Quebec, as I described earlier.

In addition, the commissioners and senior staff agreed that, in the absence of clear rules for initiating social change or a satisfactory theory of women's subjection, the legitimacy of the commission's work lay in the voices of Canadian women themselves. No one doubted for a moment that women had something to say about their status. Only the occasion had been missing. That is how, if its academic and often theoretical research component characterized the work of the B&B Commission, the public hearings marked the work of the RCSW. We of course also granted research contracts – about three dozen.

On the research side, the commission rejected numerous research submissions for their esoteric nature. We always reported our decisions to the commissioners at each of their meetings. For lack of a conceptual framework, and in light of our tight schedule and short existence, we created our own benchmarks for assessing our needs and the projects submitted, based on common sense, intuition, and judgment rather than a grid of clear criteria. Some academics were insulted by our decisions. I remember one such case, submitted by the famous and controversial sociobiologist Lionel Tiger, then at UBC, who tried every line of reasoning to convince me to fund his research on "male bonding" and his book *Men in Groups*, published in 1969, which had not impressed my three colleagues either. He had explained to me how men felt comfortable among themselves in groups. Their nature makes them work spontaneously in teams, which women cannot do. Male bonding had aggression, violence, and the need to control as its epicentre. Although no expert in sociobiology, I had read *On Aggression* by the Austrian biologist and zoologist Konrad Lorenz, later winner of the Nobel Prize, which was at another level. Tiger suggested I was backward in not understanding the obvious, while I was telling him he did not meet our research needs grid.

The contract research reports did not necessarily suggest recommendations, and our commission report contained weaker as well as stronger recommendations. At the time I was particularly sensitive to the weakness in our chapter 7, "Participation of Women in Public Life." When writing the draft of it, I included as a subtitle a quotation from Pierre Mendès-France, the short-lived prime minister of France, whom I always deeply admired: "Politics is not the possession of those who give it all their time, all their efforts. It belongs to everybody, and everybody ought to be involved in it." It was from a text he had signed, published at the time we were writing our report, in the May 1969 *Saturday Review*, entitled "The Mission of Politics." None of us knew anything about political parties and electoral campaigns when we were drafting our report. But I could see these chapter recommendations were simply pious wishes and felt frustrated by our failure to deal thoroughly with the real problems underlying the absence of women from the public sphere.

We were missing a feminist analysis of power and patriarchy, and the conceptual tools for such an analysis. Discussion was focused on whether or not gender was determined by nature or influenced by culture, but we lacked frameworks to move beyond this dichotomy. We had not heard of the concept of empowerment. Nor had we heard of the feminist process as an expression of the values shared specifically by women because of their socialization – such as nurturance and caring, service to others and self-abnegation, peace, cooperation, harmony in human relations and in one's environment – values so badly needed as an alternative to the way power has been traditionally exercised. And, above all, we knew nothing of the organizational side of electoral politics – the big Blue, Red, or Orange machine – and had no idea of how important they were. That is what we should have understood from the perspective of male chauvinism to start understanding "women and politics."

The research done in-house and the studies commissioned to academics expressed history in the making. Women's studies were about to start on the most modest scale in Canadian and in American universities, but "feminist scholarship" was still unknown. The "classics" at the time were female academics such as Mary Beard, Alice Rossi, Evelyne Sullerot, Alva Myrdal, Marie-José Chombart de Lauwe, Viviane Isambert-Jamati, Andrée Michel, Margaret Mead, or Jessie Bernard. They were from France, the United States, the United Kingdom, and Sweden. Nobody would refer to them as feminist scholars. They simply were the first to study women as legitimate subjects. In 1967–68 the commission gave Canadian researchers, often young professors, now famous feminist scholars, the opportunity to develop what would become important feminist critique and theory through research contracts and publication. One was Micheline Dumont, from Sherbrooke University, who wrote a history of Quebec women for the commission. She developed the now well-known, original hypothesis on Quebec female religious orders as a channel for women to realize their intellectual and managerial potential through legitimate social roles other than those of marriage and motherhood.

For lack of a general theory, we remained as close as possible to the women of Canada whose voices we wanted to amplify. Quite early, the commission called for a presentation of briefs from organizations and individuals. We had a special division in our offices of four mature women ready to get back into the labour market, more or less part-time, their children being old enough, in charge of getting "women's voices" to the table. They were responsible for reaching out to groups, answering telephone requests on "how to," and were privileged contacts at the public hearings. A bilingual brochure, *What Do You Have to Say about the Status of Women?*, was distributed across the country in supermarkets and libraries and through associations and the mass media. We were also the first Canadian royal commission to rethink what in previous commissions had always been a rather legalistic process surrounded with an impressive apparatus of protocol and formality. We wanted to have hearings in spaces friendly to women: shopping malls –Yorkdale, in Toronto, which had opened in 1964 – temples or church basements, public libraries and so on. We received 468 briefs and about 1,000 letters of opinion. Many of these submissions entailed substantial research from those who presented them and proved to be invaluable to the commission.

In 15 April 1968 the seven commissioners and staff began their public consultation in Victoria, BC, totalling thirty-seven days of public hearings from west to east throughout the country, concluding in Ottawa at the beginning of October. Over some ten days in August – we had no meetings in the summer – the chair, Florence Bird, Lola Lange, and I lived the then rare experience of meeting women to listen and discuss their status in Whitehorse, Yellowknife, and Fort Rae (Great Slave Lake), as well as at the Keewatin District (then Northwest Territories) and Churchill (Manitoba). In some cities we were able to set up a hot line connected to our local hearings. And Canadian women owe a huge debt of gratitude to Florence Bird for another Canadian first: she sold to CBC-TV the idea of having a team of technicians and a friendly and competent young TV reporter, Marguerite McDonald, to follow us everywhere, presentations being recorded, with a report on the air the same evening or the day after.

For me as a young woman discovering Canada through other women, the experience of the public hearings – and of the whole commission for that matter – is one of the most memorable of my life. What I discovered month after month, week after week, is how universal women's experiences were. This would be a lesson for life. Women in rural areas of Canada, women living and working in cities, native or immigrant women, young students as well as older women, francophone and anglophone women, they all said the same things. They spoke of their aspirations and the lack of opportunities, the prejudices and stereotypes, the discrimination and injustice, the need for legal changes regarding marriages and families to attain real and equal partnership. They spoke of the children they cared for. They stressed how the present political, economic, and social structures of Canada were an insult to their dignity as women. What they had to say was most empowering, and it then seemed to me that the intrinsic value of the case was so obvious that society – the state – would have to understand and readjust as soon as the report and its recommendations were released, demonstrating what needed to be done!

Back at the writing table and the challenge of a report, we survived as a group and produced an almost unanimous report by keeping to as pragmatic an approach as possible. John Humphrey decided at the end to write a minority report, as he could not agree with advocating temporary quotas as a measure of correction, although he agreed with our analysis. I had heard that a report of a royal commission no longer had any legal existence once tabled in the House of Commons and usually ended up "on the shelf." Before we concluded our work, I quietly took the administrative risk of having us solicit and contribute financially to two initiatives after the tabling of the report. Their mandate was to promote public discussion about our recommendations and nurture women's mobilization to action. The FFQ, under the leadership of Francine Dépatie, published a $1.00 *"Guide de discussion,"* while one was later released by the National Council of Women, who had commissioned an English one from the Toronto chapter of the Canadian Association of Adult Education. In addition, the commission's chair, Florence Bird, a well-known broadcaster, used the media extensively to publicize the report's recommendations, while the commissioners and myself accepted as many invitations as possible from women's associations to discuss the report.

When the report of the RCSW was tabled on 7 December 1970, a respected journalist from the *Toronto Star*, Anthony Westell, wrote,

At 2.11 p.m. in the House of Commons Monday, the Prime Minister rose, bowed politely to the Speaker, and tabled a bomb, already primed and ticking.

The bomb is called the Report of the RCSW in Canada, and it is packed with more explosive potential than any device manufactured by terrorists ...

And as a political blockbuster, it is more powerful than that famous report of the controversial commission on bilingualism and biculturalism.

This 488-page book, in its discreet green, white and blue cover, demands radical change ... not merely with relations between French and English, but between man and woman. The history of the problem it describes and sees to solve is not 100 years of Confederation but the story of mankind.

First attention focuses naturally on the Commission's 167 proposals for practical action, from reform of the law to provide

abortion on demand to rewriting of schoolbooks which teach
sexual discrimination to our children.

But controversial as some of these proposals may seem now,
they will quickly be accepted in substance, if not in every detail.
They are reasonable answers to real problems which can no
longer be ignored.

Between 1971 and the beginning of the recession (1976), the Canadian government integrated women's issues in the official discourse and
took action on several fronts that improved the daily lives of thousands
of women in Canada. It did so exceptionally rapidly and smoothly,
when compared with state action in most industrialized countries, including the United States, with the exception of the Nordic countries.
A 1979 review of the recommendations of the RCSW carried out by the
Canadian Advisory Council on the Status of Women indicated that 43
(35.2 per cent) recommendations were considered implemented, 53
(43.4 per cent) were deemed partially implemented, and 24 (19.7 per
cent) were judged as not implemented, with 2 (1.7 per cent) considered
to be irrelevant. So some three-quarters of the commission's 167 recommendations were implemented, in itself quite a feat.

The state failed to set into motion the radical changes requesting society's transformation. In the federal government, the best illustrations
are pay equity, daycare, and abortion. If we take pay equity to illustrate
the point, all that the Liberal government was able to do, after bitter
inside arguments, was to create a one-person royal commission in 1983,
at least keeping the issue alive. Judge Rosalie Abella reported to the
new Conservative government of Brian Mulroney in October 1984. She
made specific recommendations on systemic discrimination in the workplace: salary, seniority, job classification, training and development, special needs, career opportunities, promotion, and affirmative action.
Nothing of any consequence has since been discussed or implemented
at the national level, and in today's Canada, women's pay still lags behind men's salaries by roughly 30 per cent! The state has also dismissed
any attempt to fundamentally change the market rules or the family arrangements, as recommended in chapter 4, "Women and the Family,"
and chapter 5, "Taxation and Child-Care Allowances." However, I be-

lieve that a great number of citizens would welcome fundamental changes in our society. As usual, politicians lag behind the voters, thinking they know them only too well.

I had the honour to co-sign the report with the commissioners, including the recommendations making abortion by a qualified medical practitioner during the first three months of pregnancy the sole decision of the woman. It also said that the Criminal Code should be amended to permit abortion by a qualified practitioner at the request of a woman pregnant for more than twelve weeks if the doctor is convinced that the continuation of the pregnancy would endanger the physical or mental health of the woman. It included the case of a substantial risk that if the child were born, it would be greatly handicapped, either mentally or physically. But my real personal choice would have been to co-sign Elsie Gregory MacGill's minority report, a choice I did not have as the executive director of the Commission. As I said in the House of Commons a few years later, after having been elected as an MP, abortion should be decriminalized and be "a private medical matter between patient and doctor," quoting Elsie MacGill in her minority statement. Although Prime Minister Trudeau recognized women exercised a primary role in deciding on abortion, he believed that Canadian society was deeply divided on the issue of abortion and his 1969 reform was all that would be offered politically.

Readers of our report are always quite shocked that violence against women was not included. It took a shocking and revealing public incident twelve years later for the issue to become an object of public policy! I was sitting in the House as a frontbencher when the first parliamentary report titled *Wife Battering* was tabled on 12 May 1982, followed by the general nervous laugh of male MPs and a few loud trivial comments or vulgar jokes. Despite this shocking reaction, an evolution had taken place, as shown by the title of the document, produced by a mostly male parliamentary committee, bluntly referring to women as the prime victims. (Only three of the twelve members were female: Thérèse Killens, Flora MacDonald, and Pat Carney.) According to my recollection, several MPs, shamed by the indignation of the media and the protests of their constituents, attended special screenings and discussion groups of National Film Board productions such as *Not a Love*

Story, trying to understand an issue that had remained entirely in the private sphere.

Violence towards women – physical, sexual, and psychological – was not even identified by the commission as a feminist issue. Brutality, beating, rape, and incest were topics society was not yet ready to acknowledge existed, had they been voiced during the public hearings. Of course, we all knew of these facts. But they were considered personal problems, individual, not to say exceptional, and not feminist issues.

A rapid content analysis of the 1970 Hansard, when the report was tabled, reveals no serious, recurring, or systematic interest of Parliament in the problems and needs of women in society, with the exception of NDP MP Grace McInnis's questions and comments, then the only woman sitting in the House of Commons (1968–72). Policy issues of special interest to women, usually of a very specific nature, were still being discussed on an ad hoc basis. When the report was tabled in Parliament, after more than three years of media coverage of the commission, MPs had started debating the Maternity Leave Act; the White Paper *Unemployment in the 70's* (dealing with compensation during pregnancy); and Kathleen Archibald's report *Sex and the Public Service.*

Shortly after the tabling of the report, the Privy Council appointed Freda Paltiel, a feminist, middle-management civil servant, as coordinator to implement our report, an interdepartmental committee to support her work, and an Office of Equal Opportunities for Women in the Public Service Commission. Less than six months after the tabling of the report, Prime Minister Pierre Trudeau appointed Robert Andras, who was minister of state for urban affairs, also minister responsible for the status of women. I had become a civil servant, in the Research Branch of the CRTC, and was appointed to the interdepartmental committee.

Many women's associations and others, such as the Canadian Union of Public Employees (CUPE), further to consultations with their members, wrote their own report on the status of women expressing the problems and solutions regarding their membership preoccupations, thus reinforcing the royal commission report. At their national convention Grace Hartman, at the time vice president of that powerful union (then president in 1975), tabled and obtained the adoption of both our report and recommendations and theirs. A year later, in 1972, a new national coalition of women's associations was created in the wake of Laura Sabia's original coalition and under her inspiration: the National ad hoc Action Committee on the Status of Women. Their action was launched with 500 delegates from some thirty different associations, during the conference "Strategy for Change," in Toronto on 7–9 April 1972. I was one of them. A few years later, NAC had the unique privilege of making an annual presentation to Cabinet. In my first year as a Cabinet member, on 17 February 1977, NAC presented their brief. It was a historical first, and Cabinet was represented by Ministers Ron Basford, Barney Danson, Marc Lalonde, Jeanne Sauvé, and myself, then minister of national revenue. The tradition went on during the Trudeau years and for the first years of the Mulroney government.

In addition, during the more than eight years I sat in Cabinet as a minister, any memorandum to Cabinet tabled for discussion and (hopefully!) approval had to include a section entitled "Status of Women," whatever the topic being presented. The minister who signed the memorandum had to clearly express how, directly or indirectly, the request would affect women in Canada.

The Legal Education and Action Fund (LEAF) was also developing, underground so to speak, and would be officially created in 1985. Several women lawyers in the Department of Justice and other federal departments were helping women from behind the scenes. Their colleagues and friends in private practice joined LEAF further to both the new Canadian Constitution and Charter of Rights and Freedoms sanctioned in Ottawa by the Queen in April 1982. As they perfectly describe it on their website, "They tasked themselves with the job of ensuring the Canadian Constitution, and its Charter of Rights and Freedoms, would be an instrument through which women's substantive equality could be won. They also recognized that the fundamental change about to happen to Canada's laws held a promise that would only be realized if women activists kept women's rights front and centre." We owe them a lot.

I learned years later that our report of the royal commission had travelled a lot and was known in other countries. In May 1998 I was invited as a colleague researcher and speaker by the Centre for Women's

Development Studies in New Delhi. I was astonished to find that researchers and professors were familiar with our names and knew parts
of our report from memory! They even had a few copies, annotated and
a bit worn out!

To have been appointed executive secretary of a national royal commission gave me a unique opportunity to develop. Circumstances helped
me affirm my leadership; practise my sense of interpersonal relations,
including diplomacy, with many different social actors; establish valuable and interesting connections and networks everywhere; deepen my
teamwork potential; gauge the limits of the possible; learn how to re-
solve conflicts; quickly grasp trends or differences in opinions; but also
bring together, motivate, and convince; rapidly get over big dramas and
bad stress; and apply rigorous management to public finances. It is often
said that I have vision, vision being always rather relative! As to intuition, it seems that I am gifted with it, but I cannot help that. And once
I have understood an issue, a situation, I can make a decision without
hesitation and stick to it.

It was with great pleasure that I greeted the commissioners arriving
for a meeting or the public hearings. It has been a pleasure to get to
know them, to understand their internal logic regarding feminism, to
listen to them, to discuss with them, to eventually identify a fixed idea
(!), to travel, relax, and laugh together. I could count on the support
and advice of our small core group and staff researchers, hearings co-
ordinators, organizers, translators, and other support staff. In addition,
I got the best secretary there could ever be, Suzanne Richard, a mother
of eight, pregnant when we started working together! I had the great
luck, years later, as minister of national health and welfare, to work
with her again, having "stolen" her from Pierre Juneau. The commission was, I admit, one of the most exhilarating and gratifying experiences of my life and one of which I am, I confess, very proud.

◆✳◆

In the fall of 1970, preparing to move back to Montreal to work, I was
invited by Charles Lussier, a commissioner in the federal public service,
to discuss my next possible career move in Ottawa, which was very flat-

tering. The problem is that I am not really a careerist and I had nothing in mind! At around the same time, Pierre Juneau, first president of the new Canadian Radio-television and Telecommunications Commission (CRTC), contacted me to see if I would be ready to join the Research Branch of the commission as assistant director. The director was André Martin, a famous French short film director, and his team had twelve or fifteen young and a few senior people somehow involved with radio-television and cultural creation: Patrick Gossage, Rodrigue Chiasson, Liska Bridle, and Mary Wilson. The Research Branch was a most original and creative group from media, film, and humanities backgrounds. I recall one special long-term initiative: editing the Harold Innis papers for publication, somehow an unusual project, except if one thinks of his theories on media and communications and the ways this new powerful set of human activities was reshaping culture and civilization. This and other work would be feeding Pierre Juneau's thinking and speeches.

My involvement with the team was immediate and totally unexpected as the result of the so-called October Crisis. On 10 October 1970 the British trade commissioner James Cross and the Quebec labour minister Pierre Laporte were kidnapped by the Front de Libération du Québec (FLQ). Then the War Measures Act was enacted in Parliament by Prime Minister Trudeau the night of 15–16 October. On 17 October Laporte was killed in Saint-Hubert, south of Montreal. It was only on 4 December that James Cross was discovered with a group of five terrorists. Their three missing associates would be found only on 28 December. Prime Minister Trudeau withdrew Canadian troops from Quebec on 5 January 1971. A terribly tragic episode.

The Prime Minister's Office asked our CRTC Research Branch to monitor media use. With my new colleagues I set up a monitoring system, recording critical moments in a timeline, forecasting possible future moves on radio and television in Quebec. Relaying each other from early morning to 2 a.m. the next day, we listened and watched, recording media output if significant, analyzing media facts and trends, and every night I personally delivered a sealed envelope summarizing the situation to the PMO.

In normal times, my responsibility was to keep the team alive and well and protect them from unnecessary bureaucracy, which I did with pleasure. In April 1971 I sat on the jury of "Miss CRTC"! Otherwise my memory just kept titles or topics of dossiers in which I was involved, not their objectives, orientations, or recommendations to the president, such as the pros and cons of a new hot dossier, that of product marketing directed at children's television programs. Another one was multicultural broadcasting, a hot new topic, and my meetings with Casimir Stanczykowski, the founder of CFMB in 1962 and the first multilingual broadcaster in Canada, regarding the use of cable television. I cannot recall the topics of the president's speeches on which I worked, edited, or translated. What comes back above all is the team spirit, playful, modern, with bright and intuitive young people, whose talents, very different from mine, were opening new windows on the world for me. In a way, I felt one of them, I was but I was not.

On evenings or weekends I accepted invitations to speak to women's groups, as shown in my agenda: the Fédération des Unions de Familles; the Association des Veuves; the Business & Professional Women's Club of Quebec; the YWCA; the National Action Committee; the Salon de la femme; the Industrial Management Club of Canada, as well as attending the FFQ and AFDU meetings. I also accepted a few radio or television interviews, or some from *Châtelaine* magazine, always on the status of women. In 1968 I had been invited to sit on the board of the Canadian Foundation of Human Rights and continued to actively participate. Through Monique Lussier, I had become a member of the board of the Ottawa Social Planning Council, an enriching community experience.

That is how I had become a civil servant, starting at the end of September 1970, while continuing to check the printing of the royal commission report, making sure nobody changed an iota on the galleys of the recommendations approved by all commissioners. It was on 1 December 1970 that I would accompany Florence Bird and the commissioners for the personal presentation of the report to Prime Minister Pierre Trudeau, the official tabling in the House of Commons taking place on 7 December 1970.

PART TWO
Life as a Politician

6

Going into Politics, Me?

April 1971. The offices of the Canadian Radio-television and Tele-communications Commission (CRTC) were located on Metcalfe Street, facing the Parliament Buildings in downtown Ottawa. I was in my office when the phone rang. It was Marc Lalonde – Mr Lalonde – chief of staff for Prime Minister Pierre Trudeau. Out of the blue he asked if I would consider running for office in a by-election in Saint-Henri (Montreal), to replace the incumbent MP who would be appointed citizenship judge. Gérard Loiselle had been in the House of Commons for fourteen years, elected and re-elected since 1957. These technicalities were gibberish to me. As I was unfamiliar with political manoeuvres, it seemed to be a deceptive plan of action, something mischievous. Flabbergasted by this phone call, I burst out laughing, thanked him, and replied that politics was not for me!

April 1972, still at the CRTC a year later. The phone rang in my office. It was Marc Lalonde again, asking me if I could go as soon as possible to the Prime Minister's Office for a meeting. Convinced that it was another important discussion regarding the implementation of our report on the status of women, I rapidly walked up the Hill with my copy of the *Report of the Royal Commission on the Status of Women in Canada* under my arm. The afternoon was radiant, sunny, and warm. I was taken to a room where I recognized the faces of television stars: Jean Marchand, Jean-Pierre Goyer, other ministers whose names I forgot, Marc Lalonde, and a few other political staff. Besides Marc, I knew none of them. I was given the same invitation as the year before, but this time I would run for office in the upcoming general election. The riding they had in mind – Duvernay in Laval, north of Montreal – had been without an MP for eighteen months, after the resignation of Eric Kierans. I did not laugh and waited until I replied, to my own surprise, that I would need a few days to think it over and give my answer. It was agreed. I did not know it but my life had just moved into totally unknown territory.

How had I come to such a radical change of opinion on things political in one year? What had happened? On the spot, I did not even ask myself the question.

All I wanted to do was to discuss this news confidentially as soon as possible with Monique Coupal, an old friend and wise adviser, then secretary general of the CRTC. I had never belonged to a political party and knew none of their players. She organized a meeting with Jean-Pierre Mongeau, brilliant political analyst and backroom politician, a Liberal, to discuss the situation together. I was somehow ready to take the plunge but I was wondering if they were serious. We agreed on the points that were posing problems for me, and it was decided to use them as a test to see how serious the Liberal Party was with their proposal. So at my second meeting at the Prime Minister's Office, I answered that I was ready to plunge in, with three conditions: the election of a minimum of three women candidates in Quebec in safe ridings, for I had no intention of being the token woman of the Liberal Party; a safe riding for me, as I would not be able to meet all the challenges at once; and financial assistance from the Liberal Party, as I did not think I could raise all the money needed for my campaign from the private sector. I would also have to obtain a leave of absence without pay from the Public Service Commission so that I could go back to my job at the CRTC should I lose my election. This, however, should not have been a major challenge anyway and had nothing to do with the PMO group. To my surprise, the answer was yes to each of my three demands. I thanked the group and promised to provide my answer rapidly. Back with Coupal and Mongeau, I can still hear Jean-Pierre: "But they really mean business!" He was stunned by the request for financial assistance in particular. It was only later that I learned that he was very close to the key players, being one himself.

But I still had hesitations, questions of ethics, especially in the broad sense of the word. Power was dirty, not to say criminal and dangerous. That was, in a few words, what many people believed, especially women. I myself shared these views on the evening of 1 May 1972, when I went to meet Gérard Pelletier at his Ottawa apartment. I knew him from television only, but he was my minister, as the CRTC reported to him. He had agreed to see me to discuss my eventual candidacy. He had not been present at the two previous meetings in the PMO, and I candidly believed that he knew nothing of the proposal then put to me. Of all the ministers at the time, for me he personified integrity, sensitivity, and intelligence. And he was somehow an anti-politician, not a childish partisan, with whom I wanted nothing to do. Pelletier made me feel comfortable immediately, giving me hours of his busy time, discussing the possibility of reconciling honesty and politics. I recall asking him about the meaning of "kickbacks" or "payoffs" (*pots-de-vin*) and political "patronage." It was on the basis of this sole meeting with a very special politician that I made my decision to plunge in and accept the offer of the PMO to run for a seat as a Liberal. I would run for the nomination in the Duvernay riding. I had entered politics.

If I tell this old tale, it was because, in addition to issues of integrity, I had found that it was of prime importance that, as a newcomer, I would not be "stealing" the riding from someone, since Eric Kierans had resigned his Duvernay seat eighteen months before. Always the dream of well-conducted human relations!

How had I gone from April 1971 to April 1972, making that 180 degree turn: politics was not for me but then I agreed to run for office? In my spare time, following the Royal Commission on the Status of Women, I had given speech after speech to women's associations, during which, at one point of my presentation, I would always state, "And you must go into politics! At one level or another – at the school board, the municipal level, the provincial or the federal – where you feel comfortable taking the risk, for nobody will ever bring you power on a silver plate!" These words were for others; they had never been for me, never ever. The idea to run for political office had never touched my mind. And now it would be I who would go from words to action!

As usual, what motivated me was public policy for simple justice, for women, for equity, and for those who were in disadvantaged circumstances in one way or another. Policies and projects that opened windows on the world were also a passion of mine, as well as cultural initiatives doing just that. However, during my two years at the CRTC, as I participated on the Privy Council Office Inter-Ministerial Committee to implement our RCSW report, I must have registered civil service prejudices, the numerous barriers to overcome, and the administrative slowness of bureaucracy. So becoming a member of the House of Commons would bring me much closer to the decision-making arena, or so I believed. It is only years later, after I had left the political arena, that I understood a much simpler motivation for having considered running for office in 1972. I loved working for Pierre Juneau and the CRTC with the great policy objectives of Canadian content and Canadian ownership. I helped him with some of his speeches. But I was getting bored with managerial tasks such as dealing with the Treasury Board on budgeting, employee classification, and other human resources issues, and so on. In fact I needed a professional challenge.

The Civil Service Commission granted me leave without pay to run for election – a brand new rule, as my work had nothing to do with decisions that partisan politics could affect. In other words, I could still be impartial in my work in the CRTC Research Branch after having been a candidate. My next step was to become a member of the Liberal Party of Canada (LPC).

In Duvernay, at Laval, I met what remained of the local Liberal Association, a tiny but faithful long-time orphan that had had no MP for eighteen months, and its president, a man of integrity, loyal and organized. And I started learning about the riding's geography, socio-cultural makeup – a good middle-class, rather young community, very French Canadian – and local leadership, and the rules of the game of a nominating meeting. I met with the LPC (Quebec) secretariat, bringing them my CV. Horrified to see that I was born in Rome, the first thing they did without even asking me was to make me "born in Montreal"! I was rather insulted, did not argue, and concluded that politics seemed at times odd, if not narrow-minded. I paid a rapid courtesy visit to Eric

Kierans at his McGill University office. The first meeting of the heads of sector committee took place at the home of the local Liberal Association president on 12 July.

We had no budget. In a nominating meeting, the expenses are usually covered by the local association, but if needed the LPC (Quebec) would help. All publicity material, including printing, such as texts, flyers, business cards, and pictures, was designed, done, and even printed by a few local supporters and my family. My organizing committee, basically the small core group of Duvernay Liberal membership I had first met, had agreed that recruiting new members for the LPC (Quebec) to join the riding association, and as quickly as possible, was the first objective. It was to be done in the traditional way by going door-to-door and by evening kitchen parties in homes ready to invite their friends and neighbours to come meet me and discuss. The LPC (Quebec) executive director, Jean Richard, fixed the nominating meeting for Sunday, 20 August. After having spent most of June in Ottawa, I had taken a small furnished bachelor apartment in Duvernay. I had been wasting my time in Ottawa, week after week, waiting to see Jean-Pierre Goyer, the minister politically responsible for that riding, but I could never see the point. I sensed that he was not particularly sympathetic to me. The situation was all the more unpleasant for me when I discovered that his chief of staff, Marie-Josée Drouin, wanted to be the candidate in Duvernay. Once settled locally, my team and I were able to start our mini electoral campaign slowly at the beginning of July, intensifying week by week. The truth is that I was an obscure unknown, and more, the only woman running for nomination in Quebec "but backed by Jean Marchand, the Quebec federal political leader," as the rumour had it. Jeanne Sauvé would get in the picture in Ahuntsic later.

We could not figure out what was going on locally as far as other candidates were concerned. It was as if something was going wrong, but what? But who? The notorious and now infamous Vaillancourt family, involved with Laval municipal politics, were everywhere and often attended our meetings as well, as other municipal players. With my usual intuition, I never trusted them. From the federal level, one or two characters completely unknown to us suddenly appeared in our kitchen parties. I remember two in particular, who I learned later were union organizers somewhere in Montreal, talking loudly and letting their revolvers show at times. They were to become Liberal colleagues of mine in the House of Commons in 1972. My telephone line was tapped and, having spread baby powder on my floor, I would see footprints on return at night, a true *signe de piste*. It was obvious that my candidacy was in the way of someone, but we kept enrolling new members.

One day, however, the association president, who, according to the LPC (Quebec) rules, received a copy of all new proposed memberships, noticed that the whole population of some streets had been proposed for membership with one cheque paying for all of them (at five dollars per name), a socio-political impossibility. From a handful of members in June, the local Liberal association now had hundreds of members. We had already recruited 1,000 new members. But confronted with a block of 800 names suddenly tabled at the Party Secretariat towards the very end of the campaign, we requested that a special procedure of our Constitution be applied, although it had never been used yet: in *le ballotage* each new name is checked. The Party Secretariat panicked and refused my request while I, a newcomer with no experience at all, was not ready to go over the head of the party secretary and his staff and phone Jean Marchand directly, as I should have done.

I started seeing that it was becoming a big and dirty game, which I could not decode. A week before the nominating meeting, without telling anyone, pushed by my intuition, I obtained an appointment with Jean-Noël Lavoie, who had been the first mayor of Laval, then elected in 1960 and re-elected as a member of the Quebec National Assembly for the Chomedey riding; in 1970, he also became Speaker of the National Assembly. A notary by profession, quite a civil individual, intelligent, and a man of power above all, he received me with courtesy. I introduced myself, told him where I was coming from, what was my objective and why. I went on referring to the shenanigans I had observed. To finish, I politely asked him if, how, and why he would seem to be involved in federal politics. I concluded by asking him for his support for my candidacy. He answered very frankly that I had impressed him and that I had guessed the situation well, but that the die was cast and it was too late to stop the machine set up against my candidacy. What I also understood was that he, the "big boss of the Jesus Island (Laval)," had not accepted not being consulted by the feds, and by Marc Lalonde for a start, as Trudeau's chief of staff!

On Sunday evening of 20 August, the room was full for the nomination meeting and votes. We had done everything to ensure that our members would all come, a typical election problem. The local association president who was chairing my campaign recognized people who had no business there. He was nervous. I was elegant, smiling, going around, talking and shaking hands, but I did receive a few strong punches in the low back, could not see where they came from, and was more careful. It was serious. Speeches, votes, and results: I was defeated by 100 votes in a total of 3,000 votes, by the other candidate, a young unknown local accountant, to the great satisfaction and the shouting of half of the audience. He became a Liberal colleague at the 1972 election. No comment.

In the following week Jeanne Sauvé, from Outremont, then television political reporter and commentator, was also a candidate. Not backed by Jean Marchand, she chose to run for nomination in the Ahuntsic riding, against the respected local association president, Bob Kouri. She was having a hard time, although she was a seasoned campaigner helping her husband Maurice Sauvé when he was a minister in the Pearson government. Although we had old common friends, Jeanne and I did not really know each other. As soon as she learned of my defeat, *Le Devoir* having published an editorial on it and on me, she required that the Party Secretariat perform a recount, which involved checking each proposed new membership and determining if they had paid the five-dollar membership themselves. I had tried in vain to have that famous *ballotage* procedure conducted, but she obtained it. Thanks to it, she won by a mere twenty votes. She obtained that recount because the Liberal Party (Quebec) Secretariat had panicked, concluding that there would not be any woman official candidate in the impending general election. Trudeau's instructions in 1972 had been to have women elected in Canada. There was the promise the PMO had made me of at least three women candidates in safe ridings in Quebec.

On 30 October 1972 the third of this trio of the first women from Quebec elected to the federal Parliament was Albanie Morin. She had become a candidate at the last minute in the Sainte-Foy riding of Louis-Hébert (Quebec City), a safe Liberal riding if ever there was one, where she lived and had been a municipal councillor. Jean Marchand, himself from Quebec City, offered the incumbent, Jean-Charles Cantin, then fifty-four years old, a practising lawyer while an MP, who had spent ten years in Parliament and gone through four elections, the appointment of consul of Canada in Louisiana, which he assumed for eight years. So Albanie Morin had an easy nominating meeting, if any, as her candidacy might have been unanimous, which I think I recall. After the election, I was often told the story of how Trudeau had given clear instructions to his two 1972 campaign co-chairs, Senator Keith Davey and Minister Jean Marchand, to ensure the election of women. Senator Davey explained to him after the election that he had been unable to find proper women candidates ... in all of English Canada!

The weekend after my defeat, on Saturday, 26 August, Marc Lalonde invited me to his home, the family farm where he lived on Perrot Island, just west of the island of Montreal. He too had read Le Devoir and he wanted to understand what had happened. We talked, walking through the cornfields. I told him about the meeting with Jean-Noël Lavoie and what I had learned. One of my messages was very simple: the Party Secretariat did not know its ridings. They had no idea of who was who, the political life in the Liberal ridings and Opposition ridings, the trends and so on. He asked me how serious I was when I had agreed to run and had become a member of the Party, and if I was still interested in going into politics. I answered that, yes, I was. He then offered me his future Outremont riding, telling me at the same time what nobody knew, namely that he was jumping into elected politics. A dream riding and constituency from many angles! Deeply touched by his trust and fully appreciating his generosity, I replied at once that it was out of the question and that Trudeau needed him to be elected with no problem, in a riding that would let Marc easily play a ministerial role and support the prime minister.

During the next few days, I took things slowly, thanking all my organizers and the local Liberal association president, and leaving my modest Duvernay bachelor apartment to stay with friends in Montreal. Out of context, on the Wednesday, Pierre Péladeau, whom I did not know, asked to see me at his office and offered me a senior position at Québecor! Two days later I phoned him, thanking him for the offer, and gave him my answer, regretfully negative. Unexplained meteorological phenomenon. Then I went back to Ottawa, ready to return to my CRTC job.

Very early on the morning after my late arrival home in Ottawa, on 5 September, the day after Labour Day, I had a phone call from Marc Lalonde asking me to come to his office as soon as possible. What would that be all about this time? The writ for an election had already been signed on 1 September, the House of Commons having urgently been summoned to legislate the Vancouver dockworkers back to work. So we were in an election but Trudeaumania was no longer there. An anti-Trudeau atmosphere, anti-bilingualism, and general dissatisfaction with the prime minister were prevailing, while that election slogan "The Land Is Strong!" was certainly not helping the situation.

In addition, at the beginning of that year the NDP had launched a book by David Lewis that would become their campaign manifesto. *Louder Voices: The Corporate Welfare Bums* turned into a most popular slogan all over the country. Accused of being "welfare corporate bums," the first villains, Aluminium Canada, Canadian Westinghouse, and Michelin Pneus, were soon joined, further to David Lewis's rants, by Shell Canada, Denison Mines, Cominco, Dofasco, Falconbridge, Bell Canada, Canadian General Electric, and dozens of other corporate giants, all guilty according to Lewis of not paying their fair income tax share.

That morning at the PMO Lalonde and others informed me that plans were to "parachute" me during the election into the riding of Saint-Michel. I first believed that meant Saint-Michel-de-Bellechasse, an agricultural community along the St Lawrence shore, thirty kilometres east of Quebec City, facing Île d'Orléans. I did not have time to panic after I learned that they were talking of a riding called Montreal-Saint-Michel in the northeast of the island. The plan was explained to me.

The incumbent MP would be appointed Citizenship Court judge after he ensured my election as my campaign manager. Victor Forget was a strange human being, of retirement age, a former pharmaceutical salesman, intelligent, misanthropic, and cynical, elected in 1968 thanks to Trudeaumania. His claim to fame was that he had never opened his mouth in the House of Commons, hence his name was not in Hansard! I agreed to the PMO proposal, fully trusting Marc Lalonde and Jean Marchand.

A few days later, back in Montreal at the party office, I waited alone in a corridor that evening for what seemed a few hours, for Jean Marchand to call me into the room where he had been negotiating with the thirteen members of the St-Michel riding Liberal Association Executive, twelve men and one woman, Forget's close-knit guard. I followed Marchand inside. The reception was icy cold, especially from those of the former city of St-Michel and Montreal sections of the riding. (The constituency also included the city of St Leonard with a large Italo-Canadian population.)

Life slowly got back to electoral normal. My candidacy was registered. An empty store was rented for the campaign office. I was taken by car through the riding, meeting the executive individually while I connected with the local Liberal campaign volunteers and election officials. The LPC (Quebec) woke up, rewriting my CV with pride that I was born in Rome, pure gold for the Italo-Canadians!

Although not a legal requirement, I found it appropriate to live in my riding, as my new small team appreciated. I had finally found an apartment on Viau Street, south of Metropolitan Boulevard. Back in our campaign headquarters, I was immediately bombarded with questions: "Viau Street? Where exactly? That's impossible. It is out of the question! Phone Mr Lalonde immediately!" I complied on the spot and was told by Marc Lalonde to terminate the lease at once, even if I lost three months' rent out of my modest personal budget, and I was never to tell that story to anyone.

The apartment walls and ceilings were mirrors of a light smoky colour, which I had found very vulgar. But I had to live somewhere in that area of resident owners or tenants of bungalows, duplexes, quadruplexes, and so on. Almost no apartment for rent. So, unknown to me,

I had rented the apartment just freed by the most famous Madame possible: Martha Adams, whose prostitution salon it had been! Famous, for she was running as an Independent candidate, in the same general election, in the riding of Saint-Hyacinthe against Claude Wagner. She was avenging herself against the former minister of justice of Quebec, very law and order, now a Court of Sessions of the Peace judge and a federal Progressive Conservative candidate (and future MP) for Robert Stanfield in that same 1972 federal election.

Everything was mind-boggling in that constituency, in fact eccentric, exotic. First, it covered a huge territory for an urban riding – new streets were appearing during the campaign, their residents having not been enumerated! At the time, the constituency of Montreal-Saint-Michel included part of the city of Montreal (Papineau Street, etc.) (low-income workers), the whole city of Saint-Michel (rather poor), and all of the City of Saint-Léonard (French-Canadian and Italo-Canadian families covering all types of middle-class incomes, as well as the most important Haitian community after the New York one, and a few other new Canadians). With the Mafia in addition! The Vic Cotronis lived there in big nouveau riche houses, the Violi clan, Luigi Greco and his brother, as well as a number of the characters identified by the Commission d'enquête sur le crime organisé just set up. A month after my election, on 3 December 1972, Luigi Greco and his brother died in the criminal explosion of their "Pizzeria Gina" on Jarry Street.

Further to my moving to a modest apartment on Lacordaire Boulevard, south of Metropolitan East, I learned that "Machine-Gun Molly" or "Monica la Mitraille" had lived next door in the same building before being shot dead at the age of twenty-seven by the police in a high-speed run in Montréal-Nord, she driving a Camaro.

Robert Beale, a locally well-known professional boxer, was my Conservative opponent. He was the leader of both the anglophones and the Italo-Canadians, in this Saint-Léonard where the language fight had started with the provincial Bill 63, *Loi pour promouvoir la langue française au Québec*. That was the legislation requiring children who were receiving their education in English to acquire a working knowledge of French, and everything was to be done to ensure that immigrants acquired a knowledge of French upon arrival in Quebec. The legislation had passed in November 1969, sponsored by the Union nationale. The fight was still going on, with less violence, in public gatherings. Bob Beale was a character who spoke loudly and at times aggressively, protected and financed by Paolo Violi, among other sources (the Mafia hated the separatists), but who did not bother me or my campaign committee although he rented the store next door for his headquarters. Toward the end of the sixty-day campaign, to my astonishment, my campaign committee hired a bodyguard to be at my apartment door at night. This was so new to me, with no points of comparison, so wild, that I was never afraid one single minute. It was pure Agatha Christie and, anyway, nobody would believe me. All this was very far from the old Saint-Léonard-de-Port-Maurice, its farms and fields, where we, University of Montreal student friends, used to go for a Christmas sleigh ride, pulled by two horses.

The electoral campaign had not been easy at the start. Not only did I know nobody and nothing of that part of Montreal, but I knew nothing about organizing an electoral campaign. I listened, asked questions, and accepted all that was decided for me, somehow puzzled that it was about "selling" me, exactly like the marketing required to launch a new toothpaste or other domestic good. I was careful not to mix up the different communities and their leaders, and I made good human relations at all times. However, overhearing conversations, it rapidly became clear to me that their old MP Victor Forget, "my chief campaign organizer," could not stand me, and worse, that he had decided to teach me a lesson. He wanted to punish me for what was happening to him by making sure that his 1968 majority of 22,307 votes fell to 10,000 or less. But we were no longer in 1968 and there was no Trudeaumania! These figures did not mean much to me, but I knew that, if that was his strategy, I was finished, for he was not the master of that dangerous game. Without a word, I phoned Jean Marchand, asking him to take Forget out of my campaign office at once and to send me a few names of regional organizers who were trustworthy and competent. The party immediately forwarded a fine young volunteer to take over the office. And I received a few names of experienced and recommended Liberal campaign organizers from East End Montreal. I met two or three by myself, convincing an old warrior of past provincial Liberal campaigns in Rosemont, a typographer at *La Presse,* Jacques Saint-Pierre, to take over my campaign. Once more, my intuition had helped me and I could not have made a better choice. He became a friend and managed all my subsequent campaigns.

We had plenty of electoral challenges, having started late, for one thing, and lost some time after. We needed a finance strategy resting on the private sector, as the Election Expenses Act limiting electoral expenses for both candidates and political parties, as well as the first forms of public funding through partial reimbursement of expenses and tax credits for contributions, would appear only in 1974. Two legal electoral responsibilities in particular had to be filled immediately: the "official agent" and the "auditor" for my campaign. Two professionals of integrity and competence accepted and volunteered, the official agent being a Liberal from within the riding, Jean Desjardins, and the auditor, a senior partner from Deloitte & Touche, Pierre Seccareccia, from Montreal, both becoming personal friends during my four elections. We also benefitted from the voluntary work of a brilliant young Italo-Canadian lawyer, a witty, smart negotiator whose special responsibility was to make sure I did not accept any questionable financial donations – without antagonizing potential donors! We also needed someone in charge of communications and found a local discreet and responsible Liberal volunteer, and so on.

Everything was new to me. I wrote to friends and former colleagues, including commissioners of the Royal Commission on the Status of Women, for a small donation. We managed financially without having to borrow money. Members of the association made as many door-to-door visits as possible, while I did business streets and stores, small commercial malls, churches and temples at the end of celebrations, bingos (never again; people are so busy with the cascade of numbers that it is an absolute waste of time for a candidate), all while a huge double platform on wheels, with a photo of my face in black-and-white on each side, the size of billboards, was driven slowly through busy streets at lunchtime! Local publicity through business cards (with photo), badges (with photo), posters (with photo), national election platform pamphlets, interviews with the neighbourhood local papers, French and Italian, was slowly progressing.

One event stayed with me: my official presentation to the Italo-Canadian community. It was on a Sunday, and I was trying to practise a bit of my limited Italian to perform well. The future Senator Pietro Rizzuto (no relationship with the criminal family of the same name) was presiding, and I could not understand a word of what he was saying, or from those following him. Not a word. I was terribly humiliated and would have liked to disappear. I smiled a lot and shook lots of hands, repeating, "È il mio piacere! ou Grazie mille!" As a result of being parachuted in the course of the election I had not been able to do my homework and had no idea that the vast majority of our Italo-Canadians were from the south of Italy, mainly from Sicily, whose mother tongue was Sicilian, and that their Italian, spoken by a very few of them, was completely different from the language spoken in Rome or in northern Italy! But I still could not figure out why I had perceived their officials as very cold and even hostile toward me. I learned only much later that in the 1968 campaign Jean Marchand had promised these leaders and their community that the next federal Liberal candidate in Montreal-Saint-Michel would be an Italo-Canadian man! One cannot trust politics, and the 1972 schemes and strategies had instead imposed a French-Canadian woman, who at least had the elegance of having been born in Rome!

On Monday evening of 30 October 1972, surrounded by my whole team, some family, close friends, and SRC French television (who still regularly show repeats of my supporters lifting me in the air that evening!), in a local Italian restaurant at 8:05 p.m. I was declared elected by Radio-Canada, the first woman from Quebec, with 23,850 votes! It was more than Victor Forget had received during the 1968 Trudeau-mania. I was exhilarated and so was everyone around me. It is only later, in fact the morning after, that I understood that Pierre Trudeau's government was in a dangerous minority situation with 109 MPs, half of them from Quebec, having only two members more than the Conservative Opposition of Robert Stanfield, hence facing a serious imbalance. The New Democratic Party of David Lewis, with its 31 seats, clearly had the balance of power.

I was an MP. How had I managed that, I who did not trust politics? It was important and urgent that women became politicians, at all levels.

Political power is never given on a silver tray. I knew it very well and had repeated it time and again while speaking to women's associations everywhere in Canada. But I had never considered going into politics myself; it was clearly not for me, especially because of my sensibility and capacity for emotion (no reference here to crying easily; on the contrary, I do not cry). I could not envision myself developing the pachyderm skin needed in politics. And also because of the law of the jungle of such a milieu (to continue with the animal world): the extreme competition, the political calculations and strategies humiliating the Other, the violence. Did I have the killer instinct needed in politics? Not really. Finally, the total lack of transparency and the shortage not to say the absence of ethics, the disrespect of others and even corruption in its diverse forms was not for me. Accidentally, I had witnessed up close and could not forget cases of corruption of Duplessis supporters as well as physical brutality performed locally by his men during provincial elections.

Had I learned something during my first election? Yes, I had. When writing the chapter on women and politics for our *Report of the Royal Commission on the Status of Women in Canada*, I knew it was our weakest chapter. Our president, Florence Bird, was outraged the day I shared that with her, but I did not know how to make those pages forceful and punchy. It was not so much that a feminist analytical framework was missing. It was the total ignorance of all of us around the table of the operational inside of politics, its organizational dimensions, and its importance. The commission had benefited, in camera, from the testimony of Pauline Jewett, who had been an MP for two years, and from Flora MacDonald, who was working then in the Progressive Conservative Party of Canada (PC) national office. The only concrete and specific point that remained with me from those presentations was that political parties never assigned "safe ridings" to women candidates – a strong image, but meaning what, excatly? It was on the strength of this assertion that I had based my conditions to the PMO before agreeing to run for office. Besides what the two had told us of prejudice and attitudes, I had not grasped the key role of organization, of logistics – the detailed coordination of a complex operation – a fundamental element in each step of a riding electoral campaign. The public and the commission were both prisoners of the colourful image of a huge machine grinding into motion: "the Big Blue Machine" of the Conservatives, and "the Liberal Big Red Machine." It told us how powerful it is, but it kept us in the world of magic. To my amazement, what I had learned through my first election was the role and importance of the riding organization when running for office.

Informed public policies being my objective, I thought I would now be closer to where it really takes place, in Parliament. What and how exactly? I did not know, but I wanted to contribute to "a just society" and a "participatory democracy," the two major slogans of Pierre Trudeau's leadership campaign of 1968, which had really engaged me.

I was often asked why I had become a member of the Liberal Party of Canada and not of the NDP, or of the provincial Liberals. For me the decision was obvious, and I never hesitated. I had always worked on national or federal dossiers, in the course of which I met politicians and civil servants at the federal level. As executive secretary I had been in charge of a national royal commission. In addition, I had become a federal civil servant at the CRTC, and the national dimension of Canadian issues attracted me spontaneously. In the Quebec Liberal Party, as distinct from the federal one, I knew nobody and had not practised this level of organization or become familiar with the issues. But why not the NDP? What I had known of it in Quebec, when in paid employment at their CCF meetings, or the FTQ union or others, and the writings in *Cité Libre*, it was all aimed at the provincial level; I admired their struggle against Duplessis's injustices, corruption, lack of social programs and higher education development. But the party had always appeared to me utopian and doctrinaire on the other subjects in its political agenda. I resisted taking out party membership in my youth and would not have felt comfortable in it.

On another level altogether, back to private life, awaiting my entry in Parliament, my sister Catherine, a famous actress in life as well as on the stage, had sent me a telegram informing me that I now had the qualifications required to ... join the Union des Artistes (the Actors' Equity Union)! She was right: politics was also drama.

7

The House of Commons:
A Strange Universe

The twenty-ninth Parliament opened on 4 January 1973, "our" first Parliament, we the dozen new Liberal MPs, disappointed with the minority government but thrilled by our personal victories. Shortly before 2 p.m., the mass of the elected rushed through the west door of Parliament and up the stairs to the House of Commons, Albanie Morin and I next to each other. The security commissioner shouted, "Ladies, upstairs!" We explained that we were newly elected MPs, but he called to check first. Such were the times. (In the same vein, we discovered that there were no women's washrooms near the House of Commons, and it took us months to get one.)

In November we had been sworn in individually by the clerk of the House of Commons and we had discovered the offices assigned to us. At the time, two MPs shared three office rooms, our secretaries being in the middle one. Francis Fox and I shared the same office, which was fine with me, Francis being bright, competent, and charming. Later, when the Confederation Building, the former Treasury Board Building, was opened for MPs, we both chose to move there, receiving individual, spacious, and sunny offices, a new little green bus system taking us to the Centre Block of Parliament in no time.

In the morning of the day before the official opening of Parliament, the Liberal regional caucuses, followed by the national one, met for the first time. In these private groups, MPs and senators presented to Cabinet their views on what goes on and what they expected from the government in policy and strategy. All four political parties met separately in caucuses every Wednesday morning. At the Liberal national caucus, MPs and senators addressed the prime minister, who listened and concluded with marching orders for the week. The ministers were at the table with the PM, listening, not arguing, with the elected MP caucus chair facing the room. The NDP and Social Credit having no senators, their MPs made up the entire caucus.

That evening it was the Governor General's Ball, with long dresses for women and tuxedos for gentlemen! Astounding in the twentieth century, especially as we would meet together in the House of Commons for the Parliament opening the day after, again in long dresses, elegant but more business-like for the five women MPs, and tuxedos again for the men. Such pomp and circumstance seemed to me quite ridiculous and disconnected from the modern world. For this ceremony, about half a dozen of my Montreal campaign workers were able to make it to Ottawa, and I had the pleasure of entertaining them at the parliamentary restaurant, taking them afterward to the public galleries of the House.

With so many new NDP and Crédit Social members, the government benches had to accommodate some of them. Seats were distributed according to a strict protocol of the year of first election and surname. I was the only Liberal never to have been, technically speaking, a "backbencher," as I was the only new MP to sit in the fourth row. Excitement was at its height. For the first time, in person, we saw John Diefenbaker, Robert Stanfield, Tommy Douglas, David Lewis, Réal Caouette as well as some of the famous old-timers like George Hees or Stanley Knowles.

This minority government lived in a particularly electric atmosphere by its nature, and more so for receiving some sixty newcomers in the House at once. We had to discover everything. No compendium explained how Parliament functioned. There was no "Handbook of the Perfect MP," no orientation sessions, no mentors. Strangely, it was every man for himself, while I thought I had just joined the big Liberal Team. What helped me and my newcomer neighbours was that, as a woman, I never had a problem with asking questions when I did not know something. Ah! The shortcomings of men unwilling to ask for directions to the next gas station when they have lost their way. So I started organizing my office and secretariat and visiting the Parliament Buildings. Back home in my riding, I was helpless with the phone calls to my apartment asking me to help find a job as soon as possible for an unknown citizen, when I did not even know where to start. Just before Christmas, I almost went through a moment of panic when a constituent, unknown to me of course, phoned at 11 p.m., getting angry at me when I explained to him that I could not reverse a Supreme Court judgment forcing him to pay arrears of $60,000. He finally slammed down the phone shouting that I had just lost his family's nine votes in my next election. I already saw myself in Opposition. One does feel somehow prisoner of one's voters.

But real life started just after the New Year. From January to December 1973, I did not see the year fly by! My memory is of a buzzing beehive. Life had become super fragmented. I was trying to learn everything, to understand the rules of the game, while also getting to know my Liberal colleagues and the others. We had thematic caucuses – unemployment insurance, urban affairs, housing legislation, foreign investment control, and so on – almost daily, which was quite unusual. At times I felt I had slipped into a boys' college where we were all behaving a little childishly, while at other moments we suddenly shared in great high points where we attempted to survive at all costs. There were evenings when I sat until 3 a.m., with us, the new Liberal MPs, believing our humble presence in the House was essential to save the government. And it was, in a way.

Following the very formal Speech from the Throne, read in the Senate Chamber, then the replies in the House of Commons by the mover and the seconder (an honour for two newcomers), then the speeches by the leader of the Opposition, the prime minister, and finally the leaders of the other parties, all in an immutable order, we were in the first session of the twenty-ninth Parliament. More daring than I remember, I plunged in and made my "maiden speech" (an obvious sexual/sexist connotation) on 15 January, during the reply to the Speech from the Throne, the first by a newcomer. I had been sitting in the House for only nine days! After the usual compliments, I registered my pride to be the first Quebec woman speaking in the House of Commons since Confederation, and then I said,

As a newcomer to parliamentary life, and if the old-timers do not scorn too much such newcomers as myself, perhaps they will be interested in the naive observations of a woman who has yet to

get used to the rather belligerent games which honourable members at times allow themselves to play. I was rather flabbergasted,
during last week's debate on the resolution for peace in Viet Nam,
by the calm assertion of the Hon. Member for Abitibi (Mr
Laprise) [Gérard Laprise was a Social Credit MP who had been
re-elected four times] that women brought about the war in Vietnam just as they did many other wars. To my mind, if some
would reflect on belligerence, which the dictionary defines as the
love of war, they have a subject of reflection right at hand ...

The office of member of Parliament is not, as I have often
heard it described, a more or less honorary one. It is a full-time
job, with no overtime pay. I have the honour and the weighty responsibility to represent here the most densely populated riding
in Quebec, the riding of Saint-Michel, for the sole purpose of participating in that work. The men and women I represent here,
Mr Speaker, are ordinary people. I represent 150,000 of them.
[Hansard translation]

Amongst other points made, I expressed the importance of having
the debates of the House of Commons televised, for "Canadians might
get the impression of taking a more active part in the federal government if they knew more about its machinery, and televising parliamentary proceedings would no doubt help to reach that objective."
Referring to the promises of the Speech from the Throne, I voiced my
support for a guaranteed annual income program, however minimal the
proposal. But I stated that I also believed in the importance of protecting
social programs for all, like family allowances and pensions, to nurture
solidarity throughout the whole population, while in parallel developing
much better assistance for those most vulnerable, starting with the
78,000 women heads of families (and the 8,000 men in the same situation). On this latter point, I referred the House to the report and analysis of the Royal Commission on the Status of Women.

In the Parliamentary Restaurant, while eating at the "Quebec table,"
a long oval table under one of the arches creating loggias, I heard some
of the old-timers cynically observe how Gérard Pelletier was definitely
of the *pelleteux de nuages* (cloud peddlers) type, the supreme insult. I

had never heard that local expression, but my first speech in the House did not escape that putdown, making me one of them, and rather proud to be.

I also started learning of a face of Canada other than the one I had observed in the public hearings on the status of women. For example, back from the riding one Monday, at lunch again, I overheard two new Stanfield Western Conservative MPs who had just visited Quebec City for the first time, confiding to others, "I couldn't believe it: there they speak French all the time!"

The first major debate in the House, as of January, was on the death penalty, with Bill C-2 tabled by the solicitor general, Warren Allmand, and it went on for several months. The five-year moratorium suspending the death penalty, adopted in 1967 when Trudeau was the minister of justice, had just elapsed on 29 December 1972. The first amendments tabled from start by Allmand, clearly abolitionist, were defeated. It was a case of free votes, and the atmosphere was tense and emotional, reflecting the contradictory opinions of the general population. Further to long debates and numerous votes, on 29 May new legislation extending the moratorium for another five years was finally adopted by a majority of only thirteen votes.

Discovering what the caucuses were all about, especially the Wednesday morning national caucus, its nature, its role, and its power fascinated me. I saw that one spoke first and foremost to the prime minister, never to ministers, who were silently seated at the long table facing the crowd of MPs and senators. Trudeau listened closely, without a word, finally putting the record straight and setting the tone for the week ahead in his end-of-meeting talk. I observed that, for an ordinary MP and for the newcomers, the caucus was an avenue to make a name for oneself and be identified in relation to the public policies of the day and others. Whoever wanted to make a point, MPs and senators alike, just went to the mic, giving one's opinion, frustration, criticism, suggestion, then simply went back to one's seat. I concluded that if some of us wanted to push a particular point or oppose a project, it was better to do it not through a succession of speakers, which were too clearly identifiable and immediately reduced to a specific block, but through loose networks of different colleagues sharing common values, one here, one there, from various regions of the country, thus infiltrating the environment more subtly.

I was already making friendly acquaintances with Liberal colleagues of other provinces, MPs and senators. My own first initiative in caucus was a most prosaic one. I had just left my position at the CRTC where, as a civil servant, I could make as many long-distance calls as I needed, on the government line, without charge to our office. But as an MP I had to pay for all the long distance telephone calls to my constituency or elsewhere. I was shocked. In addition, I found it unacceptable not to have a secretary in the riding, not having a spouse to play the role, unpaid, starting to dream of a real riding office. I tested the grounds around me, forming a small caucus of Liberal MPs to which we added one MP for each other party caucus. It became the very formal Services to Constituents Committee. I then learned the role, powers, and composition of the Board of Internal Economy that administered MPs' expenses, among other duties. "The Board is responsible for establishing By-laws, policies and guidelines relating to expenditures and resources provided to Members in order to carry out their parliamentary functions." At national caucus we then began the siege of Allan J. MacEachen, government leader in the House and president of the Privy Council, underlining the government minority situation, the gross injustice of treatment between civil servants and elected representatives, all working for the same Canadian public, and so on. To the old-timers' stupefaction, we won, and the machinery of the House started developing the parameters of the project.

I had never heard Napoleon's battles discussed more than in the Liberal caucus of Prime Minister Pierre Trudeau! Certainly, this resulted from the solid political culture of an astonishing prime minister, but while the rules of action originate in military strategy, it is not common for most people to hear them discussed openly. My first observation, then, was that political discussion was a military metaphor. As one of the few women in politics, I felt from the start that I was in forbidden territory where I was a tolerated exception. Not that I suffered from discrimination or was singled out. Nor was I, technically, the only woman in caucus: Jeanne Sauvé and Albanie Morin for the Liberals, as well as Flora MacDonald for the PCs and Grace McInnis for the NDP, were declared elected in the same 1972 general election. However, one of them became a minister immediately and we did not see her often, and the other, an early victim of cancer, occupied a position related to the Speaker. Albanie Morin was appointed assistant deputy chair of committees of the whole, occupying the Speaker's Chair regularly. There were many Liberal caucus and committees functions she could not attend. For all practical purposes, in the daily Liberal environment I was the only woman in an eminently male world constantly punctuated by a language that I had never heard before and that was not mine.

The first task asked of a newcomer by the party whip is to stay until the end of the daily sitting to "kill a bill" (of the Opposition, of course). Discussions constantly focus on "the enemy" or "the adversary," "attacks," "traps," "ambushes," electoral "battles" and "victories." "To resort to the use of force," "the strategy" and "the strategists," "reserves," and "tactics" are expressions used in many cases. "To have your back to the wall," "trench warfare," "to go on the offensive" or on the "counter-attack," "covering the rear" are others.

The bipartite system of the Canadian parliamentary government, the adversarial design of the House of Commons, the partisanship that results, and the legalistic framework of procedures only accentuate the rhetoric that particularly repels women. It also probably puts off a number of men from community environments, small family businesses, or middle management, where the vision of human relationships still mirrors that of the family. Of course, we say that "life is a long battle," but this is meant in a moral sense. Most people in most situations trust one another instead of constantly being on their guard.

In addition to this alienating combative rhetoric, the ferocious competition among colleagues of the same political party, from MPs to ministers, is another dimension for which women of my generation had received no preparation. Furthermore, to this day, I am tempted to disappear, to return to my own territory, when faced with a situation defined by competition. I detest all of this, except if it is a question of defending ideas or values. If it is a case of competition between individuals in the flesh, I feel that I am cracking under the pressure and not in the race. Worse, I tend to condemn it.

Unfortunately for me, competition was everywhere in politics. One day, much later in the 1980s, when I was minister of national health and welfare, I had finally won an additional $50 million for medical research "against" an able Cabinet colleague who wanted it, rightly so, for his own department. My colleague Judy Erola, by then already a friend for life, told me, as I was grumbling and uneasy with my success, "You, like many women, cannot taste victory! A real Cinderella syndrome! You should read the book." I was cut to the quick. And I ended up reading Colette Dowling's *The Cinderella Complex: Women's Hidden Fear of Independence*. She was right. Mariette Sineau, the French political analyst, devotes a complete chapter to "the conduct of failure and over-compensation" in her 1988 book *Des femmes en politique*, based on interviews with French women politicians. Sheila Copps's hypothesis is that men benefit from having learned how to win and how to lose in school group sports like hockey, baseball, football, or soccer. We did not learn anything of the kind at Teacher's College in Rigaud, where the only sports in which we indulged were figure skating and croquet!

As the regiment mascot, I was treated in a friendly manner by my colleagues in the Quebec caucus during my very first year. Then, without understanding why, I began to hear nasty and slanderous remarks about me, which hurt. It was not until much later that I realized that this change coincided with my first responsibilities: co-presidency of the first national party convention to review the Trudeau leadership, appointment as permanent delegate to the United Nations, and elected vice president of the national Liberal caucus. I was no longer the charming caucus newcomer; I was a competitor, and it was war.

For a brand new MP, my new professional life was full, although I was no longer in charge of anything – a first for years. At the time, an MP's salary was a low $18,000, much less than in my previous five years. (In 2018, the MP salary alone is $172,700.) I felt I had become a social worker or local ombudswoman, without the tools for the job. For some reason, getting a job at Canada Post topped my constituents' requests, or dreams of Local Initiative Project funding. Sometimes I was sorting out people's unpaid unemployment insurance benefits, or obtaining or speeding up family reunion cases of Italian or Chinese or other families. My constituency then appeared to me as follows: "Saint-Léonard orders and Saint-Michel asks, and the section of Montreal follows"!

This being said, shortly after my election, I was contacted by a young constituent in a wheelchair, Claude Saint-Jean, and his family. A nice, likeable, and determined young man, he suffered from Friedreich's ataxia, a genetic disorder resulting in speech difficulty, muscle weakness, difficulty with walking that gradually worsens, loss of sensations in parts of the body, scoliosis, and heart disorders, while the mental capacities are unaffected. I had never heard the word *ataxia*, but it was painful to witness the obvious physical and psychological efforts he mustered to ask for my help. He had just set up a foundation to raise money for medical research on this condition, then non-existent in Canada, and wanted me to do something. Thanks to a couple of personal friends, established physicians and researchers Drs Claire and Pierre Nadeau, I started learning how researchers choose a research topic and why, the research funding reality, and so on. And yes, with help and contacts, in 1975 Dr André Barbeau, neurologist, "a real clinical researcher" as the later Quebec Prix-Marie-Victorin 1985 described him, accepted Claude Saint-Jean's challenge and broadened his research work to look specifically into Friedreich's ataxia. This educational pathway later served me well when I became health minister in charge of the Medical Research Council. I saw Claude Saint-Jean and his family (two brothers and a sister had also developed the disease) regularly during my twelve years in politics, as I then lived in Montreal. He died at fifty-four years of age, a long life for a man in his condition, thanks to his passion and efforts to find a cure.

Unemployment insurance problems, immigration cases, and jobs research kept coming in. I did Saturday evening banquets, Italian suppers, Haitian celebrations, even the openings of local junior hockey games on Sunday afternoons, balls and carnivals, receiving constituents on Saturday or Monday mornings. All of this was brand new to me. I had no idea that people regularly attended these parish and community social evenings with pleasure. It was the last thing that would have come to my mind. I immediately decided that I would do only collective gatherings and not accept invitations to family functions. The latter was not my role as an MP. In my years on the Hill, the House of Commons did not sit on Wednesday evenings. For those of us from Montreal or Toronto, it was expected that we would make a round trip and be available for similar invitations and be back in Ottawa by midnight. Piggybacking on this local agenda were regional political conventions, invitations as a speaker in other ridings, speeches to women's groups, and media interviews. I recall a women's issues panel in Vancouver where I was bombarded with questions about Western alienation. I was trying not to look too stupid, having so much to learn about our historical and political pasts.

Relationships with the media always remained mysterious for me and I learned rapidly to remain polite and open with everyone, beware of their games and modes of functioning. And I always kept my private life private. Newcomer, young, female, spontaneous, and Liberal caucus mascot, it was the time of labelling each new player while still unknown, that repeated labelling turning into a pernicious game. Ah! the nightmare of discovering one's "image," a strange and mysterious alter ego sticking to one, at times quite a dumbfounding stranger ... At my nominating meeting, the Montreal newspapers had already decided that I was "an intellectual." Now, in Ottawa, I was labelled as follows:

- *est promise à un brillant avenir*
- *désarmante de simplicité*
- *débordante d'énergie et d'enthousiasme*
- a refreshing face in Canadian politics
- the young Quebec activist
- Quebec MP makes history

In my first months after the elections, I had substantial visibility for a young newcomer! I had "made" TV *Hebdo* (223,000 copies), *Décor-mag*, and *Châtelaine*. And I even had three cartoons, one of them in *Allo-Police*!

But the real game was taking place on the floor of the House. Were we going to hold on? The spectacle in question period, further to the secret dealings between "them" and "us," rested on the performance of Allan J. MacEachen, the elusive and brilliant House leader of this twenty-ninth Parliament. He was a true poker player manoeuvring the main Opposition parties as if he were playing cat-and-mouse. He was gaining time by sending them back-to-back through the allotment of numerous Opposition Days with votes, our opponents choosing to put their pet project to a vote, not leading, by nature, to a coalition between themselves, which would have overthrown the government. It was very smart, as none of the Opposition parties, individually, had enough votes to defeat Trudeau's government. In this historic case, the balance of power being clearly in the relatively strong NDP, they proposed "leftist" legislation which the Conservatives would have never supported, and vice-versa.

Such "Opposition Days" (some twenty per Parliament) are allotted by the government House leader to one or the other Opposition party, which then chooses its topic, attacks the government, and goes to a vote, hoping to be joined by the other partiers in Opposition. And, yes, it is true that I witnessed an NDP old-timer speaking without stop during a few hours and giving, in passing, his recipe for a good apple pie, in order to block a vote! As a neophyte, I was fully living the moment, absorbing the system, and trying to find my way through these games.

It was anything but boring. In addition, in February I was asked to co-chair with Judd Buchanan (first elected in 1968, then parliamentary secretary) the next LPC National Convention of 14–16 September, the first convention with a vote of confidence on the leader. A type of challenge utterly new to me. Our common goal was, of course, to maximize the positive votes for Trudeau, against the not-yet-forgiven general discontent of the 1972 quasi-defeat. We were also keeping in mind the underground pro-Turner support network, after-effects of the 1968 leadership, still alive and active but silent, within the caucus, even in Cabinet, and among a number of Liberal partisan subgroups. The other major challenge was the teamwork that would define the priority themes for the discussion sessions, select the panellists and possible keynote speakers, and prioritize the resolutions to be voted on. I was discovering the backstage games and players that exist for better or for worse in every political party. It was with great pleasure that I closely worked with Torrance Wylie, the national director of the party, and later with Pierre Bussières, from Quebec City, who had the full backing of Jean Marchand and whom I found not only an exceptionally gifted organizer but a humanist thinker, a strategist, and a tactician, like Torrance indeed. Pierre would become a colleague MP in 1974, then minister of state for finance,

and finally minister of national revenue, a friend for life, whom we suddenly lost in August 2014. And I still see Torrance Wylie almost weekly,
with the same pleasure; wise, loyal, down-to-earth, a remarkable political analyst. After having served Pearson and Trudeau, he went into the
business sector, which always fascinated him. The 1973 convention was
a great success: 2,500 delegates, with a high number of new registrants,
participated in this convention during which 125 resolutions were
adopted. As to the vote requesting a vote of confidence on the leadership,
90 per cent of registered participants voted against. It was the highest
support for Trudeau in his entire political carrier.

Two days later I was leaving for New York until Christmas, for the
United Nations General Assembly, to which Mitchell Sharp had appointed me as the parliamentary delegate. Saul Rae, Bob's father, was
our ambassador, hence the big boss of the Permanent Canadian Mission
at the UN, with Geoffrey Bruce as minister counsellor. It would be one
of the great years of negotiations of the Law of the Sea, with Alan
Beesley as our brilliant ambassador, while Bill Barton (who would succeed Saul Rae as our UN ambassador) was the very competent one for
the Disarmament dossier. Once more I had been given a unique opportunity to discover the world, figuring out the corridors of international
diplomacy. The Austrian Kurt Waldheim had now been the fourth general secretary of the UN for the past year. Every morning the Canadian
team participated in the discussion and briefing session of the Permanent Mission. The various UN commissions sat in the afternoon. From
time to time we had to go to the General Assembly, listening to the
speeches. The days often included business lunches and suppers, as well
as cocktails of all kinds to consult with foreign colleagues or obtain
their support for our position on this or that debate.

I had been appointed to the fourth commission, that on Decolonization, under the well-advised counselling of Ernest Hébert "the realist"
(whom I would meet again with great pleasure in 1981, I as minister of
national health and welfare, and he as our Canadian ambassador in
Ivory Coast). On two votes having to do with self-determination of
Namibia as an independent country, but still under illegal occupation
by apartheid South Africa, I admit having stood up to Hébert, informing him that Canada would not vote against the motion, despite the

formal diktat from Ottawa, alone of all countries but South Africa (with Vorster as PM), Portugal (still the colonial government in Guinea-Bissau, Mozambique, Cape Verde, and Angola), and the United States! I let Ernest Hébert make his long distance calls to our Department of External Affairs in Ottawa and went on voting as I believed Canada should be voting. No crisis ensued. During that twenty-seventh UN General Assembly, I had to do a few round trips to Ottawa for key votes and spend a weekend in the riding or in Ottawa for a special national caucus. I came back home for good on 17 December.

In the summer before this modest and fascinating international learning experience, Trudeau had selected me as the MP accompanying him to the meeting of the Commonwealth heads of government in ... Ottawa, less exotic than the one before, in Singapore! It was the second meeting only of the heads of government (since the creation of this institution in 1946, participants having been prime ministers) and it was taking place at the Château Laurier on 2–10 August, during which a private retreat of the heads of government only at Mont-Tremblant, a first, was on the program to allow frank and informal exchanges. Queen Elizabeth and Prince Philip were there.

The prime minister of India, Indira Gandhi, had just spent eight days in Canada in June and did not return for the Commonwealth heads of government. Landing in Ottawa on 16 June, she had stayed three days in the capital city before travelling all across Canada to Vancouver. Trudeau gave a dinner in her honour at 24 Sussex. It was a very formal occasion, with long dresses and tuxedos and some twenty guests around the elegant table, including the three elected Canadians seated in the centre as per protocol: the host, the prime minister; our secretary of state for external affairs, Mitchell Sharp; and me, for whom this was a historical moment. We were in the living room when Mrs Gandhi arrived and I was then astounded to witness two prime ministers known around the world, incapable of the most minimal small talk! Neither was saying a word! It was a tense situation for all of us until Mitchell Sharp broke the ice by going to the piano and playing a lively tune!

Back from New York on 17 December, as I mentioned, the House adjourned on the nineteenth to reconvene on 3 January with several votes that very evening on Bill C-203, the Election Expenses Act. The year 1974 started unpredictably: we sat for ten days, this short session ending on 14 January with the installation of the new governor general, Jules Léger, a formal reception for lunch at Rideau Hall, and royal assent for three new pieces of legislation in the afternoon. We were to come back to Ottawa only on 26 February to prorogue the session the same day, opening the second session of the twenty-ninth Parliament the day after with the Speech from the Throne and its usual ritual. No need to stress that no calendar or agenda was circulated ahead of time. We usually learned the program at the last minute. We, the MPs, had therefore found ourselves in our ridings, rather confused by these six long winter weeks, far from Ottawa, with a sense of expectation while nothing was happening.

I still did not have any special responsibilities and was not looking for any, to tell the truth. During this long adjournment, I regularly went to Ottawa for meetings, a few speaking commitments, media interviews, and working sessions at External Affairs following my work at the UN. Or I was doing my MP work in the riding and, at long last, opening my hard-won constituency office, on Jarry Street East, near the St Gilbert parish church, in southern Saint-Léonard. In Quebec at the time, the parish defined socio-cultural identity and community belonging, no matter if people practised a religion or not, even in Montreal, the big cosmopolitan city. My riding included nine active Catholic parishes, one of them Italian, as well as at least three temples of diverse religious denominations, one for Jehovah's Witnesses. It was taken for granted that everyone, at least francophone, was a Catholic and "practised." The Catholic Church in Quebec has drastically declined from the mid-sixties to this day, Catholics who attend mass having gone from 85 per cent of the population to less than 5 per cent today, and with less than 60 per cent of Quebecers considering themselves Catholic. In parallel, the Catholic Church as an institution and the local parishes completely lost the French-Canadian century-old "parish civilization/culture" as well as their social role.

My constituency and I developed a real bond through the years, crossing even the lines of separatism, an important allegiance for many in the francophone part of my huge riding. With the Haitian community, with the small network of Chinese new Canadians, or older

Ukrainian ones I was one of them, so to speak. It meant quite a multiplication of work and social functions, but it was my constituency. As to "my" Italo-Canadian community, a book would not be enough to describe its activities! I recall the Sunday of my very first Da Vittorio–Labatt Italian bicycle race (I was just an official) with all the men in typical T-shirts, the excitement, the noise, the sheer number of people and the crowds – quite an exotic show in that part of Montreal. That community's Saturday-night banquets were quite different from those of local francophone parishes. Long dresses for women at their most sexy, sparkling jewels, always loud music and animated *va-et-vient* from the tables to the head table, at which would be Dr de Stephanis, Italian consul general in Montreal, the Most Reverend A. Cimichella, OSM, auxiliary bishop of Montreal, the St Leonard mayor (often an Italo-Canadian), the provincial MLAs, the federal MPs of adjoining ridings, all served great pasta and local red wine (less great). Nothing in common with me serving supper with Father Rény to the Golden Age Club of the Sainte-Angèle Parish, in the very francophone bourgeois coop!

I was spoiled with gifts from one Italian family or another wanting to thank me and my office, or from a parish, or for whatever special occasion. I brought back home unusual objects: a tall, heavy, green, marble and bronze "1920s style" telephone for my living room; a four-foot "original" Roman (or Greek) amphora on a metal stand, also for my living room; several luminous Virgin Marys made of plastic and sea shells, and so on. Always from the heart! The most unexpected was when on a Friday night I arrived home from Ottawa to find blood on the kitchen floor from the fridge. My riding secretary, the motherly and efficient Claire Doré, had warned me to be careful, but still! Inside were 2.5 kilos of veal or calf liver, worth a fortune, from two butcher brothers we had helped, which, by the way, was our job!

The French-Canadian women, especially in the Saint-Michel section of the riding, covered me with knitted things they made: a long scarf, even a sweater, and more often *des p'tites pattes de Phentex* (little night or home socks in Phentex). I must have received a hundred through the years. I gave them to my sisters and brothers for my nephews and nieces. Everyone hated them! In the 1980s, Cabinet started one day with a presentation by the prime minister of a proposed updated version of the

1965 "Conflict of Interest Guidelines for Cabinet Ministers," but no copy was distributed, and an open discussion, very rare in those years, started among ministers. I recall Gerry Regan asking the PM if the next time Lord S— — invited him for a weekend hunting party at his castle, could he accept under these new rules? I couldn't believe it! Guys started saying what they received, say, for the holidays. For example, my friend Charles Lapointe, minister of small business, always got four or six bottles of excellent wine in a wooden case. For others it might be a week in Florida, or a good painting, and so on. At one point, in French, I said to Trudeau, *sotto voce*, "Boss, I am sure I won't have any ethics problems with what I receive, especially all my *p'tites pattes de Phentex*." The Quebec ministers burst laughing. Trudeau made me repeat at least twice, trying to understand. I finally had to tell him about the Phentex company on the Montreal south shore that produced craft yarn that was indestructible, ugly, stain-resistant, unstretching, unshrinking, washable, dryable, and came only in striking fluorescent colours.

Finally, on 27 February, the opening of the second session of the minority twenty-ninth Parliament took place. I was then a member of three standing committees of the House: Broadcasting; External Affairs and National Defence; and Health and Social Affairs. At the end of March, the government announced the Mackenzie Valley Pipeline Inquiry, a royal commission to be chaired by Justice Thomas Berger, to investigate the social, economic, and environmental repercussions of a proposed gas pipeline to be built through the Yukon and the Northwest Territories. The House then sat until the evening of Holy Thursday, 11 April, and then from 22 April to 9 May 1974.

Further to the 1973 Yom Kippur War and the oil embargo imposed by the members of the Arab oil-exporting countries, fuel shortages and economic anxiety were at their height. The word *inflation* had become a home concept for Canadians, and it was used in popular language. Canadians, however, did not really suffer oil shortages, but further to the 1973–74 New York Stock Exchange major loss of value and ensuing bear market, they found themselves facing an 11 per cent average inflation rate, the cost of food being the biggest victim. Unemployment statistics were also worrisome. But the oil crisis had turned sour through a Canadian political twist with Alberta's self-sufficiency and the oil price fixing by Premier Peter Lougheed. Everyone remembers the bumper stickers: "Let the Eastern bastards freeze." The news that Trudeau had managed a compromise with the provincial premiers at the end of March 1974 was well received by public opinion. His popularity went up in the polls. David Lewis and the NDP released a long list of demands for the imminent budget as a condition for their continued support. On 6 May John Turner tabled on a budget that pleased no one. The government fell on the budget on Wednesday, 8 May, and once again we found ourselves in a general election.

I can see that I was particularly fortunate in my first eighteen months as an MP, an unknown newcomer on the Hill. I was not conscious of it at the time, living fully in the moment. I owe a debt of gratitude to Trudeau and colleagues close to him, Marc Lalonde, Gérard Pelletier, Jean Marchand, to Mitchell Sharp, and in a way to Allan J. MacEachen, for pushing me as a backbencher into high-visibility roles in the party, the media, and, by way of consequence, vis-à-vis the general public. Furthermore, and despite the fact that notwithstanding my feminism I considered international politics a men's world, fascinating, but one to which I could never aspire and was not aiming at, I had started learning it.

And we were now in an election! In June and July 1974 I was invited here and there as a new rising star, and a woman. The minister of agriculture, Gene Whelan, asked me to speak at his nominating meeting in Windsor, then I met with Peter Stollery and his team in Toronto-Spadina on my way back to Montreal. In Quebec the official launch of the campaign took place on 25 May. One of my sector heads kept resigning, then withdrawing his resignation, but otherwise all was running smoothly. I benefitted from the same team of volunteers I'd had in 1972, which was increased by new faces of constituents who joined us. In mid-June my colleague Irénée Pelletier asked me to speak in Sherbrooke. As Margaret Trudeau, very "flower power," had decided to participate in the campaign while breastfeeding baby Sacha, I was asked to accompany her, together with Marc Lalonde, to Saint-Hyacinthe. In evenings, as was customary, I participated in electoral activity in neighbouring Montreal ridings. All these activities were new to me. I was also invited to do a few television interviews in French and in English, some radio "open line" shows, and newspapers interviews. Towards the end of the campaign I went to Roberval and Bagotville to speak in support of our local candidates. Two days later it was Joliette and Saint-Donat, and two more days later I was in Matane, Amqui, Mont-Joli, and Causapscal, from where I came back late Sunday night, just in time to vote for myself on Monday morning, 8 July. (I had learned in 1972 that I could, and ought to, vote for myself!)

That Monday evening I was re-elected and we now had a majority Liberal government, with 141 seats. From my 23,850 votes of 1972, representing 48.77 per cent of the votes, I had obtained 29,822 votes, or 65.44 per cent of votes. I now had solid roots in northeast Montreal. Moreover, the campaign atmosphere in the riding, the reception during visits to industrial sites and shopping malls were in total contrast with those of 1972. This was not due to me, really, but to Trudeau's new-found popularity and firm stand on inflation, strongly opposing Stanfield's wage and price controls. Trudeau won 60 of the 74 Quebec seats, while David Lewis lost not only half his NDP seats, but his own seat in York South (Toronto), having been defeated by an unknown Liberal woman, Ursula Appolloni. However, the government did not get a single Alberta seat, in part the result of the oil crisis and the corresponding provincial electoral strategy.

From the election on, I spent my time in the riding seeing everyone, thanking them for their help and their confidence put in me, receiving constituents at my riding office. And I looked for a house, my small Lacordaire Boulevard apartment just south of the Metropolitan being too small and terribly noisy. Volunteers from my northern neighbourhood called "the Coop," in the Saint-Angèle parish, helped me find a bungalow there. But with mortgage rates at 11.75 per cent for a five-year contract and high housing prices, I came to the conclusion that it was not for me, at least not now. I would keep my small rented house in Ottawa, put money aside by no longer keeping an apartment in Montreal, and stay with friends instead. And I went for a long overdue holiday in Mexico, discovering Oaxaca and the pre-Columbian preserved Zapotec and Mixtec archaeological sites nearby, as well as Zihuatanejo, still an unknown picturesque fishing village on the Pacific Ocean.

◆ ✳ ◆

Trudeau's Liberals had gone from a minority to a majority government. How would it be different? Would our lives change?

In September 1974 we were slowly coming back to life after almost two years of electoral and political challenges. In the Liberal camp, we had a first reunion on 4 September in the regional and the national caucuses, getting to meet the newcomers, including the new female MPs: Ursula Appolloni, Iona Campagnolo, Coline Campbell, Aideen Nicholson, Simma Holt, joining the three of us from Quebec, now eight women in the Liberal caucus! But in all parties together there were only nine women among 264 MPs in the House, Flora MacDonald remaining the only one in Opposition. The Parliament of Canada had moved from 1.8 to 3.4 per cent women: still a real shame. In the October 2015 general election, forty years later, the eighty-eight women elected represented only 26 per cent of the MPs, still far from what it should be. Back to the Quebec caucus meeting that morning, it had been a delight to discover half a dozen modern, bright, newly elected Quebeckers, who were impertinent in the best sense of the word and ten or more years younger than I. We were to become friends for life, and we still see each other regularly today. We became a tightly knit core group made up of Claude-André Lachance, Charles Lapointe, Pierre Bussières, and Rémi Bujold, as well as Bernard Loiselle and Louis Duclos at times, joined shortly after by Dennis Dawson.

My swearing in by the clerk of the House took place on 24 September. The thirtieth Parliament opened on 30 September, and again I was joined by some riding organizers and family members in Ottawa, a true personal pleasure. Mitchell Sharp and Allan J. MacEachen had exchanged seats, the former now government leader in the House and the latter, secretary of state for External Affairs! We were to learn from the Speech from the Throne what was awaiting us in the months ahead: in particular, a Green Paper on Immigration, the broadcasting of the House of Commons Debates, and a new Citizenship Act.

October kept us rather busy with standing committees meetings by a succession of votes culminating on 23–25 October with questions put to vote without bell, the House being in "committee of the whole," the business of Supply taking precedence in government business. Nobody can then leave the floor of the House until the House is granted adjournment by the Speaker. The day after, a Saturday, a small multipartite group of MPs, of which I was one, left for the traditional week at the UN session in New York. For me, it was almost a holiday, compared with my months there in the preceding fall.

Turning now to unexpected events breaking the routine of my ordinary MP life and opening windows on the world, Ivan Head, foreign policy advisor of Prime Minister Pierre Trudeau, whom I barely knew, invited me to the Parliamentary Restaurant soon after our return to brief me on the work of the Atlantic Conference and their next gathering in Sicily to take place on 14–18 November. Of course it would be interesting, but I did not know that institution nor the topics they usually discussed. I had everything to learn about the actors present and the other guests, and I would find myself in an unfamiliar environment. It was all about exchanges on major international policies, not on diplomacy, nor on international security. These Atlantic Conferences, set up by the Ford Foundation, had been created to reinforce links between the United States and the Western European countries on key topics other than military ones, the latter covered by NATO. It was following the momentum of "the countries of the Atlantic," "the Atlantic movement." This particular Taormina gathering would be on "Resources and International Politics."

Ivan Head had me appointed the Canadian delegate, and I accompanied him, by plane, via New York, Rome, Palermo, and from there by car to Taormina, in Sicily. We arrived at sunset, staying at the exceptional San Domenico Palace Hotel, in the former fourteenth-century monastery of the same name. When I opened my monastic cell room shutters, I was speechless in front of too much beauty. My window was framed with bougainvillea, overlooking the Ionian Sea with Etna volcano burning against the darker sky. For a short time, the fat binder of serious documents just received was far from my thoughts. We were about fifty participants, with one-third being Americans. The conference was co-chaired by the American Democratic Senator Frank Church, who had enormously impressed me by his commitment to peace (he had been one of the first American senators opposing the Vietnam war); his passion for promoting social justice; his work for cooperation with other countries; and his integrity. Very influential and admired, Frank

Church III (Idaho) would serve as senator from 1957 to 1981. He became chair of the Senate Committee on Foreign Affairs, but his fame
would come with his work with the committee bearing his name, which,
starting in 1975–76, investigated abuses of the US intelligence agencies;
extra-legal FBI and CIA intelligence-gathering and covert operations
both at home and abroad. Co-chair of the conference was the Republican Senator Charles Mathias (Maryland), a real progressive conservative. Besides American delegates, this conference included European
personalities as well as some Latin Americans: politicians, editorialists,
business leaders, and academics. The participants were rather sympathetic and friendly, making the exchanges easy, open, and frank. I introduced myself to Claude Julien, then editor-in-chief of the newspaper
Le Monde diplomatique, an expert on the United States, and a friend
of Fernand Cadieux.

Back home, I attended a meeting of the Canadian Foundation of
Human Rights in Toronto at the end of November. Two weeks later the
PMO asked me to host a lunch at 24 Sussex in honour of Shirley
Williams, new minister of state for prices and consumer protection in
Harold Wilson's Labour government. I would meet her again, some
twenty years later in London, when on short notice I had to replace the
president of the Independent Commission on Population and Quality
of Life, the former prime minister of Portugal, Maria de Lourdes Pintasilgo, who had suddenly become very ill that night in our hotel. Dame
Williams agreed to act as master of ceremonies and help me at the
launch of the report for the media, in Regent Park.

The year 1975 opened on the theme of women, with the first UN
"International Women's Year." At the end of February and beginning
of March, Françoise Giroud, the well-known journalist and co-founder
of the magazine *L'Express*, by then appointed Secretary of State for
Women, invited women politicians and feminist senior civil servants to
Paris for a conference-celebration. Lise Bacon, minister of state for social affairs in Quebec, chaired the small Canadian delegation, of which
I was a member, together with Laurette Robillard. The UN had just
declared 8 March "International Day of Women." My memory is of a
rather elitist and arrogant attitude of the French organizers and participants towards us, although they did not have much to teach us. But I

will always remember with pleasure the grand and very elegant evening they offered us at the Opéra Garnier, which, as a poor student, I had known only from the outside!

During that time in Ottawa a very Canadian topic, immigration, started to monopolize public opinion and the political class. The government was getting ready to adopt a new Immigration Act, all the preceding ones being criticized and questioned: selection criteria, the issue of refugees, and other conditions for acceptance or dismissal. Robert (Bob) Andras was the minister of manpower and immigration and Allan Gotlieb, his deputy minister. Andras had invited provinces and interested groups to present briefs. He had also requested a study that would pragmatically define problems and solutions. Further, a Green Paper was tabled in the House of Commons in February 1975, creating a particularly heated debate across the country. At the very beginning of March the government set up a special joint committee of the Senate and the House of Commons to hold public hearings across the country on the controversial Green Paper. As far as I know, it was the first time that a committee of Parliament had a budget to travel as mandated. Over its thirty-five weeks of existence, and further to fifty public hearings in twenty-one Canadian cities, having studied the 1,400 briefs submitted, the special joint committee tabled its report and recommendations on which the new Immigration Act would be based.

I was a member of that special joint committee, perhaps the only committee work that I as an MP found interesting and productive. To tell the truth, I did not find meetings and work for standing committees of the House of much interest. Members were appointed by our government party whip, who often changed the membership at will, without explanation. One day one is in, two weeks later the same member is out. In addition, without any research capacity, pushed by time, it was impossible for an MP to develop expertise on the subject matter reporting to one's committees. I had concluded that committee work was, both for the witnesses and the subject matter on the agenda, just a kind of ritual, a liturgy for the sake of it, where one had to go through the motions, a kind of acting with no particular value, blindly highly partisan, including on the government side.

To the opposite, this Special Joint Committee on Immigration, multipartite, co-chaired by Senator Maurice Riel and Martin O'Connell, a
former minister, was articulated around a specific project and was not
an open-ended process without a clear aim and calendar, except the ex-
pedited passage of this or that, and without the needed working tools.
It was a large committee made of eight senators and fifteen MPs, the
latter including Jake Epp, Benno Friesen, and David MacDonald, as
well as two more Progressive Conservatives; Léonel Beaudouin, a Crédit
Social; Andrew Brewin, an NDP; and Aideen Nicholson, Peter Stollery,
myself, and a few more Liberal MPs. Nothing better to develop camaraderie and esprit de corps than travelling together from place to place!
Absenteeism being a major problem for committees, we were maybe
half the membership regularly travelling the country. Hard to share airplane and bus seats without exchanging with one's seatmate, or to sit
alone at meal time and so on because he or she is a political "enemy"!
We got to know each other personally, and we even discussed the controversial issues presented to us.

Following the organizing meetings on the Hill, we first covered part
of the Maritime Provinces during the week of 28 April, then stopped
in Quebec City and Montreal in the week of 12 May. A somewhat
dramatic incident occurred there, really capturing the temper of the
time. We were having our public hearings at McGill University that
particular afternoon when a Protestant minister from the west of the
island, somehow ahead of his time, started describing the way current
conditions to reject an immigrant application (especially homosexuality)
would have applied to a young man in his thirties, hippie-like, homosexual, just landed at Dorval airport, who was ... Jesus Christ! Our
Créditiste colleague, Léonel Beaudoin, was so shocked by this blas-
phemy that he had a cardiovascular incident at once. I turned into the
francophone de service: first aid, ambulance, and so on. Luckily, Léonel
recovered well and rapidly. By blocks of two to three days or a full
week, the committee pursued its public hearings across the country,
adding Newfoundland and Fredericton, the Prairies and the North,
British Columbia, and so on, to conclude with national public hearings
in Ottawa up to the end of September. Four of us – Peter Stollery,

Andrew Brewin, David MacDonald, and I – wrote a minority opinion
on a specific point but signed the report. The Immigration Bill was
tabled in 1976, based on our report, and became the Immigration Act
of Canada in 1978.

Another dimension of parliamentary life across parties was the possibility of membership in one or several interparliamentary associations.
Some were for MPS only, others for senators, but in general they had a
mixed membership of parliamentarians. The oldest of all is the Inter-
Parliamentary Union (IPU). In a way it was a predecessor of the United
Nations, the creation of which was its main purpose, and which, in my
time, was doing great work in promoting more women in politics. So I
joined but was not particularly active at first. The IPU goes back to
1889 and was born out of the context of pacific ideas that developed in
the middle of the nineteenth century. Public opinion opposed wars as
fatalities and demanded the creation of mechanisms to solve conflicts
through negotiations, further to the failure of diplomacy. Between 1870
and 1890 the idea of bringing together parliamentarians of all countries
convinced the pacifists of the most diverse nations. The IPU was
founded in the midst of the first franco-anglo parliamentarian meeting
in 1888, in Paris. It is now based in Geneva. Other such associations
included the France-Canada one, those of NATO, the Commonwealth,
the Francophonie, the United States, the Americas, and more.

Gordon Fairweather, an impressive "Red Tory" colleague, a solid
human being – I always found he looked like the ideal of a prime minister! – active in the IPU, had me appointed on an MP delegation to an
IPU meeting in Geneva, the week of 10 March 1975. There I met some
interesting colleagues from other countries, the secretariat staff, and
learned about their research projects – all precious sources of information for my speeches and media interviews. They were doing a superb
job of collecting data and providing analysis of women's political participation in many countries. I believe it was my first trip to Geneva. I
would return often after I left politics, when I got involved as a volunteer in the governance of an excellent small organization: the International Centre for Migration Health and Development, of which I still
am treasurer.

The House got ten days off for Easter, which was on 30 March that year. In the summer, the Commons sat until 30 July, in typical Canadian hot weather, meeting in a building without air conditioning, the House reconvening on 14 October 1975. I had spent the last two weeks of August on holiday, joining French friends and their two children in Languedoc-Roussillon near Perpignan, trekking, exploring old Cathar fortifications, and staying out of the strong, cold mistral wind, the Mediterranean being too cold to even set foot in its waters.

Reflecting on my parliamentary life at the time, 1975 was definitely my big year of the Inter-Parliamentary Union! In addition to discovering that institution of value in Geneva in March, I was then appointed a participant (thanks to Gordon Fairweather, I am sure) in a colloquium organized by the IPU in Bucharest, to take place at the end of May. I was accompanied by the new Canadian IPU chair, the ex-minister Bob Stanbury. The topic of discussions, for which Peter Dobell had been preparing me for weeks, terrorized me: "A new system of international economic relations," following Nixon's 1971–73 announcements and actions that led to the end of the Bretton Woods System. Dobell, whom I still see regularly, had left External Affairs in 1973 to set up a parliamentary centre, a brilliant initiative to give Canadian MPs at least a basic knowledge of international affairs. Hard to imagine today, while being constantly bombarded by world news that we wish we could lock once in a while, that forty to forty-five years ago, Canadian public opinion as well as its elected representatives, no matter the political party, did not share much knowledge of world affairs.

As I come from research, I am always particularly hesitant to talk on a topic I have not mastered. Such was the case here and I kept repeating it, but it did not impress anyone. We were four panellists: a Hungarian Communist government economist; MP Ronnie del Mel, who two months later would become minister of finance of Sri Lanka; Klaus von Dohnanyi, former minister of education and science under Willy Brandt, but at the time a Social Democrat MP; and me. Von Dohnanyi would become the German minister of state for foreign affairs in December 1976 and the first mayor of Hamburg from 1981 to 1988. In 1978, when I was minister of national health and welfare, I had the pleasure of spending a few moments with both Ronnie del Mel and Klaus von Dohnanyi, in Ottawa on business, a few weeks apart!

Again with the IPU, the next event was their sixty-second annual general assembly in London, a real spectacle, and I was a member of the Canadian delegation. I reached London directly from my holiday in Perpignan. The Canadian delegation was registered at the Savoy. Queen Elizabeth herself opened the proceedings by saying, "The parliamentary approach to world affairs offered the best hope of winning that concord between nations which had been sought for so long. It enabled change without violence, because its essence was a respect for the other person's point of view and a passionately held belief in his right to express it." All the participants were then invited to a royal banquet at Windsor Castle while a commemorative stamp for the IPU was being issued. I still have my envelope with that historic stamp, postmarked 3 September 1975 and addressed to Miss Monique Begin, Palace of Westminster, London SW1.

This chapter covered the first working year of the majority government, from September 1974 to September 1975, while I was still a backbencher. I had participated the best I could on the standing committees of the House: Broadcasting, External Affairs, National Defence, and the Special Joint Committee on Immigration – the last having priority in case of schedule conflict. I was no longer a member of the Health and Social Affairs Standing Committee. I had enjoyed international travels and meetings with other parliamentarians through the IPU and before that, the most interesting Atlantic Conference in Taormina, Sicily. And I had always remained present in my riding and close to my constituents, serving them well all year around.

At the midpoint of that 1974–75 period I had celebrated the first International Women's Year in Paris at the invitation of the French government. I would conclude these twelve months or so by being a speaker at a women's conference at Adelphi University, in Long Island, on 27 September 1975. It was a nice way to conclude my third year as a backbencher member of Parliament. I would come back after the summer to the arduous work of the Special Joint Committee on Immigration, no longer for the public hearings but to write our report and recommendations!

8

Parliamentary Secretary for Eleven Months

The Special Joint Committee on Immigration started meeting on Tuesday, 30 September, for the whole week: mornings, afternoons, and evenings, even if the House of Commons was in recess. The House reopened on 14 October when the second session of the thirtieth Parliament was called at 2 p.m. The day after, Wednesday, 15 October 1975, I was appointed parliamentary secretary to the minister of external affairs, Allan J. MacEachen. How and when had I learned it? I have no recollection. But I changed seats in the House of Commons, getting closer to the ministerial benches and to "my" minister.

What I do recall very well, however, is that Henry Kissinger was in town, and that I had suddenly been invited to the state banquet given in his honour. It was to take place on the famous ninth floor of the Lester B. Pearson Building, the Foreign Affairs Department on Sussex Drive, the evening before, 14 October. I forget the details but Kissinger, in conversation with his table neighbour, the deputy speaker of the House, Albanie Morin, made an indiscreet remark about Nixon. He did not know that his mic was open in order for the journalists in an adjacent room to hear the toasts presented. The *Washington Post* and a number of American media reported the day after that Kissinger apparently said, "Nixon is an odd, unpleasant man who was barely able to function during his last 18 months president, but said he was decisive and one of our better presidents ... Says Jacqueline K. Onassis was sexy, a hard woman who knew what she wanted." Diplomacy, where were you?

The morning after, I was at Kissinger's breakfast at 7 Rideau Gate, the opulent house adjacent to Rideau Hall (the governor general's residence), a second home for important foreign dignitaries. In that same afternoon, MacEachen had reserved a small government plane to accompany Kissinger back to Washington and pay a formal courtesy visit at his office. With us was Alain Dudoit (a future Canadian ambassador), then the young diplomat dispatched to the minister's office, as was the custom. We were no more than thirty minutes in the office of Henry Kissinger, who talked and talked. Mentally, I saw Allan J. as a big fly and me as a minuscule one, remembering how the Italian journalist Oriana Fallaci had analyzed Kissinger in her book *Interview with History* which I had just finished reading. He, always sure of himself, had boasted to her that he felt like "the cowboy who leads the wagon train by riding ahead alone on his horse, the cowboy who rides all alone into the town"! She also made him admit that the Vietnam war had been "a useless war." Unfortunately my image of Kissinger, too superficial a judgment I admit, will always be that of "the cock of the walk." We stayed in Washington for the night, back in Ottawa the morning after.

Two days later I played a new role that would be repeated often. In the absence of MacEachen, who travelled a lot, I replaced him at Rideau Hall, when Jules Léger, the governor general, received the credentials of the new ambassadors to Canada. During that ceremony I was not expected to speak, standing next to the governor general; my time would come after with small talk during the tea offered by Jules and Gabrielle Léger to the newcomer, always a man, accompanied or not by his spouse. The Légers were delightful people, cultured and subtly mocking, and I simply loved them. I felt as though I was an elegant piece of decorative furniture in these presentations of diplomatic credentials. I remember one Middle East ambassador who was wearing five (gold I assumed) watches on his left wrist. Another one I congratulated on his headdress – his fine *keffiyeh*, made of a square cotton scarf in a red-and-white checkerboard pattern, kept in place by a black *agal*. He thanked me for the compliment and explained how surprised he had been to find it at Filene's department store basement, in Boston. He had bought a dozen of them. I went on smiling nicely, knowing that it was a dishcloth in the household section.

One new role was not awaiting another one in that special assignment. I say "role," for it was like acting, with the exception that I was lucky if I received a text for the part before the show! So the following Monday morning, on 20 October, at the Lester B. Pearson Building, I was opening the consultations with the Senegal minister of cooperation and planning, Ousmane Seck, who would later become minister of finance for Abdou Diouf and develop a remarkable international career of his own. Then the same evening I chaired the official dinner given for him on the ninth floor of External Affairs, complete with long dress and chauffeur.

At question period just following the official lunch for Ousmane Seck, I replaced my minister for the first time. Answering questions in the House is a most challenging test for anyone. As parliamentary secretary I was discovering that strange heavy book ministers carried in the House for question period. In fact that strange book was a kind of giant Cardex: the subject of each anticipated question had its card and a brief overview on the topic. The practical issue was the time it took to find the topic while listening to the question, usually from the Opposition! In Canada, MPs never give notice of a question to be put in the House, contrary to practice in the British Parliament. So here the lack of preparation due to the absence of a notice affects the quality of the answer, and the atmosphere of the debates is more adversarial. As an example in my first week as parliamentary secretary, MacEachen being abroad, I was asked if Mr and Mrs Johnson of Hamilton, both missionaries in Vietnam, will be freed. Then why had Prime Minister Trudeau not given Fidel Castro a piece of his mind regarding the Canadian pilots forced to land in Cuba and still under KGB custody? Or this one: What is Canada doing to evacuate some 200 Canadians still caught in the middle of a war in Lebanon?

Question period appeared to me as a test that gave the Opposition and the Press Gallery, and now interested Canadians via the broadcasting of the House by CPAC, an image of the know-how, the skills, and the knowledge of each minister, or the PS. One must give a good answer and not try to outsmart the questioner. And above all, avoid stale language! And if one does not know the answer, make sure one is given in the following hours – provided it does not happen too often! Of course, the real role of question period should be to contribute to a serious debate of the objectives and orientations of ongoing public policy development, and not a competition of adversaries. So, with time, question period appeared to me as totally irrelevant. Noises, shouting, and insults have recently really reached an unacceptable level, completely out of place. Question period became a circus and the population took notice and has increasingly lost interest in politics. As Michael Chong, when he was a Harper Conservative MP and minister, so aptly concluded, the Q & A of a few seconds (under Harper, the rule was thirty-five seconds for each question and answer!) are purely rhetorical and do not speak to the mind. They are also, physically speaking, incomprehensible because of the ambient noise. In his analysis in 2008 in the *Canadian Parliamentary Review* he adds, "The second reason we should care has to do with Montesquieu's doctrine of the separation of powers. If we believe that it is essential that the legislature hold the executive to account for the functioning of a good democracy, then Question Period and Debate are important tools in meeting this objective."

On top of frequently replacing one's minister in question period in the House, as was my case, the PS must, according to demand, speak in the adjournment proceedings, commonly known as "the late show." PSs then read well-developed answers to the question of the concerned MP, who requests more information and calls for the adjournment proceedings, which take place in a quasi-empty House from 10 to 11 p.m. Then the PS must check "the blues" of the official transcript, in both official languages, as they will be printed during the night! The same procedure serves a member whose written question on the Order Paper is still not answered after forty-five days as he or she can transfer it to the "late show." I had two "late shows" in my first week of office.

The job also included numerous briefing sessions, discussions, and so on with senior External Affairs officials, such as Geoffrey Pearson, who chaired the departmental working group on human rights, elaborating on the stand to take at the UN. I also recall discussions on CNUCED/UNCTAD IV, the Law of the Sea. It was also very important for me to be closely associated with the work of the Standing Committee on External Affairs and National Defence and its special subcommittees: on international development with numerous witnesses testifying; the Armenians; disarmament; agricultural concerns; and the budget of National Defence.

Because I was receiving foreign ministers, I rapidly had to get acquainted in particular with the international aid and development dossiers: the Canadian International Development Agency (CIDA), the International Development Research Centre (IDRC), Francophonie, and others. Once I had acquired a basic knowledge of the hot issues and our policy objectives, I had to learn how to entertain pleasant social conversation, to become adept in the small talk of which Trudeau was incapable. My family education had not equipped me with that talent, as we never received anybody at home and could not go visit friends, so I started observing how people were behaving in formal social occasions. To my surprise, I noticed that they did start talking of rain and good weather! My instinct always made me spontaneously start straight with the issue at stake in order not to waste anyone's time and because it was the one thing of relevance and importance. My interlocutor often just froze. What a lousy sociologist (and psychologist) I was! So I learned to start conversations by talking about everything and nothing to create a good atmosphere.

At Rideau Hall, I met the new ambassadors to Canada of Kuwait, Zambia, Thailand, Belgium, Zaïre, Poland, the United States, Haute-Volta, Gabon, Botswana, and more. There were lunches and dinners to thank departing heads of mission, or frequent lunches for foreign dignitaries and visitors at the governor general's, where I was always received as a member of the family. Exceptional great pomp surrounded the visit of the prime minister of Pakistan, Zulfikar Ali Bhutto, on 23–24 February 1976, who was accompanied by a large entourage, including his personal dancers. My memory is that I was in long dresses for three consecutive days and evenings!

Lunches in one of the private dining rooms of the Parliamentary Restaurant, with or without MacEachen, were quite frequent in the first months of 1976, while hosting foreign delegations: students from Milan, the Yugoslav delegation, a New Zealand one, and the Italian

Olympic team. On Monday, 22 March, another special occasion was the formal lunch at the Lester B. Pearson Building for Manuel Perez-Guerrero, minister of state for international economic affairs of Venezuela, very active with the Group of 77 and other international groups, whom I had picked up at the airport on the Sunday afternoon. One day in May, with much emotion, I hosted for lunch the minister from Papua New Guinea, which had just become an independent country in September 1975. As for local embassy dinners, I managed to accept only a strict minimum, as they really were too great a demand on my busy time, and I did not really enjoy all the social chattering.

From 11 to' 15 June, still in 1976, Seretse Khama, his spouse Ruth Williams, and his minister of foreign affairs, A.M. Mogwe, were visiting Ottawa before continuing to other Canadian cities. He was looking for financial help to finally reach Botswana's economic independence from Rhodesia (today's Zimbabwe), which strangled its neighbouring land-locked country. At the time, Canadian economic and technical assistance to Botswana reached $7 million per year. There was a major issue with the railway system crossing Botswana but in the hands of Rhodesia, and Botswana's need to set up its own official military force. There was, of course, a state dinner at 24 Sussex for Seretse Khama, who had taken his country to independence in 1966 peacefully and had become the very first African president who could not be accused of corruption. Same protocol, same formality as for the 1973 banquet for Indira Gandhi, except that Trudeau was completely relaxed and at ease. He confided to me on another occasion that he felt close to three African presidents: Léopold Senghor of Senegal, Julius Nyerere of Tanzania, and Seretse Khama of Botswana. Margaret Trudeau arrived a little late from the Habitat Conference in Vancouver and was extremely elegant and sophisticated, no longer the "flower child." She was now in open and painful conflict with Pierre. For dessert, she had ordered plain yogurt covered with granola to affirm herself against a protocol, which she was finding intolerable. I was dumbfounded. As an MP, the protocol had me seated with the president, the prime minister, and our minister of external affairs, Allan J. MacEachen, at the centre of the table, one more privileged experience for me.

I have not yet mentioned the uninterrupted media requests on any international issue in addition to the usual topics on the status of women or my political opinion. This 1975–76 year was surprisingly busy on that front, in Quebec, in Ottawa, and anywhere I was, although the big traveller was my minister! I had to be informed at all times, being clear and specific! In my private life I also had to be flexible and ready to adjust to a thousand unforeseen events, like leaving suddenly for Chicago for the evening in order to represent Canada and celebrate the Bicentennial of the United States and present them with a beautiful unique photo album. It was the result of Lorraine Monk's talent, *Entre amis / Between Friends,* the most challenging project ever produced by McClelland & Stewart. Trudeau and Monk would later present a special edition of this album to President Gerald Ford, in Washington.

I consider myself very lucky to have been one of the last promoted parliamentary secretaries whom Prime Minister Trudeau let attend the Cabinet committees relating to our official duties, in my case External Affairs and National Defence. I recently learned from Rick French, at the time in the PCO, that my minister, Allan J. MacEachen, insisted on my participation, which I thought was the norm. That had created a quarrel: the Privy Council Office considered it unacceptable, as I had not been sworn as a privy counsellor of the Queen, as ministers are! Well, thinking of it today, I suppose the PCO's opinion was entirely justified, but I did not know about these arguments behind the scenes at the time. I did benefit from observing how Cabinet committees worked and what roles ministers played. In the absence in all my twelve years in Parliament of any notes, briefing book, or even a paragraph in the Standing Orders of the House of Commons on the role of parliamentary secretaries, I now see with surprise that PSS never talked among ourselves about what we were doing. There was no sense whatsoever of the parliamentary secretaries being a group, a specific entity. Their identity rested only on the personal, individual relationship, when one existed, between the promoted MP and the minister, then becoming a training ground towards a future ministry.

During that special mandate at External Affairs, what was the state of world in 1975–76? On the international scene, the world was slowly and painfully getting out of the horrible twenty years of the Vietnam war, going back to 1955 under the French, the United States having declared war in 1965, and Saigon having fallen on 30 April 1975. In Canada we had received 50,000–100,000 young American draft dodgers. In Africa, decolonization, which, with the second wave of feminism, I consider the two major twentieth-century achievements, was going on, and the former Portuguese colonies were obtaining their independence at long last: Mozambique, Capo-Verde, São Tomé, and Angola, the last falling back into a violent civil war. A civil war had also erupted in Lebanon in April 1975, which would go on up to the 1990s and after.

As to aid and development, in 1975–76 CIDA would enjoy a relatively positive international reach and an optimum budget, leading to an increase of new NGOs made up of younger Canadian volunteers wanting to participate in Third World development. In External Affairs I was receiving representatives from African francophone countries, not just the traditional Commonwealth countries, sensing that they were all expecting so much from our government. The fact is that Canadian aid as a percentage of GNP peaked at 0.52 per cent in that year. Canada then seemed to be getting towards the famous 0.7 per cent of its gross national income (GNI), the UN aid spending target per developed country. Unfortunately, our aid decreased dramatically in the forty years and more that followed. We never contributed more to international assistance than that 1975–76 level of 0.52 per cent. The Donor Tracker states, "Canada is the 9th-largest donor country, spending US$4.1 billion on net official development assistance (ODA) in 2016 (in 2016 prices). This represents 0.26 per cent of its gross national income (GNI). The government of Prime Minister Justin Trudeau has committed to 'restoring and renewing' Canada's international assistance and 're-engaging globally'" (www.donortracker.org/country/canada). The website then quotes the prime minister following the tabling of the 2018 budget in the House. Let us hope these are not just words.

◆ ✳ ◆

I cannot conclude this chapter on my new role in External Affairs without sharing two incredible and totally unexpected official trips, going back to my beginnings as parliamentary secretary to Allan J. MacEachen. A month after my appointment, on 20 November, General Francisco Franco, of Spain, died after a long illness. It had been repeated publicly for years that Juan Carlos de Borbon, grandson of the last king of Spain, would succeed Franco when he relinquished power. But he never did and no formal transmission of power ever took place. Western governments then consulted each other on the future of Spain, democracy, and Franco's successor, the possible violence around that situation, and so on, in order to figure out whom to send to the funerals. There were worries about that situation in all our countries. The informal decision was to send someone representative, but no heads of state of Western nations. That is how I ended up on the covers of *Paris Match*, *Holà*, and other magazines between Nelson Rockefeller, the American vice president, and Princess Grace of Monaco, in the Cortes lodges, at the young king's swearing-in ceremony!

I had had to leave Ottawa at once for the state funeral, welcomed by our ambassador, Georges Blouin and his wife, Denise, at their official residence. Getting off the plane, I was unable to escape a first radio interview … in Spanish, which I do not speak but understood enough to reply, slowly, in French! I was then received by the Spanish minister of foreign affairs, Pedro Cortina y Mauri.

The weather was gorgeous on the morning of my landing in Madrid but on the cold side. The Blouins informed me that my elegant black coat I had just bought at Holt Renfrew – not reimbursed, no need to say – was "not level" with the situation, not chic enough. Our ambassador asked me to wear his wife's fur coat, which I politely refused to do. He then had his chauffeur take us to an elegant shoe store, where he asked me to try on and purchase (at my expense, not reimbursable, of course) a pair of high heeled, exquisite, long, fine, leather, black boots, very expensive and totally impossible to wear in our Canadian weather! As a sociologist, I was starting to discover the standards of the super-wealthy and powerful Spanish aristocracy, but I was also insulted by the requests of our ambassador, otherwise a fine human being. So my first day in Madrid, besides the boot purchase episode, took me to a visit to our embassy staff and to a fancy and very expensive hairdresser, chosen by the embassy, always at my expense. I have natural wonderfully curled hair, which I did myself with no effort. Not good enough.

On the morning of the following Saturday I attended the coronation of King Juan Carlos I in the Cortes, followed by a banquet for international guests. In the afternoon, Ambassador Blouin and I paid tribute to the late Generalissimo, who was lying in state in the Madrid royal palace, the two of us escorted to the head of the line of kilometres-long rows of people waiting to pay their respects. Half a million mourners waiting in silence and slowly progressing towards the doors of the palace was tremendously impressive. I will never see so much pomp and circumstance again.

Then on Sunday, 23 November 1975, the funeral took place outside the royal palace, which faced the large plaza, full of people, with a platform built against the grey stone wall of the palace over which a canopy had been installed for the new King and Queen Sofia. Facing the royalty on the other side of that stage were Franco's widow, daughter, and her husband, the Marques de Villaverde, Cardinal Marcelo Gonzalez Martin, bishops, and other church dignitaries, an improvised altar, and rich Flemish tapestries hanging on these outside walls as a backdrop. The army was everywhere. And police and military corps in their best uniforms kept the crowd at a minimum distance. All foreign participants stood at the foot of the platform, packed against each other. I was with our ambassador, who had found us space quite close to the stage. Photos were totally forbidden. The funeral ceremony went on for hours.

At the end of the formal funeral, a double cavalcade on horseback as well as ranks of military men in uniforms, forming guards of honour on both sides of the coffin placed on a special truck between them, started riding and walking the fifty kilometres through Madrid and the countryside northeast towards the burial site. They were followed by a procession of foreign visitors' official cars, of which Canada was one. I waved to the crowd when they shouted "Canada!" after recognizing our flag. After quite some time, the procession arrived in a scary, huge, circular site without vegetation, at the foot of unfriendly mountains, La Valle de los Caidos (the valley of the fallen), at a colossal cold, modern, cement basilica built by Franco's political prisoners at the end of the Spanish Civil War, almost under the ground – a sanctuary called Santa Cruz – where Franco was entombed. This immense plaza was full of people, of which a great number of neo-fascist youth, the *Azules*, as I assumed from the colour of their blue shirts, arms raised for the Nazi salute, shouting Franco's name. The crowd had lost its Father. When entering the basilica, all hell broke loose, and the hundreds of thousands turned into a mob. I lost my ambassador and was scared for a while. His chauffeur finally found and extracted me, and we returned to Madrid. As far as I was concerned, I was attending the funeral of a war criminal and fascist dictator who, just at the end of September, had five political prisoners executed. In 1975!

The same evening, feeling like a zombie, I graciously agreed to meet the Canadian women gymnasts at the Palacio de Deportes de Madrid (palace of sport of Madrid). Back to Montreal with Iberia late Monday morning, followed by the next AC flight to Ottawa.

Three days later, on Thursday, 27 November, having received the mandatory vaccines, I left for Ceylon, now the Socialist Democratic Republic of Sri Lanka, where I represented Canada and my minister at the twenty-fifth anniversary of the Colombo Plan. Set up in 1950 to improve socio-economic development of the countries of Asia and the South Pacific through mutual assistance and the transfer of knowledge and technologies, it had started further to a meeting in Colombo of the foreign affairs ministers of the Commonwealth. In 1975 our high commissioner was a woman, Marian MacPherson, the first female Canadian ambassador I had met. She was a perfect person, competent, calm, and of good company. The prime minister, Sirimavo Bandaranaike, looked like a good "mamma" and greeted me with a huge smile and much kindness, but she had a strong personality. She chatted with me at length at the welcome banquet, where I proudly wore the long dress I had made myself in Ottawa, and at the inaugural conference the morning after she asked me to light the symbolic flame at the entry of the large conference room where delegates would be meeting. But the contrast with the city of Colombo was total, with army and police everywhere, including at my hotel room, a bodyguard following me even in the public washrooms! Students were stepping up to the barricades, and she was determined to quash the student uprising. Bandaranaike, the first woman democratically elected as a head of state, played hard. Were these upheavals due to increasing unemployment? Or were they linked to the increasing ethnic tensions between the Sinhalese majority and the large group of Indian Tamils, which would lead to the civil war of the 1980s? I did not know at the time.

Before the start of the conference, Marion MacPherson took me by car to the sea, quite a distance from the city, where I would discover the most beautiful white sandy beach, a calm sea of the most attractive light blue and turquoise colour I had ever seen. I just had time to put my big toe in the inviting Indian ocean. *Beauté, calme, et volupté*. Back at work, the discussions followed very much the UN pattern, in English, with a smaller number of delegations, more collegial and relaxed. As usual, I was the only woman, but not really, for with me was the perfect woman high commissioner!

To celebrate the end of the conference, the Sri Lankan government offered the choice of two excursions by bus: either a discovery of the south of the island or one to admire "the cultural triangle" in the north of the country. The second was my choice, on Thursday, 4 December 1975. Our bus stopped at a few cultural sites en route, the ultimate stop being Sigiriya, taking us past paddy fields, small villages, and finally arriving at the UNESCO World Heritage site of Sigiriya, dating back to the fifth century but discovered, cleared of weeds manually, and studied starting in the 1890s. The bus stopped before a dense, green, lush forest, out of which emerged a tall square natural block of granite rock, some 200 metres high above the surrounding ground, 370 metres above sea level. At the bottom of it were carved large lion paws and remnants of the giant body of the animal up the sides of the rock, the head having collapsed at one point. Between the paws and legs a series of large steps were carved in the rock.

And after those, surprise! The traveller had to climb a tiny, old, narrow, scary, iron staircase of 800 steps along the steep slopes of the giant rock, the last 250 being the most difficult and the scariest. They were often completely vertical, at times zigzagging a bit to take the traveller, at mid-height, to the galleries of the remaining eighteen to twenty-one frescoes of semi-naked nymphs of delicate and sensuous colours. Having learned that, I panicked because of vertigo and told my colleagues that I would await them near the bus, on the ground. But I had been adopted by the group, and the prime minister's cousin pricked my pride, reminding me loudly in front of all, that Prime Minister Pierre Trudeau had easily gone up the mountain, signing the golden visitors' book atop. I was stuck, again the only woman, with the men around me having pricked my vanity, and decided to do it. Today I look at my pictures and cannot believe it. And I too signed the golden visitors' book! The view from the top of that granite block was unreal. Down through the jungle were still the clearly recognizable remains of another palace and gardens – Versailles, Singhalese version! The oldest landscaped, terraced water gardens in the world.

When I visited Sigiriya more than forty years ago, the ground site had not yet been restored, and there was absolutely no tourist accommodation of any kind. Still, long alleys, tall granite columns, temples, and big sculptures were emerging from the greenery. On that late afternoon, with the sun setting, the strong blue sky, the immensity of the green plains down below, I shall always remember the image of a young Buddhist monk draped in his orange robe standing there alone, smiling.

Another trip that I was asked to make as MP and parliamentary secretary brought me to Turnberry (Ayrshire) in Scotland. Towards the end of April 1976, I landed in Gatwick with the Canadian Armed Forces, took the train for London and then for Glasgow, and from there a local train for Girvan, where a car took me to the Turnberry Hotel, a luxurious golf estate developed within a micro-climate with palm trees and the sea in the distance. We were there for the twelfth Anglo–North American Parliamentary Conference on Africa, an event sponsored by the Johns Hopkins University and the Ariel Foundation. Besides the three Canadians (David MacDonald, PC; Andrew Brewin, NPD; and me) and some Americans (Congresswoman Cardiss Collins and Professor Vernon McKay), there was an interesting United Kingdom group, rather of the left (Dr Jesse Dickson "Dick" Mabon, Scottish politician; Maurice Foley, UK Labour) and others. I had been asked to give the opening presentation: "World Price Changes and African Development." There would be sessions on Angola and the Middle East. Unfortunately, I no longer have notes on these discussions. On the last evening we were all received at the nearby Culzean Castle for a reception and a banquet. This 1777 castle overlooking the sea is as impressive as that of the televised series *Downton Abbey*, and it belonged to the Scottish Kennedy clan head, who bequeathed it to the National Trust for Scotland.

And what about our domestic policies and politics from mid-October 1975 to mid-October 1976 in all that? It's hard to sum them up without returning to the 23 June 1975 budget of John Turner and his dramatic resignation as MP and minister of finance on 10 September. If Trudeau's family life was now showing cracks, the economic situation of the country was also deteriorating amid economic philosophies diametrically opposed in which public opinion, and the Liberal caucus, were not really involved. Trudeau and part of his Cabinet identified with Keynesian approaches, while a majority of "conservative" economic ministers espoused monetarist policies. For the prime minister, when markets were left to themselves, they did not automatically generate the best economic performance and the best social balance. It thus left the state with an interventionist role to play, either in economic recovery and/or in protecting the social safety net. For John Turner, his minister of finance, reckless public spending and the increasingly uncontrolled deficit were the keys to galloping inflation and high unemployment rates. His department and he therefore wanted to reduce expenditures: in unemployment insurance, health care, social transfers to the provinces, and proposed guaranteed annual income initiatives that were being discussed behind the scenes.

What the voters had witnessed during the July 1974 general election were Trudeau's mockeries and sarcasms regarding Stanfield's wage and price controls, and the promise that none of this would take place if he, Trudeau, was re-elected prime minister. At the time, I had not connected the dots, as I was not really following economic policies and the philosophy supporting them, between actions taken by the Trudeau government as way back as June 1969. In his first term as prime minister, Trudeau had then set up the controversial Prices and Incomes Commission under Dr John Young, who had tried without success to win support in public opinion for a voluntary 6 per cent wage guideline. This commission died in August 1972 on the eve of the 30 October general election in which I was first elected. As the economic situation continued to deteriorate, Trudeau, now re-elected, started developing a strategy of voluntary price controls by collective efforts, population subgroups, and so on. Amongst other initiatives, in May 1973 he had created the Food Prices Review Board under the leadership of Beryl Plumptre, with no real power except that of "monitoring" fluctuations in food prices and reporting to the public via the media. It became rapidly clear that this approach would not be successful.

Faced with the evidence and further to Turner's resignation on 10 September, Trudeau appointed Donald Macdonald as minister of finance in a major Cabinet shuffle in September 1975. During the period mid-October 1975 to mid-September 1976, voters and backbenchers like I was, lived, in my case with great difficulty by lack of historical knowledge, a complete reversal of the situation, and a total lack of respect for the given word, when the government, on 13 September 1975, announced the establishment of the Anti-Inflation Act and Program. It was embodied in three independently operating agencies. The first was the Anti-Inflation Board, under Jean-Luc Pépin, the former minister of industry and commerce, defeated in 1972; the second component was the Office of the Administrator, the latter being Donald Tansley, also reporting directly to Parliament, in his case through the minister of national revenue; and third, the Anti-Inflation Appeal Tribunal. The AIB principal function was to monitor and identify changes in prices and wages that exceeded guidelines and encourage compliance. In cases of non-compliance, subjects would be referred to the administrator for review and legal enforcement of the guidelines, his decisions subject eventually to the Appeal Tribunal. I recall that the whole program, activities, and decisions were judged very controversial before being finally considered ineffective, and the program was phased out in 1978–79.

In the House of Commons or in the business community, Trudeau was accused of socialism, even of fascism! When defending government action, Trudeau was referring to a mixed economy model in a context of free enterprise. But the damage had been done: Gallup polls showed a five-point loss for the Liberal Party for the 1976 first six months, while the Conservatives had gained seven points under their new leader, Joe Clark.

Everything was going wrong in these twelve months of 1975–76. Further to Gérard Pelletier's resignation from Cabinet and nomination as our ambassador to France, Trudeau had appointed Pierre Juneau, the remarkable first president of the CRTC, as minister of communications. He set out at once to run as the Liberal candidate in the Hochelaga riding of eastern Montreal, Pelletier's former seat, for a by-election, where, to general surprise, he was defeated on 14 October 1975 by Jacques Lavoie, who would later cross the floor of the House to the Liberals!

The death penalty was an ongoing, emotional, and controversial issue, which would conclude during these same twelve months. As a new MP, I had had to rush back to Ottawa during my time at the UN for a vote on the death penalty, namely to extend a five-year moratorium suspending the death penalty for another five years, the bill having been passed by only thirteen votes. The five years had expired. On 14 July 1976, after long and passionate debates, Bill C-84 completely abolished the death penalty by a free vote of 130 to 124, with life imprisonment without parole before twenty-five years in the case of premeditated murder. Two days later, Bill C-84, approved by the Senate, received royal assent. The parliamentary session was then adjourned until 12 October 1976.

The 1976 summer was an exciting one because of the Montreal Olympic Games. Unknown to me at the time, in parallel with that historical vote in the House, I would have a last role to play as parliamentary secretary to the minister of external affairs, Allan J. MacEachen: receiving Queen Elizabeth on a particularly sunny July midday in the Rideau Hall gardens. It was probably on 15 or 16 July. The Queen and her entire family, a first, were in Canada for the opening of the twenty-first Olympiad in Montreal on 17 July. She had already visited Nova Scotia and New Brunswick. I cannot recall by what protocol accident I found myself alone with the Queen in the gardens of Rideau Hall, with the guests forming a large circle around us but far from us. Not knowing what to say to her and not wanting to talk of the weather, I asked her in French what unexpected gifts she had received in the course of her royal visits. In her fluent French she gave me a few examples like that of a live llama received in South America, or other unexpected animal, simply put in her limousine trunk by the chauffeur! We chatted for thirty minutes. I have always liked Queen Elizabeth.

Had I liked being parliamentary secretary to the minister of external affairs? Yes, I rather did, because I learned bilateral international relations, but in a terribly fragmented way and at a modest scale, adding to my observations in my time at the UN in 1973, about multilateral international relations. Having said that, I did have a chance to acquire a solid sense of what Canadian aid and development was all about with dossiers of CIDA and IDRC, who, with our UN peacekeepers, our *Casques bleus,* contributed to define modern Canada in the world. Of course, with no direct power base, I usually felt like doing someone's errands. However, my minister and the department, after having briefed me and discussed the topic of the day, let me do it my way and express it in my way of thinking.

In parallel with all the tra-la-la attached to being External Affairs' parliamentary secretary, with the assistance of my sisters and brothers, I had reopened "my first house" personal file, and we were looking in Montreal, just northwest of my own riding. A small two-story brick house under construction in the Sault-au-Récollet, Scandinavian style, appeared rather promising, and I set out to explore this opportunity. It was the summer after all!

9

Minister or Not? National Revenue

It seemed to me that men, in general, and political strategists, in particular, considered, without ever expressing it, that to have some women in politics looked good in modern democracies. But it was chiefly a matter of balance, not of equality, even less of equity. Not surprising then for the few of us sitting in the House of Commons to feel at times rather tolerated than true equals! As a consequence, I had to know my place, to be both an innovator and a go-getter while respecting the limits of established order and acceptable behaviour for a woman.

This image of women's place in politics became very clear to me one day in August 1976 when I was walking along Rideau Street to get to my Confederation Building office. Rumours of a major Cabinet shuffle were building up. September was becoming the month of Cabinet shuffles: Don Macdonald had become minister of finance in September 1975 further to John Turner's resignation, and we were now in September 1976. And September 1977 would witness yet another shuffle! However, according to the rules of the game, nobody knew what and when until the event actually happened. Trudeau was at only 29 per cent in the polls. Jean Marchand, then minister of the environment but previously minister of transport, had resigned from Cabinet on the *Gens de l'air* and anti-French in the air controller conflict on 30 June. The atmosphere in the House of Commons had become "sulphurous," to use the word of John English in his chapter "Off the Track," also a strong image describing these times, in the second volume of *The Life of Pierre Elliott Trudeau*. Then in September, Bryce Mackasey, at the time postmaster general (as well as interim minister of consumer and corporate affairs), resigned on some policy issue, while two older warriors – Charles (Bud) Drury (public works as well as science and technology) and Mitchell Sharp (president of the Privy Council and government leader in the House) – announced it was time to quit to make room for a younger generation.

So, while walking, I met Jean Chrétien, then president of the Treasury Board. Always sympathetic to mere MPs, he confided to me, without my asking, that I was ready to be a minister. However, I should not be disappointed if I did not become one, "because we already have one woman in Cabinet [Jeanne Sauvé] and it is unthinkable that there would be two." And he added, "Moreover, Jeanne's riding of Ahuntsic being adjacent to yours, it makes it even more impossible!" The image that sprang to my mind was that of a contagious disease. I thanked him and did not say another word. I was shocked and very discouraged by such a traditional attitude. I remember how deeply I felt about the intrinsic injustice of the established order. A few weeks later, on 14 September we were three female ministers, in true Trudeau fashion, he who could not stand preconceived ideas! Joining Jeanne Sauvé in Cabinet, Iona Campagnolo and I had just been sworn in by Governor General Jules Léger quite early in the morning of that glorious fall day. After Ellen Fairclough, Judy LaMarsh, and Jeanne Sauvé, I was now the fourth woman minister since Confederation, and my friend Iona, as minister of state, the fifth.

So I would become a minister. As I wrote, plans and schemes could be one very unpleasant reality of political life. It was because of what I perceived as a gross and dumb plan that I almost missed being appointed a minister in 1976. Early in the morning of Tuesday, 14 September, Jim Coutts phoned me at home in Montreal: the prime minister wanted to see me as soon as possible. The House was not yet sitting, following the summer break, and I took the first bus or plane for Ottawa. I reached Trudeau's office past 11 a.m., and he simply asked me if I would accept becoming the minister of state for the status of women. Although I was excited by the challenge of joining Cabinet, my first reaction was negative: not only would I be the first woman, and moreover an identified feminist, to receive this junior ministerial position, but I would also be the first to be named without the benefit of a regular port-folio, that is, without budgets, legislative and executive powers, and the usual team of public servants. I would not even have the power to sign a memo to Cabinet.

As of 1971, when a minister was first appointed to be responsible for the status of women, it had been a responsibility added to that of a male minister with a regular full portfolio, as there was no woman in the Liberal caucus between 1968 and the end of 1972. During that pe-riod of time the first two incumbents had been Bob Andras and Bryce Mackasey. The tradition continued after November 1972, when John Munro followed. The current minister was Marc Lalonde, who saw the Status of Women added to his National Health and Welfare portfolio in 1974. I should explain here that the small committee of women civil servants set up by Gordon Robertson to report to the Privy Council on ways of implementing the *Report of the Royal Commission on the Sta-tus of Women*, on which I was working at the CRTC, had recommended such a course of action. We thought that each department, in turn, and its male minister, would then have to "learn" the status of women.

Back to Trudeau's offer: negative arguments started rushing in my mind. I knew we were about to enter a recession and that there would surely be no more money for women, and this after the summer cele-bration in Mexico of the newly proclaimed UN International Women's Year and the great expectations it had generated in Canadian women's associations. Also, the Badgley report on abortion was about to be re-leased, and I already knew from the private presentation to Trudeau of the *Report of the Royal Commission on the Status of Women in Canada* in December 1970 that he would never budge on the subject. I was both angry and hurt that a prime minister like Trudeau would resort to what seemed to me a gross electoral tactic that would surely, in time, have a boomerang effect against the government. I was also quite disappointed, as I was anxious to set out on a ministerial adventure, though dying of fright beforehand. After explaining all of this to him, he gave me a few hours to think it over.

Leaving Centre Block, I bumped into Pierre Juneau and Monique Coupal, two old CRTC friends now working in the Privy Council Office, going out for lunch. I asked if I could join them. I knew I could share my dilemma very openly with these two knowledgeable and trustworthy persons. They listened to me, not giving any advice but reflecting my own reactions like in a mirrors game. I left them having convinced myself that I could not accept Trudeau's offer. At 4 p.m. he received me. I was persuaded that Trudeau's offer was a mistake for me and for his government. I explained my views and thanked him while stating my frustration. He confided that of all those individuals boasting that they had refused a ministerial appointment in the past, I was the first, and he was impressed. He was impressed, but I could have killed him. I had to rush to catch the train to return to Saint-Léonard in my Montreal riding for a stormy public meeting on Bourassa's Bill 22 that had made French the official language in Quebec. Walking rapidly towards the Confederation Building, I suddenly vomited on the sidewalk. Hard to believe but true!

Monique Coupal saw me, picked me up, and brought me to their home, stating that there would be no Saint-Léonard that evening. She made me rest on their sofa in front of the television, while she and her husband had supper in the kitchen. Commentators kept apologizing that the prime minister's 6 p.m. press conference was delayed, and delayed, nobody knowing why. At around 7 p.m., Monique came to tell me that the prime minister was on the phone. I thought it was a joke and did not like it at all. But it was true. Trudeau simply asked me, "if" his planned discussions were to succeed, would I accept being made minister of national revenue. I simply answered rapidly, "Yes, Prime Minister." He added that he could not guarantee it, but that I would learn it by watching his press conference. Snippy, I replied, "What? I would learn the answer through the media?" A few minutes later, Cécile Viau, his wonderful private secretary, phoned and said, "Mr Trudeau would like you to be at Rideau Hall for 8 a.m. tomorrow." I was sworn into office as minister of national revenue.

When I joined Cabinet on 15 September 1976, only one of the Three Wise Men (*les trois colombes*) remained in office: Prime Minister Trudeau. Marchand had just resigned, while the journalist Gérard Pelletier, minister of communications, had left Cabinet in 1975 when appointed our ambassador to France. But that day, when two younger

Quebecers, Francis Fox and I, were appointed to Cabinet, we were still joining others of "French Power" in Ottawa: Marc Lalonde, Jean Chrétien, Jeanne Sauvé, Jean-Pierre Goyer, André Ouellet, and Marcel Lessard – a strong team indeed. Not to forget Senator Renaude Lapointe, the first woman editor of *La Presse*, a courageous and lucid journalist, already the Speaker of the Senate, with great Quebecers like Maurice Riel and Maurice Lamontagne as colleagues in the second Chamber. I could add Roméo LeBlanc to the French Power, the Acadian minister of fisheries and oceans, and Jean-Jacques Blais, to be appointed with me, who always defended the Franco-Ontarians.

That fall, Cabinet had also strong colleagues from Ontario: Donald Macdonald in Finance, Bob Andras in Treasury Board, and Judd Buchanan in Public Works, for instance; Otto Lang in Transport from Saskatchewan; from BC, Ron Basford as minister of justice; or Don Jamieson, from Newfoundland, as minister of external affairs. The younger generation had Hugh Faulkner, also from Ontario, whom I liked for his openness, culture, talent, intelligence, and complete bilingualism. He was *un moderne* who was moving that day from remarkable accomplishments as secretary of state to minister of science and technology. There was also, from Manitoba, James Richardson, of the family-owned grain company, then minister of national defence, who did not seem to mix with others and who we sensed was against bilingualism and did not like us, the French Canadians. In fact, he resigned from Cabinet a month after my appointment, opposing official bilingualism, remained a Liberal MP, finally crossing the floor of the House to sit as an independent, then formed a political party called the One Canada Party, a total flop, and disappeared from national public life.

I have never been "the only woman in Cabinet." When Iona Campagnolo and I were appointed as ministers, we joined Jeanne Sauvé, sworn in at the end of November 1972, the second Liberal female Cabinet member after Judy LaMarsh, who had resigned in 1968. As minister of state for fitness and amateur sport, Iona Campagnolo, first elected in the riding of Skeena in 1974, started by reporting to Marc Lalonde for one year, and then to me when I succeeded Marc in National Health and Welfare. She was excellent in her portfolio, a very macho one for a woman, and she and I became friends for life. We met each time I was in Vancouver and I visited her regularly when she was in Victoria as the outstanding lieutenant-governor of British Columbia during an exceptional tenure of six years up to September 2007. A committed environmentalist ahead of the times, a feminist, an activist, and true friend of First Nations in her province, a strong supporter of human rights, she played diverse prominent roles, including that of the first elected chancellor of the newly established University of Northern British Columbia in 1992, where she served a six-year term. She was defeated by the NDP in the 22 May 1979 general election won by Joe Clark, while I was re-elected with 77.15 per cent of the votes in Saint-Léonard-Anjou in Montreal! In the following general election of 18 February 1980, Iona did not run for office, but I was re-elected with 81.12 per cent of the votes in my riding. Later, in November 1982, she was elected president of the Liberal Party of Canada, the first woman to preside over a federal political party in Canada. She ran again in 4 September 1984 but was defeated.

I might have been the only woman in Cabinet later in 1980 when we came back to office after Joe Clark, but for the election in that February of a newcomer who was to become another woman Cabinet colleague friend for life: Judith Erola, from the Nickel Belt riding in Northern Ontario. She had the added challenge of learning to become a member of Parliament at the same time that she was joining Cabinet as the minister of state for mines, a department of its own, reporting to Marc Lalonde, then the new minister of energy, mines, and resources. She remained in Mines for three years before becoming a full minister in her own right as minister of consumer and corporate affairs. In September 1981 she was also sworn in as the first female minister of the status of women. We both left the House of Commons after the 4 September 1984 elections, she being defeated, me leaving politics of my own volition. Because there were so few women and because I was "the official feminist," I want to clarify that I was never the only woman in Cabinet, and that I was *never* responsible for the Status of Women! Most people still state that I was!

After the ceremony and the pictures at Rideau Hall, the famous morning of the swearing in of surely half the Cabinet – sixteen old and new ministers – on 15 September 1976, at around 10:00 a.m., I aimed for the Connaught Building. Right downtown, that impressive faux Tudor-Gothic construction on the opposite side of the Château Laurier, was the national revenue minister's office. It is where Customs and Excise is located. In high heels and a Chanel style white suit, slim and tall, much younger looking than my forty years of age, I entered the Connaught dark lobby when the commissioner asked what I wanted. I explained I was the new minister. "Oh! No, Ma'am, I just heard it on the radio: our new minister is a man called Monikue Beghin!" I said my name in French and he took me, still dumbfounded – a woman and a French Canadian – to the seventh floor to Peter Connell, the deputy minister. I was taken to a splendid, elegant, and huge office but felt very lonely that morning, just by myself in one of the three federal departments going back to 1867. I slowly went around, introducing myself to the civil servants there and asking about their work. At 4 o'clock, Peter Connell very graciously improvised a welcome cocktail for the floor. I never forgot his short speech: "And, Minister, I want you to know that I am also a gentleman farmer on the Quebec side, and my favourite cow is called Monica." I did not react, kept my smile, wondering in *petto* if I should slap him in the face. Years later I told Michael Pitfield, clerk of the Privy Council, of this scene. Horrified, he wondered why I had not reported it to him at once. To tell the truth, as a woman at the time, one went through moments clearly unacceptable by today's standards, not reacting and telling oneself, She laughs best who laughs last! Two months later, the same deputy minister – at the end of my short speech during the closing dinner for his senior staff workshop in Château Montebello, the only woman at the table – pulled my chair back when I tried to sit down, and I found myself on the floor with the guys finding it very funny and laughing. I decided that that particular half on my first portfolio shared the "officers' mess" culture.

The other big half of the portfolio, that of Taxation, was of an institutional culture clearly more complex, subtle, and secretive. I much enjoyed working with my first taxation deputy minister, Sid Hobart, who was to retire a few months later. His offices were at 125 Elgin Street, but a number of the Taxation staff worked next to the Connaught Building, where the American Embassy now stands, in several World War II temporary barracks-like buildings now demolished. In

January 1977, Sid Hobart, having retired, was replaced by Dr Jack S. Hodgson, promoted from assistant deputy minister (ADM), while Bruce MacDonald would in turn become ADM. Another of my assistant deputy ministers was Harry Garland, a strong personality who gave leadership to the crusade against tax evasion in my time and after, conceding that probably $1 billion went unreported each year, while academic tax experts believed it was ten times more.

Revenue Canada no longer exists as a department today. It has been replaced by two distinct Crown corporations reporting to Parliament through two different ministers. One is the Canada Revenue Agency, which administers all tax laws for the country and most of the provinces as of 1999, under a commissioner of revenue and chief executive officer, who report to a minister of national revenue who has an organizational chart very different from in my time and with half my responsibilities. The other is the Canada Border Service Agency, created in December 2003 and ensuring the security and prosperity of Canada by managing the access of people and goods to and from Canada, through clearance, control, and examination services at close to 1,200 points of entry. It operates under a president and reports to Parliament through the minister of public safety.

The House was not yet sitting in September 1976, but my frantic life in External Affairs as Allan J. MacEachen's parliamentary secretary would rapidly calm down. In parallel to my first Revenue Canada briefing sessions, I had to complete my agenda as parliamentary secretary. So the day after my swearing in as minister, with Margaret Trudeau I co-hosted a lunch at 24 Sussex for Madam Callaghan, whom I saw again the same evening at the state dinner offered by Trudeau for her husband, James Callaghan, the United Kingdom Labour prime minister, as of April. Callaghan would be the only former trade unionist in that post as well as the only British PM to have occupied the three leading Cabinet positions: foreign secretary, home secretary, and chancellor of the exchequer.

The day after, I attended my first Meech Lake Cabinet retreat. That is when I concluded that the new political reality was light years away from my universe as an MP, a member of National Caucus and a member of standing committees of the House of Commons. This was later confirmed by my first Cabinet committees – Foreign Affairs and Defence Policy, Government Operations, Economic Policy – Cabinet or the Treasury Board meetings. What we used to discuss at caucus was years behind the realities of Cabinet current concerns.

At the time, nothing, not a single document, no information session, helped a new minister to learn the role. It would be through a colleague who was a friend of Fernand Cadieux and who became a close friend of mine, Roméo LeBlanc, that I received a first and invaluable piece of advice: "Get hold of Dick Crossman's diaries and read them as soon as possible!" Roméo LeBlanc, former CBC foreign correspondent, who had become press attaché for Pearson and Trudeau, had been elected in October 1972 like me but remained a backbencher during that minority government, before being finally appointed minister of state for fisheries and now minister of fisheries and the environment. His advice was referring to the three volumes of *The Diaries of a Cabinet Minister* then just published in London, Crossman having died in 1974. Dick Crossman, a brilliant socialist intellectual, had been Labour minister of housing, lord president of the Privy Council and leader of the Commons, to finally become secretary of state for health and social security. Every Sunday evening at his country manor, Crossman would dictate the daily notes he had made of his week and of Cabinet meetings. His book release terrified the public service by the ridicule he cast on bureaucracy and its foibles. I was to learn years after, in my second mandate in National Health and Welfare, that Crossman's *Diaries* had been the inspiration for the hilarious television program *Yes, Minister!* But at the time, what I recall learning was the unwritten true functioning of Cabinet.

I do not remember where my new desk was in the House or with whom I shared it when I became minister of national revenue, but when becoming minister of national health and welfare the year after, I became a "frontbencher," sharing Roméo LeBlanc's desk in the first row of seats, the most prestigious, relatively close to the Speaker's seat. (In the House of Commons, members are seated two-by-two at double desks, according to a protocol of first election year, role/responsibility, etc.) I was to spend all my ministerial years after Revenue Canada sharing my desk with Roméo LeBlanc, a friend – a rare treat in politics.

If I already had answered questions in the House as a parliamentary secretary, the real test was to do so as *the* minister of this or that. Bilingualism was a trap. In my years there were no paid English courses for francophone MPs as there were French for anglophone MPs, which was unfair. It was as if it was taken for granted that Quebecers were bilingual. My biggest problem was idioms, which could be identical in our two official languages, slightly different, or completely different! Which, of course, one never learns at school. So I regularly replied to questions in the House by translating the French idiom into English word-for-word: "Mr Speaker I always call a cat a cat!" I never heard a word about it. It was only when Judy Erola joined Parliament years later that she asked me what I meant that I learned the English idiom: to call a spade a spade. In one of my very first ministerial meetings as minister of national revenue, in front of the welcoming party in Halifax, a new political member of staff, older, very proper, and serious, whom I did not know well, repeated loudly to me in front of everybody, as if I was a child, "Minister, the powder room!" Well, it means needing the washroom … To which, irritated, I finally answered, "But you know I don't put any powder on!" In question period, in National Revenue, when the question from the Opposition did not make any sense, I answered, "Mr Speaker, the honourable gentleman is completely in the potatoes!" – an expression frequently used in Quebec, meaning he does not know what he is talking about, he is all mixed up. A young page immediately brought back a (friendly) note to my desk from Eymard Corbin, the Liberal MP for Madawaska-Victoria: "Monique, please don't insult the Madawaska Republic and its major crop!" The first time my young wonderful political assistant Anita Biguzs said, before a major speech, "Break a leg, Minister!," I wondered what was wrong with her until I learned she was wishing me good luck!

My ministerial role was slowly becoming a reality, overlapping with requests that had been accepted long ago: a political trip to northern New Brunswick to Chatham and Bathurst; invitations in my riding; the funeral in Quebec City of my colleague and friend Albanie Morin elected with me in 1972; and other commitments. The House reconvened on 12 October with the Speech from the Throne, the Parliamentary Ball at the governor general's, and daily question period. My trip to northern New Brunswick was the result of the new decentralization policy of Treasury Board, which aimed to have the Ottawa bureaucracy move to different regions of the country wherever possible. As far as I could see, the daring new policy was making as many happy as unhappy people. That was why I went to Rigaud to open the Customs College in a former novitiate. On the negative side, going to Bathurst, in Acadia, meant closing customs offices no longer used enough to justify them, where those few jobs lost were a drama in a region of low employment.

Almost every Wednesday evening, with the House not in session, I would fly to or be driven to a conference, or a political meeting in my riding, or a visit elsewhere in Quebec or in Toronto, unless I had been asked to welcome and pick up the Spanish minister of foreign affairs, Marcelino Aguirre, and his wife at the Mirabel Airport on a Sunday, going back to Ottawa the same evening! It could also be a dinner at the residence of the governor general, Jules Léger, for the diplomatic corps or in the honour of a distinguished foreign visitor. At the end of November I even had the privilege to be invited by Trudeau to a lunch at 24 Sussex with Alvin Toffler, the sociologist and famous futurist whose book *Future Shock* had become a bestseller. Saturdays were as busy, and Monday mornings were reserved for a full schedule of appointments at the riding office.

In my new department I immediately learned not to take the time to study in depth the individuals' files sent to the minister, as a predecessor had done, usually taxation cases, conscious as I was of the legal deadlines on each case. In a delicate international case, I learned when a minister and his deputy ought to inform the prime minister, as we did once, quietly, regarding a member of European royalty. Another case I faced was of the French architect Roger Taillibert and the income tax on his honoraria related to the Montreal Olympic Stadium, the Olympic Village, the Biodome, and more, which he refused to pay. It meant I had Mayor Jean Drapeau on the telephone or in person in Montreal, much too often for my taste, pleading and putting all the pressure he could on me to make the department and its minister change their mind. Besides his power of conviction, to which I was absolutely insensitive, the mayor was always very courteous. But what a politician! After I had left politics and when Drapeau was about to announce his leaving politics, he sent his friend Senator Maurice Riel, also a good friend of mine, to ask if I would run for mayor of Montreal and offer his assistance. Very flattering, but of no interest to me.

So I had to set up a ministerial office, which was not a simple thing to do. After discussing the situation with my two secretaries who had been with me since my first election, we concluded that my senior secretary, in need of something less frantic, would become secretary to Jean Marchand, by now Speaker of the Senate, while the second one would be promoted, taking charge of my office on the Hill at the Confederation Building, looking after my constituents, while liaising with the constituency and the new ministerial offices. My first chief of staff was Fred MacDonald, from the Liberal Party office, whom I had known and appreciated while I co-chaired the September 1973 Liberal National Convention. Calm, responsible, and serious, I could count on him with my eyes closed. At the same time, thanks to the selflessness of Henri Vandermeulen, director of the Liberal National Caucus Research Bureau, I met a rare jewel, then and now: Anita Biguzs. She assisted me during my eight years in Cabinet and, when I left politics, joined the civil service. She later became associate deputy minister of transport and retired as deputy minister of immigration, refugees, and citizenship – a formidable responsibility she carried beautifully. Then my old friend Monique Coupal chose to leave her position in the Privy Council Office to come as my special policy advisor and later as my chief of staff. She was quietly always in control, noiselessly following all that was going on, including current affairs, Canadian and international, always grounded, exceptionally frank and totally loyal. Fred knew the party from within, and Monique had practised the machinery of government when I had everything to learn. I owe Monique Coupal several of my political successes as well as the friendly atmosphere and teamwork of my political cabinet, and her credibility with my department and the senior Ottawa mandarins. I consider myself particularly lucky to have benefitted from such support. In the Saint Leonard or Anjou (Montreal) riding office, staffed with two mature local women in succession, files ran smoothly and constituent requests were promptly looked after. Demands could be of any kind: a family, back from visiting in Italy, whose salami and cheese had been seized at Customs on their return (and I was that minister!); or a Chinese restaurant owner awaiting a visa for an older parent back home for more than two years; or a local Haitian community association in need of a grant, and so on. And above all, jobs, jobs, jobs, employment at the Post Office seeming the ultimate catch. As my senior Quebec political assistant I was also blessed with Paul Delaney, always in a good mood and ready to solve any kind of situation (except the day he accompanied me to view a heart transplant operation from a visitors gallery, when he almost fainted!) then when we came back in 1980, and by a very mature helpful Montreal woman, until I left political life. In the House I was assisted by George Baker as my parliamentary secretary, with whom I got along very well. A bright and outspoken Newfoundlander, he had a reputation as a maverick that made power nervous but I loved. He would be appointed senator in 2002.

My new life was getting organized, and to complete the picture, at the end of October, finally healed from a pneumonia, I moved to my very first house, almost finished, in the Sault-au-Récollet in Montreal, bordering my riding. A dream turned into reality. I even had a rather large garden and trees. My youngest brother, an architect, and my sisters and brothers all helped get the place ready, and I would cook and entertain them as often as politics left me some time for myself.

It was with my Customs and Excise deputy minister, Peter Connell, that I worked more closely – searches, arrests, seizures of goods, confiscations, or offences or having high visibility and calling for public reactions that taxation does not generate, being more secretive and confidential by its very nature. But there were also other issues: the assembly of Canadian bishops wanting tighter control of pornography from abroad; issues of imports for our shoe industry. On the Taxation side, invitations were to address bankers associations, the Tax Executive Institute, accountants associations, John Bullock and the Canadian Federation of Independent Business, local chambers of commerce, and the Canadian Banks Association (with Donald Macdonald, finance minister). During my year in National Revenue I regularly accepted inter-

views with the media, be it in Lloydminster (a small city with the unusual characteristic of bordering the two provinces of Alberta and
Saskatchewan), Toronto, Halifax, or Montreal, wherever I was asked,
as well as in Ottawa.

At the international level, further to the successful negotiations
undertaken by Customs and Excise before me, I had the pleasure and
satisfaction of signing a customs treaty in June 1977 with the commissioner of US Internal Revenue, Jerome Kurtz, newly appointed and in
Ottawa also to meet our experts. This treaty, still in force, lets travellers
leaving Canada for the United States by air to clear customs and immigration at their point of departure in Canada, once registered for their
flight. Upon landing in the United States, they collect their luggage like
any local traveller, saving time and effort and much appreciated. The
reciprocal procedure to apply for travellers from the United States to
Canada was to be negotiated by our neighbours later, but the Americans shelved the project.

On a light note this time, another file of Customs and Excise had to
do with modernizing the customs officers' uniform. I had not been involved in it at all, this being a rather low priority, in my opinion. Anyway I had never been briefed on it. One day Peter Connell asked me
to attend the fashion show of the proposed new uniforms in the Connaught Building, and I went. He had hired a designer firm. For men,
pants would be replaced by overalls, in a thick fabric like twill, in dark
turquoise, to be worn over a shirt of a strong mustard colour. My Girl
Guide totem having been "mocking stork," I could not repress a laugh
and asked the civil servants if they could portray portly Eugene Whelan
or Don Jamieson dressed like that. It was not very smart: men wearing
overalls in Canada towards the end of the twentieth century? Even blue-
collar workers did not wear them anymore. On top of portly men having to wear that, overalls for women would raise the issue of breast size
and importance. My new department was hiring women en masse, having discovered that they were more meticulous in their work than their
male counterparts! Instead of their cap, customs officers would wear a
Russian *chapka* with three flaps, in fake fur of the cheapest quality in a
dirty brown colour. I suggested a review, the whole file. I have no idea
who dealt with it after me.

I admit that today's Canadian television series *Border Security* depicts a reality that bears no relationship to the job of a customs officer forty-five years ago! It paints a large groups of very professional, well-trained, sophisticated, courteous, even caring officers, capable of foiling the trickiest illegal traveller plots. Their first intuition is helped by all sorts of instruments that give an immediate answer on drugs and whatnot. That does not compare with the undeclared bottle of California wine of my time.

The minister of national revenue is not in the role of policy-making, which emanates from Finance. Following tradition, I was to automatically sit on the Treasury Board Cabinet Committee, which met a few hours weekly. We were four or five members, in addition to the secretary (its deputy minister) or another member of the Secretariat, usually Gérard Veilleux that year, and the president, Robert Andras. This central agency considered every memo approved by Cabinet through a fiscal lens. Each ministerial initiative approved by Cabinet was then scrutinized in terms of its financial, personnel, and management dimensions. The men all smoked cigars at that committee meeting and my clothes were stinking, and I had to wash my hair at once because of the smell. But I found it an interesting committee to be on, which the majority of ministers are not familiar with until their memo approved by Cabinet is rejected!

Quite proud of having always completed my income tax myself every year, I decided to make the taxation form user friendly by shortening it, the officials having volunteered that some questions were redundant. Each revision of a form presented for my approval still had the usual four pages. One day at lunchtime, tired of their childish way of avoiding shortening the form without valid explanation, I sat down with a pencil, scissors, and glue to develop a three-page form. My officials showed me that half a page of key information was missing. So I added the half page and left a blank below. They were so shocked and negative that I gave up and never spoke of it again. Bureaucracy is bureaucracy.

Another of my initiatives, dead on arrival, was to make the SIN card, our national identity card, mandatory for all Canadians, its current use being legal only for work in Canada or to receive government allowances.

Having been brought up in France and having travelled quite a bit, I was familiar with national identity cards in use in most countries. As soon as I started testing the idea, I was confronted in question period, more than ten years after the fact, with Diefenbaker's violent opposition to it. "The old lion" had said that it was the beginning of the dictatorship of the state.

Besides the daily routine, two files remain important in my memory, one regarding Taxation, the other Customs and Excise. The first came back on the scene in the Harper years: that of the registration of charitable, educational, or religious entities for tax purposes enabling them to give income tax receipts for donations. In my time in office, strangely, the problems seemed to affect only women's organizations. The triggering event was a meeting at my office requested by an academic, a founder of a new feminist research institute, the Canadian Research Institute for the Advancement of Women (CRIAW/ICREF), Naomi Griffiths. She was a historian who would become my dean at Carleton University, but I did not know her at the time. Her new institute regrouped academics and community leaders who, as volunteers, were developing initiatives with women's local community groups to address their problems. One such case she described to me was that of some Vancouver Chinese women who, further to a divorce, were sent out on the street with no knowledge of their rights and of the English language, and the need to teach them language and other skills needed to be reinserted in their community. This had been judged by my department as against the law for a charitable organization.

There were a few established women's associations approved for registration as "charitable organizations," hence allowed to issue official donation receipts for financial gifts received, which could be used by the donor to reduce his or her income tax. To be registered, an organization had to be established and operated for charitable purposes, devoting its resources (funds, personnel, and property) to charitable work. The description at the time was much like the one given today: "the relief of poverty; the advancement of education; and the advancement of religion." The court would decide if certain other purposes were also acceptable. Political purposes were political partisanship objectives and wanting to "retain, oppose, or change the law, policy, or decision of any

level of government in Canada." This, in the aftermath of the Royal
Commission on the Status of Women in Canada! I was shocked by the
reasoning that one could not push to change unjust or simply outdated
legislation, especially in the case of women. Enough to believe that some
civil servants had studied their new minister's CV. But if so, they had forgotten to study her special advisor's CV, a lawyer by training, but more
important, the legal advisor of the RCSW. Without a word, Monique
Coupal studied the situation, understood how the department assessed
the requests received, and calmly explained to women's groups how to
rewrite their charter in a way to not appear unduly activist or "politically active," meaning pressing for changes to laws and regulations. No
need to add that CRIAW did get its charitable organization status.

The other file that caught my eye was of totally different nature and
had to do with Customs and Excise. One day Dr Victor Railton, MP
for Welland, just south of Niagara Falls, elected with me in 1972, came
to see me. He was a man of solid judgment who had served as a surgeon
during the Second World War in France, England, Belgium, and the
Netherlands, loved and respected by everyone. His story was incredible.
He wanted justice for a family in his riding, whom he knew well, who
had had their door forced open in the middle of the night by the RCMP,
who arrested them and seized some of the wife's jewellery, all without
a search warrant. The older couple had given a reception the evening
before, during which the mother had shown a jewel that her daughter
– who lived just on the other side of the border and to whom the mother
had lent the piece – was bringing back. A guest told the story to a neighbour, an RCMP officer. My deputy minister, Peter Connell, said that
there was no problem and no incident: case closed. I disagreed. My political cabinet was as shocked as I was, knowing that a search without
a warrant was unjustified by principle, the presumption of innocence
being a cornerstone of our legal system. For a search to be legal, the
basic rule requires that the police ask for authorization beforehand, obtain a search warrant, giving reasonable and probable motives for the
search. In studying the Customs Act, the Excise Act, my special advisor
found a section of the Act going back to the Prohibition era giving customs officers and the RCMP acting for them the power to conduct a
search without a warrant if the conditions for obtaining a warrant exist

but circumstances made it would be impractical to obtain a warrant. All this had been legislated to help locate, control, and seize stills that were making alcohol during the night!

I started reviewing the Customs Act and other legal instruments Revenue Canada used to repeal searches without warrants. The opposition from within was particularly strong and nasty. We got the same reaction from the Department of the Solicitor General and its minister, Francis Fox. Customs officers felt castrated: they would lose their power. I was already in my second ministry when the Customs Act review on which we had worked was finally agreed upon. In any event, the adoption of the Charter of Rights and Freedoms in 1982 changed the situation radically by clarifying this type of police powers over individuals.

In addition to my regular meetings with my two deputy ministers, I also had a few briefing sessions with a senior civil servant who impressed me by his intelligence, competence, and vision: Donald Tansley. He was of the Saskatchewan school who had to leave Saskatchewan when Ross Thatcher became premier in 1964, wanting to have nothing to do with the remarkable professional civil servants of the previous NDP government. That is how the feds were enriched by Tommy Shoyama, Al Johnson, Del Lyngseth (who would be an excellent assistant deputy minister during all my years in National Health and Welfare), Ian Potter (future ADM of Aboriginal health after my time but with whom I worked at the Canadian Breast Cancer Research Initiative), and Art Wakabayashi. I would have loved to have had Donald Tansley as a deputy minister in National Revenue but he was then the administrator, the final authority, of the Anti-Inflation Act and Program created by Pierre Trudeau in 1975. The act and the program reported directly to Parliament through the minister of national revenue, hence these briefing sessions to prepare me for the defence of his estimates in Committee of the Whole in the House of Commons.

◆❋◆

Quite unexpectedly, on 16 May 1977, St Thomas University, in Fredericton, granted me my first doctor of laws, *honoris causa*, for my contribution to human rights, which I received with astonishment and humility. More than thirty years later, I finally guessed that I owed it to Noel Kinsella, a Red Tory, then law professor in that university. Appointed senator by Mulroney in 1990, then Speaker of the Senate, we had sat together on the board of the Canadian Foundation of Human Rights. For my speech, having no idea of the custom for such a ceremony and not ready to ask around to avoid boasting about this honour, I decided to speak about the political drama of Quebec separatism in the wake of René Lévesque's election as premier just six months before. I asked the help amongst others of Blair Williams, then professor of political science at Concordia, to develop the idea I had about a consultative process to address the situation. I was already turned off by the highly legalistic and antagonistic atmosphere in Ottawa when discussing the situation and was dreaming of this "participatory democracy" promoted by Pierre Trudeau during his 1968 leadership campaign. As a citizen, I wanted to express my dream of a sort of constituent assembly, a kind of parliamentary assembly of civil society, to rewrite the Constitution, which would be later subjected to a national referendum. It had nothing to do with relationships of power but, I admit today, it was a generous and naive utopia aiming at "re-confederating" Canadians, by redesigning the relationships and responsibilities between the First Nations and the Inuit, the founding French and English peoples, older immigrants and newcomers – with empathy, among equals. It would include leaders and ordinary citizens. Of course nobody ever spoke of that speech, and I bet it was not even mentioned in the local newspapers. All this less than a year after the June 1976 ugly airline pilot strike on bilingualism and the Official Languages Act.

My first year as a minister and Cabinet member was then coming to an end. I had been discovering a whole new world! With hindsight, I reckon that, if in my Department of National Revenue I remained on the surface of things and could successfully address only a few ad hoc cases, at Cabinet and at the Treasury Board, I learned the machinery of government and observed the political culture of my peers. I saw my ministerial role in that particular department rather as one of "support" in a huge federal architecture.

Taxation and Customs and Excise were very different in their individual institutional cultures, but their top executives shared the deeply rooted view that Canadians were all potential criminals! That is not what I had heard from our employees of either division, for I made a point of getting to talk with and listened to as many of our civil servants as I could in every Canadian city I found myself. I was always warmly received. I remember visiting the imposing historical 1936 National Revenue building in Old Montreal Place d'Youville, that of Customs and Excise. The director had taken me to visit its unreal system of underground galleries (filmed in Frank Oz's thriller *The Score* with Robert De Niro, Angela Bassett, and Marlon Brando, in 2001) filled with seized illicit goods, an antique dealer's dream! Such was the exotic side of the portfolio. I had met, listened to, and exchanged with many employees at that huge federal building in Montreal. Just after my appointment, with Jean Chrétien I had visited the then-small Taxation offices in Shawinigan and been introduced to the employees. Chrétien had just left the Treasury Board for Industry, Trade, and Commerce, and I had to turn the first sod for the future huge Shawinigan-South Taxation Centre building.

To conclude this first year as a minister, I must acknowledge – while observing Trudeau and the seniors in Cabinet and remembering that their political roots went back to Pearson for some, and, in the case of the prime minister, to his *Cité Libre* past and the "three doves" (Marchand and Pelletier having already left when I joined Cabinet) – that I had joined an old team towards the end of its time, *en fin de régime*. Trudeau was almost sixty and had been prime minister for nine years. I had missed the boat of History, those years that I had viewed full of energy and enthusiasm based on the quest for "the Just Society," the very raison d'être of my joining political life. I had observed how the regime was sagging. I never shared these feelings with anyone and forbade myself to think of it. When landing at National Health and Welfare a year later, at forty-one and of prime age I would be one of the youngest of an old Cabinet. But I would rapidly be back on my feet, thanks to my natural vitality; I would have work to do and a great objective in mind.

PART THREE

The Biggest Department

10

National Health and Welfare:
The Medical Research Council

It had been a strange summer, but were there "normal" summers on the Hill? The House of Commons had sat until 26 July 1977, despite the heat wave, in buildings without air conditioning. Then an emergency session had been called for 4, 5, 8, and 9 August, with MPs sitting past midnight, to authorize the Arctic pipeline construction and to sanction back-to-work legislation to end the three-day 2,200 Canadian air traffic controllers strike over wages. In the meantime, it was business as usual at National Revenue and Cabinet meetings were still on. After the last vote of 9 August, ministers were on holiday up to 6 September, at which time ministerial activities, caucus meetings, and other political pursuits resumed, the House itself reconvening only on 18 October, with the Queen presiding over the opening of the third session of the thirtieth Parliament.

So we were again in September, and although I had not heard any particular rumour, we were bound to have a Cabinet shuffle further to the sudden resignation on Labour Day of Finance Minister Donald Macdonald, due to his wife's health. Out of the blue, as far as I was concerned, I was called by the prime minister to his office, at 1:30 on Thursday, 15 September. The meeting lasted ten minutes. I came in as minister of national revenue and came out as minister of national health and welfare. I thanked him, and that was it. He never gave me any particular mandate and took for granted I would do my best as a responsible person. Such was the man. The swearing-in ceremony for this particular Cabinet shuffle, which affected a dozen portfolios but only one newcomer, Norm Cafik, took place at Rideau Hall, again with Jules

Léger, during lunchtime the day after. The big news was Jean Chrétien's appointment as minister of finance, the first French Canadian ever in more than one hundred years in that portfolio, a very well-received nomination. The other appointment, controversial this time, was that of Jack Horner, an Albertan right-wing Conservative, one of "Diefenbaker's cowboys" during the 1960s, who had just shocked everybody by crossing the floor of the House to the Liberal side in April. Searching the web, I found a media item covering my new appointment: "On pourrait commenter l'énorme promotion de Mlle Monique Bégin qui reçoit le ministère au plus gros budget ($10 milliards)," signed Paul-Émile Richard in *l'Évangéline* (One could comment on the huge promotion Miss Monique Bégin got by being appointed to the department with the biggest budget [$10 billion]). As regards Marc Lalonde's move, he was to be minister of state for federal-provincial relations, a new ministerial portfolio, for one year, before being appointed minister of justice and attorney general in November 1978.

So I was minister of national health and welfare (NHW), an incredibly exciting promotion and a huge challenge. I was succeeding Marc Lalonde, who had had a stellar performance in the portfolio for five years, as of 1974 holding the portfolio of the Status of Women concurrently. Because I refused the latter portfolio in 1976, Lalonde would have to keep it for two more years, up to our 1979 defeat by Joe Clark. Marc provided excellent leadership in both fields of responsibilities. He had had a high profile and much visibility. Regarding the Status of Women, women in Canada owe him the full and rapid implementation of at least two to three dozen of the recommendations of the 1970 *Royal Commission Report on the Status of Women in Canada*. He had released his famous 1974 report *New Perspective on the Health of Canadians,* an internationally praised document that changed the way people look at their health. He also drove an active campaign against tobacco and in favour of "ParticipAction." Finally, in June he had just concluded the historical agreement on provincial health-care transfer payments through "blockfunding," replacing the old 50:50 reimbursement of actual legitimate provincial expenses, and the feds and the provinces were ecstatic. More on this later, as I became its unwilling victim.

I had landed in a very big department, which was receiving more than 25 per cent of government expenditures, more than Agriculture and National Defence. That fact was known abroad, and I recall the stupefaction of some counterparts and other politicians to see a country where National Defence did not have the biggest budget! I could not recall the exact amount of money, though, and was delighted when I recently found a 1982 piece by Charlotte Gray in the CMA *Journal*, towards the end of Pierre Trudeau's last government: "Begin's empire gets the biggest portion of the government's spending. Its projected budget for 1982–83 is $19 331 765 000. That $19 billion represents over a quarter of the government's total estimate of $74 billion." She is such a professional historian that we can trust these figures. The department then counted 10,000 civil servants.

Up to the recent past, the department had had a long history of two completely separate sections, each with a senior deputy minister: one for health and another for social policies and programs. For the first time, in the year before my appointment, the two were integrated under one senior deputy minister, Bruce Rawson, with nine assistant deputy ministers. Through different venues, I had come to admire two outstanding previous senior deputy ministers who had worked with Marc Lalonde: Dr Maurice LeClair and Al Johnson, imprinting their mark on both Health and Welfare. But they had moved on respectively in 1974, with LeClair joining the Ministry of Science and Technology and, in 1976, the Treasury Board, while Johnson was appointed president of the CBC in 1975. Al Johnson had been replaced immediately by Bruce Rawson for the Welfare side of the department, while Jean Lupien succeeded Dr LeClair up to the end of 1976 when Bruce Rawson became the only deputy minister of all of National Health and Welfare.

Health and Welfare had nine branches, each under an assistant deputy minister, reporting to the deputy minister. Separate from that classical federal bureaucratic structure at the time, a special position of principal nursing officer of Canada existed to give voice to the largest health profession, that of nurses. Dr Josephine (Jo) Flaherty, a strong personality, former professor, and mentor, who had been dean of nursing at the University of Western Ontario and president of the Ontario Registered Nurses' Association, was holding the position in my years.

The nine branches were directly and entirely legally under me as minister, including the ninth one, whose working relationship was under my minister of state for fitness and amateur sport, Iona Campagnolo, simply fantastic in that portfolio. (I had not been as lucky with her replacement.) Iona, whose riding, Skeena, was in Northern British Columbia, had been made parliamentary secretary to the minister of Indian affairs and northern development upon her first election in the summer 1974. She has been committed to improving the lives and status of First Nations all her life, in whatever role she found herself. She was then appointed parliamentary secretary to Marc Lalonde, in National Health and Welfare, a year before I became the minister. Joining Cabinet with me in September 1976 as minister of state (sports), her mandate ended when she lost her seat in the 1979 election. Iona had her own political cabinet and worked with my ADM in charge of this branch, Peter Lesaux. Bruce Rawson and I overlooked their work discreetly to respect her ministerial credibility. I simply signed her memos to Cabinet and other legal documents after she had signed them. Nobody knew, and all was both elegantly done and according to rules.

The first thing I observed to myself, decoding who was who at the head of my new department, was the absence of even one physician or one woman. Some of the ADMs called "Dr" were not necessarily medical doctors, but PhDs in pharmacology, like Alex Morrison. He would be one of the most competent and resolute personalities I was to work with and appreciate. When he knew me more, I benefitted from his side talent of making delicious all-natural jams, which nobody would have guessed when watching his stern expression at work. He left his position just before I myself left politics, moving to Utah, where as a Mormon he would become one of the seventy elders of the Church of Jesus Christ of Latter-day Saints, going as he once wrote "from public health to spiritual health," constantly advocating for mental health reforms and programs.

In the power structure of my new department (in no particular order), branches' official names at times were far from describing their daily responsibilities. Medical Services, for example, was in charge of Aboriginal health exclusively, while Social Services dealt strictly with federal-provincial fiscal arrangements, especially the Canada Assistance

Plan and the welfare arrangements of the provinces. The problems of the day made me work mainly with the first five branches, and with the sixth.

Departmental structure of National Health and Welfare

Department	Assistant Deputy Ministers
Health Protection	Dr Alex Morrison, Dr Bert Liston (in 1983)
Income Security	Del Lyngseth, Dr E.L. Maasland
Medical Services	Neil Faulkner, Dr Lyall Black
Health Services and Promotion	Oscar Landry, Dr Maureen Law, F.D. Kealey (acting)
Policy, Planning, and Information	Russ Robinson, Mike Murphy, Monique Jérôme-Forget
Social Services	Brian Iverson (until retirement in 1982), Mike Murphy
Intergovernmental and International Affairs	Norbert Préfontaine
Corporate Services	Ray Laframboise, Del Lyngseth
Fitness and Amateur Sport	Peter Lesaux, working under Iona Campagnolo

These senior civil servants reported to the deputy minister. It is worth noting that at least five, even six of these branches were a world of specialized issues and activities of their own, each enough to keep several ministers busy. The easy temptation to split the department in two – Health and separately Welfare – as Kim Campbell did during her short government and remains to this day, is a really bad idea, as is demonstrated by research on the social determinants of health.

Over my seven years and more at National Health and Welfare, I had four deputy ministers. Ministers do not select their DMs and are generally not even consulted, which is not always a wise practice. The latter are appointed by the prime minister on the recommendation of the clerk of the Privy Council, the most senior non-political official in the government of Canada, also the DM of the prime minister. My first new DM was Bruce Rawson, recruited by Marc Lalonde in 1975. Rawson had been the Alberta deputy minister of community health and social development, and he had impressed Lalonde at federal-provincial conferences. Bruce and I worked together up until the May 1979 Liberal electoral defeat. He never felt really comfortable with me. I don't think it had anything to do with the fact I was a woman. The problem was that I was not Marc Lalonde! Competent, rapidly understanding the mysteries of life, Rawson was a lively and likable, hyperactive, Machiavellian senior bureaucrat helped by his two personal advisers, Paul Becker and Rick Van Loon, controlling and scheming for him. He rapidly sensed he could not really control me.

A digression is required here on the role change of Bruce Rawson, my first deputy minister, when I came back as minister of national health and welfare in March 1980. When Trudeau came back as prime minister, he gave his approval to a new Cabinet superstructure put in place by Joe Clark, as proposed by Marcel Massé, his clerk of the Privy Council, an idea probably already in Michael Pitfield's books in his first tenure as clerk (1975–79), as André Juneau, himself in the PCO at the time suggested, when I discussed these times with him recently. Under Joe Clark, Wilbur MacDonald (a farmer elected for a short nine months in Cardigan, PEI), became the first minister for the new Super Committee of Social and Native Affairs, with David Crombie, Health and Welfare minister, becoming his vice chair.

It was in March 1980 that we ministers discovered with no explanation that new structure of "Super Committees of Cabinet." In our opinion, the super Cabinet committees increased bureaucratic power over ministers' governance and role within the machinery of government, and that was a big negative. Through the years I kept a tiny piece of paper on which my old friend Roméo LeBlanc had simply written, "Monique, watch out, our deputy ministers now meet together between them before Cabinet Committees," which he saw as one more plot against elected representatives. Again, I owe an explanation to André Juneau. In the mind of the PCO, although we were never told, the concept behind these super committees was to do away with the terribly wrong "vertical silos" approach, which had each minister in fierce competition between peers for approval and maximum budget of this or that new proposal/project. Our deputy ministers – senior civil servants whose future was protected, hence making them less "territorial" – through meetings between themselves, developed a sense of the necessity of "crossing sectors" and keeping a broader view of the common good. It was a noble objective, but I wonder if they never engaged in some logrolling of their own.

On the political side, in March 1980 Jean Chrétien, by then minister of justice and attorney general, was also appointed minister of state for social development, in charge of the corresponding super Cabinet committee (followed by Senator Jack Austin), while Bruce Rawson became his deputy minister and Rick Van Loon one of his assistant deputy ministers. My two former civil servants and collaborators were now my bosses, with me "the biggest spender," as they loved to repeat, in charge of controlling ministers' initiatives as presented to Cabinet!

In a strange turn of fate, Rawson later became deputy minister of Indian affairs and northern development; western economic diversification; and fisheries and oceans, before leaving for the private sector.

For me, the Privy Council Office, the famous PCO, always remained mysterious. I knew from my royal commission time in the 1960s that the clerk of the Privy Council was the deputy minister of the prime minister. As a minister, I had noticed that some PCO officers sat at the back of the room at Cabinet meetings, opposite the PM, as secretaries of the decision-making process. I did not feel a need to learn more, as Monique Coupal knew the PCO, as she had herself left it to assist me as a minister. I had a vague idea that PCO officers might total 20. Well it was more like 200 to 300! The PCO was in charge of Cabinet committees, appointments of senior bureaucrats (deputy ministers and others), ministerial orders/decrees, the machinery of government, the public service, and some security and personal information, among their fields of responsibilities. As will be seen in chapter 13, "The Canada Health Act," starting in 1982 when Gordon Osbaldeston became clerk of the Privy Council, André Juneau would have been the PCO officer responsible for "health," dealing directly with my own senior officials, while some of his colleagues were assigned to each of the other ministerial sectors. Monique Coupal tells me that after she left PCO she did not deal with them anymore, but with our department people.

That long but necessary digression now brings me back to getting reacquainted with my old department. At the same time I had inherited Rawson and Van Loon as "my bosses" in Social Development after Trudeau's return in February 1980, I was introduced to Pamela McDougall, the DM at Health and Welfare appointed by Joe Clark; a diplomat who had been the second Canadian woman promoted to ambassador (to Poland). As a DM, she had been a bad appointment and, after a few months it became clear that the situation was dysfunctional. I then met with Michael Pitfield, clerk of the Privy Council, and Jim Coutts, Trudeau's principal secretary, to plead in favour of appointing a woman deputy minister, "recommending" Huguette Labelle. I knew her a bit and had had lunch with her to get to know more about her and get her CV. The two men reacted spontaneously and strongly: "But she does not even have a PhD!" "Oh! yes, she does!" I was able to rebut. (By the way, most of my male DMs did not have a doctorate.) "Yours is the biggest department; a newcomer could not handle it." I then reminded them, to no avail, that Labelle, the principal nursing officer of Canada in Health and Welfare under Marc Lalonde, had co-authored with Hubert Laframboise for Dr Maurice LeClair, then deputy minister, the famous *A New Perspective on the Health of Canadians*.

The Privy Council recommended instead to Trudeau the appointment of Larry Fry, who wanted to retire in June 1983. I just learned recently that he had been the ADM of Health Services and Promotion when Marc Lalonde was the minister. I then had the pleasure and satisfaction of working for three years with this experienced administrator – calm, a pleasant person to deal with, and one on whom one could rely, a classic bureaucrat who knew how to process files but not a visionary nor imaginative policy mandarin. As to Huguette Labelle, a few months later she was appointed the first woman career deputy minister of the federal government as undersecretary of state of the Department of the Secretary of State, handling, among other dossiers, that of citizenship, official languages, student loans, and more. And Dr Maureen

Law, in my own department, was then appointed assistant deputy minister of health services and promotion; there had also never been a woman assistant deputy minister in Health and Welfare before!

Following Fry's retirement in June 1983, Dr David Kirkwood took over. Trained as a physicist (Atomic Energy, Chalk River) who had joined External Affairs as a diplomat (NATO in Paris, Athens, Bonn, etc.) he moved to the Privy Council Office and to other departments (senior ADM, DM) to finally chair the Anti-Dumping Tribunal, before becoming my deputy minister, landing in Health and Welfare at the worst of the heated "medicare" federal-provincial discussions. His administrative load was considerable and I could not work with him on policy issues as much as I would have liked, which I still regret. He was very courteous, knowledgeable, listening well and of good advice, a rather reserved professional.

A few months later, Michael Pitfield, the super-powerful clerk of the Privy Council, developed the so-called pilot project of creating a few "associate" deputy ministers. Not surprisingly I suppose, taking into account the size and budget of my department, although I never even thought of complaining and never heard any dissatisfaction, Pitfield and Jim Coutts asked to see me to obtain my approval and go along with that new initiative. No need to say that I was viscerally opposed, knowing that even with twins born of the same egg, having two top managers equally in charge of a department could not work. They then suggested that the "associate" could be Dr Maureen Law; I weakened ... because she was a woman and because at the time I did not know one very negative side of her personality. I asked her, if she were to appointed, could she work with David Kirkwood and support him fully, to which she replied positively and enthusiastically. As soon as she was in the job, her loyalty to him disappeared at once, and three years later, she was the only deputy minister.

One thing became clear to me from start: if there were one federal department naturally close to the daily life of most Canadians through a number of different "constituencies," it was mine and I did not intend to let them down!

◆ ※ ◆

The very first request to me, the afternoon of my swearing in, was about appointing the chair of the Medical Research Council (MRC). Dr Jean de Margerie, the council VP and dean of research at the University of Sherbrooke Faculty of Medicine, with Dr James Roxburgh, director of the Grants Program, had asked for an emergency meeting with me. I did not know why they wanted to speak with me. All at once, I discovered that I was the minister of medical research; that its president had the rank of a senior deputy minister to me, independent of my department; and that the then relatively small medical research community – some 300 researchers at the time – was by tradition to be consulted for the appointment of its president. The very first full-time president, Dr G. Malcolm Brown, a medical researcher who was a born leader and a strong figure in setting up and structuring medical research in Canada, had passed away in May. Putting things together, I then recalled his forceful, tall figure, bordering on arrogant, as a witness at the Standing Committee on Health, Welfare, and Social Affairs of the House when I was a backbencher.

A few hours later, to my continuing surprise, when asked for yet another immediate appointment, this time by the president of the First Nations, I learned that I was also the minister of the Inuit and First Nations health, a responsibility completely outside of Indian Affairs and Northern Development, corresponding to a branch headed by an assistant deputy minister in my own department!

At the time, the MRC was one of three federal granting agencies responsible for supporting research conducted primarily in universities and their affiliated institutions. The two other agencies, the Natural Sciences and Engineering Research Council (NSERC) and the Social Sciences and Humanities Research Council, were responsible for the areas indicated by their names.

The consultation of the medical community with a view to identify candidates for the council's presidency had taken place, and names were prioritized by the MRC. I was presented with the list by the two medical emissaries a few days later. They explained to me that I was expected to meet personally and by myself the names on the list, starting with the two at the top, in order to come to a proposal for submission to the prime minister as soon as possible. I knew none of these names. Surprising coincidence: the very evening of my swearing in as health minister, I had been travelling to Montreal for the Institut de Recherches cliniques de Montréal banquet where I was the keynote speaker (and of which I would become a board member from 1998 to 2005).

The feeling of the medical research community at the time of my appointment as their new minister was that my predecessor and the government had not been particularly supportive of medical research, putting their efforts rather on public health against a very medicalized health-care system. Historically, from 1920 to 1970, milestones in Canadian medical research give the image of great research leading to immediate applications: insulin changing lives of diabetics (Frederick Banting and Charles Best); a new treatment of osteoporosis (James Collip); treating seizures and epilepsy (Wilder Penfield); the creation of Pablum for babies; the polio vaccine (Raymond Parker); the world's first external cardiac pacemaker (Jack Hopps); the Cobalt-60 "bomb" against cancer (Howard Johns); recognizing stroke, transient ischemic attacks (C.M. Fisher); treatment of Hodgkin's disease (Vera Peters); causes of children's poisoning and the first childproof medication cap (Henri Breault); stem cells and bone marrow transplantation (James Till and Ernest A. McCulloch); and, in 1969, to complete this partial list of remarkable successes, the control of rickets with vitamin D in milk (Charles Scriver). In the following years Canadian medical research shifted towards bio-medical research, the peer-review system became the sacrosanct norm for granting research money, and the MRC budget plateaued, not catching up with inflation.

Scientific research in general and medical research in particular have always fascinated me, but I felt quite humble and illiterate thinking of these great researcher names. The two at the top of the list I was given were those of Dr John Evans (whom I met as soon as 29 September) and of Dr Pierre Bois, two exceptional human beings I will always remember fondly. Dr Evans, a cardiologist, with his great capacity to spot talent, had created the McMaster Faculty of Medicine when only thirty-five years old, in 1965, recruiting a group of daring young researcher professors ready to innovate in their teaching and give a mix of students from quite different disciplinary backgrounds a "patient focus education." When students entered the first year of the program in 1970, they were introduced to patients immediately. In 1977, when I met him, John Evans was president of the University of Toronto, from which, still a secret, he would leave to run as an unsuccessful Liberal candidate in Rosedale in the 16 October 1978 by-election, defeated by David Crombie. From there he went to the World Bank and, from 1987 to 1995, would be the first Canadian to be elected chairman of the Rockefeller Foundation.

Once having obtained his MD, Dr Pierre Bois, as calm a person as John Evans but speaking in a surprisingly slow manner in a pleasant voice, had worked for his PhD in medicine and experimental surgery with the illustrious Dr Hans Selye. As an investigator, Dr Bois had studied the endocrinology of stress. When I first met him, he had moved from head of anatomy at the University of Montreal to becoming dean in 1970, where he would serve three terms over eleven years. When we met, for we met often, it was always on a Friday early evening on my return home from Ottawa, at the Ritz Carlton bar, he with his Cognac and me with my legendary Perrier water! He will always remain in my memory as one of the Three Wise Men. More on Pierre Bois later.

I wish I could have convinced either of them to accept my offer, but neither could consider it, for different valid reasons, Evans being the president of the University of Toronto at the time (and not able to mention the future political step he was already preparing to take), while Bois wanted to complete his objectives as dean of medicine at Montreal. Both are now gone, John Evans in 2015 and Pierre Bois in 2011. I had the privilege, when visiting professor at the master in health administration program, to sit for eight years on the board of the Clinical Research Institute of Montreal at Pierre Bois's request, where he was a much-respected special advisor. We had become personal friends and we visited each other in Montreal. I knew his family and medical friends, we exchanged books, discussed, and laughed, from the day I left politics to his passing away. It is only later in life that I was associated with McMaster developments in women's health in particular and got to know and collaborate with some of John Evans's best and brightest – the name of David Sackett comes to mind, the father of "evidence-based medicine" – concluding how special his mentorship of the "problems based" medical education had been. Evans and Bois were both men of integrity, brilliant minds, visionaries, with a sense of humour, team leaders and respected scientists and researchers.

I had understood from Monique Coupal the importance of a full-time president, who would re-establish and nurture connections within the government apparatus. Then, following the list, I met Fraser Mustard and Arnold Naimark separately. Both highly recommended candidates, Mustard and Naimark, with strong and intimidating personalities of a type opposite those of Evans and Bois, left me the impression that they were not particularly interested, that I was close to a nobody in their eyes. I could not really see myself working with them, or them working in teams with others. The two meetings ended up with courtesy but with no offer nor interest expressed. Mustard, in 1977, was dean of medicine at McMaster, where he would stay another five years. He had conducted ground-breaking research in his early career on cardiovascular health and the role of Aspirin in cardiovascular protection. Dr Mustard is now world-renowned for his work on the importance of early childhood education and for promoting public policies on the role of social determinants of good or bad health. In the 1990s as a member of a study group, I then got to really know Fraser Mustard and truly admired him, a formidable mover and shaker of the mind.

When I met him, Dr Arnold Naimark, former head of physiology, was dean of medicine at the University of Manitoba, where he would become president and vice chancellor in 1981. I never had a chance to get to know him later and witness his influence.

No need to explain that I no longer have with me that confidential handwritten MRC list of candidates by order of priority. I know that the following names were on it: Lou Siminovitch, René Simard, Samuel Freedman, Antoine Di Iorio, Michel Chrétien (Jean Chrétien's brother), Phil Gold, Walter O. Spitzer, John Dirks, and more. Following the priority of names given by the researcher community, and refusal to apply by some, for good reasons, I then interviewed a Notre-Dame Hospital cancer researcher, Dr René Simard, of a younger generation. He was an active researcher and would accept only if it could be a part-time job. That was out of the question. Finally, some eight or nine months later, René Simard finally accepted the position, on a full-time basis at my insistence. We collaborated easily and I continued to see him and his wife years after politics. To my surprise, he went on a tangent somehow, becoming vice rector (academic) at University of Montreal in 1985, and later rector from 1993 to 1998.

When I came back to the department on 3 March 1980, following Joe Clark's short government, my first visitor was ... Dr Simard, elegantly presenting me with his resignation! My successor, David Crombie, had immediately accepted Simard's plans to be a part-time president, his old dream. Dr Simard knew my stand on the issue and the reasons for it and knew we would then have to part, on excellent terms, he going back to his research lab in Montreal, and I looking once more for a president! Dr Pierre Bois and I started again to have a drink at the Ritz Carlton early on Friday evenings again! I finally convinced him, still dean of medicine at the University of Montreal, to take up this new national challenge. He did with success, presiding over the council's development for ten years, having been reappointed by the Mulroney Conservative government.

Medical research would be one more dossier for me, in parallel to my department, an exciting one in which I was fully involved during my two mandates at Health and Welfare. I most enjoyed working with these researchers who rapidly adopted me. All of those I got to know through medical research were individuals full of passion for their research projects and for their responsibility as deans of medicine, heads of departments, or carrying out other mandates. What a stimulating milieu! In addition to the names already mentioned, others such as Drs Maurice MacGregor and Margaret Becklake, Charles Scriver (and his wife "Zipper"), Richard and Sylvia Cruess (all from McGill), the endocrinologist Henry Friesen, and the professor of community medicine and anaesthesia John Wade (Manitoba) are but a few names of emeritus researchers and practitioners, each an exceptional human being one cannot forget and whom I often met through the years, long after I had left politics. The Goldbloom brothers, both pediatricians, Richard (at Dalhousie), and his wife Ruth, and Victor, practising in Montreal and later a politician and a minister in Bourassa's Cabinet, and his wife Sheila, a professor of social work at McGill, I also much enjoyed meeting. I consider them all true friends. From Quebec, I also got to know leaders like Drs Jacques Genest, Claude Roy, Yves Morin, and others.

Dr Charles Scriver was a very special human being. Meeting him in my time at Health and Welfare, and after, a researcher and professor in biology, human genetics and pediatrics, was both a treat and a puzzle. What would he want this time? What was he working on now? What had he just discovered? He was an only child, both of whose parents were also McGill physicians and medical researchers. He was intellectual charm personified. And very, very gently persuasive. For example, early in my new responsibility, he would explain to me his research on rickets in children, due to harsh winter and lack of UV exposure, and the remarkable victory in public policy he and his team obtained when adding vitamin D to milk was made mandatory not just in Quebec but also through Canada, the incidence of rickets then dropping from 1 in 200 newborns to 1 in 20,000. And there were the cases of rare metabolic disorders he discovered in some Quebec communities, implying some consanguinity: in northeastern Quebec, the Hartnup disease (intermittent ataxia, tremor), a deficiency of a B vitamin called niacin, and thalassemia in families who had settled more than 200 years ago in Portneuf County, for example. I recall Charles Scriver describing Tay Sach's disease to me, usually found among with Ashkenazi Jews, or B thalassemia, which to his surprise and interest he discovered among French Canadians in Charlevoix and Saguenay-Lac Saint-Jean and other locations, and in the Greek and Italian communities of Montreal. It is not easy to explain genetic problems to parents and, as St Léonard was in my riding, he asked me for contacts among local leaders who could convince schools to participate in his research projects. I introduced him to Father Giuseppe Duchini of the Notre-Dame-de-Pompei local Italian parish near my riding office, as well as other community leaders. I considered myself privileged by these conversations. Years later, in 2003, when a visiting professor in health administration at University of Ottawa, I had both the honour and the pleasure of acting as MC for a tribute to Dr Charles Scriver (and his parents): the Drs Walter, Jessie Boyd, and Charles Scriver Scholarship Dinner, in Montreal.

It was not only through the Medical Research Council that I met great medical innovators. For example, early in my mandate, an Ottawa cardiologist, Dr Wilbert (Willy) Keon, obtained an appointment with me, not for research funding but for capital funding! He was developing the Ottawa Heart Institute, which he had just officially opened in 1976 with Dr Donald Beanlands as his most crucial recruit, his founding chief of cardiology. So they needed a building and they needed equipment. I explained to him that neither the Medical Research Council nor my department had any capital funding capacity. Our funds were strictly for operating expenditures. That certainly did not stop him and he went on and on. He repeated recently, when the Ottawa Heart Institute celebrated its fortieth anniversary in 2016, that at the time, I remarked to him, "But you look like a kid!" referring to his ambitious plans. "Madam Minister," he replied, "I checked before coming and know we are of the same age!" I laughed when he told this story in public. I do not recall that exchange at all, but it sounded like me! His case was truly persuasive for something needed in Ontario, and my officials did find some money for his objectives.

And I continued to meet, discuss, and collaborate with medical researchers all through my twenty-five-year academic career. More later.

My challenge as minister of the Medical Research Council was rather banal, but huge in the more and more difficult economic times and the growing "monetarist" ideology sweeping among Canadian elites and the media. The MRC was in dire need of major budget increases, higher than the inflation rate. At the time of my appointment, the medical research community had become so discouraged that a "consumers" pressure group backing their crusade got started. Made up of the lay public, under the leadership of Patricia Guyda, it had been created in 1975. She led Canadians for Health Research, a truly altruistic initiative, for thirty-seven years. I could not make it to the evening in her honour at Concordia University when she retired in 2013 but said in my written allocution how she had remarkably illustrated the importance of *The Power of the Weak*, the title of a book dear to me, written by Elizabeth Janeway, and mentioned "how contagious her tenacity was, a nightmare for those she challenged!" The deans of the then sixteen Faculties of Medicine/Health Sciences of Canada were my "mafia," and me, their favourite victim. More money! More money! In 1979, against all odds and despite fiscal restraint, the MRC budget was increased by 17 per cent, and I was thrilled; Dr Michel Chrétien had certainly talked to his brother, the minister of finances ... and I thanked both of them then and today.

In my first year as minister of national health and welfare, the Medical Research Council received $58 million in allotted credits for fiscal 1977–78, an increase of 11.5 per cent against an average inflation rate of 8.5 per cent. I did my best for every following fiscal year, trying at least not only to protect them from inflation but to make up a bit for the previous years' losses. Then, in 1983, when I heard of a "floating" $50 million for which some colleagues would be fighting, I had the MRC prepare a memorandum to Cabinet developing a framework for future medical research: young researchers; high-quality training; balance between basic and applied research; balance between regions and disciplines, with special attention to areas of national health concern; and the utilization of new knowledge for health concerns. This received enough support in Cabinet that I won the day for the MRC and got the $50 million. That was for two years only and would not be included in its budgetary base; $20 million would be spent in 1983–84 and $30 million for 1984–85. The needs were so great that this new money allowed the Grants and Awards Program to be restored and the number of new applications assessed worthy of support by the peer review system, to be funded from 12.6 per cent before to 40 per cent. State-of-the-art equipment was approved as well as a new program in biotechnology. The ideal would have been that the $50 million be integrated in the base budget and that would become Dr Bois's next challenge with my successor, Jake Epp.

When I left politics in September 1984, the MRC budgetary estimates for the fiscal year 1984–85 had reached $157 million, having almost tripled since my initial appointment to the ministry. Increased budgets were urgently needed, not only to see medical research survive but to develop and with it train younger researchers in Canada. Many policy-makers, including a number of elected ones, and some of my Cabinet colleagues did not understand the world of academic research and even less the abstruse university financing and budgets – there were no independent research institutes and centres yet – our Faculties of Medicine being the key players in medical research. These policy-makers automatically believed that the badly needed budget increases were topping up the salaries of full-time professors in medicine. It shows such ignorance of what research means and how research functions. How many times did I try to explain how it worked, to no avail?

It was already clear to me as a minister that, resources being limited, some basic objectives should be identified. My unique "success" at the time, just before I left politics, was to convince Dr Bois to add the field of gerontology to the MRC list of priority fields of research. With horror, but without a word, I discovered that the new field of research was called ... "geriatrics." We were then still in the pure biomedical ... And it could not be otherwise, in those years.

11

Social Policies: The Child Tax Credit and Pensions

Faithful to his deeply rooted values, upon my new appointment as minister of national health and welfare on 15 September 1977, my friend Roméo LeBlanc gave me Michael Foot's biography of Aneurin (Nye) Bevan, the Labour secretary of state for health in the immediate post-war Attlee government (1945–51). The son of a Welsh coal miner, elected and re-elected for thirty-one years, Bevan always fought for social justice and was the father of the National Health Service Act 1946, the famous British medicare.

While the Medical Research Council was a good story that ended well, my new National Health and Welfare mandate did not start ideally – first, because of my own fault, and then the result of unforeseen circumstances. After I was appointed to the biggest department on 15 September, Parliament did not resume until Monday, 17 October, only to be immediately prorogued. The third session of the thirtieth legislature started the following afternoon, with the Speech from the Throne read by Queen Elizabeth II, who was celebrating her Silver Jubilee. A big surprise was that House of Commons proceedings were now televised.

In the month before the new parliamentary session began, I spent time closing up shop and looking after unfinished business in both Customs and Excises as well as Taxation, and briefing Senator Jos Guay, my successor there. During those weeks – surprisingly, as I think about it today – I never even had a chat with my predecessor, Marc Lalonde, about my new mandate. The Cabinet culture at the time was very competitive; as a woman, I would not have wanted to look weak or indecisive, and Marc didn't offer any assistance. Everybody was busy. Everybody was a responsible adult.

As I was still an unknown quantity, succeeding the formidable Marc Lalonde after his five successful years at the helm of the biggest portfolio, the media were after me through that long month, wanting to learn of my plans regarding health issues and welfare programs. I should have postponed requests for interviews until I had been briefed. Instead, I answered the press spontaneously, not protecting myself, without checking the facts of the situation. What was worse, by repeating how dear the idea of a guaranteed annual income (GAI) was to me, and so on, I was putting my foot in my mouth: the Liberal budget, which stated our deep commitment to controlling increases in public expenditures, had just been announced. With hindsight, I see I was simply repeating my 1973 "maiden speech" commitments to alleviate poverty, and that of women and children first. I was still a true newcomer to a big game.

By some miracle, as far as I know nothing negative came out of this. No one challenged me after Lalonde's failure to bring about the GAI. I never followed that topic in Lalonde's years, for I was kept too busy on other tasks during my four years as a new MP. I had no knowledge of the long behind-the-scenes fight between John Turner (Finance) and Marc Lalonde (Health and Welfare) after Lalonde's "Working Paper on Social Security in Canada" (the Orange Paper) was released on 18 April 1973. The aim of the document, which was full of bureaucratic concepts and hard to understand except by experts, was to get to a guaranteed annual income without using that name. It had been the subject of federal-provincial negotiations and Cabinet discussions for more than two years, going from what was originally a $2 billion federal project to a $350 million project. In 1975, a year before I joined Cabinet in National Revenue, the provinces had lost interest, Lalonde had lost the game, and Turner had resigned and left politics.

No one from my new department briefed me on the disheartening end of my predecessor's attempts at social security reform, nor did they try to discuss with me what exactly I had in mind as their new minister when I spoke of the GAI with the media. Reporters did not take me to task, either. While writing these memoirs, I wondered why. A former department official reminded me recently of one possible explanation:

that all the research and experimentation around the Manitoba "Mincome," our Canadian GAI pilot project, was still going on. Launched under Premier Ed Schreyer in 1974, it would be abolished in 1979 by Conservative Premier Sterling Lyon and Prime Minister Joe Clark. This is a plausible explanation, but I still wonder why no one felt I should be aware of this important initiative.

I did, however, get into trouble with the media a few weeks later in what became known as *"l'Affaire Carleton,"* but it had nothing to do with my views on social policies. It was 2 November, two weeks after Parliament opened, and I had agreed to meet journalism students for a Q & A on parliamentary affairs at Rooster's Coffeehouse on campus. (Why did I agree to this? I was not media savvy, and National Revenue had not been the place to acquire such trade knowledge. I was a true neophyte and simply acted spontaneously.) At one point, questions focused on the McDonald Commission, which had just been set up by Francis Fox to look into possible illegal activities by the RCMP in Quebec at the beginning of the 1970s. I answered that, in my opinion, the RCMP thought they were above the law with the barn burning in Quebec, and so on. The next morning, the front page of the Carleton student newspaper, the *Charlatan*, announced, "My God, the woman had broken Cabinet solidarity!" An audiotape was found, authentic or edited, and was aired on radio stations that same evening. The national CBC picked it up the morning after, and all the media jumped in. Marc Lalonde and Monique Coupal were ready to throttle me.

The House was in an uproar. Ed Broadbent (NDP) joined the fray, reading from the *Toronto Sun* what I was supposed to have said. He was joined by René Matte (Social Credit), Andrew Brewin (NDP), and Joe Clark (PC) at one point, with all questions being put to Trudeau and not to me. With childlike amusement, Trudeau provoked the Opposition, playing with words until the situation turned suddenly into a point of privilege raised by Gerald Baldwin (PC). The show went on for a full seven pages of Hansard, extending question period past 4 p.m. The day after, on a point of privilege, I simply apologized to the House. I was truly ashamed of myself – although I must admit I still did not quite understand what I had done wrong. But I had learned an important lesson the hard way: with media involvement outside the House of

Commons, one does not try to justify and explain; one apologizes and shuts up. The crisis then died of natural causes.

Back to the biggest department shortly before the Carleton Affair. On the day the House of Commons reconvened briefly for prorogation on 17 October, the media were waiting for me outside the House upon my return from Montreal. My colleague Judd Buchanan, then minister of public works, had given a speech in Brantford, Ontario, the day before, announcing that "the federal government will consider whether family allowance payments and old age pensions should continue on a universal basis." I read his comments in the *Ottawa Citizen* as I made my way to Ottawa for the end of the second session of the thirtieth Parliament. Of course, I had heard nothing of this. Caught by surprise, I cautiously answered to the media that this was not government policy. There was no question period that day. There was one on the Tuesday, but the prime minister joined it only later, as he would be making a speech in response to the Speech from the Throne that afternoon. In question period on Wednesday, 20 October, Stanley Knowles immediately asked Trudeau about the state of affairs regarding the universality of social programs. Calmly, the prime minister said that neither he nor I had seen any such text on whether these two programs were threatened, and that the government stood by the principle underlying the programs. The question was put to me again and again by MPs on all sides, in one form or another, until Christmas. I was both furious and anxious: was it just a trial balloon from Judd Buchanan personally? How destabilizing for a new minister! Or was it a decision already taken by Finance, or by the Committee of Priorities and Planning (the famous P & P – the Executive of Cabinet) showing that the new minister had no weight, did not know, and did not count? I never got an explanation, let alone an apology from Judd, from any colleague or from my department. I simply stuck to my guns, boringly repeating that the Liberal government had always been in support of the universality of family allowances and pensions.

Then, again out of the blue, some four months later, on 22 February 1978, the serious and responsible president of Treasury Board, Robert (Bob) Andras, when tabling the Budgetary Estimates in the House of Commons, stated in the House that "there was nothing sacred about social programs" and elaborated on the need for controlling those budgetary items. Still more worrying had been the complete about-face of the formerly progressive Canadian Council on Social Development, which had stated a month earlier that Canada had to end the universality of these programs, because they had not helped to eradicate poverty. They had helped to some extent, but in any event, eliminating poverty had never been the purpose of these programs, which were cornerstones of Canadian public policies.

Unknown to me at the time, as the new minister, my spontaneous trumpeted enthusiasm for a guaranteed annual income was adding fuel to the fire lit by the "monetarist" theses stemming from the Chicago school, those of Milton Friedman and others, which opposed the welfare state and state intervention in the markets. This monetarist policy would rapidly turn into the all-powerful ideology of the free market. In the fall of 1977, those words, those concepts, that vocabulary were totally unknown to me. Even California Proposition 13 (June 1978) was yet to happen. With time, however, I observed that most Canadian elites, including some Cabinet colleagues and other politicians, senior bureaucrats, academics, and the media, seemed to have read Milton Friedman, the 1976 Nobel laureate in economics, although none of them advocated publicly for his thesis yet.

Later in my life, while teaching at Notre Dame University in the United States immediately after retiring from politics in September 1984, I would see the monetarist policy at its worst with Ronald Reagan as US president. One by one, many national governments of industrialized countries concluded that the internal problems they were facing in the 1980s and 1990s resulted from what some considered their extraordinary successes in "quality of life." As the unfortunately popular American Libertarian conservative economist Charles Murray argued in 1984 and later, all social welfare programs are doomed to bring about net harm to society. Shrinking governments and withdrawal of political leadership became the background for the rhetoric employed and the actions taken. Dismantling the welfare state became the arch-objective. Most elites proclaimed the bankruptcy of social programs and the failure of the welfare state. The deconstruction of much of a country's social systems would be either brutal and done in open

confrontation with segments of the surrounding society, as in Margaret
Thatcher's Great Britain or Ronald Reagan's United States in the 1980s,
or by stealth, as in many other countries, starting with Canada. Even
worse, if that is possible, our Western institutions like the World Bank
then forced this ideology onto African countries, crushing their fragile
development. In most cases, actions undertaken were far too painful for
individuals and families and would prove to have long-lasting negative
effects on their societies. This is what I fought against with my stubborn
protection of the universality of our social programs, and later, of a
truly universal health-care system.

At the department, staff were still in "briefing the minister" mode.
As a backbencher, I had served for a while on the House Standing Committee of Health and Social Affairs without really getting involved and
was not even a member of the committee after the spring of 1975.
Health had been much talked about in the Lalonde years, first with the
internationally celebrated *A New Perspective on the Health of Canadians,* then with the long and successful negotiations with the provinces
to change the approach of the federal financial contribution for health
care to the provinces. This resulted in the Established Programs Financing Act (EPF), in effect as of 1 July 1977, shortly before my new appointment began. As the health-care system funding had been fixed to
the general satisfaction of all parties, my deputy minister told me bluntly
that there was no point in my learning all the workings of the system.
So it was only natural that I would start by looking at social policies
and programs.

As for the GAI in one form or another (basic income for all, negative
income tax, etc.), in the 1960s I had discovered with great interest the
concept of a universal support program without conditions for those in
need, whatever the cause of poverty for the individual or family. This
concept stemmed from public policy discussions in the Netherlands,
then in the United States during Lyndon Johnson's 1964 War against
Poverty. We had made it a recommendation (number 135) in our
Report of the Royal Commission on the Status of Women in 1970.
Then, while at the Canadian Radio-television and Telecommunications
Commission, I read Senator David Croll's 1971 landmark Senate report

on poverty, whose first recommendation was to establish a guaranteed annual income for all Canadians. As a new MP, I had followed the Manitoba Mincome pilot project. It did not make me an expert, but I believed, and still do, that GAI is a key public policy that I hope to see implemented in Canada in my lifetime. I do not need to add that, as best I could, I followed the 2017 basic income pilot projects in three Ontario cities (Hamilton, Lindsay, and Thunder Bay), about which media reports contained all the usual clichés for and against.

In Pierre Trudeau's time, most federal departments included a Research and Planning Branch under an assistant deputy minister. As I came from the world of research, I particularly enjoyed working with this highly competent branch under three superb senior officials: first, under Russ Robinson's leadership, then Mike Murphy's, and finally Monique Jérôme-Forget's.

In my time, as a rule, federal departments did not use outside consultants, except for highly specialized topics. This meant that departments always spoke with a clear sense of institutional memory in the various dossiers. With the passing years I remain convinced that an excellent research group inside a department, helped by outside research contracts only if needed on niche issues, is by far the optimal approach.

In these briefing sessions on our social policies and programs, it had been relatively easy for me to grasp in very general terms which programs we were directly delivering through our Income Security Branch. Its competent ADM Del Lyngseth, who was calm, pleasant, and always ready to explain, along with John Soar, his director general, Operations, and their team were overseeing big money here: over $7 billion in 1977–78, when I arrived.

Meanwhile, I was finding it almost impossible to comprehend what the Social Services Branch under ADM Brian Iverson, a committed former social worker, was all about. I never did master it. I remember the man the staff called "Mr CAP" – Des Byrne, director general of the Canada Assistance Plan (CAP) from 1975 to 1982 – who was always ready to dissect for us his complex program, whose budget was over $1 billion. (CAP, Judy LaMarsh's proposed legislation, had received assent in July 1966 and was signed by all provinces.) In very general terms, CAP was meant to support provision of adequate provincial assistance to persons in need and to encourage the development and extension of welfare services (protective, preventive, rehabilitative, and developmental) to help prevent and remove the causes of poverty and dependence. All this by federal transfer payments to the provinces – one more shared-cost conditional grant program, roughly 50:50. Leading to controversies from day one, it has nonetheless become part of the fabric of life in Canada.

A plane trip to Vancouver with Deputy Minister Bruce Rawson four months later completely reframed the situation. Even though I had been minister of national revenue for one year, I knew I was still a neophyte in Cabinet. We were on the small government jet and could speak confidentially, with at least five hours of travel ahead of us. It was mid-January 1978, and the following day I had a business meeting with my provincial counterpart, BC health minister Robert (Bob) McClelland, and his Social Credit ("Socred") colleagues – together with my own colleagues Ron Basford (minister of justice) and Francis Fox (solicitor general) – on the infamous BC Health Entry Plan, their provincial plan for mandatory detaining and treatment of heroin addicts.

Bruce decided it was time to tell me what the finances of the country, as well as of the government, really were, and how serious the situation was, in the context of "my" guaranteed annual income project. I had learned from our Research Branch just before Christmas that because the particular causes and reasons for poverty were no longer an object in a guaranteed annual income, the number of people to be covered would include not only those on welfare but all the "working poor" – those who were forced to earn a living that was under the poverty line. This meant the cost of the bill would double. Double! I was shocked. Further to that plane conversation with Bruce Rawson, I concluded that my glorious ministerial objective had gone up in smoke and that I would be lucky if I could simply save the best of our existing programs, starting with their universality. I was coming down to earth.

Like everyone else, I knew before this long conversation on the plane that the general conjuncture, political and economic, was difficult. The anti-inflation battle was raging in most industrialized countries. In

Canada, Trudeau, contrary to his key electoral promise of the 1974 election, had set up an Anti-Inflation Board for wage and price controls. Even though inflation did decrease, the board remained very unpopular, and its creation was severely judged by history. On the political side, René Lévesque had been elected premier of Quebec on 15 November 1976, with his separatist Parti Québécois (PQ) forming the government. This was a first. The PQ had defeated Robert Bourassa's Liberal government with the promise of a referendum on Quebec's independence. In early 1977 Trudeau proposed discussions leading to the patriation of the Constitution and a charter of linguistic rights, adding that he would resign if Quebec voted for independence. In July he announced the Pépin-Robarts Commission on national unity. Still I had not realized Canada's true economic situation.

Upon my return from Vancouver, in session with Russ Robinson and his colleagues at Research and Planning and looking for a more realistic possible socio-economic objective, I asked them who, among the Canadian poor, were the most destitute. Their answer was immediate and clear, confirming what I had known since our royal commission on women, ten years before: the most destitute Canadians were children living in poverty and their mothers, especially in single-parent families. After I had listened and understood that our research team had already worked on the problem, I confirmed that finding a way to address that situation within the financial constraints of the time would be our top priority. Russ Robinson and his team had already done a great job on the issue. Over the following months, they came up with an approach to distribute more money where it was needed most urgently, while maintaining the universality of family allowances, which I valued above all. We agreed that the project was ready to present to Cabinet.

In March 1978, six months into my new job, I decided to touch base with Canadians about the increasingly stealthy attacks against the welfare state. I broached the topic as the keynote speaker at a big fundraiser for the Liberal Party of Canada in Sherbrooke – ironically, a dinner priced at several hundred dollars per person. So, on the evening of 13 March, I gave a speech entitled *"Les mythes de la politique sociale"* (Myths about social policy). I wanted to speak about the scandal of poverty in Canada by debunking seven myths and challenging the audience on how they felt about them. Once more, I seemed at odds with my environment, but I had to say something. For those in the corridors of power, I probably looked out of sync now and then, during these difficult economic times: I was always an idealist trying to be as pragmatic as possible. Stunned by such an unexpected position, only one journalist covered my speech: Doug Fisher, himself a former CCF/ NDP MP for Thunder Bay who had defeated C.D. Howe in 1957. Fisher was now dean of the Press Gallery.

In the spring of 1978 my memorandum to Cabinet on the proposed Child Tax Credit made it to the Cabinet table. I had carefully studied the document and was well prepared, but also a little nervous as a relatively new minister. In addition to the old family allowance, we were proposing a targeted and income-tested child benefit to be delivered through the tax system, to provide a maximum benefit of $200 per year per child to low-income families, a declining amount to middle-income families, and no benefit to upper-income families. I had spoken privately to a few colleagues, asking for their support, but I was discovering that some big guns were opposed, without any clear argument. Then, in the course of the discussion, I suddenly understood that simply, automatically, my colleagues had taken for granted the money would go to the father of the children. I could not believe it and was at a loss to get the file back on track. A few colleagues, including Marc Lalonde and Roméo LeBlanc, supported me, and that issue was settled. What a lesson! I was astonished, I admit. When the general discussion came to an end, I thought my proposal would be approved. I will never ever forget the Politics 101 lesson I received when Allan MacEachen, now deputy prime minister, sitting at Trudeau's right, who had not yet spoken, simply turned towards him and said, "Prime Minister, do I see a demand?" Not another word was said, and my dossier died on the order paper. How can one create a demand for something new when Cabinet is held to complete confidentiality? What absurd logic!

That had been a difficult defeat, of which I still did not understand the ins and outs. I was trying to analyze some of my colleagues' opposition, with no success. It was now May and life went on. At times I functioned like an automaton; it was like being in a fog. The House of Commons sat without interruption until 30 June. In my years on the

Hill, there was no fixed parliamentary calendar for House of Commons activities, and we sat much more often than MPs do now, including on Monday, Tuesday, and Thursday evenings. The current system of three weeks of sittings followed by a week in one's riding, as well as a fixed calendar for general elections, was unthinkable. By the end of May 1978 there was no hope left for a social security program to address children's poverty, although relatively soon it would become a major success as a key Canadian social policy: "my" Child Tax Credit turned into the Canada Child Benefit (CCB).

The parliamentary session went on until 30 June, while Cabinet committees and full Cabinet meetings continued until 20 July, through summer heat and lethargy. On Tuesday, 1 August, feeling rather drained, alone and without holiday plans, I got on a plane for San Francisco to discover the California coast. The next Tuesday, 8 August, Fred Mac-Donald, my first chief of staff, phoned and woke me up in Carmel-by-the-Sea: Trudeau had just returned from his holiday in Germany with Helmut Schmidt and from other trips after the G7 Summit in Bonn (16–17 July) and had called a special full Cabinet meeting for the next afternoon! I was travelling alone; the local Air Canada team (David Young and his wife, Sue) did everything to help me, bringing me to Monterey, then San Francisco, and finally to Ottawa. I entered Cabinet, facetiously bringing for the prime minister a California T-shirt printed with the slogan "Left Is Right" ... and the rest, as they say, is history. Chrétien, the minister of finance, learned from the media that Trudeau had committed to cutting $2.5 billion in government expenditures, while also announcing that the work of the Anti-Inflation Board was to end that fall. This was unheard of! It was very serious. The Cabinet meeting was relatively short; all departments would be affected both by cuts in expenditures and in number of jobs. We would learn of the details upon our return from holidays.

My department would likewise be affected by this huge cut; we lost $86 million from our operating budget of $400 million. This included the temporary freeze of the family allowances indexation. Of the program cuts I approved, I still have a clear memory of all the innovative and worthwhile NGO grants in public health or social services that we could no longer support financially, including the Planned Parenthood

Association. I still feel bad about this. Also my department had to reduce its staff by some 850 full-time jobs, if memory serves me well.

Analysts have much castigated the Trudeau government for its lack
of ability and for his changes of direction, more rhetorical than applied,
as well as for Trudeau's inability to express and stick to a clear economic
policy in the second half of the 1970s. Between 1974 and 1979, wrote
Richard Gwyn in *The Northern Magus*, "Of all the contests Trudeau
has engaged in ... the ones he has lost most clearly have always been
the economic ones ... In his first three terms, Trudeau lacked the
courage, the imagination, or indeed the expert advisers ... to prod him
to take a dare on the unorthodox, and the necessary. So he fiddled with
'fine tuning.'" Trudeau admired the free market system, but at the same
time he believed in a strong and interventionist state, if needed. As a
lay player when it came to economics, and after a few years in Cabinet,
our national economic vision and goals were still not clear to me, but I
became increasingly irritated by our government's ad hoc bailouts for
big business. This always happened under the threat of job losses or the
promise of jobs created – new jobs that we never really saw – and without any performance evaluation or open accountability after one or two
years. (The one example of that same approach I never quite digested
happened later, in 1981: Cabinet's ludicrous massive bailout of Massey-
Ferguson Ltd, the biggest farm machinery manufacturer in Canada,
which reached $2 billion in the red due to repeated mismanagement.)

After the unexpected Cabinet meeting of 9 August, I booked a flight
back to California – this time for Los Angeles and Santa Monica – to
continue my holidays. But before I left, sensing an opening, I made a
few contacts immediately following the Cabinet meeting and spent until
midnight in meetings with Jim Coutts (Trudeau's principal secretary),
Ian Stewart (working in Finance for Tommy Shoyama, the legendary
deputy minister), Marc Lalonde, Tom Axworthy (PMO), my Deputy
Minister Bruce Rawson, and Fred MacDonald from my political staff.
I had learned about the rules of action from Fernand Cadieux, when I
worked for him: early on, he had made me read Liddell Hart, the military historian and strategist. I had immediately sensed how difficult our
political future would be, and how within such perspectives my child
tax credit project would be much-needed good news! The project had

the dubious advantage of appearing to be an excellent policy for "the right," as it was not universal, and it would please "the left" because it addressed the inequality of the weakest members of society: children. On top of it all, the United Nations' International Year of the Child was to start in a few months.

This small conspirators' network went on working secretly (it also included Michael Pitfield of the Privy Council), discussing finances, strategy, and tactics. Members of this group could connect in total confidence and trust with Russ Robinson and our research team, and with Ken Battle and Ed Tamagno, the core of the remarkable Welfare Council: a research and information group set up by legislation in 1969, funded by my department but operating at arm's length. Because Cabinet had not approved the child tax credit in May, and worse, the caucus and our MPs had no idea about this innovative project, I could not talk about it.

I went back to California for a week, returning on 17 August. The usual decision-making process was short circuited. The memo to Cabinet was approved on 22 August by the Executive of Cabinet, the all-powerful Priorities and Planning Committee, of which I was not a member. The next morning, it went smoothly through full Cabinet for approval; in the afternoon I joined the Quebec caucus in its summer meeting at Mont Gabriel for two days, presenting the fresh approach and explaining these major new benefits for children. On 24 August Finance Minister Jean Chrétien made the official public announcement. Life was great.

Then an unexpected interlude abroad: the prime minister invited a few ministers, including me, as well as some other public figures – I remember Father Louis-Marie Régis, OP, a great theologian and friend of Trudeau's – to join him for the inauguration of Pope John Paul I at the Vatican. The new pope had chosen his name to celebrate his two reformist predecessors, John XXIII and Paul VI. We would be in Rome from 2 to 5 September 1978, with the inauguration being held on Sunday, the third, followed by a papal audience the following day. Those unique events would forge lifelong memories. Meeting the pope, I spontaneously felt that I had approached a holy man, a saint. Pope John Paul I died of a heart attack less than a month later, on 28 September.

Back home, the challenge was to sell the child tax credit to Canadians, but it would not be easy to explain. In those years, our social programs – old age pensions, guaranteed income supplements, family
allowances, and others – had always been delivered by monthly federal
cheques mailed directly to the beneficiaries. Here, for the first time, the
government would need recourse to the income tax system to define
who would qualify and to deliver to the mother $200 per year, non-
taxable, automatically annually indexed, for each child under eighteen
years of age, to those whose family income was $18,000 or less. The
refundable tax credit was then gradually reduced towards zero for those
with family income over $26,000. To have the CTC approved, I reluc-
tantly had to accept that family allowances would not be indexed for
two years. I was conscious that this might be opening the door to the
monetarists around me, starting with some Cabinet colleagues, but I
kept an eye on the scene.

The first challenge, a major one, was that every mother had to fill
out a special one-page income tax form, in addition to the general basic
income tax form, even if she did not pay income tax. Even worse, those
who were not registered with Revenue Canada also had to get a social
insurance number (SIN). This included First Nations and Inuit mothers,
who were not required to pay income tax. In November I had lunch
with the pragmatic leader Noel Starblanket, chief of the National Indian
Brotherhood (now the Assembly of First Nations). Putting aside any
dogmatic attitude, after my explanations and a good discussion, he concluded that the new program would improve the well-being of Indigenous children and gave his full support to the project, which he would
promote in the some 600 reserves of Canada.

Negotiations with National Revenue were difficult: my former department was refusing to lose, if I may put it this way, its virginity in
delivering welfare cheques! This was the purist view the department
was defending. It had never done things this way and would not start
now. At the time, there had never been a "refundable" income tax
credit; that was one of the stumbling blocks. Finance finally won over
National Revenue, and the machinery slowly went into action.

When I started touring the country from west to east, as a sales-
woman, I began with a popular Vancouver open-line radio show. I was

well prepared to explain the new system in simple sentences, but this was no help at all. The only thing the mothers phoning in wanted to know was what real life is all about: How much money? When does it start? It was a perfect lesson in political science! I spoke a lot to explain and sell the new benefit, but I got tremendous help from the department with Greg Traversy, a senior advisor, and Donald Macdonald of the Research and Planning Branch. They were very committed to this new program: they crisscrossed the country to meet with provincial social affairs officials, local community groups, and local media. Beginning in January, we also set up offices that gave mothers free assistance to fill out the required forms. Along with the January 1979 family allowance cheques, I made sure the Revenue Canada form to apply for the CTC, an application for the SIN, and a tax form were included in our regular mailings to all mothers.

In the House, by a strange irony, Bill C-10 could not be better placed on the legislative calendar and piloted with the Opposition parties than by Allan MacEachen, appointed government House leader and president of the Privy Council for a third time. As this new social program was, technically speaking, a fiscal program, it was of necessity a Finance bill, even though the policy emanated from my department. Very elegantly, Chrétien asked me to present and defend it in the House and with Canadian public opinion. The bill was tabled on 20 October 1978: the government hoped it would pass before the end of the calendar year, with the first cheques being delivered around March or April 1979, still considered to be income that had to be reported but was non-taxable.

That process was far from clear! I later would dream of an academic content analysis of these debates in the House, which would result in an exceptionally rich master's thesis in social science or other disciplines: history, public administration, or women's studies, to name a few. The worst of right-wing ideologies, full of prejudices (not to mention racism, at times), made up numerous speeches of the Conservative Opposition. I can still hear a Conservative MP from Manitoba roaring, "This bill was completely unacceptable: giving money to Indian mothers for each of their kids? As always, the first thing they would do is cross the border and go get drunk in the North Dakota bars!" Several other PC MPs could not accept the fact that some parents would take that money and buy a bicycle for their child: "a superfluous expense if ever there was one." To which I answered, "Great! I rejoice and it is wonderful; nothing is better for enhancing a child's life!" There was strong opposition to the fact that the child tax credit was an annual amount of $200 per child per year and was not to be distributed in twelve tiny monthly payments. This point had been debated in my department as well as in Cabinet, but I would not consider anything but the annual amount of $200. I had known poverty and knew very well that such a relatively big annual amount was the kind of money poor families can never manage to save through the year. With this sum they would be able to afford something out of their ordinary restricted budget.

From the NDP Opposition I did not have any serious problems. Bob Rae, their young MP who was quite sure of himself, had just won a Toronto seat in a by-election two days before the bill was tabled; somewhat later, as the NDP's bright and rather arrogant new Finance critic, Rae was hassling me when his party was supporting the bill. One day I had had enough. I quietly went for help from my friend Stanley Knowles, who probably called him back to order. The debates in the House went on for only a month, but it felt like a long and unpleasant month. Bill C-10 was simply approved on Monday, 4 December 1978, by unanimous consent by the Committee of the Whole at the end of its third reading debate, without individual votes being registered. I suppose the Official Opposition would not have liked to vote against such a measure and have their vote recorded!

It is worth observing the success and evolution of this program, then a truly innovative concept, in today's terms. That long but necessary digression now brings me back to getting reacquainted with my old department. When Jean Chrétien became prime minister in 1993, that CTC was modified to become the child tax benefit (CTB) – adding to it family allowances (now targeted) and the working income supplement, which did not exist in Pierre Trudeau's time, in a monthly payment following the same rules. That year, the federal expenditures for this new CTB amounted to $5.1 billion. Further to the 1998 review, once Chrétien-Martin had not only brought Canada back into the black but had put the country in a surplus, and after successful federal-provincial negotiations, the CTB was replaced by the Canada Child Tax

Benefit (CCTB). It was made up of two components: the CCTB base benefit for low- and middle-income families with children, and the National Child Benefit Supplement, an additional benefit for low-income families with children.

When Harper came to office, at the end of January 2006, having defeated Paul Martin, he immediately killed the accords that Ken Dryden and Paul Martin had signed with each province for daycare programs. With this money, which had already been budgeted for in Parliament, he created the ideologically based Universal Child Care Benefit (UCCB) of $100 per month, per child, and taxable payment for children under the age of six that is *not* indexed to the cost of living. The following year, he announced a new child tax credit, giving additional tax relief for families with children under the age of eighteen. During the 2015 general election, Harper announced yet another increase to his UCCB, retroactive to January 2015. These programs, all taxable, would not have helped those most in need, including single-parent families.

On 20 July 2016 Prime Minister Justin Trudeau announced the new Canada Child Benefit (CCB): this benefit was no longer taxable, replaced all previous programs, was simpler, and was a tax-free family benefit that was easier to understand. The CCB is expected to lift 300,000 Canadian children above the poverty line and help many middle-class families as well. Families may receive up to $6,400 per year for each child under the age of six, up to $5,400 per year for each child between ages six and seventeen, and an additional $2,730 per year if a child qualifies for the disability amount. Around 90 per cent of families with children should be better off with this new program, whose cost is expected to reach $22.4 billion over the first five years. At the announcement, the CBC reported that Jean-Yves Duclos, minister of families, children, and social development, who was responsible for the program, stated, "The poverty rate for children in Canada will fall from about 11.2 per cent to 6.7 per cent."

I have remained particularly proud of our innovative legislation creating the child tax credit. It was a great way to end 1978 and to start 1979. Indeed, in January I officially launched the UNICEF International Year of the Child, announcing a working commission to be chaired by Doris Ogilvie (a family court judge and a former member of the Royal

Commission on the Status of Women in Canada) and featuring a team
of remarkable Canadians. Their 150-page report with recommendations, *For Canada's Children: National Agenda for Action*, was edited
by the vice chair of the commission, Landon Pearson, a long-time advocate for children's rights and well-being. The report reflected what
the commissioners had heard through meeting and listening to children
and youth across the country speaking about their needs and ideas. *For
Canada's Children*, and Landon Pearson's continued personal and professional involvement, also contributed to the drafting of the future UN
Convention on the Rights of the Child.

All through 1978, the ideology of the welfare state as a failure continued to spread, more or less silently. I rapidly observed that my wonderful Research and Planning Branch was already going in the general
direction of "targeting" social programs, as it was keeping up with the
times. For our government, that was where the money was! I had neither the time nor the means to identify and study the relevant Keynesian
works, as well as the Beveridge Report and reports by Leonard Marsh,
our own reformist of the Canadian safety net in the aftermath of the
Second World War. But I wanted to learn their theories in favour of universal programs and develop a line of arguments to counteract the monetarist theories now in circulation. So one evening I had dinner with my
old socialist friend Kalmen Kaplansky, who was David Lewis's brother
of the heart. A great supporter of human rights and anti-racist movements, Kaplansky had just returned to Ottawa from his years as Canadian delegate at the International Labour Organization in Geneva. As
he explained it, what was at the heart of the Beveridge Report and of
the welfare state – the importance of developing a citizen's identity, the
sense of social solidarity between classes and generations, the reduction
of the paternalistic role of the state – no longer resonated for Canadians
at the end of the 1970s. It meant nothing. I tried to translate these values
into contemporary images, but to no avail.

I thus simply but stubbornly kept calmly defending the universality
of these two programs in which I believed so deeply. And I continued
to hear cutting remarks from a few Toronto colleagues during Cabinet
meetings, to the effect that I was a kind of intellectually delayed person
who did not understand today's world and its new modern concepts. (I

considered these powerful but passing fads, more than anything else.) It was only some thirty years later, when I got to work with Amartya Sen – winner of the Nobel Prize – that I learned that "benefits meant exclusively for the poor often end up as poor benefits." A few years ago another commissioner, public health sociologist Fran Baum from Australia, sent me a wonderful abstract explaining and justifying universality in the fourth edition of her book *The New Public Health*. Recent analysts have captured the battled I lived through as "from rights to needs," a phrase coined by Raymond Blake, a history professor from Regina. That quite effective phrase suggests another ideological bent I lived through.

My protection of universality would almost come to an abrupt end in October 1982, when I returned from an extraordinary official three-week trip to China. Marc Lalonde had been named minister of finance. He called me to his office at once and informed me that my arguments in Cabinet using "the seniors" to save "the children" and vice versa would not work on him, and he intended to bring an end to the universality of these two programs because of the economic situation. I noted his comments without saying a word. I know when I am up against a brick wall! But the topic never came up again: not in my department, nor in the Super Cabinet Committee on Social Development, nor in Cabinet itself.

Three weeks later, entering Cabinet a few minutes late, I noticed Tom Axworthy, political and policy advisor to the prime minister. This was unusual, as political staff did not attend Cabinet meetings as a rule. Before starting the regular agenda of memos to Cabinet, Trudeau opened discussion around the Liberal Party National Convention, which was to take place in Ottawa a few days later, on 5–7 November. He then turned to Axworthy, who was standing near him, asking Tom to read "the" resolution to be presented and put to a vote at the opening of the Social Policies workshop discussions. The operative key-words of that long text were "with a view to target social programs." "To target" was a recent buzzword, never used before, meaning doing away with universality. Ministers were told that the media and the prime minister would attend the discussion at one point, remaining at the back of the room.

Having not been informed of any of this ahead of time and trying to understand the exact wording of such a long resolution, I was speechless but listened carefully. I was both totally down and mad as hell, but, being the great actress I can be if needed, I kept my expression blank. Then Trudeau asked if some ministers would be ready to go to the microphones during the convention to speak in favour of the resolution. Hands rose immediately, including those on the left! In my most neutral tone, I asked for a copy of the resolution (to study the small print: did it apply to pensions *and* family allowances, or only the latter?). I knew nothing about this strategy, and I felt very alone. Then the Prime Minister added, "It would be great if the resolution against universality was approved, but not with too big a majority." Everybody around the table understood what this meant. Such a cynical observation from a person like Pierre Trudeau shocked me deeply. After all, I had not been consulted, let alone informed; I had not seen any document. I realized that I had been quietly isolated. But what hurt most was that our caucus, including strong supporters of universality, had no idea of any of these manoeuvres. Our Liberal riding associations were also unaware of this plot: universality of family allowances and pensions was a fundamental tenet for the Liberal Party of Canada. I quietly left the room for a few minutes, passing the information to a trusted friend and colleague MP, who told me to leave it in his hands. At 7 o'clock that Friday morning, I received a phone call at home from Marc Lalonde (who had never phoned me before), telling me that I would sit in the middle of the front row of that meeting room surrounded by my riding delegates and would immediately raise my hand very high to vote in favour of the resolution, with most delegates following my cue. I did not say a word. I simply loathe that kind of authoritarian behaviour, which, I admit, also frightens me emotionally and almost physically.

The day before the convention, the *Montreal Gazette* published the Broadbent-Lalonde exchange during Question Period the previous day under the headline "'Keeping Baby Bonus Universal Favoured Option,' Says Lalonde." The article added that, answering media questions at the door after question period, I said to the media, "People are going through a very serious economic crisis, and it's really not time to change the rules of the game and hurt the family budget."

At the party convention, the vote by a show of hands was called. The room was packed. The prime minister was standing at the back of the room, and all the media were there. The resolution was defeated 95 to 5 per cent! Without a word, and nervously, I admit, I had done what seemed to me the only right thing to do: I had raised my hand as high as I could, *against* the resolution. I never heard a word about it afterwards.

Seven months later, on 13 July 1983, at what would be the last Meech Lake Trudeau Cabinet retreat, Cabinet received a serious and detailed picture of the economic situation. Then Lloyd Axworthy, minister of employment and immigration, and Ed Lumley, minister of industry, trade, and commerce, jointly presented a credible set of proposals for job creation, a first as far as I was concerned. Assessing their approach and the seriousness of our economic troubles, I stated that I was ready to personally lead the dossier of ending the universality of family allowances and pensions, and I knew how to justify it to Canadians. The $5 billion or so left after a cut-off line protecting the beneficiaries most in need had been decided would be entirely and directly applied to the realistic job creation programs that Axworthy and Lumley had just presented to us. We were already facing the end of an era, with the team at the centre lacking the energy and savoir-faire they once had. But nothing ever came of that extraordinary Meech Lake Cabinet meeting.

On 15 February 1984 I was flabbergasted to hear Finance Minister Marc Lalonde, in delivering his budget, announce that public pensions would be increased. Two weeks later was Trudeau's dramatic announcement that he was leaving politics. My new Canada Health Act (1984) was discussed as a priority bill in the House; it passed unanimously on 9 April, while the Liberal leadership campaign was in full swing. John Turner would become prime minister for ten short weeks on 16 June: he called a general election right away, and lost. Those pension increases never saw the light of day.

It would therefore be Mulroney's legacy, through his minister of finance, Michael Wilson, to do away with the universality of social programs, through Wilson's first budget in May 1985. Family allowances were politically easy for them to cut, nobody fighting for women and children. But for pensions, Madame Solange Denis got in his way in front of Parliament with her famous "You lied to us! Goodbye, Charlie

Brown!" He did away with universality of pensions later, in the most disingenuous way: through a thick Finance omnibus bill in 1989, to make it easier to pass through the House of Commons. The federal government would continue to send out monthly old age security cheques to all Canadians sixty-five or older, but required upper-income seniors to pay back part or all of their benefits the next spring on their income tax return. But first, Canadians reaching sixty-five still have to complete a form requesting their pension, even if they have to reimburse the government at tax time because of their income level. Out of principle, I didn't apply for old age security when I turned sixty-five.

Once in a while I wonder if my struggle to save universality was worth something. One thing is certain: it gave Canadians some ten more years, from the early talks about monetary economics, to see things coming and to adjust their personal finances and family budgets as best they could.

The broader issue of universality did not stop me and our team in the department from addressing pension issues all through my seven years in Health and Welfare. The team was ADM Del Lyngseth's branch and his own quiet reformist leadership, as well as that of the small group of the National Council of Welfare, and the Research and Planning Branch under its three successive ADMs – Russ Robinson, Mike Murphy, and Monique Jérôme-Forget. In Canada, usually a country of small steps and incremental changes, reforms to public pensions have often been rather modest improvements to the daily lives of seniors, but what satisfaction to have won one more reform! This despite the fact that public pensions amounted to 20 per cent of the total National Health and Welfare budget. The cost had reached $4.4 billion when I took office at National Health and Welfare in 1977–78, growing to $10.4 billion in the 1983–84 Public Accounts when I was about to retire from politics. In comparison, family allowances (not counting the child tax credit) totalled $2 billion in 1977–78 and had increased to only $2.3 billion in 1983–84. It is also worthwhile remembering that in 1980, for example, the poverty rate among seniors was double that of the active labour force.

It would be hard to list all that pension reforms entailed. Besides drawing up a shopping list of specific improvements, which appeared small, we signed our first international agreements on pension reciprocity, and jointly set up a National Pensions Conference with Finance. The conference was held from 31 March to 2 April 1981. It was opened by the prime minister himself at the Ottawa Conference Centre and was co-chaired by Finance Minister Allan MacEachen and me as minister of national health and welfare. This conference happened at half-time in the long saga of a key dossier of public policy that included the future stability of the Canada Pension Plan (CPP) and the need for decent private sector pensions for all workers. Prime Minister Trudeau had called the conference on 27 April 1979. Unfortunately, this initiative died a first time when Joe Clark took office on 4 June, after Trudeau's long-awaited general election, but it came back on the agenda in 1980. This initiative created a genuine exchange between very different and very powerful partners: federal and provincial governments, small and big business leaders, unions, seniors' associations, women's associations (who insisted on being present from the start through their minister, Judy Erola), CPP officials, and others. Michael Kirby of the Privy Council Office was appointed coordinator of this initiative.

The federal government confirmed the two objectives of the federal public pension system: to ensure that all seniors would have a minimum revenue at retirement (to fight poverty), and to help maintain a reasonable balance between seniors' revenue before and after retirement (revenue replacement). The ultimate objective was that several vehicles would correspond to a satisfying revenue replacement: universal Old Age Security (OAS), the targeted Guaranteed Income Supplement (GIS) and Spouse Allowance, based on revenues; CPP or Régime des Rentes du Québec (RRQ); employer pensions; and personal savings (encouraged through special tax privileges, such as the Registered Retirement Savings Plan). The ideal situation would rest on three pillars: OAS/GIS should represent 25 per cent of old age revenues; CPP/RRQ would add 10 per cent to public pensions; and employer-sponsored pension plans would yield 15 per cent more to individual retirement income. The other 50 per cent would come from personal savings, investments, or other post-retirement work revenues. This aim of the conference was to face the problems and agree to solutions related to the second and third pillars: the urgent and important reforms of CPP/RRQ and the private sector pensions (or lack thereof).

The then 14,000 private employer–sponsored pension plans were clearly insufficient when it came to indexation; improved portability between plans; qualification to receive a pension after two years; expansion of mandatory pension arrangements; and improved treatment of spouses, usually women, through credit-splitting or otherwise. The business world, the private pensions industry, and Ontario wanted improvements from the private sector. Meanwhile, the public sector approach was shared by the unions, women's associations, Quebec and Saskatchewan, and NGOs in general.

Several excellent official background documents were produced, in addition to numerous briefs submitted by participants. The Economic Council of Canada released its study and recommendations as early at 1979, the same year that the research commissioned by Finance from the federal Task Force on Retirement Income Policy, chaired by Dr Harvey Lazar, was published. Also in 1979, Senator David Croll contributed with the *Report of the Special Senate Committee*, which he chaired. The following year we received the *Report of the Royal Commission on the Status of Pensions in Ontario*. The *Report on the Parliamentary Task Force*, chaired by Doug Frith, my parliamentary secretary, came in 1983. As to our National Health and Welfare Green Paper, "Better Pensions for Canadians," it finally became public in 1982, after countless delays. The introduction gave the tone of the dialogue: "Many Canadians have expressed concern over the adequacy and fairness of the retirement income system. In response to these concerns, the Government of Canada is putting forward for discussion and debate a number of proposals for reform … The government invites all Canadians to study and discuss these suggested initiatives, and to recommend ways in which they might be improved."

At National Health and Welfare, we were particularly interested in an expansion of the CPP/RRQ, while Finance wanted private-sector pension reform above all. The Super State Minister/Ministry of Social Development found itself in an intermediary position. In fact, both objectives were much-needed reforms. Briefs were coming from everywhere: the Canadian Federation of Independent Business, the Canadian Chamber of Commerce, the Canadian Manufacturers' Association, the Canadian Life and Health Association, the National Pensioners a nd Senior Citizens Federation, the Advisory Council on the Status of Women, the National Action Committee for the Status of Women, and many others. My colleague Judy Erola, who had the Status of Women portfolio, was closely associated with our work; I fully supported her requests for women's pensions.

In the end, nothing immediate was achieved during these years of sustained work on a key but complex file: the entire overhaul of the pension system in Canada. Sadly, in the fall of 1983, Lalonde as minister of finance and I agreed to call an end to this reform process because of the terrible economic situation. How could I sell better pensions at work when people were losing their jobs? The recession of the early 1980s was one of the worst economic slumps since the one that started in 1929–30. I shall never forget the forty-two-day national postal strike in the summer of 1981: numerous small businesses went bankrupt, not able to mail out their bills or receive payments by mail. I also vividly recall, in August of that summer, the number of homeowners having to renew their mortgage at 22.3 per cent, a major handicap for family budgets. In December 1982 we were in stagflation, with unemployment at 13.1 per cent and inflation at 11.3 per cent.

It would take decades, and the deterioration of the already inadequate company pensions and defined-benefit pension plans, for the provinces and Ottawa to finally agree in 2016 to an expansion of CPP that will particularly benefit today's young workers. It should provide higher payouts at retirement time. This will be funded by a 1 per cent increase in contribution for employers and for workers, phased in gradually over the coming years.

Back on public pension issues and thinking of Canada as a country of immigrants, the team of Social Security under my ADM Del Lyngseth had managed, when I was first appointed to National Health and Welfare, to develop and negotiate rules for the payment of bilateral reciprocal public old age pensions with countries from which we had received immigrants – at the time, mainly European countries. These international agreements applied to Old Age Security, the Guaranteed Income

Supplement, and the Canada Pension Plan, including benefits for persons with disabilities and for survivors. The agreements allowed for partial/ proportional Canadian pensions for immigrants who had not been able to accumulate forty years of earnings in Canada but had contributed something in their country of origin.

In October 1980 I would sign the first such agreements with four of my Western European counterparts. It was quite a celebration after the very hard work the department had done. With me on this quick trip were two ADMs, Del Lyngseth and Mike Murphy, as well as Ed Tamagno from the department, Jean-Claude Malépart, an MP who was a strong supporter of social programs, and my political staff, Anita Biguzs. I had received permission from the Prime Minister's Office for this rare opportunity to be accompanied by those who had done the work. We left for Europe on Friday, 17 October. In Paris, our first stop, we met with Minister Jacques Barrot, a democrat centrist, a man of conviction and values who would be in politics for forty years. Afterwards we took part in meetings at his ministry and in a working lunch at the Canadian Embassy hosted by Alec Pelletier, with Jean Farge, Barrot's Secrétaire d'État (minister of state) and the person responsible for cost control of their health-care system. It had been organized that I would then meet with our OECD ambassador, Randolph Gherson, that evening, as the next day I would chair a working session there on "Equity and Redistribution." At lunch I met Alfred Sauvy, the famous demographer whom I had studied as a sociology student. A working session resumed before a banquet hosted by Jacques Barrot in our honour and for the signature of the reciprocity agreement.

The Wednesday, 22 October, saw us fly to London for a brief stop, where I met with Minister Patrick Jenkin, secretary of state for social services, and signed the agreement. The meeting, signature, and gift presentation were done in less than an hour! We had discovered upon landing in London that this was the very day our high commissioner, Jean Wadds, would receive Prime Minister Margaret Thatcher for dinner, to which I was automatically also invited. I was seated opposite the British prime minister, with Dennis Thatcher to my left. Everything in London was "Conservative," including Flora MacDonald, who was passing through that day. After the meal, the women moved to the drawing room for conversation and tea: a most interesting historical moment for me. I liked the prime minister as a person, but not her husband, who asked me loudly during the meal why there were still some French Canadians. I gave him an answer *à la* Jean Chrétien.

Our next stop was Stockholm: also a Conservative government, but open, convivial, and egalitarian. My counterpart, the friendly Karen Söders, minister of social affairs, picked me up at the airport. She explained that ministers there do not have cars and chauffeurs – she usually travelled by public transit, but that day was given one of the six official government cars in honour of Canada! Stockholm was very cold and snowy; I merely got a glimpse of downtown before the signing of the agreement and official dinner. I still regret not having had time to walk through that archipelago of the Baltic Sea, to admire its historical districts as well as its modern architecture, beautiful glasswork, and textiles.

Bonn was our final stop, where our remarkable Ambassador Klaus Goldschlag was in his last posting. He was a historical figure in his own right, having escaped (thanks to a Toronto benefactor) his German orphanage in the mid-1930s before the worst of Hitler's "final solution" was put in place. (Klaus was reunited with his mother years later.) After the official part of the trip, he arranged for our cultural attaché, Serge Marcoux (a friend of my colleague Charles Lapointe, himself an ex-diplomat), to take us to visit Cologne, which suffered so much damage during the war; the Allies' massive bombardments left the city in ruins, with not many residents left. We rapidly visited the well-known Gothic thirteenth-century Catholic cathedral, as well as the famous, then new, glass museum *Römisch-Germanisches*, which has the greatest collection of Roman glass in the world. Back in Ottawa at the end of October 1980, Jean-Claude Malépart – a a natural leader committed to social justice, MP for the low-income southeast part of Montreal, who ate only hamburgers at McDonald's, even in Paris, for breakfast – was bragging to his colleagues that he had eaten little birds (quail with grapes) at Jacques Barrot's banquet, and even tasted raw dried reindeer in Sweden!

I would sign one more reciprocity agreement, with Jamaica, on 8–10 January 1983, when Pierre Trudeau sent me there unexpectedly during the holidays just after New Year's, in preparation for his own visit with Prime Minister Edward Seaga, who had succeeded Trudeau's friend Michael Manley. Our high commissioner gave a lovely luncheon for us at his residence, and we were the guests of Neville Lewis, minister of social services, for dinner.

It was hard to forget this trip for another reason: our small reciprocity of pensions team – Bob Allen (then director-general of operations in that branch), Ed Tamagno, Anita Biguzs, and I – were on our return trip in a small government plane when it suddenly dropped 10,000 feet over the ocean. We heard glasses and dishes in the galley flying around (and probably smashing). None of us could recall if the oxygen masks came down automatically; I think they did. But I do remember that one of the men started praying loudly as soon as we lost altitude.

Ed Tamagno told me recently how after our trips he made a career of negotiating similar reciprocity agreements with countries in different parts of the world, up to his retirement.

Last but not least, a word about those numerous non-sexy improvements needed to seniors' pensions in general. The "power of the weak" had not really played a role in the creation of "my" Child Tax Credit (or in the fight for universality of family allowances). But while the CTC owes its origin to a strategic coup I spearheaded, the positive reforms of the Old Age Pension and of the Guaranteed Income Supplement still clearly needed the power, modest at first glance, of civil society. In my years at Health and Welfare, we could count on the political activism, rather courteous but determined, of a remarkable number of golden age clubs and grassroots organizations of or related to seniors or those fighting poverty, all over the country. This is no longer the case. From 1975 to 1985, there were the Quebec Fédération de l'Âge d'Or du Québec and Association québécoise de défense des droits des personnes retraitées et préretraitées, while across the country there was the National Anti-Poverty Organization (NAPO, stemming from the Poor Peoples' Conference, Toronto 1971, that was organized by Len Shifrin, the future social policies media advocate; in 2009, NAPO changed its name to Canada without Poverty), the Canadian Association of Retired Persons, and parish or local seniors' clubs. In Quebec alone we counted 500 such clubs, which regularly denounced pension shortfalls or inhumane regulations of our old age programs. Any MP, of whatever political party and from wherever in Canada, received these repeated requests for change, the minister included.

At one point in 1980 I had the idea of asking Thérèse Casgrain for a favour. She had completed her nine months in the Senate in 1970–71, had no public pension, and was still a young-at-heart, active, and healthy eighty-four-year-old. We would reimburse her travelling expenses and she would replace me at seniors' functions and invitations all over the country. She accepted the offer, and it was a great help for me. We lost her suddenly when she died in her sleep on 3 November 1981. I attended her funeral in Montreal on 6 November and had the chance to speak with her four children, already young seniors themselves. In 1982 a few Quebec women set up the Thérèse-Casgrain Foundation to continue her social justice action through various projects.

That same year, in National Health and Welfare, I created the Thérèse-Casgrain Volunteer Award to honour this feminist icon and social reformer. The award was given annually to honour a Canadian for lifetime achievement of exceptional citizenship and social commitment. Selection was of course completely non-political and non-partisan, and the minister had nothing to do with it. Sometime in the second half of the 1990s I learned from both Thérèse's daughter and the Thérèse-Casgrain Foundation that Brian Mulroney had quietly killed the award. I wrote to Jane Stewart, minister of human resources development, on 8 March 2001 (International Women's Day), explaining the situation. The award was rapidly re-established under Jean Chrétien's government. But then it was killed again, this time by Stephen Harper, who took Thérèse Casgrain completely out of the picture and changed the purpose of the award. In 2016, under Prime Minister Justin Trudeau, the award, aptly renamed the Thérèse-Casgrain Lifelong Achievement Award / Prix Thérèse-Casgrain pour l'engagement de toute une vie, was re-established. It is administered by Minister Jean-Yves Duclos's Department of Employment and Social Development.

We were able to bring a number of these small reforms to public pensions. In 1978 we introduced the credit-splitting provision to the Canada Pension Plan in cases of divorce or separation. This change benefited women in particular – especially those who had not been able to build their own credit because they were full-time homemakers or were in the labour market only from time to time. The general idea was that the credits accumulated by the two spouses during their marriage could be split equally between them following a divorce, at the request of either spouse.

We also improved pensions and services to persons with disabilities, after government action on this file had mounted over the years. The United Nations had proclaimed 1981 the International Year of Disabled Persons. We owed a lot to the remarkable work of the Special Parliamentary Committee on the Disabled and the Handicapped, which was set up by the House of Commons and chaired by David Smith, with Thérèse Killens (Lib) and Walter Dinsdale (PC) as vice presidents. Their report, *Obstacles*, released in February of that year, offered an inventory of programs, financial support, and services that persons with disabilities required and made thirteen recommendations. It was a first in Canada. People I met across the country started telling me about the most basic tools they were missing in order to enjoy a fuller life and greater participation in society. For example, our city sidewalks did not have curb ramps in the early 1980s: these are now a common feature everywhere in the country. This is only one symbol – an obvious and basic one – of the exceptional physical, sensorial, and cognitive adaptations that the country, cities, workplaces, and governments would embark upon as they renovated, adapted, and designed with people with disabilities in mind. We were also able to improve CPP disability benefits.

In that same International Year of 1981, my office received a bizarre invitation to all ministers of health of the "Americas" from the minister of health of Spain, Jesus Sancho Rof, to attend a conference to celebrate the Year of Disabled Persons in Madrid at the end of October. Everything was unacceptable in that Spanish event. For one thing, it suggested the Spanish colonization of the Americas. There was no translation into English or French, even though many participants from the United States and Canada, as well as Haiti and some Caribbean countries, did not speak Spanish. On the day of our arrival, while trying to get over jet lag, ministers and their delegations had to attend a dinner in a noisy commercial restaurant far from downtown Madrid; it started after 10 p.m. and went well past midnight.

The next day, our host stayed on the auditorium stage, talking, without introducing or even shaking hands with any of us, his guests. We did not understand at all what was going on. No documents were provided to participants. The US Secretary for Health, Richard (Dick) Schweiker, could not be there. At the last minute, he had asked the newly appointed US Surgeon General, Dr Everett Koop, a courageous and brilliant pediatric surgeon, to represent the United States. Koop was alone, without even a single aide, so I invited him to join us. He was a man of faith with whom one could talk, despite his strong conservatism and total opposition to abortion, for he would always remain a man of science. At future international meetings, I would see him again with pleasure. It would be said later that "Koop was the only Surgeon General to become a household name."

The same Spanish minister of health who invited us to the conference made international news in the weeks following when a scandal involving the illicit sale of toxic cooking oil claimed at least 210 lives. Early in December 1981, Minister Rof lost his job for "apparent incompetence." This unfortunate international trip had a redeeming moment: on the last day, our ambassador to Spain, Jacques Dupuis, took our small group for a fascinating day in Toledo.

Back home, in 1982, seniors did not stop pressing the government for action. I selfishly wished Thérèse Casgrain had been with us longer. The year marked the tenth anniversary of the New Horizons program – a National Health and Welfare program of grants and contributions for projects led or proposed by seniors to positively influence seniors in their community. For example, projects could encourage volunteer work, improve infrastructure used by seniors, raise awareness about and prevent and eliminate elder abuse, and promote seniors' health, lifestyle, and more. My department team was far from idle that year!

In March 1984 there were 2.5 million seniors (age sixty-five and up) on universal public pensions; about half of them also received the Guaranteed Income Supplement. Del Lyngseth's team was working with Monique Jérôme-Forget's Research Branch on all feasible amendments, subject to being approved by Cabinet, for a kind of omnibus bill as soon as possible before the Trudeau government came to an end. Several technical amendments were simply correcting past drafting mistakes or oversights that affected at times only fifty people or 3,000 pensioners who had been deprived of their entitlements for the OAS and/or the GIS, or who were not able to register for their pension in time, and thus received only one year of retroactivity. It also included numerous former immigrants to Canada who were now covered by the reciprocity agreements we had negotiated and signed.

In June 1984 one of these Old Age Pension amendments inadvertently had a feminist twist worth telling. Historically, Canada had decided that a pensioner living alone would get half the pension that a couple got. I had the pleasure of presenting in Cabinet the evidence-based calculation of the cost of living alone – housing, food, and so on – which amounts to 60 to 75 per cent of the cost of living for a couple. In terms of demography, it applied to women living alone in a great majority of cases. Adjusting to this evidence-based recommendation meant an immediate additional expense of $250 million, then an additional $460 million for the financial year 1985–86. My Cabinet colleagues were not finding it too difficult to accept this amendment, especially as I had the support of the finance minister, Marc Lalonde, and other colleagues who were conscious of the cost of daily living – with one exception: Allan J. MacEachen, no doubt thinking of all the widows and other single women offering him lunch or supper and pampering him in Baddeck, Lake Ainslie, or anywhere else in Cape Breton! He was profoundly shocked by my proposal, not imagining for a minute that these women could have difficulty balancing their budgets. But, contrary to what happened when MacEachen killed my Child Tax Credit the first time I presented it in Cabinet in May 1978, Trudeau did not pay the slightest attention to his deputy prime minister's idiosyncrasies. My omnibus bill was approved for immediate tabling in the House of Commons.

Numerous changes, small and big, to our public pensions were finally on the House of Commons agenda in the last months of the Trudeau government, with Bill C-40, an Act to amend the Old Age Security Act, tabled on 29 May 1984. The amendments – several of which stemmed from constituents' problems reported to me by MPs of all sides of the House, whom I recognized in my speech – were rather well received. I gave my speech explaining the numerous clauses of the bill on the fourth. The debates occupied the legislative calendar over the whole month in the House of Commons, and for the full day on 4 and 12 June, and 22 June, the day of its adoption. It then went to the Senate, which considered it uninterruptedly on 25–28 June and adopted it in third reading. Royal assent was given on Thursday, 28 June 1984, with most amendments coming into force on 1 July. These amendments were particularly dear to me: for the first time in Canadian history, seniors would now be living above the poverty line. What a wonderful way to complete one's mandate in social policies!

12

Aboriginal Health: Inuit and First Nations

What a surprise it had been to learn the day of my appointment at National Health and Welfare that I was also the minister directly responsible for the health of Aboriginal Canadians: First Nations and Inuit.
Like everybody else, I thought that responsibility fell to the minister of
northern development and Indian affairs. That universe was unknown
to me, with the exception of our 1968 Status of Women rapid meetings
at Fort Rae, on Great Slave Lake, NWT, from where I left with an impression of shocking poverty, traditional life, and a cultural gap miles
long between "them and us." Otherwise, at the time, I often holidayed
in Mexico, visiting and staying in villages and towns with a majority of
Indigenous Mexicans, seeing them at markets, in eating places, around
historical sites. I had little knowledge of their cultural and spiritual practices and their history.

Norway House, of the Cree Nation, at the confluence of Nelson
River and Lake Winnipeg, in northern Manitoba, is the first reserve I
visited in the first days of July 1978 after less than a year in my new
portfolio. It had an important nursing station. This trip was a very
happy experience. I was there with Bruce Rawson, my deputy minister,
Dr Lyall Black, the ADM of medical services, and George Campbell, our
regional director, himself a Cree from there, a warm, solid, competent,
and smart senior civil servant. From there we went to Garden Hill, the
largest and most populated of the seven reserves of the Garden Hill
First Nations, all this by seaplane, another first for me. The reserve was
located on the shore of Island Lake, a rather good-looking small com-

munity. We probably slept there, as we were expected by that reserve for a formal dinner. Early next day we flew to Gods Lake Narrows, a "designated place," not a reserve, with a small population of Cree and Métis, and from there directly to Gods Lake, for it would be my great and first fishing expedition!

An explanation is in order. Over a drink and just chatting, a few women friends who knew how power worked explained to me that men in power settled issues and made deals in informal settings between them, such as tennis clubs, cross-country skiing, and fishing trips. For example, in these years, playing squash was the big thing with business executives, senior bureaucrats, and politicians. Marc Lalonde and Pierre Juneau were regulars. Lalonde also went fly fishing for salmon at Anticosti Island with others. I had heard these stories and knew Bruce Rawson was party to such encounters, when big decisions were made. As I did not practise any sport, I had an idea: going fishing! My first year was progressing and Bruce was not hinting at any such expedition. I obviously did not know how power worked. So I innocently started asking when we would be going fishing. Without any explanation, it turned into this trip northeast in Gods Lake, organized by Bruce, who must have wondered what I had in mind. I had brought with me my godson François, who was eleven, and the men and the boy enjoyed themselves fully. They showed me how to fish and I caught a few pike: Gods Lake merited its name as fish kept jumping into our small boat! No need to add that no business was ever even mentioned and I did not learn any secret public policy or future objective. I am still terribly ashamed of myself thinking of it all. Not very smart for a sociologist!

That first visit to some reserves ended in a morning in Winnipeg, where I met the staff and learned about the work of our Regional Office of the Medical Services Branch. I did not go to any other reserve until the summer 1980, once I was in my second mandate as minister of national health and welfare. In question period in the House before I joined Cabinet, even as minister of national revenue, I had noticed questions, not the partisan type, to Marc Lalonde, my predecessor, on issues completely foreign to someone urban: "radiation level in river water at the Serpent River Indian Reserve," "mercury contamination in Arctic communities," "arsenic poisoning problem up in Yellowknife." I could see that it was often in relation to some mining enterprise being the polluter and the fish diet of the local First Nations.

I do not recall other topics relating to Aboriginal health, and the answers usually referred to ongoing "studies and monitoring." In those decades, Aboriginal health was not on the national radar as it should have been. Later, in the 1980s, I would face the same terrible health problems caused by mercury-contaminated rivers for First Nations communities. I recall discussing the situation with Dr Margaret Becklake from McGill, who had done a detailed health assessment of the situation for my department. Later with my Cabinet colleague Ed Lumley, we were in the St Regis Mohawk Reserve in his riding, on the shores of the St Lawrence. Industrial plants both on the US side and in Canada were dramatically polluting the waters of the reserve with fluoride, caustic soda and chlorine, PCBs and more contaminants, released by Alcoa, the General Motors foundry, and the Reynolds Metals factory. Each time the department contracted medical researchers for an in-depth study and recommendations.

It was only in 1945 that Health and Welfare assumed direct responsibility for health services to reserves and to Inuit communities, establishing nursing stations, health centres, and a few regional hospitals here and there in towns close to reserves. These minimal services were not available to Métis and non-status populations. The nursing stations had developed more slowly for Inuit communities in the Arctic, while Inuit patients in need of complex care or surgery were still being flown to Edmonton or Montreal during all my years in politics. To put things in perspective, when I was responsible for Aboriginal health there was a traditional formal rapport between my department and Aboriginal communities including the beginning of a change in that relationship. This change started, to put a date on it, in 1978–79, gathering speed in 1982, and continuing to develop considerably in the 1980s, with a gradual devolution of powers and responsibilities from Health and Welfare to First Nations reserves. It bears no relationship, however, with today's challenging and key mandate of Dr Jane Philpott as the new and first minister of Indigenous services, the former NHW Branch described in this very chapter now repatriated to her new ministry, where it belongs. Her new department of Indigenous Services has an unusual long-term goal: its own eradication! One of her priorities is the provision of drinking water in the some 600 reserves still awaiting action, while she is also working on "providing long-term funding, ensuring mutual accountability, respecting different visions, facilitating the establishment of Indigenous-led programs and services to be provided through Indigenous institutions and governments, and ensuring flexibility in government responses," as she explained in her 23 January 2018 briefing to the media at the National Press Theatre in Ottawa. This is the way to go, and if someone can do it, it is Jane Philpott.

There was lot to learn about Aboriginal health, starting with the fact that the peoples' health status was well below the national average, and their infant mortality far above. Infant mortality due to crib or cot death – sudden infant death syndrome (SIDS), the leading cause of deaths for infants in their first year of life – is still today at least three times higher in First Nations communities than in the rest of Canada. It was far higher in the 1970s and started to fall after 1980 in the general population but not on reserves. If their neonatal mortality by SIDS (during the first twenty-seven days of life, associated with access to neonatal care and obstetrics) is close to the national average, the post-natal deaths (between twenty-eight days and one year, and reflecting socio and environmental factors) remain extremely high. So the total infant mortality rate of Status Indians on reserve, for 1976 to 1980, during the years of my first mandate at National Health and Welfare, our Medical Services Branch registered 29 deaths for 1,000 live births against 11 for 1,000 for the Canadian population. Twenty years later, these rates had fallen to 8 per 1,000 deaths for First Nations, still seven times higher than for the general population. The 1992 research work of Tina Moffat, an evidence-based study of infant mortality in the Fisher River Cree Ojibway reserve in Manitoba, just 200 kilometres north of Winnipeg, from 1910 to 1939, established infant mortality to be 249 per 1,000 live births. That study published in 1999 attributed the major causes of infant mortality to poverty and malnutrition, SIDS at the time unknown to health personnel and Fisher River Methodist Church records. These facts, both historical and contemporary, about first Nations infant mortality rates, I discovered years after I left political office.

What I came to learn while in office was that life expectancy at birth for First Nations and Inuit, for men or for women, was around seven years less than for other Canadians. Diabetes on reserves was five, six, or seven times higher, and tuberculosis regularly reappeared among Inuit communities. On-reserve family and other violence, whatever its causes, was devastating. I recall some of our nurse practitioners living on reserves telling me how, waking up on weekends, they repeatedly found bloodied women at their doors or abandoned newborns. Suicides among young Aboriginals were of epidemic proportions, as well as drug use of all kinds. A great number of Aboriginals, both young and old, male and female, were alcoholics. That was the reality I faced.

Very early I was briefed on the rapid development of glue sniffing among young members of First Nations, and these youths, even kids, too often lost their lives because of it. Other volatile solvents were also abused among First Nations as well as Inuit, such as hairspray, spray paint, deodorant, nail polish remover, and gasoline. On a trip to Winnipeg with my officials, with the staff and management of a large downtown pharmacy we studied where these items were displayed and how access could be made difficult on higher shelves or behind glass. Not evident! Even very young children sprayed solvent into a paper bag, then sniffed it repeatedly, or sprayed a piece of cloth they put against their mouth or nose, sniffing it again and again. I was told some even sprayed their mattress. The brain was rapidly attacked. Repetition had very serious consequences and could cause death.

General demographic statistics on Aboriginal people for the sixties, seventies, and eighties are not easily available, hence this reference in Historica Canada / Canadian Encyclopedia, which touches on a specific trend, that of the remarkable increase in the Canadian Aboriginal population in recent years:

Between 1996 and 2006, the Aboriginal population grew by 45 per cent, compared with 8 per cent for the non-Aboriginal population. Between 2006 and 2011, the Aboriginal population fur-

ther increased by 232,385 people, or by 20.1 per cent. By comparison, the non-Aboriginal population grew by just 5.2 per cent
during that same time period ... According to Statistics Canada,
approximately 799,010 people, or 3 per cent of Canada's population, identified themselves as having an Aboriginal identity
in 1996. Ten years later, the census reported 1,172,790 people,
or 4 per cent of the population. The proportion of people reporting an Aboriginal identity continues to grow, according to
the most recent data.

By now Canadian public opinion has registered that almost 50 per
cent of the total Aboriginal population is aged twenty-four and under,
compared to less than 30 per cent of our non-Aboriginal population.
During work with the Royal Commission on Women, I observed that
the Western provinces counted numerous First Nations, although Ontario had the most Aboriginal people, mainly First Nations, counting
301,425. However, considering proportions of their total population,
Nunavut, the Northwest Territories, and the Yukon comprise 86 per
cent, more than 50 per cent, and 25 per cent Aboriginal peoples. "Down
south," Manitoba records the highest percentage of Aboriginals in its
population, at 16.7 per cent. In the 2011 census, Aboriginals made up
4.3 per cent of the Canadian population – 1,400,685 people – 97 per
cent stating they were First Nations.

Approximately three-quarters (73.1 per cent) of Inuit in Canada
live in Inuit Nunangat, which comprises four regions: Nunatsi-
avut (Labrador), Nunavik (Québec), Nunavut and the Inuvialuit
region (Northwest Territories). Nunavut has the largest population of Inuit (45.5 per cent) and the largest proportion of Inuit
as total population (85.4 per cent).

A little less than half (45.3 per cent) of all persons with registered Indian status in Canada lived on a reserve or settlement in
2011, while more than half (54.7 per cent) lived off reserve.
Québec had the highest proportion of First Nations people living
on-reserve (72 per cent).

In 2003 Health Canada stated that of the First Nations and Inuit communities living south of the Arctic Circle, 77 per cent comprised fewer than 1,000 people. It also made the point, so difficult to grasp for our super-medicalized health-care system, that all Aboriginal people view health holistically, as a product of interrelated factors: mental, physical, spiritual, and emotional. Another statistical source of 2010 reported that Canada counts 615 First Nations reserves, eight Métis settlements, and fifty-three Inuit communities. "Many Aboriginal people in Canada live in the large metropolitan areas such as Toronto, Vancouver and Montréal. However, the 2011 NHS indicated that among the major metropolitan areas, Winnipeg (78,415), followed by Edmonton (61,770) have the largest Aboriginal identity populations. In each of these two cities, the Aboriginal people represent 11 and 5.4 per cent of the total, respectively. Regina and Saskatoon have sizable Aboriginal populations as well (9.5 and 9.3 per cent, respectively)."

None of these basic and fascinating statistical data were available to me and my team while we were involved with Aboriginal health. It would be decades before research on socio-economic determinants of health demonstrated how unemployment, poverty, isolation, family violence, lack of education, lifestyle, and other conditions of life define good and bad health. And I blame the federal government, directly and indirectly responsible for the long-lasting human damage rooted in the residential schools policy and that due to the imposed relocation of Aboriginal people. This being said, the complete absence of intersectoral work in Cabinet committees or otherwise at the time was such that I never had any kind of meeting with my counterparts in NDIA during more than seven years of direct responsibility for Aboriginal health.

I invested as much time and effort as I could, for very modest gains. The team in the department and its leadership were remarkable, and I basically supported their work and the initiatives they presented me with. However, First Nations politics was a labyrinth. I had the wisdom to stay as far from it as I could. It was only on rare occasions that I dealt with the president of the National Indian Brotherhood (NIB), today the Assembly of First Nations (AFN), as when I negotiated with success with Noel Starblanket for his agreement and support on registering status Indian mothers for the new Child Tax Credit. Later, in January 1981, the AFN first president, Chief Delbert (Del) Riley, came to see me. A tough, determined, and learned individual, he was lobbying me to support the entrenchment of Aboriginal and treaty rights in the Canadian Constitution. He was the national chief, during the 1980–81 constitutional discussions, who led 200 Canadian Indian chiefs to England to make their point, taking no chance with government representations. With great pleasure and satisfaction, I worked with provincial or regional chiefs like Joe Dion in Alberta or Billy Diamond of Quebec, who were examples of vision, strong leadership, and pragmatism in improving their members' daily lives. It was, however, with tribal councils and at the reserve and local community levels that I forged a few links in working together for reform. And, to my pleasure, with the Native Women's Association. Ovide Mercredi was a grand chief whose calm and wisdom I greatly appreciated. Long after politics I sat with him as a patron of honour, as well as with Joe Clark and Ed Broadbent, all of us elders in fact, on Canada without Poverty. I also met Phil Fontaine, the longest-serving president of the Assembly of First Nations, several times but never really collaborated with him.

Still at the beginning of my mandate, at their request, I once received an impressive group of Indian chiefs in ceremonial clothes. They gave long formal presentations accompanied by traditional music, with messages that seemed to me rather negative, indeed menacing, to which I listened with attention and empathy. I had not been invited to speak but the chiefs presented me with several brand-new Hudson Bay blankets. As I was learning that morning, those famous blankets had transmitted smallpox and other contagious diseases, at times deliberately, from the white men to British Columbia Aboriginals and other Indians in the three Americas, decimating populations. Regarding Canada's West Coast Indians, Historica Canada / The Canadian Encyclopedia reports, "Major epidemics of smallpox introduced by European carriers, killed large numbers of Indigenous peoples in the 1780s, 1830s and 1860s, while other diseases dramatically reduced the population throughout the 19th century and early 20th century. A major smallpox epidemic may have killed 20,000 people in 1862, when, after infection broke out in Indigenous camps around Victoria, authorities forced them to their home communities, spreading the disease."

I was quite moved and shocked. I had never heard these horrible historical facts of past centuries, even of the twentieth century. As I was
holding the pack of blankets just received, my deputy minister, Bruce
Rawson, briskly took the blankets out of my hands, put them in a large
bag, and I never saw them again nor heard a word about why it had
happened. This day rested with me as troubling and menacing. I was
all the more surprised as Bruce Rawson was from Saskatchewan, lived
near reserves, and had Indian friends. Had I been political that morning,
I would have immediately understood that my DM was doing the right
thing, dissociating ourselves – the government – from the symbolic accusation of an unacceptable event. Besides this strange encounter, my
friendly relationships during fieldwork more than once seemed rejected
by the local Indians in power without anything being said. We could
not "be friends."

To advise me and travel with me in support of our Aboriginal health
mandate, the department appointed an Aboriginal nurse who had been
with the department for twenty years. I then got to know two generations of remarkable and rare Aboriginal nurses, one with traditional
hospital training and the other with a university degree in nursing sciences; the first from a traditional milieu, the other very modern; one
older than I, the other one younger. I first got to know Jean Goodwill,
the first Aboriginal registered nurse in Canada, daughter of a traditional
chief of Saskatchewan. A Plains Cree, she was born in Little Pine First
Nation near North Battleford, obtained her nursing degree at the Holy
Family Hospital in Prince Albert, then was hired by the Fort Qu'Appelle
Indian Hospital. At one point, with my full support, the Medical Services Branch managed to have her set up and develop the independent
Aboriginal Nurses Association of Canada.

When the Liberals came back to form the government in 1980,
Madeleine Dion Stout became my special advisor. We worked so well
together than she became a personal friend, and we see each other a
few times a year! We both left office at about the same time, when she
decided to get a master's in international affairs at the Carleton Patter-
son School, and then created the Centre for Aboriginal Culture and Education at Carleton University. Madeleine was born and raised in the
Kehewin First Nation, in Alberta. When she was very young she was

taken away from her family and sent to a residential school. Her beautiful and wise testimony to the Truth and Reconciliation Commission (2008–15), when she spoke of "resilience," has been published. It was only in recent decades that I learned the history of these residential schools, including her own.

We could travel to reserves or Inuit communities only during spring and fall, whenever was the least bad time for blackflies and mosquitoes, which bit us alive. In the far North it was possible only from the end of June to sometime in July. We used seaplanes, very small ordinary planes, even helicopters. I usually slept in our local health clinic or at the nurses' residence. Reserves varied enormously, some happy, some sad. A "dry" reserve on an island in northern Ontario was really terribly poor and all the children, quite numerous, suffered from impetigo, in the twentieth century in a land of plenty like Canada! I had developed impetigo on the roads of France during our exodus during the Second World War, and I knew those wounds took so long to heal. What a shame! The reserves I went to that appeared the poorest, the most disintegrated, the least developed, with the most problems that appeared sometimes intractable were in Northern Ontario, including the shore of James Bay. Grassy Narrows, Webique, and White Dog (today, Wabaseemoong) were such examples. In Sioux Lookout and Moose Factory we had to negotiate Indian participation on hospital boards and services for the surrounding Native population. Because of the dominant and closed-minded white populations, it was very difficult and brings back both sad and angry memories.

The most pleasant communities were in BC, including Vancouver Island, where I went twice: Bella Bella, Alert Bay. I also enjoyed Blue Quills First Nations College University, in Alberta, the first Aboriginal one, and the first with McMaster and Dalhousie to create an academic program for nurse practitioners, key to the health of Indian and Inuit communities. Through the decades I have admired the work of these nurse practitioners. In July 1982 I had the privilege to tour reserves and communities in Labrador: Goose Bay, Makkovik, Postville, and Rigolet, where people were so openly welcoming.

One particular trip west, this time to Prince Albert, Saskatchewan, was not to a reserve but would play an important role in health services to Aboriginal communities. I had been asked to officially open the National School of Dental Therapy there. There was no such thing as dental assistants at the time, and dentists were completely opposed to them. But all our efforts to have dentists work on reserves in the summer did not succeed. So National Health and Welfare took over the role played by the Faculty of Dentistry of the University of Toronto, which had started a dental therapy school in Fort Smith, Northwest Territories in 1972 but was forced to close it at the end of the 1970s, the patient population being too small to sustain the school. The Prince Albert School graduates were then hired by our Medical Services Branch to service Indian reserves and Inuit communities. Unfortunately the school was forced to close in 2011 after the Harper government would no longer fund it.

I take for granted that it is during the same trip to Prince Albert in the fall of 1981 that I visited the small community of Melfort, Saskatchewan, where I officially opened the Natahowin Health Centre at the service of the James Smith Band.

My very last trip was a memorable Arctic tour of mainly Inuit communities. Aboard were Madeleine Dion Stout and Anita Biguzs from my office, and Christine, my twelve-year-old niece, as it was my only way to be with my family. The Ottawa Jetstar flew us to Churchill, Manitoba, where we picked up the department team of George Campbell and Barry Brown and a rented Cheyenne would take us to Baker Lake, Spence Bay (Taloyoak), Cape Dorset (Kinngait), Iglooli and Frobisher Bay (Iqalit) in the Northwest Territories, now in Nunavut. When we landed in Igloolik, we had already crossed the Polar Circle, in the heart of the Northwest Passage, as we had first visited Spence Bay (Taloyoak), which is also north of the Polar Circle!

Following are the only notes I took in my twelve years in active politics in the House of Commons! I wrote them while in the Arctic during that trip:

First, one panics landing in the total silence, the immensity, and the apparent nudity of these lands without trees of the Arctic. The first shock is Churchill (Manitoba), the flat and bland ground, the end of the short and quirky evergreen trees. In fact, the tundra starts 50 miles north of

Churchill, as if cut with scissors. Desperately looking for some sign of life, flowers hidden in plain sight finally show up as tiny purple flowers at ground level. And slowly, some yellow, some white ones.

But as soon as we gather the group, we have to go again, this time to the central Arctic, below the Arctic Circle. First at the mouth of the Churchill River we see hundreds of beluga whales going upriver, having given birth to their babies. White, but golden in the ferruginous water, they really look like big sardines in oil. After hours, we land at Baker Lake. Pebbles, stones, rocks, sharp gravel, and water. Panic. No roads in or out! NO ROADS! *And these houses on stilts or rocks, without any foundations because of the permafrost, which is one foot thick. Tufts of grey green grass, the same purple, yellow, or white tiny flowers, the Arctic daisies with almost no stem and the famous Arctic cotton: a flower that is like a tuft of white fur on top of a bare straight stem.*

The entire Inuit community welcomes us at the airport. No Cabinet minister has landed here, for as long as people can remember. We are dressed for late fall as told in Ottawa: it is 90°F, astonishing, as it usually does not go over 45°F, but we will freeze later in other settlements. And the blackflies and mosquitoes will not leave us until the next day. We can't avoid eating some. I have never ever sweated so much. Visit of our nursing station, exchanges with the nurse practitioners, who are real "bush doctors," meeting with the hamlet council and the health committee. Everything takes place in Inuktituk and we are helped by an interpreter. Traditional. Exotic. Sun-dried caribou, its antlers on the roof, fish hanging like old socks on the washing line to dry, seals just caught lying there, dogs baying at the moon. Always this feeling of disorder of objects lying everywhere: large sleighs, three fat Honda tires, covered Skidoos. Empty crates, packing cases, wood, construction remains, all of this out of the last visit of the barge that had come from the south with the annual supply of all kinds. A village that had not done its spring cleaning. The Inuit smile or laugh all the time.

That evening, great honour, everyone who had not already left to camp for the summer at a few miles from the village offer us the famous drum dance. In their community centre, covered with wood veneer, really cheap-looking like a barracks, 300 residents with children and elders, accompanied by the fattest mosquitoes possible, slowly proceed

*with official presentations and gifts, and then with the dance. But the
most extraordinary is the unforgettable throat singing performed by old
toothless women, creating an echo by beating a large cauldron. Sensuous, animal, incredible. And the old women who giggle all the time!*

*While writing these lines, I note that as our health workers are
mostly women, as is the case for the local interpreters and all the aides
surrounding us, as is it is generally in the world of primary health care,
of midwives, it is with women that I can best communicate. To my great
surprise, they had all recognized me from television! I hear all sorts of
personal comments that open windows onto this culture where sexual
relations in families seem so "open" for us Westerners. When I ask a
woman who is her husband, and when the old woman points to a man,
then burst laughing and points to another one, and so on, and all the
women giggle ... Or when a young woman explains to us that the man
there she is pointing is at the same time her uncle, her brother, and whatever else! Girls often give birth at 13–15 years of age, and her parents,
as seems to be the custom, adopt the baby. Then the young mother may
marry the young father, or another man when she reaches age twenty.
Also several intermarriages seem happy; no racism here, as exists on Indian reserves.*

*We have a too short visit to the local coop. I love and have known
Inuit art since 1967 when I first arrived in Ottawa. Here the stone
sculptures do not really catch my attention but the prints are outstanding! Baker Lake has several extremely famous printmaking artists. One
of them, my favourite, is Jessie Oonark, whom I never met and is already 77.* [She would die two years later. Her life and pedigree were
then unknown to me. But I was chasing one of her tall colour prints
that I had discovered in a Vancouver Gallery and fell in love with: *Two
Birds Guard Sleeping Kiviiuk*, created and printed in 1981. It came
from Baker Lake and they had it in their catalogue but the local men
could not find the print when we were there. However, the Department's
Barry Brown later found me one, bought it for me, and had it shipped
to Ottawa!]

*The party is over by 10:30 p.m., in full sun! I fall asleep, always in
full sun, around midnight. Little children are still playing outside, while
the adult males are having a softball game. At 1 a.m., a siren signals to*

all that they must *go to bed. Nothing works: it will be full sun all night long. The howling dogs keep waking me up. The morning after, break-fast with Gordon Rae,* MLA *for Keewatin, a very pleasant young Lib-eral. And we leave for Spence Bay.*

Spence Bay is really in the middle of nowhere, the most desolated place possible. Panic and re-panic because of the endless vast space of land and sky. One of our nurses shows me a picture taken late May, just two months before this trip: impossible to distinguish between sky, land, and sea. Everything is white, without any visual cues. I am reminded of the cold solitude of some Jean-Paul Lemieux paintings. Slowly, however, Spence Bay is setting in and a charm works. Why and how? I don't know. But I become quite sensitive to this tiny community of 454 souls that makes handicrafts at the end of the world. They make miniature animal sculptures in narwhal ivory, whale bone, or caribou antlers, as well as a few traditional soapstone sculptures. But Spence Bay is known for its unique and famous packing-dolls from 100% duffel material: a 14" stuffed animal wearing the typical Inuit hand-embroidered parka, with its baby, dressed the same, coming out of the hood. We go back to childhood and buy some with great pleasure; I choose an Arctic hare. These are made by the women and it helped the community to survive when times were really bad. Their other sewing work is that of the gorgeous embroidered parkas they make, which at that time will sell in West Germany for $1,500 apiece! All this beauty mixed between tomato cans, Kleenex boxes, Carnation milk (a pint of milk is $5!).

Spence Bay is also a model of democracy in action. All the proce-dures are properly followed, everyone is recognized and can talk. They look stubborn (in a good sense), determined, clear, articulate in their demands. Between them and us, no animosity. Completely egalitarian and respectful on all sides. But, as an example, a vote at 52% is no good. They always look for a consensus of at least 80% and work at it until they get it. Several active women elected for different roles, older and younger. I will always have a soft spot for Spence. But we are lit-erally freezing ...

Then, the next stop is Igloolik on Baffin Island, 810 inhabitants, where we land at suppertime. We have no mitts, not even gloves, and

we freeze. Supper is the special of the local Coop chef: Yorkshire pud-
ding and roast beef, as in every official meal it seems, to honour us. But
the truth is that we were dreaming of Arctic char or other fish or
seafood ... I had to talk with our nurses and it was a drink at midnight.
Their life is so difficult. A young one there, 26, nice and friendly, is leav-
ing on her holidays for Nepal, but who will first walk the 100-mile trail
between Broughton Island and Pangnirtang. She is very revolted by all
that does not work in the system. She won't be able to stay long; she
will not accept it. That night, we will sleep in hospital beds in the health
personnel mobile trailers as there is no hotel of any kind. And that un-
interrupted sun for the last 48 hours ...

Traditional visit at the local Coop. As usual, the manager is a white
man. Superb polished, top quality, soapstone sculptures, some in an
exquisite soft green stone. And next to them, these new massive sculp-
tures of complex scenes of hideous neo-realism. Later, in meetings, I
observe that community, very formal, has already refused access to tele-
vision by the Anik *satellite three times. Igloolik is the most traditional*
settlement of the Arctic as far as I can make out, and I find it unbear-
able. I also leave with the impression that their young people do not
enjoy the atmosphere there.

I have no personal notes for our final stop, for a good reason. We
concluded this unique experience in Frobisher Bay because I had been
invited to open the Third General Assembly of the Inuit Circumpolar
Conference/Council (ICC), a major international NGO. Taking place in
what is now called Iqaluit (Frobisher Bay), the conference was scheduled from 25 to 31 July 1983. It was the first to take place in Canada,
with fifty-four delegates – eighteen from each member country: Alaska
(USA), Greenland, and Canada. Meeting officially in 1977 further to a
first meeting in 1973 in Copenhagen, the ICC was officially founded in
1980. Its General Assembly takes place every four years and holds Consultative Status II at the United Nations as of this 1983 Assembly.

Their early submission reads, "We Eskimo are an international community sharing common language, culture, and a common land along
the Arctic coast of Siberia, Alaska, Canada and Greenland. Although
not a nation-state, as a people, we do constitute a nation." Russia finally

joined the ICC through the special regional government of their easternmost peninsula in Asia: the Chukotka Peninsula (Siberia).

The theme of the Third General Assembly was "The Arctic: Our Common Responsibility." It was also the first meeting of the Inuit elders, who were celebrated with jubilation. Some thirty resolutions were debated and adopted, from the demilitarization of the Arctic to the recognition of their role in the Arctic environment management, energy conservation, their traditional hunting and fishing rights, and more. Several resolutions addressed to the governments of Canada, the United States, and Denmark requested that they be consulted, protected, or equal partners, depending on the issues at stake: communications systems, toxic waste dumps, and eventual nuclear or oil disasters. Finally, they voted to prepare a draft policy on Inuit educational approaches for their next such assembly. Impossible for me not to have privately observed that Canada wanted to affirm and maintain its sovereignty on the Arctic, which represented 40 per cent of its territory, on which 110,000 persons were then living, our government being particularly worried by climate change in the Northwest Passage.

The regional directors of the Medical Services Branch were open-minded and loved their work and the Aboriginal world. I can still picture George Campbell with warm feelings and admiration for his talent, a Cree from Norway House, who from regional director had become the director general of all our medical services. Or my ADM, Dr Lyall Black who, on his holidays every summer, went back to practise as a family doctor in PEI, to name only two of the civil servants of the Medical Services Branch. Years after I had left politics, I would consult and exchange with the current ADM, First Nations and Inuit Health Branch (at long last, a fitting branch identity), Ian Potter, who had joined the federal civil service from Saskatchewan probably around 1975–80, whom I admired and still do. Both when I chaired the Canadian Breast Cancer Research Initiative, where he represented Health Canada, and when I was a member of the WHO International Commission on Social Determinants of Health, I sought his advice and benefitted from his knowledge and wisdom. Nurse practitioners, non-Aboriginals, remarkably well-trained by Dalhousie, McMaster, and Blue Quills, delivered health services on reserves and Inuit communities in my time. The Dalhousie and McMaster post-graduate programs "died" for years basically because of opposition from our provincial medical associations, but also because the 1980s witnessed an Aboriginal rebellion against anyone (white) from the "South," especially these nurses.

I mentioned earlier our policy of gradual devolution of powers and responsibilities from Health and Welfare to First Nations. In 1979, under the short-lived government of Joe Clark, when I was the official National Health and Welfare critic in the Liberal Opposition, that "The Federal Indian Health Policy," which had been prepared in my time was presented and approved by Cabinet. Sometime before I took office in Health and Welfare, the department had realized that only Indian communities could change the root causes of their unacceptable poor health, and that full support by other Canadians was also required. So better health would be generated and maintained by the Indian communities themselves, hence the beginning of the devolution of health services directly to the bands. First steps were agreements negotiated one by one with the band councils, which then slowly took over 75 per cent of budgets and programs such as the Native Alcohol and Drug Abuse Program as well as the Community Health Representative Program. To start the process, a few pilot projects were designed, negotiated, and put into place. As with all births, it was difficult at times. Devolution also created local jobs on reserves for community public health activities. This had all been studied and discussed in consultations with all interested parties and by the Berger Commission (1980) and the House of Commons Special Committee (1983) in the Penner Report, our MP from the Cochrane-Superior riding, Keith Penner, having chaired this work. This devolution of services, budgets, and responsibilities was based upon three pillars: community development (reserves fighting the conditions of poverty and apathy); making the best of the traditional relationship of Indian people to the federal government; and linking the complex Canadian health system to better health on the reserves. That first step of devolution of health responsibilities culminated under the Mulroney government with the 1989 Health Transfer Policy Framework.

When the Liberals returned to power in early 1980, I had the opportunity and many occasions to meet and befriend the former Supreme

Court Justice Emmett Hall. Each time my work took me to Saskatoon, until his death in 1995 at age ninety-seven, I would see him. I also had the singular honour, in 1988, to receive an honorary doctorate from the University of Toronto, together with Justice Emmett Hall and Dr Fraser Mustard. Justice Hall remains known especially for two commissions of inquiry he chaired – one creating medicare (1964) and one on education in Ontario (1968) – although he chaired several more, all significant. I got to meet him later, after my successor David Crombie and the Conservative government of Joe Clark appointed him to conduct a follow-up inquiry into the current state of our health-care system. More on that in the next chapter.

In my last years in office, while sharing with Emmett Hall how discouraged I was with the slow progress of devolution of health programs to band councils, he told me about an initiative he had spearheaded in the early 1970s: federal grants and scholarships were awarded to Indians who wanted to study law in a Canadian university and become practising lawyers. Everyone close to government, even the general public, then observed the remarkable number of Aboriginal lawyers fighting for land claims settlements. That was Emmett Hall's making! This is how he gave me the idea of creating the First Nations and Inuit Health Careers Program (FNIHCP). The need for Aboriginal community health professionals on reserve was becoming acute and would only grow with the departure of white nurse practitioners, who were rejected on the political grounds of growing Indian autonomy. At one point, I brought the issue upfront at a major four-day conference of nurse practitioners on reserves as well as the department staff involved with these issues in Ottawa and those posted in the Yukon and the Northwest Territories. After I described the practical issues involved in devolution of health services and a possible timetable involved, I begged them not to resist the social change that they were living, which was not of their making at all, and instead to assist their communities in the passage towards self-governance in health. They were already faced with increasing local aggressiveness, which was politically motivated and understandable, but not deserved. After they came back south from the reserves and, later, from the Inuit communities, for decades they faced the fierce opposition of Canadian organized medicine, contrary to the attitudes in the United States, and were reduced to move to the United States or practise conventional nursing here at much lower pay.

The First Nations and Inuit Health Careers Program was developed in-house by the Medical Services Branch with the following objective: "Encourage and support Indian and Inuit participation in educational opportunities leading to professional careers in the health field and provide a learning environment designed to overcome many of the social and cultural barriers that currently inhibit the native student's educational achievement." The program would provide generous financial assistance in any of the health field professions offered by Canadian universities, tailored to the students' needs. The program was approved by Cabinet on 7 February 1984, one of my very last memos to Cabinet. Cabinet included in its decision the request for an evaluation before the budget renewal of 31 March 1987, and that evaluation was conducted under the Mulroney government in the fall of 1986.

When the program started on 4 July 1984, the Treasury Board had allotted $7.8 million for its first three years. Our Medical Services Branch then granted financial credits to five universities to develop these special programs. The branch also immediately hired ninety Aboriginal students for the summer to familiarize them with university health programs and encourage their future involvement. For the September 1984 academic registration, scholarships were allocated to the five first Aboriginal students. And I was leaving politics at the time with a sense of "mission accomplished."

My memory was that FNIHCP was my very last piece of legislation, in June 1984, but the Parliamentary Information and Research Services of the Library of Parliament could find no trace of such a bill tabled in the House of Commons. However, I have a copy of my presentation and discussion of this program as a witness at the House Standing Committee on Health, Welfare, and Social Affairs on 22 May 1984. I suppose that the lack of time on the legislative calendar in those last weeks of the Trudeau government made us choose a simple Cabinet decision instead of a bill to be introduced and passed. As far as I can judge, that will be the weakness of the program. I refer here to the quiet and repeated efforts of the Harper government to eliminate the program. It is hard to access any serious evaluation of today's needs for Aboriginal human resources. I can only observe that, over the last fifteen years, at meetings, conferences, and commissions, I have met and discussed with remarkable Aboriginal medical doctors, nurses, health administrators, and health researchers. And in 2000, with the creation of the Canadian Institutes of Health Research replacing the Medical Research Council, one of the thirteen institutes is the Institute of Aboriginal Peoples' Health. Its scientific director is Dr Carrie Bourassa, a Métis who belongs to the Riel Métis Council of Regina. Later, in the wake of the who International Commission on Social Determinants of Health, when Public Health Canada set up the six National Collaborating Centres (NCC) in 2005, one was the NCC for Aboriginal Health, at the University of Northern British Columbia, in Prince George. Its academic lead is Dr Margo Greenwood, of Cree ancestry, with a PhD in education, whose interests have always been Aboriginal child health, especially through early childhood education and children's rights.

If this chapter of my mandate as minister of health and welfare has any message to leave, it is one of hope. My only personal initiative was creation of the First Nations and Inuit Health Careers Program. What I did mainly was support a very capable Medical Services Branch. It makes all the difference in the world to see how much First Nations and Inuit Canadians have accomplished over the last three decades in health status. But I still feel terrible each time we learn of more suicides, especially of young people, on reserves or in settlements. I feel the same when hearing of more First Nations girls and young women murdered or going missing. We, the other Canadians, have a serious responsibility to do away with the "them" and "us" mentality and approach.

13

The Canada Health Act (1984)

It was 27 February 1979. A Tuesday. The day started at eight o'clock with a meeting of the Quebec Cabinet ministers. Then, as on every Tuesday, there was a work session with my deputy minister, Bruce Rawson, and one or more senior officials. Towards the end of the morning, I was surprised to receive a phone call from Dennis Timbrell, the Ontario minister of health. That call stuck in my memory. On the other end of the line was one of the most senior ministers of Canada's largest province. And he was worried about my reaction if he were to institute a user fee of $9.80 per day for each chronically ill person, usually seniors, after their sixty-first day of hospitalization. It was an unusual call; provincial ministers did not usually check their projects with the federal minister. I asked myself, "What does that fee for Ontarians have to do with me?"

Dennis Timbrell was a young, bright, self-assured (not to mention arrogant) Conservative minister of Premier Bill Davis and was already a seasoned politician. At my first meeting of federal-provincial health ministers, long before we had had any disagreements, Timbrell, in front of his provincial counterparts, presented me with a T-shirt printed with his little welcome speech: "Minister, you will learn that in federal-provincial conferences, Ontario decides and the others follow!"

I had no idea at the time that this simple phone call in 1979 would be the beginning of over five years of more or less uninterrupted negative, and then very unpleasant, mostly public interactions between the provincial health ministers and me, the federal minister, about our health-care system. I had no idea that it would turn into serious accusations from the provinces, followed by vicious public comments about how stubborn I was – actions supported and amplified by the powerful medical establishment and other key health-care actors. And yet on 9 April 1984, five years later, just after Trudeau had announced his departure, the House of Commons would vote to approve Bill C-3, the new Canada Health Act. Unanimously! How did all this come about?

Though I had been minister of national health and welfare since September 1977, nearly a year and a half before Timbrell phoned me, I knew almost nothing about medicare, as our health-care system is called, and for good reason. My predecessor, Marc Lalonde, had just accomplished a major restructuring of the way the federal financial share of provincial health-care costs would be paid. That restructuring changed, and in fact abolished, the daily working relationships between federal civil servants and their provincial counterparts who administered the original concept of 50:50 joint funding. We now had a new, simple annual financial book transfer for health between ministers of finance and their officials. The results – referred to as "block funding" – of these four years of high-level negotiations, involving Trudeau, Don Macdonald as minister of finance, and Marc Lalonde as minister of health, had been applauded by all parties. The feds were thrilled, because they could now plan ahead for their fiscal health-care expenditures. The provinces loved it because they were getting more autonomy. They would no longer have federal civil servants to answer to on their purchases or health-care initiatives, so they felt free to spend on health care as they wished.

I was a brand-new minister in National Revenue when that legislation came to Cabinet for approval: the Federal-Provincial Fiscal Arrangements and Established Programs Financing Act (EPF). I had not understood a word of that document, which was tabled by Finance. What a surprise it would be for me later, during the worst years of the medicare crisis, to witness senior economic Cabinet colleagues – I can still hear Bob Andras – admitting spontaneously that they had not understood what that proposed legislation was about either. I was obviously not the only one. We had all trusted the word of Trudeau,

Macdonald, and Lalonde: everything was fine! The EPF bill was passed by Parliament on 31 March 1977; it came into effect on 1 July of that year, two and a half months before I was to become minister of health.

In the department the general attitude was that I did not need to worry about or be briefed on the health-care system: "Things on the health side are now just fine" was repeated often and in good faith. There were regular and numerous health issues in which I would be involved, which I studied, questioned, and eventually supported. They originated with or belonged to branches such as Aboriginal health (under the Medical Services Branch), or critical issues under the Food and Drug Act, such as banning urea-formaldehyde foam insulation and controlling blood and blood products, which fell under the Health Protection Branch, or tobacco control and healthy lifestyles, which were covered by the Health Services and Promotion Branch. It was this last branch that was above all responsible for the health-care system: medicare.

But even more than that odd telephone call from Dennis Timbrell, questions in Queen's Park and in the House of Commons the following day aroused my suspicions that something serious was happening. A week later, on 9 March, New Democratic Party leader Ed Broadbent started the day by directing questions on the health-care system to the prime minister: "Considering that the countless doctors in Ontario currently withdrawing in massive numbers from OHIP [the Ontario Health Insurance Plan] are forcing increases in their charges from 25% to 30% above OHIP rates and beginning virtually to destroy the universality of medicare, would the right honourable gentleman tell the House what the government plans to do to preserve this essential service in Canada's largest province?" Trudeau replied, "The medicare plan ... is founded on the principle of universality and accessibility. If anything is done by any province to depart from that principle, we would have to review the very high payment the federal government is making to the province in respect of half the cost of medicare."

I had read the newspapers, as usual, but they had not given me any idea of the magnitude of the situation as described by Broadbent. In addition, in itself a signal of trouble, questions regarding medicare should have been asked by the NDP health critic to the minister of health, as

would be done in the days following. I received only vague, general answers to offer as department officials – the deputy minister, Bruce Rawson, and the assistant deputy minister for medicare, Dr Maureen Law
– kept reassuring me that there was not really a problem. I had to trust
them, but the situation did not make any sense to me. The next day, the
president of the Alberta Medical Association, Dr Robert Clarke, stated
that Trudeau was clearly intimidating the provinces in the hope that
they would intimidate the doctors. What was going on? On 19 March
the Canadian Medical Association (CMA) got its views out: "Doctors
right across the country see themselves as political pawns ... Doctor-
bashing has become as prevalent as violence in hockey." That is when
I learned the term *extra billing*, which I had never heard before. So we
now had extra billing by doctors and user fees by hospitals.

I had no bone to pick with doctors and had always greatly enjoyed
working with the medical research sector. I found myself, as I thought
at first, unfairly accused. Clearly it was a delicate subject. I decided to
figure out whether there was a real problem, as appearances seemed to
suggest, and if it was in my jurisdiction, or whether to dismiss the whole
matter as a red herring.

A word of explanation is in order here about Canadian medicare –
not to be confused with Medicare with a capital *M* south of the border:
their federal health insurance program for almost all US seniors aged
sixty-five and over. Here is a summary of what our system was all about,
and the political environment against which this would unfold.

Between 1958 and 1961 Canadians learned that being hospitalized
was no longer an expensive, often prohibitive, out-of-pocket item in
any family budget but was becoming "free," or prepaid by general
taxation. This happened with the passage of the federal Hospital
Insurance and Diagnostic Services Act (1957) under Prime Minister
Louis St-Laurent, thanks to the leadership of Paul Martin Sr as minister
of national health and welfare. Ten years later, between 1966 and 1971,
Canadians learned that visiting their family physician or specialist was
also becoming "free." The legislation passed to accomplish this was the
Medical Care Act (1966), pushed by Allan J. MacEachen, then minister
of national health and welfare, under Lester B. Pearson as prime

minister. The minister of finance, Mitchell Sharp, then extended its implementation by one year, to 1967. Both pieces of legislation had taken a few years for all provinces to sign in. It would be up to Pierre Trudeau, the newly elected prime minister, to sign the royal assent in July 1968 that finalized the Medical Care Act.

The situation was simple. Health care at the time was about doctors' visits and hospital stays – although, from the start, Tommy Douglas, premier of Saskatchewan and "the father of medicare," explained that these two components were only the first two steps of his ideal comprehensive system. Who paid whom for what was also simple: half came from the feds and half from the province. Throughout the year, provincial ministers of health sent bills to the federal Department of Health and Welfare justifying the cost of new beds, equipment, renovations, and so on, although they needed approval from National Health and Welfare for construction of a new hospital or hospital wing. When the bills arrived in Ottawa, after being audited, a cheque for half the amount spent was sent to the provincial minister of health. Quebec was the exception, as it had finally agreed to participate on condition that it would receive the value of the cash equivalent in tax points moved from federal finances to the province's finances. The public also learned of the four boundaries of our original "medicare." What was not yet covered were ambulances, drugs outside hospital, dentists, and optometrists. Canadians also knew that some of these "outside medicare" costs could be covered provincially for welfare recipients, seniors, or children up to age twelve, depending on one's province of residence and what additional programs it offered.

The two federal shared-costs health programs required provinces to respect four general conditions of the legislation:

1 universality (covering 90–95 per cent of people in a province, with identical conditions for all);
2 comprehensiveness (of medical services);
3 portability (between provinces and, to a certain extent, to other countries); and
4 not-for-profit public administration.

The agreements with each province were exceptionally detailed and precise. Yet the Canadian system was not one national integrated system. It was the sum of ten provincial plans and two (at the time) territorial plans that had the same basic standards and characteristics, while respecting regional differences.

The rigid and costly bureaucratic federal cost-control system over the provinces, and the built-in unwanted incentives leading provinces to build new hospitals instead of developing outpatient clinics, are only two examples of the reasons for changing the shared-costs programs system to what became the block-funding system, which is still in place today. It started as a somehow behind-the-scenes federal objective for a good ten years before it became a concrete set of negotiations that were finally approved in a joint general federal-provincial government euphoria in 1977. All this being said, the famous Federal-Provincial Fiscal Arrangements and Established Programs Financing Act (EPF) also covered post-secondary education, but I am not familiar with its terms and conditions as applied to universities and colleges. Both parts of the EPF were to be renegotiated with the provinces every five years.

So what exactly was the situation in federal-provincial financial participation in medicare, and what was the economic and political situation at the time? In March 1979 Pierre Trudeau's government was already an old government that had not renewed itself much. It first took office in 1968, then in 1972 for eighteen months; now, in July 1974, the Liberals had been in power for four and a half years, with a rather disappointing record of economic management. In the spring of 1978 Trudeau surprised everyone by refusing to take our political advisers' recommendation to call the election then, as the polls were naming us the winners. In Cabinet work we found lots of reasons to stall decisions, putting this or that dossier off for the future – for example, not releasing the key Lazar report on private pension plan problems, because we were terrified at the thought that it might upset the business community. We would take this or that decision upon our return to office, we thought, for we assumed our government would be re-elected. The election would be fought over the economy, but even after the Bonn Economic Summit and despite major cuts to federal departments and programs, we were drifting. Then, on Monday, 26 March 1979, without warning, the prime minister called the election.

The morning after, at my request, we had a long brainstorming session on medicare in my office. Like me, my immediate political staff found the situation unclear. With my top civil servants (Bruce Rawson, Dr Maureen Law and Mike Murphy), we were trying to make headway. I saw once more that there was strong resistance from my department to acknowledge a problem and an inability to propose a plan of action. My political staff and I started to figure out a few things. A few days earlier we had learned that the billions of federal dollars were paid monthly to the provincial ministers of finance only if the province adhered to the four basic conditions that had existed since the 1960s. These EPF payments by federal bureaucrats to the provinces were now quasi-automatic, and no form or letter needed to be signed by the minister. I had never heard a word of this or seen any document about it.

When one of my political staff tried to get more detailed information on the situation, the senior department officials gave us news clippings, which was quite unlike them. The reason slowly surfaced: the department was uninformed about extra billing by physicians and specialists or user fees in the provinces. To the credit of my deputy minister, Bruce Rawson, as he was the DM of social affairs and not of health care (which was then under a separate DM, when he joined the department under Marc Lalonde), he had probably not been privy to the EPF negotiations. The newspapers had been my source, which was normal, but were they also the source for my department? Who? What exactly? Where? and How much? were questions without answers. I learned that for the past two years, no information on health insurance, statistical or otherwise, had been exchanged between provincial and federal governments.

Amid my disbelief and impatience, I finally also learned, long after the beginning of the crisis in 1979, that the section of my department that had dealt daily, for at least fifteen years, by letter, phone, and in person by visiting their counterparts in the provinces to approve financial payments – and this was up until the new federal EPF Act in March 1977 – had dropped from about 200 civil servants to 12, including sec-

retaries. My political staff and I also found that the regulations following the EPF Act had never been drafted, let alone negotiated and
adopted, nor had guidelines been developed. So, for example, we were
not sure whether these extra billings and user fees contravened the law,
which provided for universal access for all, because there was no operational definition.

I told my deputy minister what I had just announced in the House
during the last question period: that we would immediately start developing the four basic conditions of health insurance into operational
proposals. This should be done as quickly as possible. It seemed a reasonable approach to me: before turning an Act upside down, let us
explore the implications. I took for granted at the time that the Act had
been well drafted and that only its regulations had not been developed.
Trudeau, Macdonald, and Lalonde knew their business. In the meantime, I would stick to the fundamental philosophy of the system: no
financial barrier should hinder access to health care. And I would do
everything I could not to bring medicare into the election campaign.

But I could not control this latter point. The debate was already off
and running. In New Brunswick, Premier Richard Hatfield had announced user fees just two days after our election was called. I sent him
a telegram requesting details, but he never replied. At the same time,
Ontario announced an increase in its health premium, a special tax that
had existed for some years in Alberta and British Columbia – not acceptable for free universal and accessible medicare services, but of
provincial jurisdiction.

From the start of the 1979 campaign, questions whizzed from all
sides, and reporters all over the country did their usual best to trip up
members of the government on an election campaign. Since a national
caucus meeting was not possible, I decided to give a speech outlining
the official Liberal position. As it happened, I had been invited to address the annual meeting of the Canadian Nurses' Association in Ottawa on 29 March, three days after the election was called. I did not
give an impassioned speech that day but simply stated strongly that
medicare was here to stay, that the 1977 Act was a good one, and that
the rules of the game, once clarified, would be fully enforced. No details,

no finger pointing. The ballroom of the Skyline Hotel was packed, and the nurses applauded the federal position wholeheartedly. I was to repeat the main themes of this speech throughout the two-month campaign, from Newfoundland to British Columbia.

I still remember that campaign as a long, draining, confused, and unfocused exercise. I crisscrossed the country as usual at the party's request to help some of our candidates, opening our department's new "one-stop offices" offering all our social programs and services under one roof, visiting New Horizons projects for seniors, discussing the pension reforms already in the air, and inevitably answering questions on the state of our health-care system. Public reaction was very positive when I touched on the health-care situation.

Overall, however, the campaign was awful. At a certain point, I could not stand the atmosphere anymore. Fed up, and without a word to anyone, almost three weeks into the two-month campaign, I took an Air Canada flight to Paris for the Easter long weekend, returning home four days later. As ministers got free first-class seats, I recognized René Lévesque in the Maple Leaf Lounge. I quickly explained my awkward situation to the desk, asking for their help. The staff pre-boarded me, assigning me a first-row window seat and protecting my space. I remained nervous until the plane took off. What a potential scandal I escaped in the middle of a difficult election! Those few days alone in Paris were peaceful, as I visited two good friends and otherwise just walked, getting back to my inner self.

In early May the department informed me that they now had more accurate information. They had discovered that in Ontario and New Brunswick, the provincial share of the health-care budget "had decreased from the customary 50 per cent to, in Ontario, for example, 36.8 per cent, representing substantial cuts to their health-care system." The DM and Rick Van Loon, one of his advisors (the successful future president of Carleton University), wrote me notes for the press conference: I was in Fredericton on 8 May, two weeks before voting day, speaking to the media. I was sure that I was on solid ground at long last. I did the same in Toronto the following week, accompanied by Dr Van Loon, who could answer more technical questions. For my speeches and interviews, he and the department had coined the expression "diversion of funds," with strong images like "Money from health care is now invested in roads or anything else but health care." It was a powerful accusation, which I repeated, convinced that my DM's office had fully mastered these statements written for me.

It was powerful – but completely false. In addition, it was my big strategic mistake to have accused New Brunswick, a poor, defenceless Maritime province, and that accusation worked against me. I also learned once and for all that nothing is more unproductive in Canada than number wars between the two levels of government. The voters were trying to figure out whose leadership would be best for the economy – old Pierre Trudeau or young Joe Clark – while the federal minister of health spent her time attacking the provinces! Worse, my accusations were unfounded. In fact, they were erroneous, and the provinces felt they were right to accuse me of bad faith. The two dossiers that my department put together on the New Brunswick and Ontario situations contained major errors and statistical interpretations that would backfire. These days, it seems acceptable for the public and politicians to criticize and distrust bureaucrats. I feel differently. The civil servants in my department were always competent, conscientious, and concerned about the public they served. After evaluating me and figuring out my interest and concerns, they quickly took me in and stood solidly behind the work we did together. The incident I described above was an isolated one, but with negative consequences of unexpected proportions. I shall never forget or forgive it.

Unfortunately, it became impossible to correct what had been said. In the eyes of the provinces, my accusation of provincial diversion of funds from medicare to, say, roads infrastructure was obviously done in bad faith, on grossly rhetorical partisan grounds, and was pure nonsense for them: the 50:50 rule no longer existed, as the new 1977 block-funding agreement had replaced it. After 1977 the provinces would be told by Finance annually what their federal contribution would be; it was up to them to decide how much more they would put into their health-care system. In theory, the provinces could have devoted only the federal share to their health-care system.

There was no way for me to have read the thousands of pages of minutes of the federal-provincial negotiations from 1971 to 1977, or the EPF Act; I had to rely on senior officials of my department to brief me on the topic. Of course, before this "diversion of funds" accusation, I had trusted them. I finally learned of the detailed functioning of block funding long after that election campaign by probing and probing during departmental meetings. This would be much later – in fact, after we were back in government, in 1980, for on 22 May 1979 we had fallen from 141 Liberal MPs to 114, and I was now a simple member of the Opposition, although I had been re-elected with a majority of 40,480 votes over my closest opponent – the largest majority in Canada. Of course I had been named Opposition Health and Welfare critic. The new minority government was sworn in on 4 June, but Joe Clark didn't convene the Houses until 9 October. The likeable former mayor of Toronto, David Crombie, became the Health and Welfare minister. The political atmosphere in the country remained tense.

These events meant that for 226 consecutive days in 1979, or around seven months, the House of Commons did not sit. After Clark's victory, it was as if nothing was happening on the Liberal side, except for a long, hot, lazy, and empty summer. Luck was once more on my side when I needed it. At the end of June a phone call from the Prime Minister's Office invited me to accompany Walter Dinsdale, a former minister in the Diefenbaker Cabinet and a former social worker with the Brandon (Manitoba) Salvation Army, who was known for his life's work for people with disabilities, to the Third International Conference of Rehabilitation Engineering Centres in Poznan, Poland. The conference would take place at the Institute of Orthopaedic Surgery and Rehabilitation. The Poles had insisted that it was I they wanted, although I was by then a member of the Opposition. Dr Marian Sliwinski, a cardiologist and Poland's minister of national health and social welfare since 1972, had insisted on my presence. He was a strong and lively personality – a hard-line Communist since his youth, as he had told me when I welcomed him on his visit to Canada in February 1978. He wanted to offer me a grand tour of his country, starting with his chief of staff and English interpreter, Lidia Rytkowska, an elegant and determined lawyer. He would then join us in Kracow for the last part of the trip.

There I met remarkable experts from Poland and other European countries during the five days of the conference: Dr Lesrek Klimaszewski (from Gdansk), Prof. Senghor and Dr Marian Weiss, as well as the Drs Dega, the father and mother of rehabilitation treatment in Poland. I also enjoyed meeting Dr Paul Dollfus, the medical director of the Centre de rééducation of Mulhouse, France. Minister Sliwinski had organized one more week across Poland for me and Walter Dinsdale, who repeated how lucky he was to have found himself in Poland with the Opposition! We were there for twelve full days.

As our Canadian party of two with Lidia Rytkowska left Poznan by car for Gdansk-Gdynia-Sopot, three neighbouring cities on the Baltic Sea, something strange happened. We were invited for an official dinner aboard a huge ship being built in the Gdynia shipyard, where shipyard workers who spoke among themselves, all in Polish, served us a wonderful meal. I had been informed at the last minute that I would be joining Walter Dinsdale on this trip and had not had time to read anything on Poland. But the workers' behaviour that evening made me suspect that there was something in the wind for Poland's workers – I had perceived a subtle air of rebellion. Poland made the headlines a year later with the uprising of Solidarity, *Solidarność,* the workers' movement. (I am known for having good intuition, but I am not psychic! I didn't tell anyone at the time about my suspicions. In his *Up the Hill* memoirs, my Cabinet colleague Donald Johnston refers to three situations where I told him ahead of time what would happen – and it did happen.) This first attempt to protect the rights of the workers rapidly became the beginning of the fall of communism in Central Europe.

I will always remember what I heard, observed, and lived in that car trip through Poland – my first communist country: the shockingly good life of the medical and political elites thanks to the *nomenklatura,* in sharp contrast with the daily misery of the people: lack of food, empty stores or with one shoe instead of two in shoeboxes, and the attempts to fool foreign visitors. The charming and comfortable dacha of Dr Marian Weiss, in a forest not far from Poznan, contained bottles of every type of alcohol to offer his hosts, as well as various delicacies, with everything served on fine china or in crystal glasses.

Besides my trip to Poland, the summer was quiet, except for the controversy about Joe Clark moving the Canadian Embassy to Jerusalem in Israel. The only event I remember is the Forty-Eighth Annual Conference of Public Affairs, held in August at Lake Couchiching: the theme was "Institutions in Crisis." The active presence of philosopher Ivan Illich and theologian Gregory Baum stimulated the exchanges. The plenary session on medicine, doctors, and hospitals was spirited. As a panellist, I insisted on the provinces' responsibility for safeguarding comprehensive health insurance by attacking its serious erosion.

On 17 September 1979, after the shortest federal-provincial meeting in history, David Crombie suddenly announced that he had given Mr Justice Emmett Hall the mandate to investigate and report on the state of the health-care system and to make recommendations for improvements. It was a clever move by Crombie, giving himself at least a year of breathing space. That fall, in early November, I attended the kickoff conference in Montreal of the first national public coalition, s o s Medicare, under the leadership of Jim MacDonald of the Canadian Labour Congress. Present also were Tommy Douglas, David Crombie, and Justice Hall. This was to become the Canadian Health Coalition, which defended medicare for decades afterwards. Around the same time, I also met Dr Michael Rachlis, who had created Friends of Medicare.

Then, on 13 December, the Conservatives were defeated on the Crosbie budget and we found ourselves back into an election with no leader. Trudeau had resigned the month before. We succeeded in bringing him back and started working on the election policy platform. The policy committee that Roméo LeBlanc and I co-chaired during the Clark government recommended to the election strategists, Keith Davey and Jim Coutts, that the consolidation of medicare be included in our platform. However, only pension reform would become a key Liberal proposal. On 18 February 1980 Trudeau won a majority government, and on 3 March (by telephone – I was in Mexico) he reappointed me to my old Department of Health and Welfare, to my delight.

I met my new deputy minister, Pamela McDougall (appointed by Joe Clark), who would soon be replaced by Larry Fry, to my relief. I got reacquainted with department officials, leaving politics at the door. In a pragmatic way, I simply stated that the department would no longer study how to terminate the family allowances program, and I put an end to other changes in orientation. All this went very smoothly. Meanwhile, Justice Hall was conducting his public hearings. In time, I would get involved in topics other than medicare, such as our new policy of devolution of health services to First Nations and Inuit communities. But at first, most of my time would be devoted to the first Quebec referendum for sovereignty association, participating in meetings of Les Yvettes, the spontaneous women's grassroots movement rallying for the "No" side. That made me more of an enemy in the eyes of the separatists. I was crisscrossing the province of Quebec while continuing my parliamentary and ministerial work in Ottawa as best I could. By 1 June I was finally able to devote all my time to the Department.

In 1979–80 all the provinces except two had Conservative governments. Quebec was under the separatist government of René Lévesque, with Dr Denis Lazure, a psychiatrist and true left-wing social democrat who admired China, as health minister. Lazure agreed with me completely but attacked me viciously in public. Saskatchewan had an NDP government. Its minister of health, Herman Rolfes, had been the minister of social affairs during the negotiations to replace the old 50:50 payments with block funding. He had agreed to the system with great reluctance and continued to distrust it, he told me repeatedly. Officially, he had to be against me, he explained to me, as he was being watched by his Inter-Governmental Affairs minister. The other provincial ministers of health (all Conservatives, with one Social Credit in British Columbia) were, like me, newcomers to the portfolio: they had never worked under the 50:50 cost-sharing system. With time, some confided to me that they no longer knew the figure of the monthly federal health cheque sent by my department to their provincial treasurer. They also did not know the value of the tax points they received, as they were not informed by their own Finance Department. They told me how they felt being at the bottom of the invisible ladder of power of their respective Cabinets, deprived of any bargaining power. I listened with empathy but had never felt I was in the same position in Ottawa. Slowly and cautiously at first, then openly and without apology, but never criticizing a Cabinet colleague, I had begun to define my own position on the meaning of a "Just Society." For me it was a matter of common sense, but in those years of monetarist economic theory, some contemptuous colleagues in the caucus or Cabinet often saw me as fighting a rearguard action. It was a very uncomfortable feeling to be like the opposition from within.

There was no action from the feds on the medicare front. On 11 June I was the speaker in Toronto at the 100th anniversary of the Ontario Medical Association – a time to celebrate, more than anything else. We were all awaiting Justice Emmett Hall's report and recommendations. My assistant deputy minister for medicare, Dr Maureen Law, and her team had mentioned to me that she wondered if he was up to the job due to his age (he was then eighty-two) and health, suggesting that his memory was failing. I had seen him in Montreal the summer before at the SOS Medicare conference and did not think there was any problem. Without a word, I decided to go and see for myself very informally, which I did when I was in Saskatchewan early in June. I was most impressed by him. I met him again in Saskatoon on 21 July. In the meantime, Trudeau had launched the constitutional reform project. On 9 September the federal-provincial conference was devoted to family law and integrated tribunals issues. I had to be there.

While awaiting Justice Hall's report, a year and a half since the start of the medicare "crisis," the problem was still undefined. There was, however, no shortage of indicators of a problem:

- The Ontario Medical Association was very angry at receiving from Dennis Timbrell only a 6.25 per cent increase when the consumer price index was at 9.5 per cent.
- Of the 14,000 Ontario doctors, 17.9 per cent had opted out of OHIP.
- In April 1979 Ontario had announced a daily user fee for the chronically ill in hospitals.
- Also in April, Ontario announced an increase of 5.3 per cent in OHIP premiums.
- The Manitoba Medical Association settled with an 8.1 per cent increase in its fee schedule for the year.
- In Prince Edward Island, doctors opted out en masse for six months, agreeing to reaffiliate with provincial medicare once

a quasi-automatic system of extra billing patients had been instituted.

- In May 1979 New Brunswick approved a bill imposing user fees: $6 per outpatient visit, $10 for admission, and $8.50 per day in hospital.
- Half of Alberta's doctors and specialists extra-billed their patients. During their negotiations with the province, the Alberta Medical Association (AMA) asked for a 37 per cent increase. The minister, Dave Russell, then talked of legislation banning extra billing.
- During Justice Hall's public hearings in Edmonton, the AMA raised the spectre of a doctors' strike for the first time.
- The CMA made much of the fact that extra billing by doctors represented only 2 per cent of their total fees, which many people considered reasonable, according to the CMA.

I had determined that medicare as an institution was a fragile equilibrium between three parties: physicians (organized medicine), the federal government, and the provincial and territorial governments. They could each block the smooth functioning of the health-care system, but none could take control of it. This delicate equilibrium had to be constantly renegotiated. Despite the above list of negative situations, it was hard to figure out what side the provincial governments were really on. The issue had been completely politicized through two general elections and had turned highly partisan.

Justice Hall's report was released to everyone at the same time, by personal delivery, the day he tabled it on 3 September 1980. Now that I was back in my old job, I accompanied him to the National Press Gallery. The report was very clear. The federal government and its minister had been wrong: there had been no "diversion" of federal funds. Extra billing by doctors was unacceptable. Equally unacceptable were the premiums charged by three of the provinces, and the user fees in most provinces. At the same time, Justice Hall opened three new fronts: in case of a stalemate in negotiations between doctors and their provincial government, binding arbitration should be instituted. Immediate action should be taken to reduce the enrolment in faculties of medicine, as there were too many doctors. And finally, the poorer provinces, especially the four Atlantic provinces, should receive extra money from the federal government. At long last, a famous expert, also one of the founding fathers of medicare (through the Hall report under Diefenbaker and then Pearson), had taken a clear position on the issues. We should have been able to act on the recommendations quickly. As it turned out, at least two long years would go by, during which time the federal government's position was never clear.

My department officials were pleased with Justice Hall's report. I was very satisfied as well. We concluded that the first thing to do was to hold a federal-provincial conference, with Emmett Hall as our guest. A meeting was set for 29 September in Winnipeg, where the provincial ministers were having their annual conference. The intervening three weeks gave me a sense of what would be one of the most unpleasant federal-provincial conferences I ever attended, matched only by the 1983 Halifax conference. In the meantime, provincial ministers, national and provincial medical associations, and individual physicians from across the country kept giving partisan interviews for or against, making warlike statements and threats. On the whole, however, the response was rather confused. I still hoped that when we were together, in camera, we could come to an agreement. We were all in it together; we had all been singled out in the report. The future of medicare was what counted now.

The meeting last barely half a day, and the only scenario I had not envisioned happened: Justice Hall was ridiculed, and several ministers laughed in his face, completely rejecting his report and recommendations. They would not be the only ones. Later, the *Ottawa Citizen* reported that some doctors had answered the report by saying, "This country does not need to listen to the report of a man with one foot in the grave." Several provincial ministers attacked me outright – in particular, Dennis Timbrell (Ontario), Denis Lazure (Quebec), Brenda Robertson (New Brunswick), and Rafe Mair (BC). This was the first time I had met most of them, as I had mainly worked with the provincial ministers of social affairs who, in eight of the provinces, were different from the health ministers. This meeting poisoned relationships right off the bat.

The two Opposition parties in Ottawa responded well to the report: for the Conservatives, former minister David Crombie (who had appointed Justice Hall) and Jim McGrath (my new shadow Cabinet counterpart), and for the NDP, Bill Blaikie. In that 1980 election, the Créditistes had been forever wiped out from the federal scene. My two Opposition counterparts gave numerous interviews. In general, health professionals other than physicians – nurses, hospital administrators, and others – were satisfied with Justice Hall's report. As for the CMA, it had begun a study of the possible unionization of doctors. Its outgoing president, Dr Larry Wilson, condemned the Hall report, while the new president, Dr W. Thomas, encouraged doctors to take overt political action. War had been declared by organized medicine.

It could not have come at a worse time. The federal Liberals, at the time of the Hall report release, were doing pretty well at 50 per cent in the polls. The 1980 Quebec referendum had just been won by the federalist forces. The idea of repatriating the Canadian Constitution had created a climate of good faith and generosity throughout the country.

For Trudeau, repatriation was the only issue that counted. It was truly the dream of his life. The resolution for repatriating the Constitution was tabled in the House of Commons on 6 October 1980, a month after the Hall report was released. With its ups and downs, successes and dramas, this fundamental question for a nation, together with the Charter of Rights and Freedoms, would stay in the limelight until Queen Elizabeth II signed the documents in Ottawa on 17 April 1982. But although the first year of the Constitution debate had been more or less in the federal government's favour, provincial governments were soon in conflict with Ottawa as much over constitutional issues as over Marc Lalonde's national energy program and Allan MacEachen's budget, both of which were announced on 28 October 1980.

With hindsight, I can see that my problems with medicare were not on the government agenda at that point. It had a very busy agenda tuned to totally different questions, starting with the constitutional dossiers. More dossiers had been given priority in the meantime – the issue of private pension plan reform, pushed by Finance, supported by the Privy Council and that I co-chaired with MacEachen, being one of them. It would be the first conference of this kind, with everyone involved in the issue present and participating: the pension industry, business, academic experts, union leaders, employers, and women's associations. The first three months of 1981 saw me much involved in preparing this dossier. Prime Minister Trudeau opened it formally in the Conference Centre in Ottawa on 31 March. It continued until 2 April, as discussed in chapter 10. So, besides not having a clear critical path to consolidate medicare, all I could do was to keep track of events at the provincial level. I met some provincial health ministers on a one-to-one basis, at their invitation. Two weeks before, on 17 March, the Cabinet Committee of Priorities and Planning, which was always chaired by the prime minister (I, although the biggest spender, was not a member), had set up a parliamentary task force on the Established Programs Financing Act (EPF), to be chaired by Herb Breau. Then came the summer of 1981, with its potent combination of high unemployment and high inflation, the long postal strike, and interest rates above 20 per cent.

On 17 July of that year, the House of Commons adjourned for a three-month recess, to reconvene on 14 October. Just before the vexatious trip to Spain that October, as chronicled in chapter 10, I had, again out of the blue, been asked by External Affairs in the name of the prime minister to pay a visit to the Ivory Coast president, Félix Houphouët-Boigny, to deliver to him an important personal letter. That trip would take place on 5–11 September. At the time I was in the midst of pensions issues and involved with the provincial ministers of health as the result of my opposition to extra billing and user fees. This invitation was like a great holiday and my first trip to Africa south of the Maghreb. (During the 1980–81 Christmas holidays, while going to spend a personal short week with a friend at the seashore in Morocco, my time in the sun had turned into two weeks of a ministerial tour and role when our Canadian ambassador, Gilles Duguay, "kidnapped" me on my arrival,

at the door of the plane from Canada, even though I had not told anyone of this trip.)

What a pleasure it was to be met at the plane in Abidjan late that evening by our ambassador, Ernest Hébert, and his wife, Ellis. Ernest had become a good friend when he was the diplomat in charge of the UN Fourth Committee, to which I had been assigned for the entire 1973 session when I was a new MP. The morning after our arrival on Sunday, 6 September, Ernest took us (with me was Anita Biguzs, my political staff member) by car to the lakeside Laguna town of Tiagba, greeted upon landing by the entire village with loud dances, songs, and flowers. Strangely, I felt completely comfortable right away, although I had not yet been briefed at all. Well, people are people, everywhere! The day after, in Abidjan, we visited hospitals, including the University Hospital of Treichville, a populous suburb. It would remain for me an experience of true culture shock: the poverty, the lack of basic hospital resources, the horror of tropical diseases, especially in Africa – in particular, the numerous children fighting Burkitt lymphoma (an endemic cancer of children who have malaria). Then, on 8 September, I was received by the president himself. Seventy-six years old at the time, he was called "the Grand Old Man" – amiable and authoritarian. I presented Trudeau's letter to him. Houphouët-Boigny had been the father of Ivory Coast independence in 1960 and would remain in office until his death in 1993. Two years after our visit, he moved the capital city from Abidjan to Yamoussoukro, his village birthplace, where we visited the palace and gardens (and caimans surrounding the palace fences) that he had already ordered to be built. In the evening we were received at a magnificent banquet given by the minister of health, Lazeni Coulibaly, which was also attended by the minister of finance (the Canadian International Development Agency was at long last investing in realistic development projects). I met and spoke with Jeanne Gervais, minister of the status of women. Then we crossed the country towards the north with multiple stops: Bouaké, Korhogo, and Fakaha (and its beautiful paintings on cloth made by the men), and the next village of Waraniéné (with the men who were master weavers).

The highlight of the trip was the day I officially opened a few of the eighty brand-new wells paid for by CIDA – not a big investment, but one that offered profound benefits for the life and health of the villages, especially the women and their children. The ceremony was followed by the wildest outdoor party I have ever attended, in the village of Napiéoledougou. We were in Senoufo country, at the time a tight-knit network of communities, animists who were famous for their handicrafts. Only photographs can depict the dances of children disguised as animals, the food, the songs, with children overlooking us, perched in every tree, hundreds and hundreds of people dancing together, Anita, Ernest, Ellis and me included. I made a speech and received gifts – a grand robe and a live animal (a goat?), which our ambassador put in the trunk of his car as if he had been doing so all his life.

Back home I did not know more than before what to do about medicare. Under the Constitution, the feds could not ban extra billing by individual doctors, nor could they ban hospital and other user fees – all of which were surcharges of clearly provincial jurisdiction. On the other hand, the issue of medicare would not die on its own; the fact that it was constantly fed by the NDP, some Liberal members in several provinces, some committed reporters or the media in general, and groups that had submitted briefs to the Justice Hall hearings kept the matter at the forefront. I could not plead ignorance, having been reappointed by Trudeau to the same portfolio. What I really missed during those two long years were free-flowing, in-depth discussions with my peers: Cabinet colleagues and senior Liberal politicians. Our governmental system, extremely rigid and dictated by the top, does not allow for teamwork and real but unofficial (not sanctioned by Cabinet minutes) exchanges. Under Michael Pitfield as clerk of the Privy Council, with Trudeau's full approval, the Cabinet system had become extremely rigidly managed. Collegial exchanges between colleagues simply could not be tolerated. The prime minister once told us that he did not want a few ministers meeting among themselves. With medicare I was faced with a serious and complex problem where the policy and the politics were intrinsically linked. I could not be political or assess political situations with my senior department civil servants, including the roles of pressure groups and of the public, and I could not benefit from a true informal exchange with some Cabinet colleagues, either in Cabinet or otherwise. It would have been considered a conspiracy, a power plot, or worse. Anyway, like me, most colleagues were overworked in their own portfolios, and I would have needed them for hours of free-flowing discussion.

From the outside, it looked as if the health insurance dossier was going nowhere and the federal minister was either uninterested or totally indecisive. I was repeatedly depicted as such by the press in the most unflattering ways, including comments that I was not up to being a Cabinet minister. I had good reason to look the part. Immediately after the Hall report was released, I received a letter from the prime minister reminding me of my budgetary restrictions and insisting that delivery of an integral health-care system was the provinces' responsibility. Through all my eight years in Cabinet, I had never heard of a minister receiving such a letter. Mandate letters such as those that Justin Trudeau's ministers received in 2015 did not exist at the time. It was obvious that the Privy Council, the "department" in charge of the government's general direction, had informed the prime minister that there would be no way out for me if it was based on a request for more money.

I was caught up in action and reaction, via the media, without any real strategy. The situation in British Columbia seemed the most out of control. At the end of March 1981, at the time of the National Pension Conference, that province gave the doctors an astounding 40 per cent increase but tabled legislation prohibiting extra billing. Four months earlier, Alberta had tabled a bill allowing extra billing at the same time that its health minister set up a special committee of the College of Physicians to investigate patients' complaints about extra billing. In mid-May 1981 the Ontario treasurer, Frank Miller, increased health premiums for all of the province's taxpayers by 15 per cent. Around the same time, the president of the Ontario Hospital Association, Peter Wood, raised the possibility of a $50 user fee for admission to hospital, in front of the minister of health, Dennis Timbrell. And so on. A letter in the *Ottawa Citizen* on 13 April 1981, by a Dr George O. Taylor, illustrated the state of mind of organized medicine: "We in the medical profession accept the fact that there are Canadians in economic straits unable to pay for hospital care. These have the right to be covered for.

My grandfather looked after them for nothing; my father accepted whatever the medical welfare would allow. I will look after them for nothing.
Just let me continue as a free physician." (In *Medicare: Canada's Right
to Health*, the detailed book on the medicare dossier from 1979 to 1984
that I wrote and published shortly after I had left politics, I quoted numerous other astounding public and official statements or moves by
medical associations or individual physicians, or by provincial health
and other ministers.)

In the middle of multiple challenges without apparent solutions, I
concluded that it was time to start participating in the annual meeting
of health ministers of the world – the World Health Assembly conference
held every May in Geneva. I was a strong supporter of good multilateral
organizations and was fully behind Dr Maureen Law, the department
"medicare" ADM, for her election to the executive of the World Health
Organization. So I went to Geneva for my first encounter with international colleagues at the thirty-fourth assembly. With me were ADM Dr
Lyall Black (Aboriginal health); Ken Fyke, Saskatchewan's deputy minister of health; William (Bill) Morrissey, Fyke's counterpart in New
Brunswick; and a few civil servants. Several ministers came to my desk
to congratulate me after my first speech; I could gauge how great a reputation Canada had in supporting public health and health promotion.
In September 1981 I had also attended my first Pan American Health
Organization meeting in Washington, where I participated in the plenary
session for a day. (I would attend the thirty-fifth WHO General Assembly
in May 1982, where I again met the US secretary for health and human
Services, Dick Schweiker, a Rockefeller Republican and "Red Tory," and
a pleasant counterpart to deal with.)

Back home, in the last six months of 1981 and through 1982, medical associations purchased costly full-page ads in daily newspapers in
an attempt to terrify the public with ridiculous statements such as "Civil
servants will now decide what to do about your health problems and
health treatments. Don't let them!" The CMA also paid for sickening
radio ads, which I heard for myself in the car on my way to Parliament
Hill: "As a practising physician, I want you to know what Monique
Bégin is doing is dangerous for your health" – along with the fable of
civil servants taking over – against a strong background sound of the

heartbeat, slowly vanishing, suggesting death. I could not believe it. At the beginning of April 1982 Dr Lionel Reese, president of the OMA, announced that rotating strikes could start at any time. These strikes started on 27 April and continued for ten days. Larry Grossman forced a sudden return to work by tabling a three-year contract with increases of 34 per cent instead of the 72 per cent asked for by Ontario physicians. With such a generous settlement, the minister could have banned extra billing, but he did not even try. In Quebec, on 28 April, 5,500 general practitioners started rotating strikes to back up their demand for a 63 per cent before-tax increase. In June the province legislated them back to work with an 11.3 per cent increase. During this time, the new Conservative premier of Saskatchewan, Grant Devine, made a somewhat bizarre declaration: "Extra billing is a right doctors have fought for." (He probably meant "opting out," a completely different concept.) Jim Nielsen, the new BC minister of health, increased taxpayers' health premiums by 77 per cent over eight months for single people.

The thought of a doctors' strike terrified me – this had to be avoided at all costs. I knew the history of health systems and the case of the twenty-three-day strike in Saskatchewan in July 1962. I had learned that when faced with doctors' strikes, people first support their government and oppose doctors as a group, resenting their high standard of living and arrogance, then reversing their stand at the speed of light when they think they might lose their own doctor. (I will never forget the Monday morning in June 1983 when I spotted the *Globe and Mail* headline "M. Begin to Face National Strike by Doctors" on my way back to Ottawa from Montreal. It turned out this was about Menachem Begin as the physicians of Israel carried out a hunger strike!) Because it is my personality and my sense of human relations, and my preferred tactic, I have never given a reason for my adversary to attack me; whatever the disparaging pieces were about me in the media at the time, I never attacked personally or insulted any player, publicly or behind the closed doors of in camera federal-provincial meetings, on medicare or any other topic.

In 1981 and through 1982 I had nourished the hope that the provincial health ministers, whatever their public attacks and the apparent contradictions, all wanted to get rid of extra billing by physicians and save medicare from erosion. I thought that the goal was the same and that only the means were different. By the beginning of 1982 it became obvious that the provincial ministers and I should meet to take stock of the situation, as I had been depicted as refusing to negotiate. I started our 26 May meeting with a call for cooperation. I had met the four Atlantic ministers earlier in 1981, at their request, for a delicious lobster dinner in Halifax, which was rather friendly; I also met with some one-on-one, also in Halifax, and usually on courteous terms. To my great surprise, after a whole day of debate, everyone agreed to a joint federal-provincial communiqué recognizing the problem and accepting "control" of surcharges, in particular extra billing. It was not the ideal, but my pragmatic side was seeing a solution for the first time. It was agreed that a small team of my officials would start out on the road right away, asking each province how "control" would translate for them. I had "retreated" and was given hell from the NDP in the House of Commons and from the "save medicare" constituency. Towards the end of October, when my officials reported and assessed the situation, it was obvious that the 26 May communiqué had been a big joke and no provincial minister intended to do anything. The provinces' actions left no room for doubt: it would be a confrontation. I admit there were days when I thought, without telling anyone, that maybe "they" were right and I alone might be wrong. But then there was the public's support, which should mean something.

In late July 1982 I opened health clinics in Labrador and took a few days to fly to Goose Bay, Makkovik, Postville, and Rigolet. It was a change, if a brief one, from the Ottawa scene and its constant confrontations and insults. Then my office learned that External Affairs wanted me to visit China with a small health delegation! I had been fascinated by China for many years. When I was nineteen, I gave most of my first paycheques from my teaching job to Mom for the family's needs, but I managed to buy myself a modest gramophone and one record: Chinese traditional music from some region of which I knew nothing. It was a terribly aggressive type of music for our ears, and my siblings and Mom were quite shocked.

All my life I had longed to go to China. I had read what was available at the time: novels, history, politics, biography. This was a dream come true. I do not know to this day if the invitation came from the Chinese or from Canada. I simply learned that my delegation was to explore possible Chinese-Canadian cooperation in medical knowledge and experience, and eventually sign first exchanges. Basic medical research, acupuncture, the training of Chinese bush doctors, and the value of medicinal plants in the treatment of cancer had been identified as topics that could lead to joint research projects. In Beijing I would announce a CIDA contribution of nearly $600,000 to finance a five-year project between the University of Toronto and the Sichuan Medical College for the training of health-care workers.

There would be ten of us in the Canadian delegation, including the brilliant Canadian government interpreter-translator in English-French-Mandarin, who was also learning Urdu: Jean Duval (originally from Lyon). I pleaded with my chief of staff, my old friend Monique Coupal, saying that this time she had to come: she was a great traveller who had always wanted to explore China. Because she had a young daughter, the only trip she had gone on was a weekend visit to the Vatican with Trudeau in 1978. I was glad when she accepted.

The other members of our delegation were my parliamentary secretary, MP Doug Frith; the president of the Medical Research Council, Dr Pierre Bois; my ADM (Aboriginal health) Dr Lyall Black; Dr Denise Leclerc from the Food and Drug Administration; Jean-Claude Martin, president of the Canadian Hospital Association; Agnes Hall, a great Manitoba volunteer in child health; and public health nurse Ann Harling from New Brunswick. Within twenty-four hours we would all become friends, and it made for a most extraordinary three weeks. What a wonderful break from the toxic political confrontation around medicare and two years of wondering what the solution to the problem could be.

It is impossible to describe day by day all we did, lived, and saw during this trip. After being hosted by the Canadian Commission (Embassy) in Hong Kong, including a boat trip and a swim in the South China Sea, Monique Coupal and I joined our delegation in Beijing. We were received with great warmth and honour everywhere. This had nothing to do with me, the minister, and everything to do with the living memory of Dr Norman Bethune and with Pierre Trudeau's diplomacy in recognizing China; Canada was the first Western country to do so. Bethune was still seen as a great hero and role model in China. Children and students everywhere, when we were introduced as Canadians, would spontaneously shout, "Bethune! Bethune!" (I was later flabbergasted to learn that Dr Bethune spent only twenty months of his life in China. Arriving in January 1938, he joined Mao Zedong on the battlefields, serving as a surgeon. He continued his work even when he was weak from septicemia after cutting himself badly when performing emergency surgery. He died of his wounds in November 1939.)

I retained a good memory of meeting the minister of health, Cui Yueli, upon arrival, and again later. He had lived through the worst of the Cultural Revolution, "disappearing" from 1967 to 1975. He had been made minister of health only two months before our trip. He seemed to me a solid, calm, and agreeable person. A few days later we were received at a banquet given by Dr Qian Xinzhong, who had served as the minister of health twice previously; I had received him at the WHO ministers' meeting in Geneva in May of that year. He was now minister of the delicate task of family planning. For that banquet he was accompanied by a close personal friend of his, with whom I had a long conversation: Dr George Hatem ("Ma Haide"), a Lebanese-American dermatologist who had marched with Mao in 1935, had welcomed Bethune and helped him get started and had eradicated venereal disease in the People's Republic of China. The day after, we were received by the vice premier of China, Bo Yibo, by then seventy-four years old; he was a former military leader and one of the most senior political figures in China in the 1980s and 1990s. He had been one of a select group of veterans supporting Deng Xiaoping in the late 1970s after Mao's death; Bo Yibo then commanded vast influence, as he was in general a moderate conservative politically.

In and around Beijing we visited every historical and cultural museum, garden, or site we could, interspersed with demonstrations and briefings in major hospitals as well as in medical and pharmacology institutes. Then we travelled by train to Norman Bethune International Peace Hospital in Shijiazhuang, about 300 kilometres southwest of Beijing. A thyroidectomy under acupuncture "by electricity" anaesthesia, with the patient speaking, impressed me to no end. It would be the first of several surprising acupuncture demonstrations. Then we were off to

Xi'an for two days, an additional 900 kilometres by night train – most uncomfortable. From Xi'an, we went further to the southwest, another 700 kilometres, to Chengdu, to the Sichuan Medical College and the presentation of the cheque from the government of Canada. We were there for two days (and saw the pandas and the bamboo forest). From Chengdu, we flew to Guilin (1,400 kilometres by road), to the southeast, where we were received officially and visited all its famous natural attractions, starting with the Lijiang River (in the rain).

The plane then took us Shanghai, where we would spend four days; there we were received officially, elegantly, and warmly by the mayor, Wang Dahoan. In 1982 the city already had twelve million inhabitants! It was a more modern place than anything else in China; a few teenagers wore coloured skirts instead of the Mao-style navy, grey, or black outfits, but there were none of today's skyscrapers. We began our visit at the Ruijin University Hospital and its burn unit, where they performed miracles – burn injuries being a major problem of daily life in China, both in homes and at work. (As my much-loved brother Thomas had recently died in a fire, I had to leave the group at one point, as it bothered me too much.) We attended more incredible medical demonstrations at the People's Hospital No. 6, the International Peace Maternity and Child Hospital, and the Shuguang Hospital (both traditional Chinese and Western medicine), and we visited the Hong Qiao model People's Commune of 7,600 families. In the lobby of one of their apartment buildings, I was horrified to see, posted publicly, the menstruation dates of every adult woman living there. It was social control: their husbands were often sent to work far away for months at a time, and the government wanted to make sure the women remained faithful.

At one point in that busy Shanghai schedule I could no longer take the feeling of being constantly watched and followed, thanks to the "hidden" bodyguards (in fact, they were always there, and very visible) and polite police atmosphere. So, with the help of our Canadian interpreter, Denise Leclerc, Doug Frith and I escaped for the day, walking freely in the 400-year-old classical Yu Garden in Old Shanghai. That's where I discovered the delicacy of sweet glutinous rice! On 18 and 19 September we went to Hangzhou by train, about an hour southwest, returning to Beijing for 20 and 21 September, where I gave an official thank-you banquet to China's minister of health. It was the end of an extraordinary, one-of-a-kind but exhausting ministerial trip. We had brought gifts for every stop (two of my delegation looked after a heavy trunk that followed us everywhere); we offered, in keeping with the wishes of our hosts, sturdy Canadian briefcases made of buffalo leather and stunning Inuit sculptures, as well as the first world index of geographic cancer mapping, presented in a beautiful large book.

Upon our return to Ottawa at the end of September 1982, Marc Lalonde, the new minister of finance, called me to his office to tell me that the universality of our social programs was coming to an end (I tell the story in chapter 11).

The situation regarding our health insurance problems and that of the national health minister never stopped making the news. This dossier of public policy was taking unusual pathways. For instance, on 5 October 1982 the very wise and open-minded (and powerful) Ontario premier, Bill Davis, had come to see me in my office – a most unusual visit. Later that year, on 26 November, Senator Maurice Riel, who would be appointed speaker of the Senate a year later, and his spouse, Laurence (they were a couple I saw regularly and loved), organized a fine dinner at their Westmount residence with me and Pierre Marc Johnson and his spouse, Marie-Louise, "in order to get us to know each other better." Maurice had been a friend of Premier Daniel Johnson, Pierre Marc's father, and of his mother, Reine Johnson. Pierre Marc Johnson was René Lévesque's minister of health and social affairs and a future (short-lived) Quebec premier himself. He and I knew each other pretty well already, as we shared the same constituency. Both of us had been elected with a large majority. We had also been together at numerous constituency activities. I had sensed from day one that he could not stand me. The dinner was delicious, the atmosphere, civilized, but no more.

Then we entered 1983, which would be the turning point in the medicare saga. A small team and I started exploring possible legal action by the feds and imagining an implementation strategy. In parallel, 1983 was also the high point of personal attacks against me as the federal minister. Many of the "opposed" letters then received at the department were virulent, vulgar, and sexist. One doctor from southern Ontario personally signed a letter to me on his letterhead (but sent it to the department's official address, not even the House of Commons), with "a prescription for hormones to combat your menopause, as it is clear that you are crazy."

From the beginning of 1983, my objective had been to actively clarify Ottawa's constitutional limits. We set to work with our Justice Department. My department senior officials, starting with my very professional DM, Larry Fry, seemed neither interested nor supportive, much less encouraging. Larry would tell me that he believed disputes with the provinces should always be avoided. I could not agree more! I would have loved to go through my eight years in Cabinet without a federal-provincial confrontation. Early on, I had asked Jean Chrétien privately, in earnest, how to be successful in federal-provincial meetings. He had replied that there is only one way: "Give them more money!" Fry's attitude coloured almost all the documents that crossed my desk. (Only in the final year of the medicare crisis, when we were going to win, did the department, under the leadership of my new DM, David Kirkwood, back me up.) Once I realized that I would receive little help from my senior officials, I went back to my request two years before to draft the regulations for the block-funding EPF Act that was passed in 1977. It could not be done. Too complicated. That killed my idea of taking a regulatory approach, documenting breaches of the 1977 agreement and applying penalties – which, by the way, had not been not contemplated under the EPF legislation. It was a law without penalty.

Some Cabinet colleagues and MPs gave me active support in favour of medicare by providing concrete unacceptable examples of erosion from their region and by defending health insurance in their speeches. One of them, Claude-André Lachance, a personal friend, was particularly helpful; he became my partner in crime, so to speak. He had been elected in July 1974 in a Montreal riding bordering mine, having just turned twenty, and was re-elected twice until leaving politics by choice in September 1984. While in Parliament, Claude-André, underused and somehow disinterested, had studied law while carrying out his active parliamentary role. He passed the bar exams in 1976, then did a master's in law with thesis, which he had completed in 1980. A born strategist, he is one example of how the system would benefit from smart, indeed brilliant, MPs who cannot all be appointed ministers. If only he had been my parliamentary secretary. But the system did not permit a real working relationship with an exchange of Cabinet information between us. I was, however, blessed with his friendship, trust, and talent.

The first thing Claude-André helped me with was clarifying our strategy. We concluded that it had to be the strategy of small steps – the Sino-Japanese Kaizen strategy, in which a lot of barriers can be overcome one by one when everyone is involved, from top to bottom. In this case, that meant middle management in my department, colleagues in the House (through relevant committees), the supporting health professionals, organized nursing, and especially the public. Our code words would remain "the strategy of small steps." Herb Breau, who had chaired the Special Committee on the Federal-Provincial Arrangements with great courage and political astuteness, also offered much support. This task force had been set up by MacEachen as minister of finance on 17 March 1981; it finished its work in 1983. I really did not need that task force, as every province was then decoding it as health cuts. In the chapter on health in its report, the task force recommended a joint federal-provincial approach to consolidate in a new law the four basic conditions for health insurance, supported Justice Hall's conclusions, and had the courage to speak out against any potential cuts in federal budgets for health insurance.

According to the Constitution Act, 1867, health is first and foremost a provincial jurisdiction. It is true that historically speaking, the federal government has intervened with success in areas not under its jurisdiction under the concept of national interest, starting in 1946. But in 1976 the Supreme Court had returned to a strict interpretation, rejecting the argument that inflation fell under that concept. So the only other approach worth exploring was the concept of spending power, recognized by Canadian jurisprudence since 1937. However, its parameters were vague. We were walking a tightrope. All the draft Cabinet memoranda that the department presented to me were full of the wording found in the British television series *Yes, Minister*: "On the one hand ... On the other hand ..." The only solution was to convince experts in the Justice Department to draw up a bill. Then we would have something concrete to work from. On 14 December 1982 the Cabinet Committee of Priorities and Planning authorized Justice to immediately draft a new bill.

Having just completed its demanding work on constitutional reform, Justice did not greet this task with much enthusiasm.

A week later, on 21 December – at the Cercle universitaire of Ottawa, then a private club with excellent cuisine, where we could talk confidentially – Claude-André Lachance organized a lunch for the two of us to meet with Professor Gérald Beaudoin, the former dean of the Civil Law section of the University of Ottawa and a recognized constitutional expert. He had been a member of the Pépin-Robarts Commission on National Unity, and the law expert who had just been responsible for the French version of the Charter of Rights and Freedoms. Thanks to Claude-André, his former student, we easily established a safe and open space for discussion. I described my challenges and what would be going on, with Justice having the mandate to draft a bill. Then I listened to him explain, in language I could understand, the constitutional challenges that Justice faced. He suggested having Justice invite three top constitutional experts to give their legal opinion independently, and he suggested names. This lunch became a pivotal moment in the dossier. How to sell the idea to Justice was another story, and a delicate operation, but Roger Tassé, the Justice deputy minister, was someone I knew and respected: he was a positive, open-minded legal scholar and a responsible and trustworthy senior civil servant. We met and he bought into the idea; he also loaned Mary Dawson to my department to help develop the case. She had played an important role in relation to constitutional matters and had just been the drafter for the Constitution Act, 1982.

Justice needed to know what our objectives were for new legislation for health insurance. My political office started working on it under Sharon Schollar and a core group of officials, colleagues of Madeleine Côté: Don McNaught, Alistair Thomson, Ray Lachaîne, and Bill Tholl. I had first met Madeleine Coté by chance when she accompanied me to Calgary for the Canadian Hospital Association annual meeting. Answering my question about what the problem was with medicare, she replied politely that the problem was the lack of political leadership, and that irritated me. But as we continued talking, I learned of past regular relationships by a team of federal civil servants of National Health and Welfare with each provincial Health Department; these had been abolished with the block-funding agreement and EPF Act of 1977. In the 1980s Madeleine Côté, the first (lay) woman hospital administrator in Quebec (she was appointed executive director of the Centre Hospitalier Universitaire de Sherbrooke in 1967), was one of the twelve middle-management civil servants of my department who remained on the team dealing with the provinces for health reimbursements in the 50:50 cost system. Impressed by her medicare system knowledge and openness, I had managed to have her transferred to my political staff until the end of my mandate, as she was close to retirement age. (I had never heard of these twelve people, as deputy ministers had the bad habit of bringing only assistant deputy ministers or very senior civil servants to the minister's weekly or special briefing sessions. Like me, most of them were generalists – not in the line of fire and usually not very knowledgeable about the intricacies of the cases under consideration.)

From the outset, I was clear on one thing: the mood in the country and in the House of Commons was such that I believed we could win a bill to clarify the existing medicare legislation, but I could not risk losing everything by reopening the very concept of our "free" health insurance through a new ideal medicare legislation that corrected points or added new ideas. On the Conservative Opposition benches in the House of Commons, Joe Clark's leadership was visibly questioned (he would lose to Brian Mulroney a few months later: one more big new unknown). We simply wanted to clarify the four basic conditions and reformulate penalties accordingly, to consolidate what existed. I also had to make sure nothing we did or said could justify work stoppages by physicians.

Since we had to mobilize public opinion, we decided to focus on user fees by hospitals and provinces rather than on extra billing by doctors and specialists. Our approach would isolate organized medicine in the debate. By focusing on the provinces' responsibility, we were putting them on the defensive for both types of surcharges. We could not go before Parliament without strong and visible public support. Before putting our still vague draft strategy on paper, I wanted to check with Trudeau, the ultimate strategist.

So one day, during question period, as soon as he was freed from questioning by Opposition leaders, I walked to his seat, bent down near his desk, and rapidly asked him his opinion: "Boss, I just don't know where things are going with medicare anymore."

"Who are the players and where do they stand on the Canada Health Act?" he asked.

"The ten provinces are opposed: not just their ministers of health, but their ministers of finance and their premiers. All of organized medicine is opposed. All the official elites are opposed," was my reply.

"Where is the population in all of that?"

"In favour of the bill."

"That's a sure win," was his stern answer. "Like the Constitution," he added.

I always knew he trusted me completely, and his reassurance was extremely important: the information he was receiving from those around him kept telling him that the public's support was neither assured nor obvious, if it existed at all.

I can't avoid referring here to the powerful and very secretive Cabinet Committee on Communications. It was made up of ministers (my friends on it were Roméo LeBlanc and Judy Erola) and communications experts – in particular, in Judy's words, "the Toronto Cabal." I couldn't have agreed more with her assessment. Consultant Martin Goldfarb and communications lawyer and businessman Jerry Grafstein (who would be appointed to the Senate in 1984), among others who ran market research and consulting service firms, made a life out of contracts with the federal Liberal Party. For example, Goldfarb Consultants was the official pollster of the party for years. "The Toronto Cabal," Senator Keith Davey (the "rainmaker"), and Jim Coutts exercised enormous influence on Prime Minister Pierre Trudeau. From what I saw and heard of their views and strategies over the years, I had concluded that they were manipulative and had a wrong reading of the public's views in many instances.

I wanted to move as quickly as possible. Nobody knew when Trudeau would step down, when a leadership convention would ensue, and when an election call would follow. Several people around me and among the Liberal Party strategists started saying that "saving medicare" as the central platform of the next general election program was the best guarantee of finally doing it. I was totally opposed to that approach but could not give my reasons: I was leaving politics and, above all, it was already crystal clear to me that whoever replaced Trudeau as Liberal leader, and whatever election date was chosen, we would lose the election. So my department started preparing a memorandum to Cabinet of our proposed legislation and recommended asking the opinions of three prominent constitutional experts. We recommended J.J. Robinette of McCarthy and McCarthy, Professor Peter W. Hogg of Osgoode Hall Law School, and Michel Robert of Robert, Dansereau, Barré, Marchessault, and Lauzon. I had to pass the Priorities and Planning (P & P) test before going any further. Our recommendation was approved by P & P and later by the full Cabinet. Our memorandum to Cabinet detailed the fines each province would be subject to, corresponding to the total amounts of surcharges in their province, amounting to some $118 million per year – no small sum. This came as a shock to several ministers, who had not realized that the situation was serious.

In the meantime, the medicare situation had greatly deteriorated, especially in Alberta, where, at the end of March, Dave Russell had announced that starting on 1 October, hospitals could charge user fees of up to $20 per day (over and above the rate of private rooms), at their discretion. Alberta's other user fees – for admissions, outpatient clinics, and visits to Emergency – were also increased. In addition, the province had 38 per cent of extra-billing doctors charging patients on average an extra 33 per cent on their fees. Around 160,000 Albertans had not paid their provincial health premiums (a tax over and above their general taxes). The province's treasurer had announced that health insurance premiums would increase by 47 per cent in 1983. In that first of a series of Cabinet meetings, I had obtained permission to negotiate with Alberta towards full compliance with the existing legislation. If no agreement was reached, at the end of May I could announce the federal intention to hold back the total monthly federal payments as soon as user fees were implemented. The current EPF legislation gave me no other option. I spoke with Dave Russell on 13 April, to no avail.

In early May 1983, upon my return from the thirty-sixth World Health Assembly in Geneva (where I had met the new American secretary of health, Margaret Heckler, who had just been appointed by

Ronald Reagan), I had to stop off in Paris to meet, at France's request, their secretary of state for seniors, Dr Daniel Benoist. In the afternoon, accompanied by our ambassador, Michel Dupuy, I had a working session with Pierre Bérégovoy, an impressive senior Socialist politician who would become Mitterrand's prime minister in 1992 (and would dramatically die by suicide in May 1993). At the time, Bérégovoy was the super minister of social affairs and national solidarity, with at least three secretaries of state under him, before becoming minister of finance. We discussed issues of our health-care systems and of possible new Socialist welfare policies for France.

By that time, Justice had received the three independent constitutional opinions. These experts all agreed that our different possible approaches would be acceptable in the courts as a reasonable exercise of spending power. This was the first good news I had heard since the crises had started in 1979. This information remained completely confidential; at last we had a strong hand. We then worked on a Cabinet memorandum for final approval to move towards tabling a bill in the House. Convinced as I was that it would be the Canadian public who would save medicare – or lose it – I insisted on as short a bill as possible, and of relatively easy reading. Bill C-3 would have thirteen pages. To the four conditions of the Hospital Insurance and Diagnostic Services Act (1957) and the Medical Care Act (1966), I added a fifth condition, clarifying the concept of "universality" with that of "accessibility." The five conditions were as follows:

- Universality: requires that all residents of a province be entitled to public health-care insurance coverage.
- Comprehensiveness: requires that all medically necessary services provided by hospitals and doctors be covered under the provincial health-care insurance plan.
- Accessibility: requires reasonable access unimpeded by financial or other barriers to medically necessary hospital and physician services for residents, and reasonable compensation for both physicians and hospitals.
- Portability: requires that coverage under public health-care insurance be maintained when a resident moves or travels

within Canada or travels outside the country (coverage outside
Canada is restricted to the coverage the resident has in his or
her own province).

• Public administration: requires that the administration and
operation of the health-care insurance plan of a province be
carried out on a non-profit basis by a public authority
responsible to the provincial government.

I had been thrilled when Mary Dawson had proposed a non-punitive
penalty, a new concept in law at the time. Each year, each province
would see deducted from its federal payments the total amount of user
fees and of extra billing in its jurisdiction: $1 of penalty for $1 of sur-
charge. Those penalties would be put in a special account of the federal
Consolidated Revenue Fund. The provinces would have three years to
put their house in order; once that was done, they would get the penalty
money back. (With no interest, as I joked with the public.) In addition
to the penalties, our draft bill imposed an annual report to Parliament:
this report was also to be published, with the details of the situation for
each province, always in line with the thought that medicare was to be
in the hands of the Canadian public for medicare's very survival.

The memorandum was ready for submission to P & P before Cabinet, and I presented it on 24 May. Our medicare dossier was unfortunately of the least interest to P & P ministers, who had many more
pressing issues (in their view and that of the Privy Council): the Crow's
Nest Pass situation, cruise missile tests over Alberta, and others. Medicare was relegated to the domestic, family sphere and was therefore seen
as less important. Week after week, my medicare proposed bill and
strategy were on the P & P agenda, with no decision being taken, then
were sent back to the Social Development Cabinet Committee and back
again. A few ministers were strong supporters; some were strongly opposed, and others were uneasy about it or were convinced that the public was not following at all. As I had to leave the P & P meeting once
my file had been discussed, I will never know the truth about its group
dynamics on medicare.

After more than a month of this game of hide-and-seek, I requested
a private meeting with the prime minister, who had never said a word

in these P & P meetings when I was there. I got an appointment for 22 June 1983 and spent about thirty minutes with him. As he was not good at small talk, and I was not much better, I started the conversation a bit abruptly, asking him politely if he was for or against the proposed Canada Health Act. He looked at me, a bit puzzled, and, very much à la Trudeau, replied simply, "The first royal assent that I signed as prime minister in 1968 was for the Medical Care Act." He said nothing more. I thanked him, immediately understanding that his last royal assent would be "my" Act. Then I informed him of my plans to leave politics at the call of the next election but asked him not to tell anyone, as I still had lots to do and did not want to be seen as a has-been. I needed him to know my real motivation for being in a hurry, as any minister with personal popularity was considered to be doing this or that uniquely to boost their leadership chances. He was surprised; we talked a bit and he complimented me on my intuitive sense of reading public opinion.

"My" Canada Health Act bill finally passed the P & P, but only after I assured Marc Lalonde, the minister of finance and Quebec political lieutenant, that nothing in it would affect Quebec, as Quebec had no user fees – the spectre of separation being a constant preoccupation in Ottawa. (When I was in my Montreal riding on the weekends, people talked to me about anything and everything but health insurance. It was not an issue for them.) Before the next Cabinet meeting, to be held on 30 June, I took an unusual initiative: I wrote a personal two-page letter to each Cabinet colleague and hand-delivered the letters, asking my colleagues for their support and explaining the issue at stake. In Cabinet, a majority of ministers finally decided in favour of my proposal, but only after a long discussion.

On 11 July I sent a letter to the provinces informing them of our plan of action. Privy Council emphasized the pitfalls. They would not believe the public was supportive. It was very bad faith at that point. In fact, I think the bureaucracy was retreating in a passive way, preparing for the new government. They worked on immediate issues only and tried everything to delay the passage and implementation of the Canada Health Act.

At that time our systematic public information campaign was launched, and it didn't cost millions. A small team under Michael

Mendelson and Pat Simki, with Ray Lachaîne, David Stewart, and Don McNaught, prepared texts and charts, a wonderful set of four large posters entitled "Keep the Care in Medicare / L'assurance-santé c'est pour la vie," and so on. We released a modest, typical red-covered Document of Canada position paper entitled "Preserving Universal Medicare / Pour une assurance-santé universelle" – an informative seventy-page bilingual text with a few charts and tables, which I signed. More than 300,000 copies went out to all physicians, all registered nurses, the media, groups, associations, universities, and the general public. Information about the pamphlet was publicized with each pension and family allowance cheque. I had rejected the Cabinet Political Communications Committee's request for a barrage of television advertising tied in with the future election strategy, with a budget of $2–3 million or more. I found this idea distasteful and felt it would be counterproductive, as I was sure the Liberals would lose the next election, although I could never say that.

On the basis of past experience, I favoured a different communications strategy, one that was community based, which the department's small middle-management team adopted spontaneously. I had learned from my friend Roméo LeBlanc the power of the Canadian Press (CPP/RRQ) in every small town, village, and place in Canada. Steve Kerstetter was a wonderful CPP/RRQ reporter who covered medicare. We loaded him up with all the information we had. My senior officials wanted to use the relatively small promotion budget that is automatically attached and approved with any Cabinet document, including new legislation, to buy a page in the *Globe and Mail*: I opposed this, and the money was used instead to cover expenses only (tea and coffee, doughnuts, public hall rental, etc.) for such debates – up to $5,000 for every community group interested in organizing a public debate on medicare anywhere in the country. The funds were administered entirely by the department; there was no political interference in who would get it. It was a huge success everywhere. Nobody opposing the Canada Health Act could pack meetings: I knew there would always be people in favour of medicare everywhere in the land. Hundreds of thousands of promotional materials were distributed across the country. The silent majority had a voice. And busy ministers around the Cabinet table came back from their weekend at home having been told by their constituents that they wanted medicare to be protected.

All through 1983 extensive media coverage of the medicare debate was provided. During those months I accepted as many major conference invitations as I could handle, although some were a complete waste of my time. I recall going to Brampton, Premier Bill Davis's constituency, to speak to ... twelve people in a local restaurant! I also met with many newspaper editorial boards, a new experience for me; I rather enjoyed them, because we had time to discuss and explain.

Publication of the federal government's position paper in the summer of 1983 had given the project new legitimacy. The impending Canada Health Act was a compelling reason for all parties to get involved. The provincial ministers' strategy had been to invite me to their annual meeting in Halifax that September to try to stop the bill once and for all. On 1 September, in Saskatoon, the *Financial Post* had held a major conference on medicare, with extensive publicity throughout the country. Dr Marc Baltzan, the CMA president, predicted a doctors' strike, while Dr Sam Freedman, a renowned oncologist and researcher from McGill, put the responsibility for the increased cost of health care on specialists practising excessive surgery. Both agreed there were too many physicians in the country and that perhaps two of the sixteen Faculties of Medicine should be closed. That same day, Dr Pat McGeer, the BC minister of universities (and a noted medical researcher himself), said he would grant 300 doctorates in medicine instead of the usual 80! Also in attendance in Saskatoon were the economist Bob Evans, MP Herb Breau, Dr John Rayson (BC Medical Association), provincial ministers of Health Keith Norton (Ontario) and Jim Nielsen (BC), and the Saskatchewan minister of finance, Bob Andrew. I was not invited.

I arrived in Halifax on September 7 alone, "invited" by my provincial counterparts. The meeting was behind closed doors, with provincial politicians and senior officials there in full force. It looked as if all the reporters of the country were awaiting the outcome of the game at the doors of the hotel. I was feeling ill at ease. I outlined my position, now the official federal position, again: the reasons for our actions and our projected schedule. I repeated that as soon as the bill was fully drafted, they would be the first to get a copy. Then we would begin the usual parliamentary process and contemplate eventual changes. The atmosphere of attacks and jibes reached a peak. Those in the meeting – one against ten, with me the only woman, an Ottawa "French power" francophone Quebecer – used all sorts of abusive arguments and personal remarks meant to humiliate me. Luckily, I don't cry easily, and I didn't cry then. After three hours of this very stressful exercise in which the dice were loaded against me, I returned to Ottawa. The media all agreed that with such unanimity from the provinces, I was the loser at the conference and this was a no-win situation.

On 30 November Trudeau adjourned the thirty-second Parliament. A week later, on 7 December, the Throne Speech opened its second session. Our House leader, the marvellously controlled and bright Yvon Pinard, had put the Canada Health Act bill first on the legislative list, after the bills dealing with financial matters. It became Bill C-3, tabled on 12 December. Two days later, after caucus, in the middle of question period, Yvon Pinard suddenly came to my desk and whispered in my ear that the Progressive Conservative health critic, Jake Epp, had just announced to the media the Conservative caucus's support for Bill C-3! I had always predicted to those around me that this would happen, after having studied their new leader, Brian Mulroney, but no one really believed me – except Trudeau, who reminded me of it afterwards. The Opposition's reactions ranged from the sublime, with Mulroney stating that "medicare is a sacred trust that we will always preserve," to the vulgar, with the Conservative MP from Calgary Centre, Harvie Andre, describing me to the *Calgary Herald* as "Bégin, that disgusting woman." The comment from the CMA president, Dr Everett Coffin, was a gem: "Surely the Canada Health Act is a rape of the spirit, if not the legal stipulations of the Canadian Constitution." I'll conclude with the *Medical Post*'s repugnant comment: "Although I can't for the life of me recall the source of the line, it's something to the effect that if you're going to be raped, you might as well lie back and enjoy it."

On the other hand, intense lobbying and support through the years by the Canadian Nurses Association, the professional voice of registered nurses in Canada, was instrumental in the bill being passed. (The Canadian Federation of Nurses Unions, which actively defended Canadian medicare in the 2000s, was still in its infancy at the time of Bill C-3, having been founded in 1981.) Organized nursing became a big player during the Canada Health Act (1984). It made the difference: it is as simple as that. Their executive director for all those years, Ginette Rodger – the former director of nursing at Notre Dame Hospital in Montreal, with her bright, decisive, and strategic mind – was committed to medicare. The association president, Dr Helen Glass, took on this additional leadership role. When the bill was in committee, they managed to have an amendment passed, enlarging the wording and scope of the Act by including "other health care workers" in addition to physicians as providers of insurable services.

As decided by Cabinet, we got on the road as soon as the Christmas holidays were over: my small team from the department (Don Mac-Naught, Madeleine Côté, ADM Dr Maureen Law, and press attaché Bernard Daudier) and I. We needed extraordinary team spirit to cover nine provinces and the Yukon in less than a week, through rain, fog, wind, snowstorms, and jet lag, followed from one provincial capital to another by reporters and flashing cameras. We started in St John's on 9 January, finishing in Toronto four days later. As Pierre Marc Johnson, the Quebec minister of Health, was abroad on holidays, Don Mac-Naught, Madeleine Côté, Bernard Daudier, and I met him at his Montreal department on Friday evening, 20 January, when he returned. The second reading of the bill, where the arguments are first deployed, had just finished that day. In the car to Montreal, I felt uneasy. That afternoon, one of my officials – I believe it was Don McNaught – had discovered that the *Quebec Official Gazette*, dated 3 and 10 August, contained proposals changing the hospital classification of patients and stating that "adults in hospital ninety days after their admission date pay a daily fee for shelter." From their understanding of the text, our civil servants estimated that Quebec would take in $75–100 million in 1984–85. It was a classic user fee. (Extra billing by physicians had been prohibited by law in Quebec under Minister Claude Castonguay as of 1970.) But because of René Lévesque's Parti Québécois's social democrat philosophy, I did not believe these hospital user fees, nor did Christiane Beaulieu, my new chief of staff, or the other Quebecers at that work session. This text had been published almost six months before and we had heard nothing, much less received complaints.

The four of us had driven through a terrible snowstorm, but the weather outside was nothing compared to the storm that blew up indoors on that January evening. Pierre Marc Johnson was accompanied by his deputy minister, Jean-Claude Deschênes, and press attaché, Guy Versailles. I could not quickly review Bill C-3, as Johnson interrupted me, declaring the project unconstitutional; he accused me of breaking the "federal-provincial agreement signed between me and his predecessor, Denis Lazure." He seemed genuinely angry – much angrier than when he had to challenge me publicly to satisfy the Quebec Ministry of Inter-Governmental Affairs. The Bégin-Lazure Agreement? What agreement? Then he started questioning this or that paragraph of the bill, and I saw at once that the French version had a few unfortunate and major translation errors. I immediately apologized and promised the necessary corrections. The whole meeting was most unpleasant, but I managed not to lose my patience. My suspicion on the way back home from that unreal encounter was that Johnson's theatrics were a smoke-screen in case I were to learn of his adopted user fees; this suspicion proved accurate. This evening meeting was merely the dress rehearsal for the public show he would give over four weeks, culminating in his appearance with busloads of the Quebec hospital elite – medical school deans, top civil servants, medical directors, and administrators of all major hospitals, pressure groups – a total of some forty notables. He succeeded in the role of the ultra-nationalist shaking Ottawa's constitutional confidence. And he had misled me, assuring me that Quebec did not have user fees. And here I had sworn to Marc Lalonde that there would be no penalty for Quebec, as they had no user fees!

There would be hurdles and major problems until the unanimous final passage of the Act, amended in its preamble for the better, in the House of Commons on 9 April 1984, and royal assent on 17 April; these are described in detail in my 1987 book on the medicare saga. But, more important to me, the traditional allies of medicare were disappointed by the limits of Bill C-3 and its proposed reforms. Dr Helen Glass, the president of the Canadian Nurses Association, speaking on behalf of its 165,000 members, described her deep disappointment that the power structure and doctors' fee system continued to recognize only hospitals and doctors. I couldn't have agreed more. Recognizing the role of nurses and nurse practitioners was an important objective, but at the time my strategic analysis clearly showed that the most we could get through a new piece of legislation was to fix the new charges added for the patients, restoring medicare to its original definition. In the country's state of affairs at the time, if we had opened up more fronts, to use a military term, it was obvious we would have lost everything. The Friends of Medicare group was also disappointed about loopholes in the law.

After the unpleasant and often painful last few months of the Canada Health Act showdowns and clashes, I welcomed a change of scene – a chance to decompress, relax, and get some distance from the situation. I wanted to participate in the first few days of my last WHO World Health Assembly, the thirty-seventh, scheduled for 7–17 May 1984. I also had meetings in Paris and Brussels. My small delegation and I would be out of the country for ten days. Upon arrival in Paris on my way to Geneva, I touched base with Edmond Harvey, a longtime French Socialist politician who was secretary of state for health for a second time.

During my final WHO conference, in a special session of the WHO Medical Society, I was honoured with the first Dr Brock Chisholm Medal, named for a Canadian physician who was the first WHO director general and the first Canadian deputy minister of health. I wanted to know more about him; I learned that the image that sticks to Brock Chisholm is that of "Canada's most famously articulate angry man," which I liked. There were several very formal speeches. An engraved medal, as is often a European tradition, was presented to me by the president of the Medical Society, Dr S.W.A. Gunn, a very European Canadian international health official. An added honour was some time talking with Dr Halfdan Mahler, one of my heroes; he was the third WHO director general, a promoter of the historic 1978 Alma Ata Declaration and a champion for primary care.

On the way back to Canada we stopped in Brussels to meet a few ministers and sign reciprocity agreements for pensions and other social programs with Belgium, my mother's country of birth. Each exchange and signature took place in a splendid castle. I even managed to give a speech at the Club Richelieu. Brussels would be my last official international trip – a too brief but pleasant stay, thanks to our ambassador, D'Iberville Fortier.

Back in Ottawa in July and August 1984, in the midst of a federal election, I had to impose the dollar-for-dollar financial penalties on seven provinces, totalling $9.5 million; the three others (Newfoundland, Prince Edward Island, and Nova Scotia) had ended their financial surcharges before the federal election. I felt bad having to do this twice in the middle of a federal election. In Quebec, penalties were imposed for their user fees every month up until Robert Bourassa's election on 5 December 1985. In July and August 1984 Quebec lost close to $800,000. In 1986 the new Quebec Liberal government reluctantly abolished the user fees. At the end of the first three years of enforcing the Canada Health Act (1984), in July 1987, penalties totalling close to $250 million that the federal government had retained were fully reimbursed to the provinces, as they had all finally put their house in order.

Was the Canada Health Act (1984) perfect? No. Basically, it addressed the problem of the day with great success: the erosion of a free health-care system for all by additional payments "at the door." It killed user fees by physicians and extra billing by provinces through an innovative and visibly fair, non-punitive penalty. But as this was the only problem of the day, none of us, the political players or the civil servants, could have forecasted today's major attacks against medicare. At the time the Canada Health Act (1984) came into force, physicians either had opted into medicare and were paid by their province, or had opted out and could not enjoy both the private and public payments. In 1984, only twelve physicians in Canada had opted out.

Surreptitious delisting or de-insurance of services by provincial governments; private clinics operating both within and outside provincial plans for "medically necessary services" (and their medical practitioners keeping hospital privileges and having it both ways); treating GPs or specialists directing their patients to private labs and clinics for regular procedures for the full out-of-pocket cost; hospitals charging partial costs for exams because these might not be "medically necessary" (wanting an MRI is not like choosing to colour your hair!) – these are all erosions of Canadian medicare. But a huge barrier leading to these breaches of accessibility is the unacceptable wait times at emergency departments and for surgeries.

In the years after the Canada Health Act (1984), however, things became even more complicated. We started learning that health was much more than physicians and hospitals. Today's system has to rethink and accommodate seniors' needs at home and in various types of institutions that are totally different from hospitals. It has to reform its culture from within, and it is not first and foremost more funding that will assist. What we need to develop is a de-medicalization of the health-care system. Above all, then and now, it has always been clear to me that "virtually all the problems in our health-care system are engineering and administrative failings, not failures of medical care," as long-time health reporter André Picard wrote in the *Globe and Mail* on 23 May 2017, repeating the assessment made by the last report done by five Nova Scotia authorities for fixing their provincial system.

My contention is that the Canada Health Act is the only set of rules people in Canada have for knowing their entitlements to health care. These rules are blurred; citizens no longer understand what they will or should receive for the heavy taxes they pay. Since they are not familiar with the financial and administrative aspects – and why should they be? – and have lost a sense of what they are entitled to, individuals either accept ideological arguments about being able to pay or worry endlessly about what will happen. And they purchase more health insurance, forgetting in the process that they have already paid high taxes for a "free," universal, comprehensive health-care system.

14

Under the Microscope: A Few Very Public Files

A sixth branch of the department in the business of policies and pro-grams was the Social Services Branch, under Brian Iverson. If I worked far less with its officials in my daily ministerial life than with the five other branches already covered in previous chapters, it is because of its "object." Called "Social Services," it was basically responsible for one of the most arcane, expensive, delicate, and key pieces of machinery of government: the Canada Assistance Plan (CAP). This is made of all the federal-provincial fiscal arrangements covering provincial "welfare," a shared cost program distinct from the medicare one but as important a product of the Canadian system of federalism. It is also far less well known and understood in its many dimensions by the public. But, there too, when I signed a ministerial order, it would affect the income main-tenance programs and the social services programs offered by the provinces. The CAP Directorate also administered other joint programs, such as the Vocational Rehabilitation of Disabled Persons Act. So, for obvious reasons, this branch and its activities would not have been under the microscope.

When I started in Health and Welfare, I immediately learned, almost like a new theology, the phrase *health-promotion-and-disease-prevention*. It was like one new thirty-five-letter word that, for quite some time, I did not even understand to what branch it belonged nor what it did. It had forty letters in French: *promotion-de-la-santé-et-prévention-de-la-maladie*. It appeared to me so basic and so vague that I had difficulty knowing what fell under it. But I always knew who incarnated it: Ron

Draper was its hero, surrounded by a very dynamic small team of civil servants. (Shortly after his death in 1998, the Canadian Association of Public Health set up the annual Ron Draper Health Promotion Award.) I had rapidly sensed that those speaking that language were "the good guys," and, like any good guy in my huge portfolio, they were under-financed and did not count much in our bureaucratic power structure. Finally, in 1978, my department created a new Directorate of Health Promotion ironically inside the most medically oriented branch, the one in charge of medicare ... a branch labelled Health Services and Promotion (!) under Dr Maureen Law as ADM. After the Health Promotion group had worked on defining with precision its role and action priorities, these were launched, so to speak, by Ron Draper at a national forum in January 1980, at the First Canadian Conference on Health Promotion. Later that year, in September, their six priority areas had been selected and approved: tobacco, safety, nutrition for pregnant women and preschool children, health promotion for adolescents, alcohol use among adolescents and young adults, and emotional well-being. This Action Plan document, including the creation of a national health promotion survey by Statistics Canada, was approved by Cabinet in 1982 when I was back in the health portfolio.

In hindsight, what I should have received from the department together with the first meeting on *health-promotion-and-disease-prevention* is a short briefing informing their new minister what "public health" was, exactly, historically speaking, how it was evolving, and at what point of its evolution we were finding ourselves, so I could have made the connection between those concepts. I would have seen that they were not really "opponents" to the medicalized services for individuals, but a key parallel continuum involved with collective health, the health of populations. Today we would have added "global health."

Before politics, I had questions about the limits of medical science and practice. I sensed, learning about "public health" – a term that was new to me and to most, and a complete misnomer for the public – that its proponents were almost "opponents" to our medical approaches, but why? That medical super-specialization was both essential and terribly negative for patient care had been easy for me to figure out. It was

also obvious to me that the over-medicalization of many natural phe-
nomena, like giving birth, menopause, and many more, was leading to
numerous negative, unnecessary (and expensive) outcomes. Now in my
role as health minister, further to the emergence of "patient self-help"
and "patient support groups" coming to me for funding and recognition, and the fact that my officials were completely opposed to them,
as was part of organized medicine, my critical view of medicine was revived. Concurrently "palliative care units" also emerged, very slowly,
as a new idea in Canada. Long ago I had read Elizabeth Kübler-Ross's
On Death and Dying (1969) and admired the person, her thinking, and
the science behind it. Now, in the department, I was faced with the case
of the Montreal Hôtel-Dieu's medical establishment, which was viciously against an in-house initiative for palliative care. I started observing and asking questions.

Not surprisingly, Ivan Illich's *The Medical Nemesis* came to my
mind. As I could not read it for lack of time, I asked the officials to present me with a summary of his views. I did not know at the time that
this philosopher, whom I would meet in the summer 1979 at the Couchiching Institute of Public Affairs in Orillia, a particularly erudite professor in the best European tradition, was above all an essayist with a
quasi-pamphleteer style. The top of my department opposed a clear
"No!" to their minister's request for help and understanding. It was not
good reading for me! So I had to read it by myself, and others of his
works – an epiphany, a defining moment. And I even had the honour
and pleasure, a few months after politics, at Penn State University, in
mid-January 1985, to be invited by Ivan Illich to participate for two
days in the graduate seminars he animated. More later.

In Ottawa, the Directorate of Health Promotion was also made responsible for a program launched under my predecessor, in 1975, further to Lalonde's internationally recognized *New Perspective on the
Health of Canadians*: the National Health Research and Development
Program. The program was intended to finance health promotion and
research into disease prevention to counterbalance the basic medical research approach of the Medical Research Council. Between 75 and 80
per cent of this new budget supported peer-reviewed pilot projects,

demonstration projects, symposia, and workshops, often tackling topics like child abuse and elder care well ahead of their time.

Provinces also began their own basic and applied health research programs, including the inevitable pilot projects. Later, private foundations jumped in. All of these funding streams launched thousands of pilot projects across the country — projects that usually die when their initial funding runs out, regardless of their merit. Hence my now famous rant about "Canada as the country of perpetual pilot projects" that I first mentioned at the Canadian Public Health Association in Vancouver, in May 2006 repeating it in other public speeches and written articles. Unfortunately, when it comes to moving health-care practices forward efficiently, Canada is a country of perpetual pilot projects. We seldom move proven projects into stable, funded programs, and we rarely transfer the outcomes of pilot projects across jurisdictions. This approach is not serving our health-care system well.

That waste of time, talent, and energy is the first tragedy of this approach. The second tragedy is that our provincial and territorial health silos have no horizontal collaborative mechanisms to share lessons learned from pilot projects across jurisdictions. I am thinking of a national approach, not a federal one. If a project does become integrated into a provincial health budget, that initiative usually stalls at the provincial border, no matter how strong the evidence of its success. New Brunswick's extramural program Hospital without Walls, which delivered home health care, including oxygen services to seniors, was a good example that other provinces could have learned from. The project started small in 1981, and by 1993 it would be offered across the province, becoming the health-care delivery option of choice for more than 19,000 clients in 2005–06.

Two other priorities of the Health Promotion Directorate – tobacco control and safety – were often spearheaded in coordination with Alex Morrison, the ADM of the Health Protection Branch. I still hear him briefing me on his latest encounters with the Canadian Tobacco Manufacturers' Council, or with Paul Paré, their perennial president, himself in charge of Imperial Tobacco. These four big players also included Rothmans of Pall Mall Canada Limited, Macdonald Tobacco Inc., and

Benson & Hedges (Canada) Limited. We were in an uninterrupted trench warfare with them. We could not give them an inch in our step-by-step war towards reduction in tar and nicotine levels in Canadian cigarettes or in the type of publicity the industry wanted, nor how much of it. Marc Lalonde had been an ardent fighter against the tobacco industry. When I came in, the industry had learned by its moles and were pleased that I had been a smoker (of Benson & Hedges!). In fact, I had quit cold turkey sometime before I joined Cabinet. I used to smoke with a cigarette holder refilled regularly with a tar/nicotine filter. The white silica gel crystals in the filter were like dark molasses when replaced. One morning I woke up to the fact that this molasses would have gone into my lungs! I quit at once. At first, my past as a smoker did not help and all players tested me. No need to add I supported fully Dr Morrison's strategy and endeavours, including the menace, in 1983, of a 30 per cent increase in cigarette prices and labelling reforms. When such possibilities came to Cabinet, my friend Gene Whelan would become my worst enemy as minister of agriculture, elected near the Southern Ontario "tobacco belt"! In July 1981 we hosted the fifth World Conference on Smoking, in Ottawa. Fighting tobacco is still a key public health issue, but Canada has done pretty well compared to other countries.

Did I advance Prevention and Health Promotion in any major way? No. I just protected its very existence. It had not been hard to convince me that "public health" workers are more than a delivery system, as can be said of medicare. They are the change agents for the health of the public.

Then, there was my *boîte à surprises,* my surprise box: the Health Protection Branch, where most of the department scientists worked. It was made of five directorates:

- Drugs Directorate
- Food Directorate
- Environmental Health Directorate
- Laboratory Centre for Disease Control
- Field Operations Directorate

Scientists do not ask their minister's advice. Generally speaking, they do not trust politicians and, more to the point, in no circumstances do they accept any kind of interference in their research, and I understood that. In any event, they rather consider us ignorant, indeed stupid, and we are at times. They come to see the minister on two grounds only: in cases when science is uncertain or if they want supplementary budgets! It can be intimidating, at first sight, for a sociologist to inherit a portfolio where one should at least have a law degree, but even better, a doctorate in pure sciences! In fact, Health and Welfare employed graduates in physics, chemistry, biomedical science, even earth sciences, mathematics, and statistics.

I recall a Friday morning question period in November, probably in 1978, as I was still a relatively new minister of national health and welfare. Everyone was tired after a difficult week and dreamed only of going back home for the weekend. Lorne Nystrom rose in the name of the NDP, always self-righteous and a bit arrogant at all times, addressing his three questions to me, with no notice, as usual. He wanted me to urgently issue a warning against eating peanuts from the United States, as they were probably carcinogenic, as suggested by my ADM, Dr Morrison, in a talk in Guelph (probably at its famous agricultural research centre), Nystrom stated. In fact Dr Morrison had mentioned as quoted that day in the *Globe & Mail* that "he will not eat peanuts or any other nuts that taste stale, are misshapen or are discoloured because a microorganism linked with cancer could be present. The organism, aflatoxin, will cause cancer in about 15 species of animals."

We had devised an excellent early warning system on anything related to Health Protection, in particular to prepare me for question period, and I had nothing on the topic in my large Cardex.

I replied calmly that there had not been any such warning issued and that imported peanuts were systematically inspected and seized at the border if they were considered not conforming. As he went on, pushing me "because families were just out of Halloween and kids had received peanuts everywhere in the country"(!), I just repeated that there were no problems and I added, "I want to conclude by indicating that peanuts are still a provider of vitamin E, which is the sexual energy vitamin, and I invite people to eat lots of them this weekend!" The House broke out laughing. But my department received 200 letters from scientists around the country correcting the ignorance of the minister, as that vitamin was vitamin D, not E.

BC salmon and tiny round mushrooms from China badly canned had to be withdrawn from the market until the situation was corrected. The mushroom episode happened shortly before my official trip to China. Upon arrival, at the welcome cocktail given by my Chinese counterpart, my delegation and I were served … those little round mushrooms, which we were supposed to pick and eat with chopsticks. Try it! Authorizing aspartame or banning saccharin, approving or rejecting "natural and non-prescription health products" were other ad hoc issues for me. Below follow a few files that gained high public visibility for whatever reasons.

A day in the life of a minister is rarely the same as the day before. At 10 a.m. on Friday, 16 July 1982, out of the blue, carriers brought into my office huge plastic bags filled with the 40,000 letters of petition organized by Dr W. Gifford-Jones (*nom de plume* of Dr Ken Walker) in favour of legalizing heroin for pain control in palliative cancer care. Upon arrival that morning I had received an express thirty-minute briefing from officials. It became very clear to me that Dr Alex Morrison, the ADM for Health Protection, had found the petition inadmissible and the visit of Dr Gifford-Jones a waste of time, when everyone was so busy. I had one hour to give him, as question period was to start at 11 a.m. (The House would be sitting until 4 August that summer.) Gifford-Jones was a colourful character, elegant and very sure of himself, with the gift of gab. I listened to him, accepted the petition (what else could have I done?), and told him that I would study the issue and get back to him. He had already convened the media, who were waiting at my door, where he gave a short press conference.

I vaguely knew that Gifford-Jones had a very popular syndicated newspaper column for years, that he was criticized by the establishment, but that he was particularly convincing on this particular dossier. He was not always scientifically right in his battles, as his battle against microwaves causing cancer, or later, against cell phones, had the same consequences. However, his fight in favour of controlled medical use of heroin, based on long British experience in palliative care at the London St Thomas Hospital, appeared a valid argument to be considered. I learned that this petition was the consequence of years of public campaigning from him and repeated opposition from the Canadian Cancer Society, the Canadian Pharmacists Association, and a number of his peers. On my side, I had been able to satisfy myself that narcotics controls in institutions and pharmacies were satisfactory. I had a few long working sessions with my ADM and his team on the topic, until Alex Morrison finally informed me, as a last-effort negative argument, that my American counterpart would totally oppose it. I had developed good rapport with Dick Schweiker, secretary of health and human services under President Reagan. I phoned Dick at once, explaining the case to him. He answered that he would not see any problem should we move positively on the petition demand. I acted sincerely the whole time, not arguing nor being provocative. We had a problem, and I needed a decision one way or another. As soon as he was back in his own office, Morrison phoned his contacts in Washington. A day or two later, Dick phoned me, apologizing because he could not, in fact, support me. The worst is that the use of heroin against pain for terminal cancer was already an established practice in the States, but I did not know it.

In any event, a behind-the-scenes campaign against my intentions had developed back home, and Bob Kaplan, then solicitor general, and his civil servants, including the RCMP, who had heard of the petition with Gifford-Jones and had been contacted by my own public servants, had declared war, were constantly after me and informed Cabinet and the prime minister that I was opening Canada to trafficking in hard drugs, starting with heroin! Rational discussion had become impossible. Kaplan and the RCMP were scared stiff that they would become a major target for the United Nations Program on International Drug Control because of me. I went on quietly exploring the issue. Again and again, to my satisfaction, I had checked pharmacies' control of hard and/or illegal drugs, in particular morphine. Later, in October 1983, I had an unexpected, very interesting working session with two British experts in pain management: Drs Sellers and Robert Twycross. I kept thinking of all the parents of dying relatives, deprived of what could ease their pain when morphine did not help, but heroin could.

Of course I finally lost the battle, but a mere three months after Brian Mulroney's electoral victory, my Conservative successor in Health and Welfare, Jake Epp, won it in December 1984.

I became interested in this file because, quite early in my mandate at Health and Welfare, I had learned with amazement, as a patient and a lay person, that medical practitioners were not interested in their patients' pain, nor did they have scientific training in its management. For doctors, pain was an obstacle to treating this or that condition. In June 1978, at the Seventh International Nephrology Convention in Montreal, I met Dr Ronald Melzack, the McGill psychologist-neuroscientist expert in pain study. He was also a remarkable human being who spent his summers in Arctic communities, having learned the language, collecting tales and legends, which he rewrote and published in English. At home I still read *Raven, Creator of the World, Why the Man in the Moon Is Happy,* and *The Day Tuk Became a Hunter* when soothing is required. He first became interested in "phantom limb" pain, which is suffered by those who have lost an arm or a leg. Then in 1965, with Patrick Wall, he developed the gate-control theory of pain, as he knew that pain also had a subjective dimension. Then came his internationally adopted pain scale, the pain pathways, and mechanisms and approaches to control pain. At my request, the department then created an Experts Advisory Committee on acute pain management to prepare a small information document on best practices for medical practitioners. It was distributed to every Canadian doctor, and publicized for the general public.

In 1980 a very different, infamous, and very public dossier ended up at the door from my scientists: that of urea formaldehyde foam insulation (UFFI). We were back in government, following Joe Clark's short government. The Health Protection Branch informed me that quite a number of individuals complained that after exposure to UFFI they were suffering from nondescript allergic reactions: headaches, respiratory problems, throat or eye irritation, runny noses, nosebleeds, and rashes.

Further to the 1970 energy crisis, in 1977 our government had offered a $500 grant through its Canadian Home Insulation Program to home owners to increase the insulation levels in their houses. Pumping UFFI into walls and attics, under plumbing fixtures and in other semi-enclosed space, had been the solution for many. It was relatively cheap, easy to install, and an excellent insulation. But it was often badly installed and used where it should not have been. A number of small homes, cottages, and bungalows had not been properly insulated.

What to do? Science was vague, even contradictory, providing decision-makers with no solid foundations for moving ahead one way or another. Were these complaints psychosomatic, as some believed? Were they the beginning of a collective psychosis? So we first opted for an external Canadian Experts Committee. From their report, we learned nothing new. I then agreed to set up an international Experts Commission. Same results. So, in the absence of clear scientific evidence, I was confronted with deciding in favour of public health or recognizing other valid interests of an economic dimension. We could imagine costs of UFFI removal, depreciated house values (it would become mandatory to declare the presence of UFFI in any home transaction), and costly legal suits from homeowners (which took place), even from manufacturers to government(s). My own riding of Saint-Léonard-Anjou, of relatively recent construction, had numerous UFFI cases. However, this fact never influenced me.

With no benchmarks to reach a decision, with the Health Protection team, without knowing it, we had applied the "precautionary principle," which was formulated in 1992 as Principle 15 of the Rio Declaration on the environment: "Where there are threats of serious or irreversible damage, lack of full scientific certainty shall not be used as a reason for postponing cost-effective measures to prevent environment degradation." Although this principle was adopted in relation to the environment, it was later extended to other fields of human activity by governments and some industries. This Rio principle is more recent and developed than John Stuart Mill's "utilitarian principle," which can be summed up as "Always act for the greatest good for the greatest number of people."

In 1980–81 I had to inform Cabinet of the situation because of its economic consequences. Several ministers and their departments would

have to be involved. We even held a meeting of a Special Cabinet Committee on a Saturday. A few weeks later, after interdepartmental consultations, I came back to Cabinet with recommendations that the use
of UFFI be banned in Canada, as it was in the United States; that it be
listed under the Hazardous Products Act; and that its production, im-
port, and sale be prohibited, and all recommendations were approved
in December 1980. My public situation was most unpleasant. Other
Cabinet colleagues were involved, and I kept a low profile, trying to explain the situation without passing judgment. At later Cabinet meetings,
in 1981, a financial assistance program up to $5,000 to individual home
owners was approved for removal of UFFI from one's premises. It was
later estimated that this amount was insufficient for the work needed.
In the spring of 1984, André Ouellet, who had been involved while minister of consumer and corporate affairs, revealed that only 58,000 home
owners registered for this grant.

In fact, our government had promoted the use of UFFI with our
energy grants, then learned of a "possible" important health problem,
reversed its stand on UFFI, creating major economic losses for home
owners, and then offered far too little in compensation. A regrouping
of Quebec home owners paraded a pig's head with my name on it
through the streets of Montreal. It goes with the job.

Then in 1993, after having tried every route, six Quebec home owners sued two UFFI manufacturers, the Canada Mortgage and Housing
Corporation, the Quebec attorney general, and UFFI installation specialists. An Association of UFFI Victims had already been set up with a
membership of over 5,000. The trial went on for years and cost millions; the victims lost, the judge ruling that they had not proved a
causality relationship between UFFI and their health problems! Years
later, long after I had left politics, a man coming out from his hotel in
the Sixth Arrondissement, in Paris, stopped me suddenly. I had no idea
who he was. He identified himself as Judge René Hurtubise, the one
who had ruled against the victims in the UFFI case. I did not have time
to say a word when he added that he despised me for having banned
UFFI purely for crass politics, and he left rapidly. There is no such thing
as zero risk in politics.

The most dramatic and public disaster I was involved with during the last two years as minister of national health and welfare was that of 1982, on HIV/AIDS-contaminated blood. The first case of AIDS was reported in Canada in February 1982. Nothing was then known about that puzzling new disease — defined at the time as "a relatively rare form of pneumonia." By the end of 1982 the American Atlanta Centers for Disease Control referred to four "identified risk factors" for acquiring AIDS: male homosexuality, intravenous drug abuse, Haitian origin, and hemophilia. Two years later, towards the end of my ministerial mandate, it had become clear that HIV was the causative agent of AIDS, and it was more and more conclusive that blood and blood products were a mode of transmission.

However, issues of blood regulation and supply were not new to me. It was an important dossier that would pop up from time to time in the course of my mandate. Despite my insatiable curiosity and love of learning, I never found these dossiers interesting or even pleasant. That was in response to the leader of the Canadian Red Cross Society, George Weber, who was quite arrogant and acted as if he were in charge of an ivory tower, monopolizing the country's blood supply, not ready to collaborate at all, and despising having to be "controlled" by my Health Protection Branch. However, my senior civil servants had an excellent and close working relationship with Dr Roger Perrault, the Red Cross medical director, a scientist of great competence and total integrity. He became the choice victim of the activist Canadian Hemophilia Society, which would later vitiate the Krever inquiry by identifying culprits on its own, even before the start of the inquiry. After more than two decades of persecution – the word is not too strong – Dr Perrault was finally vindicated of all accusations by the Court in October 2007.

The Canadian Red Cross Society was established in 1909 and had operated since that time as a charitable institution. During the Second World War its new role of collecting blood for the Canadian Armed Forces led the institution to start, at their request, collecting and providing blood and blood products to some provincial hospitals until it became the new norm. Connaught Laboratories in Toronto provided plasma fractionation for the blood products required. As time went on, problems started to develop. These years are captured by Law Professor Sanda Rodgers in her 1989 analysis of our blood delivery system:

> In 1972 Connaught Laboratories was purchased from the University of Toronto by the Canadian Development Corporation. The sale resulted in part because the University of Toronto had realized that a large capital investment would be needed to improve the existing Connaught facilities. Both the construction of new buildings and renovation of existing structures would be required. Prior to the sale, the Government of Ontario had declined to finance the necessary improvements. It is significant to later conflict that the objectives of the Canadian Development Corporation at that time were to develop and maintain Canadian control in the private sector, to widen investment opportunities for Canadians and to operate at a profit in the interests of shareholders.

She rightly concluded that this played a key role in the federal-provincial conflicts I would face, for it was the federal-provincial dimension of blood supply issues, the provincial health systems being the customers without consensus on the topic of the day, that I also found quite unpleasant in the blood dossier. So, of all the nonsensical governance situations I observed in my long tenure at Health and Welfare, the worst started with the blood products governance in the course of my first ministerial mandate, 1977–79.

All blood products had to be licensed by the Bureau of Biologics of my department under the Food and Drug Act. When I started in the fall of 1977, the Canadian Red Cross wanted the federal and provincial governments to finance a plasma fractionating facility, preferably in Hull, Quebec. We would all pay but have no say in the objectives and decisions. Quebec Dr Denis Lazure, René Lévesque's minister of health then, stated that he wanted to use only blood from Quebecers, fractionated in Quebec! I forget which Maritime province wanted the facility to be in its territory, and Winnipeg wanted one in Manitoba! And then there was the future of the Connaught Labs in Toronto, owned by

Americans by then, but still operating in Canada, and of the Institut Armand-Frappier in Laval, Quebec.

When I came back as minister of national health and welfare in March 1980, I received the Chapin Key report, commissioned by David Crombie in the Joe Clark government. He was recommending three plants for blood products: Connaught Labs, the Armand-Frappier Lab, and the Rh Institute in Winnipeg, in addition to a national new body to fully manage the Canadian Blood Program. We had a long federal-provincial meeting in December 1980, followed by more meetings in 1981. Finally, Dr Key's recommendations were rejected and a hybrid approach was adopted. (Connaught Campus Lab is now the Campus Connaught of Sanofi Pasteur Ltd. In my years, Dr William A. (Bill) Cochrane was its president and CEO.)

The only decision finally taken by the parties concerned – which I reluctantly approved and set up at the request of the provinces to manage blood products – was the creation of a new body, the Canadian Blood Committee, made up of and run by the provincial health deputy ministers, with no authority structure, all amongst equals, with a new federal secretariat that we paid for. I appointed Dr Denise Leclerc-Chevalier, the director of the Bureau of Drug Quality Assessment of my Health Protection Branch, as its secretary, *une main de fer dans un gant de velours*. Despite her talent, the scene remained structurally completely fragmented among players, including the absent Red Cross. The first meeting of the newly created hybrid took place on 1 December 1981. The provincial deputy ministers elected Ambrose Hearn, the DM of Newfoundland, as their chair. We would put up 50 per cent of the costs for an operational budget of $300,000. My ADM Dr Maureen Law was the only federal representative on the committee. This permanent Secretariat with Dr Denise Leclerc-Chevalier was located in my ministry's office at Tunney's Pasture, in Ottawa.

It was in 1982 that I became regularly briefed on what would become known as AIDS. *Acquired immune deficiency syndrome* (AIDS) was a term that had just been coined at a CDC scientific meeting in Washington on 27 July 1982 to describe the symptoms and risks factors. There were then eight cases in Canada, of which six had died, the first

having been identified in February. The notion was that an unknown
agent attacked the immune system through blood and bodily fluids. As
if it were yesterday, I recall Dr Maureen Law explaining to me that
handshakes might transmit the new disease: not much was known! It
then seemed to attack homosexual men, drugs addicts through their
needles, and heterosexual hemophiliacs because of the blood concen-
trates they were injected with to survive. In mid-March 1983 the Red
Cross issued a press release mentioning recently landed Haitians as a
group at risk; and there were already a few Canadian and American
cases. The large Montreal Haitian community, concentrated in my own
riding, reacted angrily. What could I say? It is true that the Red Cross
had not communicated or consulted with the Haitian community. Later
we developed a small information pamphlet. At the same time, the official line was that there was no conclusive evidence that AIDS is transmitted through the blood or blood products, and no cases of AIDS in
Canada could be linked to blood transfusion.

In May–June 1983 the ADM Dr Morrison recommended that I support creation of a National Task Force on AIDS, which I immediately
approved, with names of Canadian expert researchers on the subject
suggested by his branch. Dr Norbert Gilmore, a McGill University research pioneer on HIV and AIDS and a human rights voice for these patients, agreed to chair the committee on a voluntary basis. The task
force met immediately but was announced only in August. When I came
back from my holidays in early August, a briefing note from the department informed me that "the cause of AIDS had not been discovered,
despite two years of studies." It added that we totalled thirty-three cases
in Canada, of which twenty had died. In the fall I obtained Cabinet approval for new projects on AIDS, including information for the public,
the National Task Force, a supplementary budget of $1.49 million, as
well as an additional $525,000 for Dr Phil Gold's team research project
under the Medical Research Council.

And on 23 April 1984 the historic Washington press conference
given by Dr Robert Gallo announced the discovery of the AIDS virus,
the human immunodeficiency virus (HIV), first identified a year before
by Dr Luc Montagnier in France. However, despite Gallo's article pub-

lished at once in *Science,* this virus discovery remained controversial for quite some time before making history.

When I left politics on 4 September 1984, four months after the Montagnier/Gallo discovery, no treatment to inactivate the virus had been found. Whatever our deep concerns in the department, HIV/AIDS was still so marginal a topic in Canadian public opinion that, at the end of May 1984, the Opposition (and the Liberal) MPs did not ask a single question on the topic during the House Committee's public hearings on the estimates of National Health and Welfare. And during those two years, I might have had one question during the daily question period in the House of Commons.

The link between blood and blood products on the one hand, and the transmission of HIV/AIDS or the health deterioration in hemophiliacs on the other would only start to be slowly decoded in 1984–85. The screening test called enzyme-linked immunosorbent assay (ELISA), which identified HIV antibodies as a marker of HIV exposure in the blood collected from blood donors, was set up for use by the Red Cross only in November 1985. The expressions *contaminated blood* and *tainted blood* applied to hemophiliacs or otherwise would appear in Canada much later, in the 1990s.

To conclude momentarily on this file, during my life after politics in the 1990s, this tragedy left 20,000 Canadians infected with HIV and hepatitis C. And it would cost the taxpayers more than $5 billion in compensation.

Now that I think of it, if the Social Services (Canada Assistance Plan) or the Health Services and Promotion Branches (medicare) were the product of federal–provincial relationships, the Health Protection Branch was the one where my department required constant relationships and regulatory action with the industry or with powerful NGOs like the Canadian Red Cross Society. Food manufacturing, even agriculture (jobs threatened by tobacco control, for example), meat and fishery quality control, pharmaceuticals, natural health products, blood products, tobacco manufacturers, and drug control were topics of negotiation, legal action when needed, and full-time follow-up with the world around. To maintain vigilance and preparedness was an all-time objective.

My years in National Health and Welfare were wonderful years. To be reappointed in 1980, after the short Conservative government, was a recognition from the prime minister; I was thrilled. And then to be reappointed a third time to the same portfolio, by Turner this time, was my last moment of pride, even if I knew but could not say that it would not be for long this time. The department and the MRC knew me well, and so did the constituencies of whom I was the special voice around the Cabinet table. Practising power can be quite strange at times. This was when I discovered that the ambition of ministers and the game of Privy Council were to change departments' political heads every year and a half, two years: that was the ideal. For ministers, I heard some say to me, it would give them new contacts, new connections, new openings "for their future leadership bid"! I felt as if I were from another planet and concluded that it made no logical sense at all. A few close friends, Cabinet colleagues, meaning well, offered their sympathy when Trudeau reappointed me in March 1980! The years in Health and Welfare form part of my happiest memories of great challenges, successful battles of all kinds, and less successful ones. I dealt with extraordinary and visionary scientists, mostly very competent and committed civil servants, four helpful, reliable, and friendly parliamentary secretaries (Ken Robinson, David Weatherhead, Doug Frith, and Russell MacLellan), and some very decent provincial counterparts in either Health or Social Affairs. I also met some nasty and vulgar provincial politicians and media prima donnas, sexist if not to add racist, probably because I was a woman and from Quebec. We did not win all the fights, but when we did, I knew it would generally improve the lives of millions, at least hundreds and thousands of Canadians. It was most stressful, most challenging, and most rewarding. And it would somehow remain part of my professional life for some twenty more years under one form or another. But that I did not know!

I spoke of hard work, challenging dossiers, exhausting trips from coast to coast to coast, great colleagues and less pleasant ones, and I will try to speak of Pierre Trudeau as prime minister in the coming chapters. Through all these years, maintaining a balance in my life and sleeping enough to maintain my health were also very important. Luckily, with a few days of holidays, I can rapidly recover from exhaustion. Besides holidays with a friend or two in Morocco or Mexico (a country I loved), Guadeloupe, the Algarve in Portugal (where I went often in the summer and even once in the winter!), I did spend great long weekends ... at colleagues' homes in Canada. Two come to mind. Following the July 1974 election and arrival of the young, modern, and brilliant Québécois MPs (C.A. Lachance, P. Bussières, C. Lapointe, D. Dawson [in 1977], R. Bujold, L. Duclos, and B. Loiselle), we rapidly became a group of friends, especially the first five named above. Just after question period, past three o'clock and when I could, I joined them in the Liberal caucus lobby for a rapid coffee, just for relaxing, mocking whatever, and reorganizing the world. André Maltais (Manicouagan) would have been one of us, but he was elected too late, in 1979 and in 1980. Our friendship cemented at Charles Lapointe's great large and charming traditional Quebec home in La Malbaie, his riding. With wives and companions and Charles's Quebec City and local friends joining us, we enjoyed unending long parties, usually on the rare long weekends when one cannot do politics in the riding: 24 May, June, Labour Day, or Thanksgiving weekends. We danced, wore costumes, played games, drank (moderately), ran around, visited the region, went to the famous local hotel overlooking the St Lawrence River, and ate very well.

When Judith Erola was elected on 18 February 1980 and appointed to Cabinet on 3 March we became friends for life almost immediately. A year later, when the Canadian constitutional bill was referred to the Supreme Court, parliamentarians got the last week of April 1981 off. Judy and I had our first holiday trip together. We spent the week in Key West, visiting Hemingway's house (and cats), swimming and snorkelling in the coral reefs. And I would later discover her Northern Ontario world: her home and large fruit and vegetable garden on small Lake Panache/Penage and her large summer camp on big Panache/Penage near the Whitefish reserve, which could be reached only by boat. Judy's parents were Finnish immigrants, so I discovered the Finnish sauna tradition and some special food and legends. Judy still spoke Finnish, and her bathroom had an impressive collection of newspapers in Finnish. Her riding being the "doughnut" around Sudbury, her way of life, that of her organizers – "the old girls" who looked very ordinary but defeated the candidate the local party men wanted – and her family lifestyle were completely new to me. These "old girls" were lots of fun. As Judy had told me, they had been secretaries and office managers, not president of anything, organizing men's lives all the time. Liberals since forever, they took me around the wonderful region, to Manitoulin Island, to Espanola, Whitefish, or French River.

I still recall being wakened during the night by a bat circling my head in Judy's house, and Judy being terrified (!), or having the Vandermeulens – Monique Coupal, my chief of staff, her husband Henri, on Gene Whelan's staff, and their young Catherine – and her big white Samoyed jumping out of the car on arrival at night at the lake and getting sprayed by a skunk within five minutes. Then Judy and Monique Coupal rushed to the marina before it closed to buy big cans of tomato juice, spraying Cosaque, brushing him, sending him into the lake, which he did want to do at all ... Well, my urban riding was not exotic at all in comparison. She still likes to tell the story of me preparing her garden for the winter on our first long Thanksgiving weekend together, and I suddenly shouted, "Judy! There is a flying moose! It's attached to a helicopter!" What did I know of hunting season in the north? Yes, she had her family hunting rifles in a special case in the house and wanted to show me how to operate one. Two of my close friends, a woman scientist from my department and one from my riding, became good friends of hers after politics, and we would go to her home there, travel to Provence together, and more. While ministers, it was just the two of us escaping Ottawa in those too few long weekends without politics. Once, while swimming in small Panache, the lake being totally quiet, we started kidding about which male Cabinet colleagues we would be interested in but couldn't find one, although some were definitely better than others. We almost drowned laughing. Then Judy recalled that sound carried all around the lake in the very quiet air and we swam back home without a word.

My birthday parties, generally given by Monique Coupal and Henry Vandermeulen, through the years brought together Judy Erola and my young Québécois MP friends, as well as Marc Lalonde, Pierre Juneau, Rita Cadieux, and others, enjoying life to the maximum and not talking shop. Our very last wonderfully happy gathering of friends while in politics was at Lloyd and Denise Axworthy's wedding on 3

August 1984, in the middle of the general election called by John Turner. The wedding took place in Parliament followed by a fine reception at the Château Laurier. Judy and I were there with Ed and Pat Lumley, Roméo LeBlanc, Lorna Marsden, Dennis Dawson and Anne Laberge, Keith and Dorothy Davey, and John and Geills Turner. We were delighted by the happiness of our friend Lloyd, and we adopted Denise at once! And on 4 September 1984 Lloyd would be one of only two Liberals elected west of Ontario!

And my own family in all that? Except for my childhood and student years, I have kept my private life very private. That was a decision I made at the age of fifteen, probably as my family life was so different from that of my friends, and I wanted to protect it, however painful life at home had become. Much later in life, almost out of the blue, I became a politician. Politics can become a powerful drug, engulfing any private life, as I observed around me. I am one of those people who value and give priority to a personal life, a family life. Through all my years on the Hill, I remained as close as possible to my sisters and brothers, my nieces and nephews. My ministerial life was so full, and I gave it not only my best but so much time that I would not allow myself to be penalized because I was single. So, for example, when my sister Marie needed a break as a young working mother of two, I took her to Paris with me on an Armed Forces aircraft. (When their planes to our Lahr or Gatwick bases were not full, MPs of all parties could apply for seats for the immediate family.) On my first trip to northern Manitoba reserves, I took my nephew and godson François to God's Lake, fishing with my officials. Or my niece Christine on the great ministerial Arctic trip to some Inuit communities in the Far North in early summer 1983. My eldest nieces, Sophie and Julie, came to Ottawa and Parliament a few times. When home in Montreal, we would cook great meals, enjoy ourselves around my large dining room table, and play all sorts of board games and literary games during Christmas or summer holidays. In later years, especially after the death of my beloved youngest brother, Thomas, in March 1981, our paths somehow parted, although we still see each other from time to time.

In the meantime, another kind of family took shape, made up of friends of all ages and kinds, including a few significant others. I now have four adoptive families: in Ottawa, Paris, Toronto, and Sudbury/ Savannah/Wilmington. I never had children of my own, but I have always been surrounded by young people – tots, teenagers, or young adults – with whom I have a special bond: my three godsons, the daughter of very close friends, a niece, and others. I am a child at heart (j'ai toujours gardé la vertu d'enfance), in many ways. I consider myself very lucky and I am still astonished at the gifts of friendship and affection I have received.

After one year, Trudeau announces a Cabinet reshuffle and I receive the biggest portfolio in terms of public expenditures, that of National Health and Welfare (16 September 1977). Credit: Jean-Marc Carisse Photography.

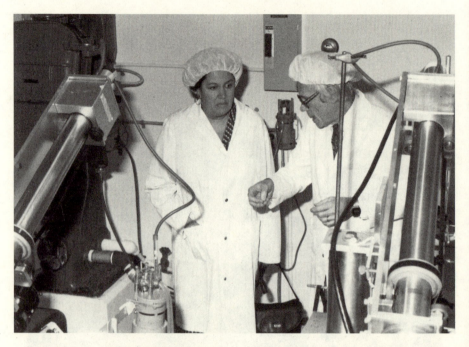

I am also the minister of the Medical Research Council. Here is a visit to the
Institut Armand-Frappier in Laval, QC.

Aboriginal health being one of the nine branches of National Health and Welfare, I went to visit at least twenty First Nations and ten Inuit communities (as much as weather and mosquitoes permitted). Here I am in one of the numerous different First Nations of a Northern Ontario reserve.

In Ottawa at National Health and Welfare, discussing with young Aboriginal leaders the future policy of devolution of community health services to the reserves.

On 3 March 1980, with Pierre Trudeau returning with a majority government after defeating Joe Clark's government, I am thrilled to be reappointed to my same old department. Credit: Jean-Marc Carisse.

After meeting Cui Yueli in Beijing, just appointed health minister of China, I was invited by his predecessor, Qian Xinzhong, whom I had received at the WHO in Geneva and admired. Minister of health from 1965 to 1982 (excepting a few years during the Cultural Revolution), he was now minister of family planning. I shared with him the purpose of my three weeks in China to negotiate academic research partnerships. September 1982.

My Cabinet colleague and friend Judy Erola and myself with
Céline Hervieux-Payette, just appointed to Cabinet as a junior minister to me
(Fitness and Amateur Sport), leaving the House of Commons for a Senate ceremony,
7 December 1983. We are again three women in a Cabinet with thirty men.
Credit: Jean-Marc Carisse Photography.

The minister of finance, Marc Lalonde, supports the 30 per cent tax increase on cigarettes I am requesting from Cabinet to prevent tobacco's damage to health!
Credit: Tom Innes, *Calgary Herald*, 13 July 1983.

I found myself fighting the provinces for five years to get rid of hospital user fees and doctors' extra billing until the unanimous passage of the Canada Health Act in 1984.
Credit: Tom Innes, *Calgary Herald*, 27 July 1983.

During my seven years in National Health and Welfare, there were numerous great cartoons of me. Here is one of my favourites!
Credit: Merle Tingley, *London Free Press*, 14 April 1983.

Chairing the largest Commonwealth health ministers meeting (forty-two out of forty-eight) in Ottawa, focusing on preventive health care. To my left is the long-serving Commonwealth secretary-general, Sir Shridath Ramphal. October 1983.

While a visiting professor in health administration at University of Ottawa, from March 2005 to the end of August 2008, I served as a commissioner on the WHO International Commission on Social Determinants of Health, here in Santiago, Chile, at our first meeting. Working with our chair, Sir Michael Marmot, was a precious experience. To his right in the photo is Chile's then president Ricardo Lagos, also a commissioner. Credit: Alex Ibanez.

Further to retiring from the Telfer School of Management, University of Ottawa, in December 2010, after four years in women's studies, seven years as dean of Health Sciences, and many more years teaching in the master's of health administration, President Allan Rock and Dean François Julien name a study room for me.

Receiving my honorary doctorate in laws, Dalhousie University (Halifax), 1987.
Photographed by Carlos, Dalhousie Photographic Services.

A Holocaust survivor, elected president of the European Parliament,
twice minister of health of France, Simone Veil, whom I met a few
times in Ottawa, Montreal, and Paris, remains one of my heroes.

PART FOUR

Working with Pierre Trudeau

15

The First Quebec Referendum (1980)

The 18 February 1980 general election, further to the defeat of Joe Clark's government on John Crosbie's budget, on 13 December 1979, brought Trudeau back to power with a solid majority of 147 Liberal MPs against 103 for the Conservative Party as the official Opposition, and 32 for the NDP. Significant from a strategic viewpoint, Trudeau had received 68.2 per cent of the Quebec votes, corresponding to 74 Liberal seats out of a possible 75. The prime minister and I had both obtained the highest percentage of votes of all of Canada in our respective Quebec ridings: 81 per cent! For the first time, the Social Credit did not have even one seat and would never come back on the federal scene, further to its appearance in 1962.

The prime minister formed his government on 3 March, and I was reappointed minister of national health and welfare, to my great satisfaction. I learned of it in Mexico, where Trudeau reached me through our Ambassador Claude Charland as I was taking a well-earned holiday. Like others, I had been sent to campaign for colleagues in the worst winter cold: shaking hands at the corner of Portage and Main with Lloyd Axworthy in Winnipeg, a May 1979 newcomer to the House, or doing the same with Judy Erola at 6 a.m. at the INCO mine entrance in Sudbury. I had also been sent to support our Liberal candidates in Toronto, Timmins, Windsor, Hamilton, Burlington, Temiskaming, Kirkland Lake, New Liskard, Cobalt, Verner, Haileybury, Moncton, Shediac, Saint-Calixte (Joliette), Sydney, Baddeck, New Waterford, Glace Bay, Verdun, Saint-Henri, Sainte-Marie, in Beauce, at Brome-Missisquoi – a list that today reads like a train itinerary!

The Quebec Referendum question on its independence, the very first referendum, promised by René Lévesque for Christmas, had been in fact released on 20 December 1979, a week after the start of the federal election. It is worth reading it again:

> The Government of Quebec has made public its proposal to ne-gotiate a new agreement with the rest of Canada, based on the equality of nations; this agreement would enable Quebec to ac-quire the exclusive power to make its laws, levy its taxes and es-tablish relations abroad – in other words, sovereignty – and at the same time to maintain with Canada an economic association including a common currency; any change in political status re-sulting from these negotiations will only be implemented with popular approval through another referendum; on these terms, do you give the Government of Quebec the mandate to negotiate the proposed agreement between Quebec and Canada?
>
> Le Gouvernement du Québec a fait connaître sa proposition d'en arriver, avec le reste du Canada, à une nouvelle entente fon-dée sur le principe de l'égalité des peuples; cette entente permet-trait au Québec d'acquérir le pouvoir exclusif de faire ses lois, de percevoir ses impôts et d'établir ses relations extérieures, ce qui est la souveraineté, et, en même temps, de maintenir avec le Ca-nada une association économique comportant l'utilisation de la même monnaie; aucun changement de statut politique résultant de ces négociations ne sera réalisé sans l'accord de la population lors d'un autre référendum; en conséquence, accordez-vous au Gouvernement du Québec le mandat de négocier l'entente pro-posée entre le Québec et le Canada?

Television having been installed in the Legislative Assembly in Que-bec City, the parliamentary debates on "The Question" started on 4 March. We had just formed the government in Ottawa the afternoon before. This Quebec parliamentary debate went on for two weeks and amounted to a resounding success for the Parti Québécois, Claude Ryan's provincial Liberals seeming unprepared and totally lost. However, public opinion polls were describing the two camps as running neck-and-neck.

As soon as we were back in government, Trudeau chaired a special weekly Quebec ministers Monday breakfast meeting at the Langevin Block, with the presence of Pierre Juneau (then in the PMO, further to having been defeated in a by-election in Montreal), as well as De Montigny Marchand, from the PCO, and Claude Lemelin, a former *Le Devoir* editorialist, Carl Goldenberg, and one or two more. Other names formed the core group of actively involved advisors, including Gérard Veilleux, Bob Rabinovitch, George Anderson, and Tommy Shoyama (just retired). They all met every Monday at noon. One morning, quite early in the game, De Montigny Marchand suggested to the prime minister that we should start trivializing (*banaliser*) the referendum. My heart immediately skipped a beat, and I strongly reacted against such a defeatist approach. It was not a good start.

Jean Chrétien, whom Trudeau had made the official federal spokesperson on the referendum, took over the Canadian Unity Information Office / Centre d'information sur l'unité canadienne, set up by Paul Tellier before Joe Clark's time and just revived. What I saw of what they did was trivial: distributing coffee mugs or card games with a red Canadian maple leaf that we were supposed to distribute in our ridings. The centre, under the two key players Pierre Lefebvre and Richard Dicerni, was a very secretive operation, with lots of money, focused on heavy-handed advertising of every program, pension, allowance, or federal money going to Quebecers. It was embarrassing, tantamount to incomplete not to say dishonest statements. Of course my department – with all the pension cheques, family allowances, and new Horizons grants – offered a natural vehicle for political inserts heavily praising the financial benefits of federalism.

In hindsight, either I was too busy with a very demanding portfolio, with speeches and meetings all over the country all the time, or I was deliberately kept aside for being too demanding, but I learned through books years later of the federal war machinery of these days. Or maybe I was "the minister with the Yvettes movement," which was a world on its own, almost outside the mainstream game. Reading L.

Ian MacDonald's *From Bourassa to Bourassa: Wilderness to Restoration* when it came out in 2002, I learned, for example, that every Monday afternoon in March, April, and May 1980, Chrétien met with a committee of the Quebec caucus – Jean-Claude Malépart, Rémi Bujold, André Maltais, Dennis Dawson, and Irénée Pelletier – to discuss the state of affairs relating to the referendum.

Things were not going well at all through March 1980. The feds were not allowed to campaign directly in Quebec or take initiatives, unless specifically approved by Claude Ryan, on an ad hoc basis, as he was by provincial legislation the leader of the No campaign. In Quebec, Montreal, or Ottawa I came to think that our male colleague politicians did not know where to go or what to do and were unable to answer or even see the emotional dimensions of what was at stake as lived by the public.

Then came *Les Yvettes*! The name is that then used in school books to describe "Yvette the little girl doing dishes to help Mom, when her brother Guy was practising tennis, boxing, and diving to become a champion," which Lise Payette, former TV personality and the Quebec minister of the status of women, had used with contempt while referring in a public meeting, on 9 March to Madeleine Ryan, Claude Ryan's wife, as "just a mother at home," the ultimate insult. Minister Payette then repeated it several times in a press conference, attacking the Liberal leader Claude Ryan: "Des Yvettes lui, il va vouloir qu'il y en ait plein le Québec ... il est marié avec une Yvette!" On 11 March *Le Devoir*'s Lise Bissonnette signed a resounding editorial accusing the minister of despising women at home, hence breaking women's solidarity. Erroneously, the media rapidly assumed that they were detecting an anti-feminist backlash in the population. But it was the opposite, as will soon be demonstrated.

Still nothing visible was happening in the official No side under Claude Ryan's leadership. In the federal ranks, Jean Chrétien was repeating with passion his love of the Rockies, but this image was going nowhere in comparison to the "the great Quebec collective project" of the Parti Québécois, and Gilles Vigneault and Pauline Julien and other artists' songs and poems about the country Quebec.

Towards the end of March one of my political staff heard of a brunch of federalist women to take place at the famous Château Frontenac hotel in Quebec City on Sunday the thirtieth. No program, no organizers' names, no agenda. I decided at once to go to Quebec City, picking up Thérèse Casgrain and Lucie Dion by plane from Montreal. Once there, in the ballroom of the Château Frontenac, I lived one of the most extraordinary brunch gatherings I ever experienced: *le brunch des Yvettes!* The meal ticket at the door was only six dollars. Titles, social classes, famous people – none of that meant anything anymore. Along narrow refectory tables were seated 1,700 women, all equals. None of the usual famous hotel white damask tablecloths and napkins, no elegant china, no crystal glasses. One had to look for a place anywhere in the room, sit down, and in my case, introduce oneself to a woman on my left who worked in a launderette and a nurse on my right, and eat a casual breakfast. It was so warmly egalitarian, a dream come true, a situation that does not exist in politics, whatever we brag about. A few local Liberal women organizers went onstage with Thérèse Casgrain and Madeleine Ryan, the first Yvette, accompanied by Thérèse Lavoie-Roux, a Quebec Liberal MLA, one or two other women, and myself, when the organizers saw me at a ballroom table. None of this had been pre-orchestrated except for having Madeleine Ryan there. We were each invited to say a few words, no more than five minutes, about what we wished for our country, and we each spontaneously concluded acknowledging, "I am an Yvette!" Everything was positive and full of hope. An American journalist, passing through the Château to cover a business meeting, intrigued by this huge, unusual gathering, inquired and wrote about it. This is how the rest of Canada heard about it!

The origin of this first gathering of Les Yvettes came from the same overwhelming helplessness that I felt: our men in power seemed powerless and incapable of thinking, strategizing, even reacting. I had never experienced that before. So, six or seven women from Quebec City, Liberal organizers both at the federal and provincial levels, from the Jean-Talon and Louis-Hébert ridings, who regularly lunched together, decided to take charge. As far as I was able to verify decades later, they were Andrée Richard, Monique Lehoux, Elisabeth Goodwin, Lucienne

Saillant, Jeanne Painchaud, and Lyse Audet. So they decided to give voice to the federalist Quebec City women, across partisanship and neighbourhoods. They did it without financing, only through volunteers, and against the will of the provincial Liberal Party strategists. English Canada still does not know much, if at all, about an initiative that would become a powerful spontaneous social movement all over the province, a key factor in defeating the first referendum on sovereignty.

This would be followed, a week later, by the huge gathering of 14,000 Yvettes at the Montreal Forum, on the evening of 7 April 1980. Women came in by bus from every town and village close enough to Montreal. I remember buses from the Eastern Townships, De Lanaudière, Quebec City, and farther. The provincial Liberal politicos had finally woken up, trying to take ownership of that first success, and reluctantly gave Louise Robic, future Premier Bourassa's MLA and minister, then working at the party head office, the responsibility for logistics. She took over renting the Forum, organizing intercity buses, light and sound, music, decorations, badges, water bottles, even minimum fast food. She was given a very limited budget, for the provincial Liberal Party was sure it would be a complete flop. The entrance ticket was four dollars! I was there that evening. It was a huge party of women, old and young, students, farmers and nurses and secretaries, and businesswomen! And women at home! They were singing, there was music, flags. It was most convivial and very noisy! The French SRC-TV legendary host Michelle Tisseyre was acting as MC and about a dozen established politicians and other known women leaders were on the stage, not to make a speech – that was not at all the style – but to give a testimony of a few words of how they felt, their hopes for the results and why. Testimonies came from Thérèse Casgrain, Madeleine Ryan, Renaude Lapointe (Senate Speaker), Jeanne Sauvé (House Speaker), Thérèse Lavoie-Roux and Solange Chaput-Rolland (Quebec MLAS), Yvette Rousseau (senator), Sheila Finestone (president of the FFQ), me a federal minister, and maybe one or two more. We were celebrating Canada, and the times were not for grand theories. In the audience one could hear Lise Payette's name being booed here and there, but that was not the spirit of the evening. Without saying it in words, everyone knew that evening that politics was too important to be left to men!

Most Quebec editorialists and later feminist academics, of all political persuasions, put down these gatherings as an anti-feminist backlash from "women at home," "just housewives," "completely manipulated Liberal women," but they did lousy research, if any at all. As far as I could check, they did not interview the original Quebec City organizers, or Senator Dennis Dawson, then their MP (who, by the way, learned of the brunch in the newspapers the day after!). Exceptions to this severe judgment of mine include Renée Dandurand and Evelyne Tardy's chapter in the 1981 *Femmes et politique*, and decades later, Stéphanie Godin's UQAM master's thesis in 2003. The majority of participants in these Yvettes gatherings were of the silent majority of citizens, and they were "natural" feminists, without a label, as I was myself learning about branches of feminism when teaching in women's studies a few years later.

During the next six weeks of the referendum campaign, the Forum gathering was followed by local meetings of Yvettes all over the province. It became quite exhausting to be in Ottawa during the day when the thirty-second Parliament reconvened for its first session on 14 April, and to cover Yvette meetings in the evenings. But besides those in Montreal and its South Shore ridings, I managed to participate to some twelve other Yvette gatherings, including the Saguenay cities and some Laurentians towns.

I lived this first Quebec Referendum with great emotion. Although it was almost won by the Yes camp in favour of separation, the second referendum, in 1995, appeared quite different to me. It seemed to be more of a game, less of an emotional adventure, a unique moment in time. In 1980 families were divided and so were working colleagues, businesses, and associations of all kinds. We were all bombarded with media messages. Television was thrilled to exploit politician brothers or sisters on opposite sides on of the issue: Pierre Marc Johnson, Péquiste, and Daniel, Liberal; my sister Catherine, a separatist and prominent actress, and myself, the federal minister. The two of us played the roles with elegance, even wit!

As it is certainly clear by now, I was quite sensitive to the attraction of the PQ rhetoric of a better future, that *grand projet de société* – whatever it meant – to which citizens were invited, while we had not much to offer other than the Rockies or the statistics of federal transfers of money. All publicity from the Yes side was modern, sophisticated, and smart; it went brilliantly straight towards its objective. One day Simon Dorval, a Montreal publicist who had done excellent TV and other media publicity work for our health promotion programs against tobacco or alcohol abuse, asked to see me. He reminded me of one of our billboard panels against alcohol abuse. I interrupted him, suddenly seeing the light! His office had created a great image: against a dark plain background, a hand empties a wine glass on a table, nothing else, with only these words: "No, thanks, is a great thing to say!" / "Non, merci, ça se dit bien!" I saw immediately how brilliant this ad would be in the circumstances. At the end of March, when the Yvettes had just not yet started filling the vacuum of a pro-Canada presence, I submitted the idea to the Quebec ministers weekly meeting where, after a thirty seconds of discussion, everybody said, "Go ahead!" I was able to obtain approval from the Chrétien special Referendum Committee, find a bit of a budget, which was not much, and we put the ad back on Quebec billboards. According to L. Ian MacDonald in his book quoted earlier, my "Non, merci!" message "had emerged as the principal slogan of the NO campaign." Lévesque was furious, acknowledging the coup, and took legal action against me, my department, and the advertising agency, but he lost in the Quebec Provincial Court. Our public health message was completely legitimate and was not new. But at the following national caucus in Ottawa I was reprimanded by Trudeau, further to Warren Allmand's strong emotional accusation against my French billboards, as I had not rescheduled the same in English for NDG and the West Island.

It was almost impossible for Trudeau to play an active role in the referendum campaign because of the Quebec rules of the game. We discussed this often at the special Quebec ministers meetings in Ottawa. Trudeau would make only a few measured interventions; in fact he first gave two speeches in the province, at the Montreal Board of Trade and at a large rally in Quebec City. Towards the end of the campaign, it was decided to go for broke: Trudeau would give a major speech in Montreal, at the Paul-Sauvé Arena, on Wednesday evening, 14 May, the week preceding the vote, to a crowd of 9,000. I missed this historic speech, as I had promised to speak at the No gathering in Huntingdon with Gérard

D. Lévesque, the Opposition parliamentary leader in the National Assembly. In his speech, the prime minister attacked the hypocrisy of the referendum question, decoding what it really meant: language that never once uses the words *separatism, independence,* and *sovereigntist,* with a view to fool people. The speech was a huge success but left an impression of future socio-political major changes, undefined but not strictly constitutional. His last words were, "Il faut du changement. Faites-moi confiance!" I never for one minute believed that Trudeau had deliberately misled the voters. He lived, worked, and thought as a particularly well-learned jurist, and he was in a unique position to appreciate the fundamental value of the rule of law for a country.

On the evening of 20 May the referendum vote gave 59.4 per cent to the No and 40.6 per cent to the Yes camp. The day after, in the House of Commons, Trudeau announced his intent to patriate and renew the Constitution, the British North America Act 1867, resting in London, England. He then sent Jean Chrétien to meet each provincial premier, but Lévesque refused to receive him. The rest is history.

It has always been crystal clear to me that Trudeau's speech at the Centre Paul-Sauvé and the Yvettes social movement won the first referendum, the 1980 one, defeating the Yes vote in favour of Quebec's separation from Canada. I have found it fascinating that when analyzing the spontaneous socio-political Yvettes movement, the media and the academic world systematically gave positive recognition to Trudeau's historical speech as what "won" the referendum while the Yvettes "defeated" it. Official federalist voices never recognized that the Yvettes too won the No victory.

It is hard to appraise and fully understand Trudeau's action and passion following the 1980 referendum without backtracking ten years. Ramsay Cook, the great historian friend of Pierre Trudeau over nearly forty years, considered the aftermath of the 1970 October Crisis as the beginning of deliberate strategies from Trudeau to respond to French Canada's alienation from the federal government. The adoption of the first Official Languages Act in 1969, shortly after he became prime minister, had been a first step. While it gave statutory recognition to the country's linguistic duality, it fell short of clearly entrenching bilingualism. Around the 1970s, according to Ramsay Cook, the prime minister's "consistent plan ... was to implement a constitutionally entrenched bill of rights, reform such federal institutions as the Supreme Court and the Senate, and then deal with the division of powers on a case-by-case basis." At the infamous 1971 Victoria Conference with all the premiers, he nearly achieved just that. The detailed description of the conference can be found in Cook's book *The Teeth of Time,* the historian being in Victoria at the time. A sticking point, Premier Robert Bourassa asking for more power in social affairs, became a stumbling block, with Claude Castonguay and Claude Morin's feeding the opposition to an accord. After a week back in Quebec City, Bourassa rejected the Victoria agreement. Everyone lost, Quebec in particular.

Back in Ottawa, very few ministers dared speak in Cabinet about the Constitution patriation and the Charter of Rights and Freedoms. The file was the prime minister's. Even Marc Lalonde, an accomplished constitutionalist, was once put in his place in Cabinet. If a colleague had something to suggest or to add, the prime minister would politely listen, then go back to his reasoning and the argumentation from the start. Although not trained in law and finding judicial rigidity and formality spontaneously rather off-putting, but interested in its unremitting logic, it was clear to me that on this subject the prime minister was not surrounded by equals in Cabinet, with the exception of Lalonde, even if many colleagues were lawyers by training and past profession.

One exceptionally dramatic occurrence among many stemmed from the 2–5 November 1981 meeting of the provinces and the prime minister, and the final agreement of nine of the provinces to "the Kitchen Accord" (in Quebec called "the night of the long knives" when its delegation did not attend). In that accord, a rider was agreed upon to give the provinces the power to override certain rights. It had the power to render Section 28 inoperative, including the equal rights of women. At the next Cabinet meeting, while ministers were congratulating each other, Judy Erola took the floor, saying to the prime minister, "Sir, there is not much point in being minister for the status of women when women have no status in the country." The party pooper, she then stated in no uncertain terms the new problem affecting 52 per cent of the Canada's citizens due to this accord. The prime minister was clearly annoyed. There was a heated but polite exchange between the two, Judy making the point that the Charter was not good enough to protect women's equality. She then asked permission to convince the nine provincial premiers to change their positions. "You, Judy, are going to change the premiers' position when all the federal negotiators could not?" She replied, "Not me, Prime Minister. The women of Canada!" At a minimum, all ministers should have known by then that the Women's Ad Hoc Committee on the Constitution had been watching and commenting in public on the constitutional negotiations for twelve to fifteen months. Trudeau told her she could not get involved as a Cabinet member, could not speak publicly, attend press conferences, and so on. I just had the courage to state that I supported her. Not a word from any other ministers. She was given two weeks. It was understood she would resign if the campaign did not succeed. Social media and the internet did not exist at the time. But telephones did – not the smart ones, of course – and Rolodexes. Women MPs of all parties got into the fray as well as Quebec's Yvettes, activist networks, women's associations, and the Ad Hoc Committee. They marched on provincial legislatures and flooded provincial MLAS offices. Flora MacDonald, Pauline Jewett, Margaret Mitchell, and Marian Dewar got on the phone personally to the premiers they knew well. After a little more than two weeks, on the evening of 23 November, the last premier capitulated.

I easily understood and agreed that Trudeau was right that Quebec separatists would use any inaccuracy, vagueness, or logical ambiguity to obtain more power, always more, as negotiations went on, until the separation of Quebec. And yet in 1990, after three years of public discussions and shortly before Mulroney's Meech Lake Accord would die in the hands of the Manitoba MPP Elijah Harper because of unmet Aboriginal claims, I agreed to be a *MacLean's*/Hunter TV panellist for the Yes side, in June, with I believe a Torontonian established constitutionalist, Peter Russell, against Sharon Carstairs and Al Johnson opposed to the accord. Carstairs called me "a traitor," while Al Johnson remained above the fray, a friend whom I always admired. It would be the only time that I would take a stand on the Meech Lake Accord, and I somehow still regret it. In fact I was torn. By opposition to Trudeau and some of my male friends, I hate intellectual debates and verbal jousting just for the sake of it. I was affected, as many others were, by

the importance of bringing Quebec back into the large Canadian family
and by the need to erase the damage of the symbolic power taken on
by "the night of the long knives." I knew the power of symbols in society, and the shortcut they offer to attract and win people's trust, loyalty, and heart. We had legal concepts, fundamental ones, but abstract.
For a sociologist, it is evident that Quebec can be called "a distinct society" in the cultural sense of the word. But I had trouble then seeing
clearly the bear trap due to the legal lack of precision of the term.

I had always taken for granted that Trudeau's Just Society – the slogan from Trudeau's 1968 leadership campaign – included all faces of
justice, and of course, social justice, meaning the action, in fact the fight,
against socio-economic iniquities and others.

Way back at the beginning of the 1960s, listening to Fernand Cadieux or reading *Cité libre,* including texts signed by Pierre Elliott
Trudeau, I had also absorbed their critical analysis of nationalisms and
the dangers of *l'étapisme,* that step-by-step approach to achieve independence. I also knew, or thought I truly understood, Trudeau's rigorous
thinking about the Constitution and the Charter of Rights and Freedoms, but I will always remain a sociologist, a social analyst, and not a
lawyer, a legal expert. For Trudeau, in the matters of those two documents as well as his natural, spontaneous analysis of separatist issues,
of language and cultural challenges, federal–provincial relationships, the
B&B report and recommendations, and more, besides resting above all
on super-rational thinking, his standpoints and decisions were grounded
exclusively in the rule of law and the administration of justice by the
court. This does not mean that his thinking and actions were not also
based on deeply entrenched values of social justice and redistribution of
wealth, or openings to the world, for which he fought.

16

Trudeau's Two Departures

On Friday, 24 February 1984, after my meeting with my deputy minister, I took the plane for New York, as the House of Commons would not sit for the whole following week. I would celebrate my forty-eighth birthday with very dear friends: Anne-Marie Galland and her father, Senator Chauvin, my adoptive Parisian family, the three of us in New York for a few days, and Alec and Gérard Pelletier, at the time our ambassador to the United Nations, a couple dear to me. A wonderful escape from the medicare federal-provincial crisis and other political millstones.

The weather was nice, and after a short walk through Central Park I joined my friends for a dinner at the Pelletier residence, in the old elegant official Park Avenue apartment of Canadian permanent representatives to the UN. On that Saturday evening we were all meeting at the Public Theater for the play *Cinders,* a theatre of the absurd *à la Kafka,* a parody of the totalitarian nightmare imposed on the citizens, a brilliant text by a dissident Polish author, Janusz Glowacki. I had never forgotten my official twelve-day trip to Poland in early July 1979, delegated by Joe Clark to accompany Walter Dinsdale to the third International Conference of Rehabilitation Engineering Centers in Poznan. The minister of health and social affairs had organized a wonderful cultural trip in my honour from the Baltic to Cracow. But everywhere I noticed examples of communism at its worst: poverty, lack of elementary goods, restricted food, police atmosphere, and unkept environments. To complete this perfect New York holiday weekend, I spent the Sunday walking through town.

An invitation to speak at New York University, in Greenwich Village, one of the biggest and most dynamic private American universities, established in 1831, had taken me to New York. On the Wednesday afternoon I would present to the Social Work Department, the other social sciences being also invited. So, to start the week, I visited some UN agencies, starting with our Canadian Mission, where I had sat for four months in 1973, as a new MP, following my first election. From there I spent some time at the offices of the United Nations International Children's Fund (UNICEF), an institution that I admired for their wonderful humanitarian work for the development and the rights of children. Later in the afternoon I was at the United Nations Population Fund, which we strongly supported with their key role in "delivering a world where every pregnancy is wanted, every childbirth is safe and every young person's potential is fulfilled."

On the Wednesday, Gérard Pelletier asked his driver to take me to the university campus and bring me back. Shortly after I had left midtown, he phoned his driver, asking him to inform me that Trudeau had just resigned! It was now official, but the prime minister had talked with him in the morning. I was flabbergasted. It had already been four years since Trudeau had won the 18 February 1980 general election, including all Quebec seats except one, and he still had almost a year ahead of him before calling the next election. He had played a key role in winning the first referendum against Quebec separation on 20 May 1980, had patriated the Constitution, and had seen the Charter of Rights and Freedoms adopted. He had reached all his crucial objectives. Such a sudden departure was bound to happen sooner or later, we were in a leap year, it was 29 February, and he had had a long walk in the snow in Ottawa.

Trudeau had announced his resignation first as leader of the Liberal Party on 21 November 1979, remaining an MP until the leadership convention and the election of his successor, while in Opposition during Joe Clark's government. Everyone had been taken by surprise, but his heart no longer belonged to the daily parliamentary struggle. Unknown to anyone, he had been to see Don Macdonald in Toronto a few days before, informing him of his decision and his desire to see him as his successor, adding he would do his best to accommodate him in taking over the leadership. Further to his departure from politics in September 1977, Macdonald had joined the McCarthy law firm, and his family was most happy that he had left active politics. Don had always said that he would not run for the leadership, for he did not have "the royal jelly"!

The leadership convention would take place in Winnipeg in March 1980. Late in 1979 Don was tempted, and a Macdonald organization was developing without fanfare. I was one of the ministers pressing him to run. On 7 December in Ottawa, I had lunch with Kathryn Robinson, a brilliant lawyer with Goodman & Goodman, whom I liked a lot. She would be Don's chief campaign organizer. Don requested that I co-chair the campaign presidency with my colleague Bob Andras. We expected that Turner would not run, for he had no interest in being the Opposition leader. And then the unthinkable happened, a few days later, on the evening of 13 December, on the floor of the House of Commons, when we defeated Joe Clark's government by a majority vote against his budget! The rest once again is history, including Trudeau's return as Liberal leader further to a few days of intense and emotional days of caucus discussions.

But this time, coming back from New York to Ottawa, a lot of water had flowed under the bridge. Trudeau had come back, after winning a majority government in 1980. And I had gone back to my beloved Department of National Health and Welfare for another four years and more. On the Friday morning, straight from my landing in Ottawa from NYC, I was in my office for the signature of a special accord to accommodate Quebec, found most satisfying by my guest Pauline Marois, my counterpart as minister of social services. The balance of the day was spent in meetings on the proposed Canada Health Act (Bill C-3) with my small team: my MP friend Claude-André Lachance, Don McNaught from the department, and Madeleine Côté, now on my staff from the department, the two latter having worked with health provincial officials for years while applying the old federal legislation regulating the 50:50 cash transfers to provinces for hospitals and medical care. Working with them was most enjoyable. My bill, tabled in the House on 12 December 1983, was now being scrutinized by the House Standing Committee on Health, Welfare and Social Affairs. That evening, with Trudeau, I was a guest at a dinner given by the Mexican ambassador in honour of Ivan Illich. I had finally read this original thinker, with great interest.

A week later, on 6 March in the afternoon, Cabinet met for the first time since the dramatic announcement of Trudeau's departure. I remember the general atmosphere of this meeting and the prime minister's soliloquy to us, his ministers. Quite rapidly, the "Boss," shy and uncomfortable in such circumstances, incapable of banalities, started by addressing his colleagues' future in a somehow disillusioned not to say crass political way, not at all reflecting the refined human being he was. He informed us that, should we need an appointment – I think he said "a job" – for the future, whatever it would be – a court nomination, a diplomatic posting, a Senate seat, a position with a federal agency, a national council or other – one simply had to go see him and ask. I was deeply shocked; it was somehow humiliating for all of us, his team. I am sure, however, that this was not his intention. I also immediately thought it was also an abuse of power not at par with his acute sense of democratic ethics. When we left the room I discovered that Judy Erola felt exactly like me; she just murmured to me, "Over my dead body!" Not so long ago we had reminisced about that unexpected moment of Cabinet life with Pierre Trudeau. In the years after Judy and I both left politics, people would ask her or me why we had not been appointed Senators, suggesting we had done something wrong!

I would have qualified as an applicant, as I knew I would be leaving politics by choice at the next election and in need of a job, although I had to keep it a secret, but I would never have considered asking him. It had been obvious to me for a good two years that the Liberals would be defeated, whoever was to replace Trudeau as Liberal leader. We would be crushed by the Mulroney Conservatives, and I had no intention of being in Opposition for ten years. I was a builder, and my nine months in Opposition under the Joe Clark government had been enough. I had already determined, with the help of Claude-André Lachance, that I could take a chance at academic life as a professor or in the media as a commentator. But while doing this exercise, I rapidly concluded and explained to Claude-André that I would never enter the media world; I would rather become a silent Carmelite than speak daily to say nothing new or repeat clichés!

However, I did ask to see Trudeau for my friend Roméo LeBlanc, without mentioning it to him or to anybody else. This old proud friend too had been hurt by Trudeau's lack of feeling for his colleagues at that Cabinet meeting, after all these years of having devoted his talent and loyalty to the prime minister. He had confided to me that if "the Boss" did not guess his need for an appointment insuring his financial future for his younger family, he would not be one to beg! But Roméo could not go back to his international job of CBC foreign affairs senior correspondent – London, Washington – that he had left to serve Prime Minister Pearson in 1967 as his press secretary, then Trudeau up to 1972, before running and being elected himself and becoming a Cabinet member. I simply informed the PM of LeBlanc's situation, of his sensitivity, at my personal initiative, not wanting any reaction or reply. Trudeau appointed him to the Senate before leaving politics at the very end of June 1984.

The public has long remembered this business of political appointments, as well as Turner's very machismo patting the bum of Iona Campagnolo – president of the Liberal Party during the following election campaign – in front of the media. It helped him lose the 4 September 1984 general election to Mulroney. The political appointments were the final nail in the coffin of Turner's dreams. Trudeau himself had signed some forty to fifty appointments at the end of his mandate on 30 June, as Turner was sworn in as the non-elected prime minister by Governor General Jeanne Sauvé, one of his loyal supporters since 1968, on Saturday, 1 July. We did not know that Trudeau had made an agreement with Turner to some seventy-five more appointments. The famous television debate of 24 July between the contenders underlined this fact, with Mulroney accusing Turner of the Liberal endemic political patronage with grossly partisan appointments as his first gesture. Everyone remembers the debate with Turner replying, "I did not have the choice!" and Mulroney responding, "You had a choice, sir. You could have said, 'I won't do it.'"

So with Trudeau announcing his departure, a leadership convention was called for 16 June 1984, with John Turner as the star contender.

It was obvious to me that he would be elected Liberal leader in mid-June and would become prime minister two weeks later, Don Macdonald being no longer a contender. In 1982, at Trudeau's invitation, Macdonald had agreed to chair the Royal Commission on Economic Union and Development Prospects for Canada, an important enterprise needing two more years of work before presenting its report to Prime Minister Mulroney.

It was exciting to discover who would run and on what program, but it was also a toxic race, with ministers watching each other, considering each political achievement, not for what it was really worth, but as a move on the chessboard towards a leadership bid. The first to declare his intent, in the very first week of March, was Donald Johnston, president of the Treasury Board, the youngest candidate at forty-seven, very rapidly labelled "the man of ideas." He was followed by Jean Chrétien, Mark MacGuigan, John Munro, John Roberts, and Gene Whelan, all Cabinet colleagues.

Parliamentary work was going on in parallel with the electoral fever of any leadership campaign. March to June 1984 was very busy for me, as I had unfinished pieces of legislation, on important issues, that I wanted to see adopted before the end of Trudeau's government – the Canada Health Act (1984) before anything else. Bill C-3, tabled in Parliament on 12 December 1983, was finally adopted unanimously by the House of Commons on 9 April and sanctioned on 19 April, despite daily attacks by the Conservatives, the provinces, and organized medicine over five long years. The day before, I had predicted unanimous passage of the bill to Yvon Pinard, our wise and competent House leader, as I had observed that Mulroney had managed to gain control of his caucus relatively rapidly since his own election as Conservative leader, and that he was a smart politician who wanted to be prime minister before being an ideologue.

Shortly after unanimous passage of the Health Care Act, to my total surprise, the Prime Minister's Office and External Affairs asked me to spend the Easter week (23–29 April) on an official trip to Israel.

Travelling with me for that visit were my last chief of staff, Christiane Beaulieu, and one assistant. I was of two minds during that trip. First, I found the war atmosphere there and the Palestinian question awful, but I could not raise either with government officials. But there was also the emotion of paying respects to the Holocaust victims during the visit to Yad Vashem, the unforgettable discovery of how small the country was, and how vulnerable its geographic location, and for someone like me brought up a Christian, the historical meaning of the Holy Land, Jerusalem locations, Tiberias, the Sea of Galilee, Caesarea, then Masada, and the Dead Sea Scrolls.

After the visit to Yad Vashem I was invited by Minister Shostak to visit the Hadassah Jerusalem Medical Centre with its ultramodern 130 departments and clinics distributed through twenty-eight modern buildings, and to meet with clinical investigators at their research centre. I reviewed the equipment and facilities, trying to understand the space organization, and listened to the presentations, which were meant to impress me with how advanced they were. Impressed I was indeed, as we could not favourably compare at the time. We had lunch at the hospital, then were taken to visit the famous twelve Chagall stained glass windows, dedicated in 1962, in the adjoining Abbell Synagogue. I have always love Chagall's work, and this was a unique occasion of colourful beauty and joyful biblical life expression. On the following day, a meeting was organized at my request with the minister of social services, Ben-Zion Rubin, a member of the National Religious Party.

Then, thanks to the elegant and generous assistance of our Canadian ambassador, Vernon G. Turner, we were taken to the north to visit Acre on the Bay of Haifa, in the Mediterranean Sea, a key site of the Crusades. Acre is a beautiful old city, rich in history, and the holiest city of the Baha'i faith. There I understood the complexity of the state of Israel after passing through towns and villages, seeing mosque followed by synagogue, again and again. Jewish history, the relatively short-lived Christian one, then the Muslim ancient and current Arab one, and again modern Israeli history are so deeply entrenched that the Arab-Jewish tensions are almost unavoidable. I dreamed of going to the Occupied Territories to see for myself what it was really all about in the early 1980s. Again, Ambassador Turner asked his driver to take me to Nablus and part of the West Bank, alone, with no Canadian flag on the car. I had a terrible shock: the poverty was in your face, as well as the half-demolished housing compounds, the barefoot kids wandering in the streets or what were called "streets," the garbage, the dirt. I could not believe what I was seeing. And never forgot. Years later, I hoped with many around the world that the 1993 Oslo Peace Accord signed by Shimon Peres would finally create a Palestinian state. It would not.

The week after the unexpected experience of my penultimate official foreign trip, I was in the House on 3 May, announcing my support for John Turner, to the surprise of many, before taking the plane again, this time en route to my last participation in the thirty-seventh WHO World Health Assembly in Geneva. We stopped in Paris to meet the socialist politician Edmond Hervé, minister of health, at his request, with his deputy minister, Dr Jacques Roux. I was impressed by their seriousness and sense of commitment. I shall never forget that meeting, for both men, and a few more French politicians and civil servants, were later accused of manslaughter in the dramatic contaminated blood tragedy that we would also live through in Canada. They were found guilty and served prison sentences, which were later reduced.

In Geneva I first attended the traditional Commonwealth health ministers meeting, then the first three days of WHO Health Assembly, scheduled for 7–17 May. The discussions that year considered vitamin A deficiency and ensuing xerophthalmia in children, dramatic in Asia, where it affected ten million children, but also serious in Africa and the Western Pacific, leading to early blindness, followed by death. The resolution was about the development of adapted local nutritional programs and training and the production of appropriate food, as well as the usual call for an international effort and special financial contribution. As a layperson I felt it sounded more like a pious wish than an action-oriented decision. Before leaving, I was honoured in a special way, not me but Canada through me, when I received the first Brock Chisholm Medal, as related earlier. It gave me the occasion for a good conversation with the long-serving Dr Halfdan Mahler, the remarkable WHO director general (from Denmark) who had convened the 1978 Alma Ata Conference "Health for All by the Year 2000," which aimed to revive research and action around primary health care, a precursor to the social determinants of health approach. To attend that historical Alma Ata conference was the only request I ever made to the Prime Minister's Office, but Joyce Fairbairn, one of Trudeau's staff, later a senator, turned it down without explanation. On my way back to Canada from Geneva, I signed more reciprocity agreements for social programs, this time with Belgium. My small delegation was delighted, as I was, to visit Brussels and Liège, every ministry appearing to inhabit a historic castle! Upon our return, on Monday, 14 May, I came as rapidly as I could from home in Montreal to Ottawa, to be in a long dress at 10 o'clock at Jeanne Sauvé's installation as governor general in the Senate Chamber, followed by a reception and, after question period, by the official Cabinet photo with her at Rideau Hall.

The busy political and parliamentary life of the end of a mandate was multiplied by the leadership electoral fever. Besides the Canada Health Act, passed in April but still requiring work at the operational level, I had to make sure that Bill C-40, an Act to amend the Old Age Security Act, was on the agenda every step of the way. The passage of this legislation was dear to me and my officials, including our National Council of Welfare, because, when it was implemented, Canadian seniors would live for years to come above the poverty line for the first time in our history. In March 1984 we had 2.5 million pensioners sixty-five years old and more, and half of them were receiving the Guaranteed Income Supplement in full or in part. Bill C-40 was passed in time, with all the details described in chapter 11.

My biggest problem during the months following Trudeau's walk in the snow announcement was that nobody should know that I would soon leave politics myself. I was at the height of popularity, and telling of my decision would have had two negative consequences. First, it would have turned me into a "has-been" while my work was far for being completed, and, second, it would have been interpreted as a rejection of Turner, the favourite of the Liberal traditional right wing of the Party, a slap in the face he did not deserve.

For the last two years I had known that the Liberals would be defeated at our next general election, under whatever leader. An important segment of the population, in Quebec and elsewhere, hated Trudeau – the word is not too strong – for all sorts of contradictory reasons: bilingualism, our energy policies, our economic ones, or others. People wanted a change of government. It was already exceptional for a prime minister of the fast-changing and media-based modern democracy to have been in power for seventeen years, minus nine months. On the other hand, I would have been certain of being re-elected in my Montreal riding of Saint-Léonard-Anjou, no matter what damages my colleagues suffered. In the last two general elections I had obtained the highest majorities, both in numbers of votes and in percentages of votes. Without even knowing that such statistics were being collected, I had learned that I was enjoying an exceptionally high national popularity rating.

But I did not want to find myself in the Opposition ranks and had no appetite for the Senate, as its members were non-elected. I would fulfill my responsibilities until the next election at which I would not be a candidate. But how and when to make this public without damaging the party and the next Liberal leader? I did not take myself for someone else, but I represented the "progressive" wing of the party, its "leftist" side, as media clichés would have it, and I definitely had electoral value. Writing these words decades later to describe my political role at that time, it seems as though I am talking about another person, in fact outright pretentious and presumptuous, as I never felt comfortable with these roles. My ego has never been big enough for me to care how others defined me. So if timing was a problem regarding my leaving politics, my immediate issue was about announcing whom I would be supporting in the leadership race.

Early in March, while we were both on duty in the House of Commons one afternoon, Jean Chrétien came to sit next to me, asking me if he could count on my support for his bid for the leadership. At the time, alternating between a francophone and an anglophone for the Liberal Party leadership was a sacrosanct tradition. I then explained to Jean that I would vote for an anglophone candidate, the more so as Trudeau had been there for more than fifteen years, had imposed a measure of bilingualism, and was considered a factor in the Western alienation as a Quebecer. I was therefore waiting to see who would be running. He used every argument to demonstrate that my reasoning was worth nothing, that he was the best, and that "his time had come." Despite my sincere efforts to tell him how good I thought he was and my admiration for his role as negotiator (with Roy Romanow and Roy McMurtry) in the Constitution patriation and the passage of the Charter of Rights and Freedoms, he was furious and holds a grudge against me to this day. The same with his spouse, Aline Chrétien!

When all the candidate names were known, pressure from the media, colleagues, caucus, and party membership became stronger and stronger to learn whom I would support. Dr Michel Chrétien, Jean's brother, whom I liked and knew well as an established medical researcher, on Jean's behalf, went as far as to visit my Liberal association in Montreal in my absence (I was on duty in the House!) without telling me, to ask my thirteen delegates to vote for his brother! A real dirty trick, unheard of. Any manoeuvre, wheeler-dealing, and dirty politicking was on, and there seemed no limit to play harder games. I was resisting pressure to announce my support for a candidate. I might have voted for Donald Johnston; he was right-of-centre but not an ideologue, and he was a true democrat, open and modern in his approach to public policies, including the idea of guaranteed annual income! But my sense of *realpolitik* won the day.

As winning the leadership had already been a done deal for Turner for two years, I privately discussed my plan with two colleagues, good friends of mine, who were in Turner's support organization: Lloyd Axworthy and Ed Lumley. With their help I prepared a short "contract" in which I would give Turner my full support if he would commit to apply the Canada Health Act as of 1 July 1984, and to keep the universality of family allowances and of old age pensions. These exchanges were very civil and, a month before the leadership convention, on 3 May, my support for Turner was announced.

Turner based his leadership campaign on the promise of more fiscal restraint and economic growth; Chrétien promoted his problem-solving ability, giving a few examples, with a sense of entitlement. As ever in a leadership convention, the atmosphere was electric in the vast Ottawa arena where the leadership vote took place on 16 June. From the first ballot, one could see that the game would be between Turner and Chrétien, Don Johnston taking the third spot. Turner was elected on the second ballot with 54 per cent of the votes against 40 per cent for Chrétien. The party remained quite divided in the following days. Turner shared that his challenge would be to preserve unity by keeping the most competent of Trudeau's ministers while finding ways to project the image of a renewed team with a new government orientation.

This being said, he reappointed twenty-three of Trudeau's ministers in his own first Cabinet, including Jean Chrétien, to whom he gave the External Affairs portfolio and whom he named his deputy prime minister, and Marc Lalonde, whom he re-appointed minister of finance. As one of the twenty-three, I was reappointed, for the third time now, minister of national health and welfare. But I still had my problem of when to inform Turner of my decision to leave politics without unfairly influencing the immediate future of the newly elected prime minister and the Liberal Party of Canada. We did not know that he would call an election almost immediately. Anyway, unknown to all, I had already accepted the offer to be a visiting professor at the University of Notre Dame in South Bend, Indiana, starting in September 1984.

So Turner was elected leader, and the House went back to its scheduled agenda until the prorogation of Parliament on Friday, 29 June 1984. Partly because of my Bill C-40, on the amendments to the old age pensions, also supported by the Opposition, the House of Commons sat from 11 a.m. to 9 p.m., without interruption for the last two weeks of June.

Early the day after, a Saturday, 1 July, the new Cabinet members were sworn in by our former colleague Jeanne Sauvé, in her new role as governor general, beaming in welcoming "her" candidate since 1968, John Turner. On the way back to Parliament from Rideau Hall, we had our first Cabinet meeting immediately. Around the Cabinet table we were observing who had been Turner supporters. The atmosphere was not formal at all, but rather buddy-buddy (*copain-copain*), quite a surprise for the old-timers, totally opposite Trudeau's disciplined Cabinet meetings. Needing to share our observations, after our usual personal signal, Judy Erola and I escaped to the women's washroom, sure to be alone there. "But he is a pussy cat!" was our spontaneous and mystified reaction. Where was the powerful Bay Street lawyer, the outstanding financier, the big-business candidate who would assure us a new lease on power? We were both amazed to discover a prime minister who needed to be loved and surrounded with comradeship, like one sees on television in male locker rooms after a great game of hockey.

If particular dossiers were discussed, I have no memory of them. In fact, I don't think there were any! But what I will recall all my life was the *tour de table* Turner started, inviting each one to tell him if he should call an election now or wait one more year. Like Mulroney, some assumed that Turner, whose election had boosted the poll numbers in favour of the Liberals, would wait at least until after early fall and tour the country before receiving Pope John Paul II during his twelve-day visit across the land in early September, as well Queen Elizabeth and Prince Philip's in September and October. I was trying to make sense of opinions going in all directions, trying to figure out the new "Turner" ministers – and they were many – who were basically in favour of an immediate election. I did not speak. Then Jean Chrétien, whose viewpoint was most important to me because of his experience and his great electoral sense and intuition, insisted that Turner should wait and that it would be the end of the Liberals if he were to call an election now. No decision was made that morning.

We had a rapid lunch at 24 Sussex, each of us wanting to get back home as soon as possible for what remained of the 1 July long weekend. The next Wednesday, on 4 July, we learned on the news that Turner had asked the governor general to call an election for 4 September. What to do became suddenly very clear to me. I still see myself, the day after, at the *Cercle universitaire*, informing in confidence my Medical Research Council president, Dr Pierre Bois, a great scientist and a truly wise man with whom I had loved working, of my impending departure and personal future. It appeared to me more elegant to let Turner explain his decision through the media and start talking of his electoral platform before announcing my own departure from politics. So on Wednesday, 11 July, in the early morning, I took the first plane to Toronto, arriving at Turner's residence at 9:30 a.m. Stunned, he greeted me warmly, starting to cry when I told him of my decision to quit politics.

At noon, back in my office, I phoned David Kirkwood, my deputy minister, to tell him about the situation and my decision. At 2 p.m., I had a meeting with my entire Ottawa political staff, both from Tunney's Pasture and those on the Hill, who did not suspect anything. The balance of the day was spent on the phone with my Montreal office team. The media started running to my Confederation office on Parliament

Hill to such a point that my press secretary pressed me to give an impromptu press conference right there and then. Everyone had been taken by surprise. The following weekend was devoted to explaining the situation and my decision to the Saint-Léonard-Anjou Liberal Association Executive. I apologized for letting them down, and during the electoral campaign at that. Then, faithful to a promise I had made, dear to me, I suggested that the candidate replacing me should be not only an Italo-Canadian but a female one and I recommended the remarkable young lawyer Liliana Longo who was working in my office. (André Ouellet had made me responsible for recruiting women candidates from Quebec.) My executive, French-Canadians and Italo-Canadians, were almost all males. Totally forgetting my presence, they exclaimed in unison, "Not another woman!" Within a few minutes, they had chosen Alfonso Gagliano, a local accountant, then also president of the second-biggest Quebec schoolboard, that of St Leonard, despite my strong resistance ... and with good reason, as the future would show.

On Wednesday, 18 July, Dr Sam Friedman, former dean of medicine of McGill, renowned medical researcher, then vice principal of McGill, phoned to offer me a one-year contract as visiting professor in the Department of Sociology. I thanked him warmly, informing him of my contract with the University of Notre Dame. He simply replied that he would be expecting me a year later, upon my return in September 1985! That was very good news.

As of 14 July I had been appointed acting prime minister until my holidays to start on 8 August. Life on the Hill continued, and so did a few trips across the country, campaigning for colleagues, such as Lloyd Axworthy's nominating meeting in Winnipeg, a few more in Montreal: those of Arthur Portelance in Gamelin, Raymond Savard in Verdun, Jean-Claude Malépart in Sainte-Marie, Thérèse Killens in Ahuntsic, and Marcel Prud'homme in Saint-Denis. I also agreed to attend the nominating meeting of a newcomer, Françoise Drolet, in Trois-Riviéres, and of my friend Judy Erola in her riding of Nickel Belt in Sudbury and region.

On 6 August I returned to South Bend, IN, to meet the provost, Prof. O'Meara; Dr Michael J. Loux, a philosopher and the dean of the College of Arts and Letters, home of the large Department of Economics, where

I would teach; and Sister John Miriam Jones, assistant provost, who welcomed and guided me. Finally, before leaving for holidays, in Montreal I had the special pleasure to meet once more with the international public figure I so admired, Simone Veil, who had been appointed minister of health of France once more and on that day was keynote speaker at the International Council on Social Welfare. Senator Maurice Riel, Speaker of the Senate, and his wife Laurence had organized a lunch for Simone and Antoine Veil, with Claude and Monique Forget, Thérèse and Robert Sévigny, and myself, at Les Halles, a unique occasion.

I finally left for a two-week holiday in the Algarve, Portugal, at the seaside property of Anne-Marie and Yves Galland, my beloved Parisian "adoptive family" going back to January 1976. When I returned home on 29 August my department and the Medical Research Council jointly celebrated me in a huge joyful ceremony in the Judy LaMarsh Park outside the Tunney's Pasture offices of National Health and Welfare. On Tuesday, 4 September 1984, Brian Mulroney and his Conservative Party won the federal election with 211 seats out of 282, the Liberals being reduced to 40 seats, from the 147 we had! John Turner had been prime minister–elect for seventy-nine days.

In 1971 I had refused to run for office when invited by Pierre Trudeau's chief of staff, Marc Lalonde, having never thought of it, but also because of my keen sensibility, knowing that politics operated by the law of the jungle. I have to admit that when I accepted the same invitation a year later, it was in a way because I needed a professional challenge. I never regretted it! An idealist, from an early age I had developed a sense of realism. With my sense of humour, I can criticize myself and even laugh at my dreams. As I have a natural suspicion of dogmas, ideologies, and formulas, I am also a pragmatist.

Political life can be brutal, destructive, betraying, and alienating. I find myself blessed to have left it unscathed and personally enriched. And I had the good fortune to leave active politics with major policy accomplishments affecting the daily lives of millions in Canada for the better. On top of it all, I left political life with new friends for life!

17

"The Boss"

Earlier in these memoirs I included three or four short anecdotes describing Pierre Trudeau in a particular situation, some to his advantage, others not so much. I find it very difficult to speak here of Trudeau, telling how he was, who he was, what it was like working for him, how I related to him as a colleague. There are so many texts about Pierre Elliott Trudeau: more than 100 books and chapters in books – biographies and his own autobiography: *Memoirs / Mémoires politiques* (1993) – not counting articles, television programs, albums, photo albums, even cartoon booklets. I have more than a dozen such books in addition to his own writings before, during, and after politics. When I was writing this chapter, two more books on Trudeau, written by academic historians, were reviewed in the media (by Robert Wright and Paul Litt). And then several portraits and/or analyses of Trudeau are found in the memoirs of some of his friends, past Cabinet members, or political staff. I won't borrow from any of these sources.

That said, I will admit that two texts on Trudeau are especially dear to me: Edith Iglauer's long and extraordinarily perceptive 1969 *New Yorker* "Profile of a Prime Minister," and Ramsay Cook's book *The Teeth of Time (Remembering Pierre Elliott Trudeau)*, released in 2006, although written immediately after Trudeau's death in 2000: the history of their intellectual friendship over forty years. Ramsay Cook's book is the one that helped me understand the value, key role, and importance of the cerebral Trudeau's approach to the Quebec 1980 referendum. I was finally able to reconcile myself with his promise of "change" amounting to the patriation of the Constitution and the Charter of

Rights and Freedoms and to understand the fundamental democratic asset he left to Canadians and Canada.

There are several different Pierre Trudeaus, and there are not, as he has always been true to himself. If I can state that, it is because I came to know of Pierre Trudeau at different moments of his public life, starting long before he became an elected politician. It was in 1949, as a young Girl Guide, that I first heard the names of Pierre Trudeau and of Jean Marchand, although I cannot say that they meant much, except that these two were "the good guys." So was the archbishop of Montreal, Mgr Joseph Charbonneau, who had asked the Girl Guides to take up a collection every Sunday at every mass, for the asbestos miners in their four-month-long labour dispute, during which they were savagely beaten by Duplessis's provincial police. I was thirteen or fourteen at the time and faithfully collected money at the door of the Saint-Antonin church, to which I had been assigned, with a sense of a special mission. Later, in 1956, I was then twenty years old and had left teaching children to work as a secretary at the University of Montreal and study by myself towards a BA. My friends were already full-time students and I would join them for the lunchtime talks by Quebec public intellectuals and activists, listening and learning. Trudeau came a few times, not yet a law professor at the University of Montreal, further to Duplessis's veto to his appointment. It was only after Duplessis's sudden death in September 1959 that Trudeau saw his dream realized when he was hired as chair of public law in his alma mater. At the time, Trudeau was a name, an exciting personality, an original, and some of my friends would tell me about him and parties they had attended or famous individual causes he had defended. He was depicted as a fun and brilliant dilettante.

He slowly became a recognized public intellectual in Quebec. It was when working for Fernand Cadieux while studying in sociology, in 1958–61, that I met most of the authors of the famous first issue of *Cité Libre*: "Pour une politique fonctionnelle" jointly written and signed as the magazine's manifesto of June 1950, the second part following in February 1951. *Cité Libre* was born! While checking a few dates on the web, I found this pearl from the CBC Archives describing the appearance of *Cité Libre:* "When the host of CBC *Soundings* described *Cité Libre* as a 'little' magazine, he wasn't far off the mark. The French-language,

political magazine – co-founded by Pierre Trudeau and Gérard Pelletier
– had a tiny circulation of 2,500, but was highly influential. *Cité Libre*
was the only voice in Quebec openly criticizing the corrupt rule of Premier Maurice Duplessis. Ten men put up $25 each to publish 500 copies
of *Cité Libre*'s first issue in 1950." I already knew personally three of
the seven authors of this *Cité Libre*'s famous manifesto, then professors
in the Faculty of Social Sciences at the University of Montreal: the
economist Albert Breton and his brother, sociologist Raymond Breton,
and Maurice Pinard. I would meet three more at Cadieux's office or at
their lunches where he often invited me: the lawyers Claude Bruneau
and Marc Lalonde, and the psychoanalyst Dr Yvon Gauthier. I did not
participate in any discussion with them; I was there, listening, observing,
learning, and trying to follow public policy and political concerns new
to me. I knew of the seventh author and co-editor of the magazine,
Pierre E. Trudeau, but had not yet met him.

This being said, despite having moved often in my life, each time
throwing away tons of papers and texts, I still have a clipping of a long
interview of Pierre Elliott Trudeau by Jean-Marc Léger in the *Le Devoir*
series "Où va le Canada français?" in the 6 May 1959 issue. Trudeau
was the third to be interviewed over the weeks in a list including André
Laurendeau, Raymond Barbeau, Michel Brunet, Marcel Faribault, Jean-
Charles Falardeau, Father Richard Arès, s.j., Gérard Bergeron, Jean-
Louis Gagnon, Paul Gérin-Lajoie, and other Quebec intellectual leaders.
These interviews covered political critical problems of francophone
Quebec, where its nationalism stood, its safeguards and its future, its
fight for autonomy.

Significant is the fact that Trudeau's interview is the only clipping I
ever saved. And kept for decades! A *Le Devoir* journalist used a quote
from Trudeau's interview as its title: "Pour restaurer la liberté et la justice, supprimons l'alliance des tenants et profiteurs du statu quo." No
need to remind the reader that nobody, no one, could imagine on 6 May
that Maurice Duplessis, the autocratic premier who had suffocated all
Quebec institutions in the name of "provincial autonomy" and "nationalism," surrounded himself with corrupt ministers, and abused all
human rights would suddenly die four months later, almost to the day.

Re-reading this interview today, with the distance of time, reveals the fundamentals of Trudeau's reasoning on Quebec's future. The photo is of a man in his prime (he was forty), with answers full of ideas and anger. Right from start he said, "Je rêve d'un people dont l'esprit et le cœur seraient ouverts sur le monde, qui ne redouterait aucun changement dès lors que celui-ci procéderait d'une passion de vivre, d'un amour de la vérité et d'un goût vif de la liberté." He then launches into institutions and players, without names, that were colluding with the retrograde Duplessis government to maintain the people in poverty and ignorance. Towards the end of this long interview, he answers the journalist about how the future should come about: "Je ne vois qu'une règle essentielle: pragmatisme, ... audace, ... agitation."

Such were the days of the growing Quebec public intellectual Trudeau.

Then would come his decision to join a political party and run for office. What I remember vividly, and identified with, was the decision to accept the Liberal Party of Canada's invitation to run federally of "The three wise men / Les trois colombes": Marchand, Pelletier, and Trudeau. One evening, probably in late 1964 or early 1965, at Dyname, Fernand Cadieux's research group, Cadieux asked me to do him a favour and stay to take notes during an evening private strategic meeting. I saw to it to that we had a meal delivered. Besides Fernand, present were Marc Lalonde and Michael Pitfield as well as one or two others. Lalonde and Pitfield had become great friends while serving in Davie Fulton's political staff while he was Diefenbaker's minister of justice. Then both moved to Lester B. Pearson's office. The discussion went on for hours. I was simply taking notes, loyalty and discretion being of the essence. Throughout the evening the group discussed the pros and cons but more importantly, the conditions under which the "three wise men" should run for office in the impending general election, and why. The reasoning was very clear and it appeared to me very exciting. The three had to go together. Not just one of them, or two, but the three, as if that symbolic number carried a special power, becoming a critical mass. Having seen them in Fernand's entourage, I knew that Maurice Sauvé and Maurice Lamontagne, both federal ministers at the time, were secretly manoeuvring to attract Jean Marchand into federal politics. Not many, not to say nobody, were interested in recruiting Gérard Pelletier and even less Pierre Trudeau. The big plus was Jean Marchand, the great Quebec union leader. Later, as a new MP, I observed that Marchand was an even better political analyst and strategist than Trudeau. The idea that particular evening was that one does not get into politics alone. The three had to get in together. It was urgent not only to replace but to renew the Quebec team in Pearson's Cabinet, by Quebec leaders coming from different horizons, more open to the world, who had seriously thought through the national question. In September they announced their decision to run for office, and on the evening of 8 November 1965 the three wise men were elected as federal Liberal MPs.

The Trudeau I had observed or heard about now and then had become an elected politician and, almost immediately, Prime Minister Pearson's parliamentary secretary, conducting several international missions before being sworn in as minister of justice of Canada in April 1967, less than a year and a half after his first election. In the same month of April, thanks to Marc Lalonde, by then principal secretary to Mr Pearson, I had become the executive secretary of the Royal Commission on the Status of Women in Canada, first under Pearson, then under Trudeau as prime minister. I would follow Trudeau in his new roles through the media, especially the newly televised federal-provincial conferences and his public defence of his omnibus bill modernizing the Criminal Code with his famous quip, "The state has no place in the bedrooms of the nation." That's how he started becoming known to English Canada.

So, from a public intellectual, Trudeau had become a political figure whom I would first meet in December 1970, at his office, when accompanying the Status of Women commissioners to present the prime minister with our report. In what remains of my newspapers clippings, other than those in my files at the National Archives (basically from my time as a Cabinet member and later), the second and only other old one I kept is a photocopy from La Presse dated 15 July 1980, less than two months after the 1980 first referendum on independence had been lost by René Lévesque. We were back in power in Ottawa and it was the beginning of the constitutional debates. The piece consists of two parts:

a text by reporter Gilbert Lavoie introducing a second long text, an "Open Letter to Quebeckers" by Trudeau arguing against the "two nations" theory. This is a great Trudeau fundamental discussion on the meaning of the "Statement of Principles for a New Constitution" as it had just appeared in Hansard on 10 June 1980 and in the document sent to each premier.

> We, the People of Canada ... Born of a meeting of the English and French presence on North American soil which had long been the home of our Native Peoples, and enriched by the contribution of millions of people from the four corners of the earth, we have chosen to create a life together which [transcends] the differences of blood relationships, language and religion, and willingly accept the experience of sharing our wealth and cultures, while respecting our diversity.
>
> We have chosen to live together in one [sovereign] country, a true federation, conceived as a constitutional monarchy and founded on democratic principles.

The opening phrase "We, the People of Canada" immediately led to a major debate in Quebec about the word *nation*. Referring to Lincoln, Trudeau clarifies in *La Presse* that there are no English or French nations, but "'sociological nations' or 'ethnicities' (the French Canadians, the Canadians of Anglo-Saxon ascendency, the Inuit, the Dene Nation and others)" – free translation. With distance and hindsight, it can be concluded that these two press clippings, of 1959 and 1980, are exemplary of Trudeau's idea of Canada and of federalism, and of his fundamental political objectives: the patriation of the Constitution and the Charter of Rights and Freedoms.

It was fascinating how Trudeau the politician could much more fully express his ideas about the country and its governance through a national political life than through *Cité Libre*. Did I agree with him? I sure did. To take only one example, I considered he had no choice but to use the War Measures Act during the 1970 October Crisis in Quebec, faced as he was with the terrorist abduction of a British diplomat and of a

Quebec provincial minister, followed by the assassination of the latter.
That outdated and shocking legislation, the only one in existence, was
later to be replaced by the more limited Emergencies Act.

But what about Pierre Trudeau as a person? From day one, I felt like
a member of his extended family: the younger sister or the cousin of a
brilliant and original elder brother, not so much in terms of shared
friendship and life, or work experiences, but because of a community
of common values and objectives. When we came back in office early
March 1980 and entered the renovated Cabinet Room, I saw the new
wooden frieze sculpted with words that I knew from Fernand Cadieux
"Justice being taken away, then, what are kingdoms but great rob-
beries?" from St Augustine in the *City of God*. This addition to the
room made me deeply happy. I belonged. I was not necessarily always
in complete agreement with some of his political moves, but I always
trusted him, and he had my full loyalty. That symbolic and spiritual
family, in the non-religious sense of the word, included Fernand
Cadieux, Gérard and Alec Pelletier, Marc Lalonde, Jean Marchand,
Roméo LeBlanc, and a few others. I just felt I belonged. I also knew
Trudeau was a man not afraid of solitude, which he not only was comfortable with but he needed. From that to be a very private person and
to actively protect his private space, it was only a small step.

One of his great assets was his extraordinary personal discipline,
deeply rooted in his education from home. In everything, from keeping
in shape physically to protecting the eight hours of sleep he needed,
toughing it when he did not get them but becoming nasty or stubborn.
He was also always controlled in what and how much he ate and drank.
Shortly after the 1972 election, he invited half a dozen of the new young
Quebec MPs for an informal lunch at 24 Sussex. We were all around
our thirties, quite excited, getting to know each other at the same time:
Francis Fox, Irénée Pelletier, Jacques Olivier, Raymond Dupont, and
myself, and maybe one or two more. We simply sat with Trudeau at the
family round table and were served a healthy and relatively light meal,
perfect for people who would be sitting all afternoon and evening in
the House or at their office. All I recall was the fresh asparagus, which
I enjoyed. The prime minister left as soon as the meal was over, letting

us go back to Parliament by ourselves. But my colleagues were still so hungry that the first thing they did was run to find a hamburger before question period!

Easily piqued by a remark, a situation that aroused his competitiveness, he could not easily miss the opportunity to enter the game! Although exuding self-confidence, sometimes to the point of arrogance, Trudeau was a shy individual, and on a one-to-one basis, starting the conversation could become awkward. This being said, I would not conclude that he was not fully comfortable within himself. He knew himself, his superb accord between physical and mental capacities, his good mental hygiene focused on the present moment and positive about the future. He was also a very sensitive person. I saw him cry at Fernand Cadieux's funeral in Ottawa in February 1976 and at Gérard Pelletier's – his true closest friend and his conscience referee – at St Léon-de-Westmount in June 1997.

With children, his and others', he became another person! It was marvellous to watch. It was as if he let himself be fully himself: spontaneous, open, loving the moment, playing, laughing, protective. Pierre Trudeau was also a very good listener. But he was not someone to pay compliments for a job well done. It did not come to him naturally to acknowledge a good job, as one would expect of a "boss." That was absolutely not his style, and I attribute his attitude to his upbringing and deeply rooted belief that each person is before all a responsible individual who will do her or his best in the job occupied. Always courteous with his collaborators, he was particularly elegant and silent, he whose privacy and private life, so precious, were exposed for all to see at the worst of Margaret's very public behaviour with male rock stars. His hidden suffering was painful to watch in Cabinet at the time.

I recently learned from a literary friend the term *eidetic memory*, which runs in her family, and I wondered if photographic memory could be the root of Trudeau's great power of recall. His show of spontaneous quotes of classics or recollection of foreign languages – quoting Paul Valéry in French or Rainer Maria Rilke in German, speaking in Spanish with Castro, was impressive. Two months after my appointment at Health and Welfare, in mid-November 1977, I was accompanying

Trudeau when Italian prime minister Giulio Andreotti came to Canada
on an official visit. The two statesmen were of the same age, and Andreotti's reputation had not yet been tarnished by criminal charges.
They knew each other and obviously enjoyed themselves, exchanging
spontaneously ... in fluent Italian. When my sister Catherine (Bégin)
was playing at the National Arts Centre, he would invite the two of us
for a walk in the woods at Harrington Lake with the kids on Saturday
morning. Whatever lead role she was playing, the two would exchange
passages from the play or other playwrights: Euripides or Chekov or
Beaumarchais! Reminiscing about Pierre Trudeau, Jean-Louis Roux recalled that when he was playing Claudel's *Tête d'or*, Trudeau, who liked
the poet very much, started quoting him a verse. In his own *Memoirs,*
published in 1993, Trudeau offered literary quotes particularly mean-
ingful to him. He had a deep appreciation and knowledge of culture and
arts, and not surprisingly, he has been called a Renaissance man.

Now, what about the government organization Trudeau favoured
and approved? Having not really studied the way the PMO and PCO
functioned before I joined Cabinet in September 1976, I recall the huge
number of academics and experts who joined the PMO in 1968–72 and
the rationalization of every step of the way in the political process.
Critical path methodology applied to public policy development. I
often heard about the disaster it was and a partial cause of the 1972
minority government.

Earlier I described what the power structure had been for me in my
department and what I thought of it. We certainly lived a consolidation
of power in the PCO and in Cabinet and committees structure when we
came back in 1980, seriously curtailing the role and power of ministers.
I was told that the idea originated with Joe Clark and was adopted at
once when we returned to office. So super cabinet committees with a
super minister in charge surrounded with a mini super team of senior
civil servants was then consolidated. So I became a member of the Super
Social Development Committee of Cabinet, chaired by Jean Chrétien
and his top senior civil servants' mini department. The key invention
of these Cabinet committee meetings was a special meeting called
"Banking Day." None of that was ever explained, even less discussed
with us, and one would or not slowly discover, for instance, that our

deputy ministers met before our own Cabinet. The Executive of Cabinet, the Committee of Priorities and Planning (P & P), operated in total secrecy. Even the Political Committee of Cabinet, that of Communications, also a powerful tool of government, never reported to us Cabinet members, let alone sharing any information.

An interesting 1999 study by Mark Schacter with Phillip Haid for the World Bank – rewritten and published for Canadian consumption by the Institute on Governance, an independent NGO created in 1990, based in Ottawa and Toronto – clarifies this new governance. Trudeau backed his clerk of the Privy Council, Michael Pitfield, for these reforms, both believing "strongly in technocratic decision-making built on formal systems and analytical techniques." The idea was to come to collective decision-making among ministers. This points to the primary barrier to optimum collective decisions: the vertical "silos" approach to Cabinet work, which had started bothering me seriously in the early 1980s. I never heard a colleague ever talk of this "silos" system, but I thought it was counterproductive. I had then even given a contract to an excellent researcher for her to inquire if and what other countries had managed to do to overcome the vertical "silos" system. Even more than thirty years after my time in Cabinet, the biggest challenge to common Cabinet decision-making, the collective endorsement of decisions made to the satisfaction of the common good, has not yet been achieved, despite all the research on intersectoral ways of working and its benefits. The 1999 study authors also identified the need to free the ministers from the grip of their own departmental officials.

Reverting to the "Banking Days" of the system, bearing the bureaucratic name of Public Expenditure Management System (PEMS), the theory was that each super committee was given resource "envelopes" to cover the sectors for which they were responsible, and we, the ministers, were collectively to decide on allocations to departments. In reality competition between us was at its maximum, and I always had the impression that the final decision, whatever the discussion between ministers, had already been made.

Full Cabinet meetings themselves were more structured than ever. Each minister's office got the heavy binder of Cabinet documents at around 6 p.m. on the day before Cabinet met. But we had to give the

PCO notice of any oral intervention planned for a specific memo to Cabinet the evening before! Like squaring the circle. I do not remember much spontaneity in the Cabinet system, if any, during Trudeau's last government. Ministers could not spontaneously raise questions or make interventions if not on the agenda.

Very rarely a key politico gave us a short partisan presentation at the opening of a Cabinet meeting. I never forgot Senator Keith Davey instructing ministers "to regularly take one's favourite journalist for a drink," to "cultivate a few journalists," and so on. I also recall him explaining poll results and concluding that political organizers, pollsters, and publicists – he the first one – knew very well and on the basis of their strategies that "the public was the equivalent of a five-year-old." I found such statements quite offensive but, more so, completely erroneous. As I have observed, the public is not stupid at all. It was during these years that I observed that Cabinet started including discussions on the news of the night before and the morning newspapers, based on nothing except impressions. We then massaged our communications accordingly for question period, or with the press later. Public policies and government were not the essence of Cabinet discussions anymore. I saw that quite quickly. At around the same time, in 1981 or 1982, Monique Coupal made me read me *L'Illusion politique / The Political Illusion,* the work of the French sociologist, philosopher, and humanist Jacques Ellul, a name I did not yet know. It made me understand that the very nature of politics was changing with modern communications technology. The daily, constant, uninterrupted interplay between the media and policy deliberations aiming at approval for action was being replaced by an action-reaction only at the level of images and short messages.

In lieu of a last paragraph on this chapter on "the boss," how did being in politics under and with Pierre Elliott Trudeau rank in my life? At the top! Not that I do not cherish other life experiences, but to have been a politician, at the national level, and then a Cabinet minister for some eight years, and to have served Canadians under Pierre Trudeau remains a unique experience. I consider myself very lucky. I was later asked to run for political office at the municipal and provincial levels, but I would not even consider it. Trudeau's leadership, with its ups and downs, remained rooted in "the Just Society" and "participatory democracy," which was what I related to. A political leader almost against himself, I believed him when he replied to Alain Stanké in his famous early seventies interview that he did "not really want to become a leader." But he understood that as a leader he could undertake constitutional reform and introduce the Charter of Rights. He was interested in the general (very general) orientations of his government. But the workings of each ministry did not captivate him.

I would not have worked with any other prime minister than Pierre E. Trudeau because his notion of governing included discussing ideas, ideals, and values.

Reflecting on my political life, I must conclude that so often I was the right person at the right place at the right time. So much for talent or hard work! But I also often felt as if I should shout that they had the wrong person! I had *un sentiment d'imposture,* feeling as if I was a fraud, not exactly who they thought I was. A bit of a misfit, a little marginal, a little different. Just enough to feel uncomfortable and to cultivate doubt about the world. Then I remembered home, where my patriarchal but totally anti-conformist father had enacted improbable, nightmarish, and crazy situations to "build your character and to overcome your fear of judgment of others"! I realized that even if textbooks did not mention it, a patriarchal, far from ordinary, and anti-conformist education might have been the best possible preparation for a woman of my generation to survive, to even enjoy, the male worlds of power of government and politics. I had long been familiar with the ambivalent feeling of not being like others, and it did not hurt!

◆ ✳ ◆

Let me conclude these chapters with my thoughts on the way I lived and understood being a woman in Cabinet. I will also develop how, during my time in office, I saw the general question of women ministers and in Cabinet.

Two of the questions I am still asked – on the bus, during cocktails or meetings, at the restaurant or in the hallway – are these: How was it to be a minister under Pierre Trudeau, and how was it as a woman in

Cabinet under Trudeau? In fact, these questions sum up two key dimensions of the world of power: the mystery of its organization and its special culture. If women have now learned how political parties and elections are organized and won, the mechanisms and procedures to get from A to B in the power structure, they are still deeply and instinctively put off by the world of politics. I have been one of them. And yet several of us have experienced this political power and even registered a few historical successes.

As one of the rare women entering the House of Commons, and then Cabinet in the 1970s, how did I live that transition to elected politics and its world of power? The newcomer to the House or to Cabinet must assert herself, but within the limits of what is allowable by her new chauvinistic and patriarchal universe, while remaining true to herself. However, paradoxically, she has entered into the egotistical world of a personality cult, where one must have an extreme style on more than one account and know how to come through the screen as a virtual exhibitionist! The experience is difficult and uncomfortable, and I never lived in that way – at the Federation of Quebec Women, nor at the Royal Commission on the Status of Women in Canada. Of all my new experiences, the most stupefying was the enormity of the male ego. I remember example upon example of a minister, a senator, or an MP fishing for compliments for an ordinary performance related to his everyday role. The exploitation, pretensions, bragging, and need to save face are all facets of what at home we used to call "*la bella figura.*"

In all my years as a minister, although I had the good sense to never admit it to anyone, I often thought that I was very inadequate in authority and felt guilty without reason. Shortly after I began my mandate as minister of national health and welfare, in a stupefying "psychological profile" that one occasionally reads about oneself, a well-established senior journalist, Doug Fisher (who had never interviewed me), wrote, "Marc Lalonde [whom I succeeded] was strong, but Monique Bégin was aggressive." This short sentence bothered me for a long time. I was certainly not succeeding a lamb! Unable to recognize myself as an aggressive woman, I was conscious of the type of personal failure that this image represented. I knew from experience that I had not changed and that this judgment of being "aggressive woman," with all that it implied, was completely unjustified. Certainly I knew where I was going, but I believed in teamwork and sought consensus above all. A good listener – another notable so-called female role – I let others say what they wished and tried to convince, rather than impose my views by banging my fist on the table at the end of the discussion.

Yet my visceral feminism was not enough to make me understand that by occupying a position of authority and exercising leadership at the top of a pyramid in a bastion of male power and in the eye of the cameras, I had simply deviated from the traditional roles expected of men and women. As I mentioned years later to Simone Veil, former minister of health in France and former president of the European Parliament and someone I admired and like very much, I was extremely happy to read in another of these famous "profiles" that she sometimes got angry! As I then told her, so did I!

As a woman in politics, I always felt that I was exceptional, special, and out of the ordinary, a feeling reinforced by the inevitable "My wife likes you very much!" and the high visibility of such a small number of women. In fact, although I had always resisted the idea, we were token women. (Feminist theory has it that "tokenism" in large corporations is finding 15 per cent or less of minorities in the dominating group.) Consequently, we did not have the right to diversify among ourselves, and symbolically we had to obey models of excellence in the name of all women. In the rare instances where the subject lent itself, we were to give "the woman's point of view." I also felt that I existed for male colleagues as a woman rather than as an individual or a person.

I recall discussions between male Cabinet colleagues to that effect, the dream being to have Adrienne Clarkson or Marie-José Drouin (when she was with the Hudson Institute) agree to run for the Liberals. I often felt that men, even remarkable men, and this includes Pierre Elliott Trudeau, did not understand the marked abnormality of women's absence in their work world. They did not understand what the group was missing, what we had to contribute, nor the increasing subtlety of injustices and barriers that we had to conquer. Some women in the ranks, a sparing presence, was understandable, even important, they thought. Obviously they did not realize that these were always overqualified women who were generally twice as competent as their male colleagues. But simply wanting as many women as men in politics (or in business, senior university administration, or elsewhere) is exaggerated, even extremist. In fact, it is uncalled for. They were really convinced of this.

Did this general prejudice affect my work? I don't think so. I quickly learned what everyone knows on the Hill: all ministers are equal, except some are much more so than others. In our British-based parliamentary system, other than the prime minister who has all powers, the only minister above others is the minister of finance, whose intrinsic power is the budget for which he need neither consult nor inform the Cabinet. The rank given to the other members of Cabinet by protocol means not much in and of itself. (Of course Treasury Board and Justice also have huge powers over whatever project from any of us, ministers.) What counts first is the personality and political will of the person, the ingredients by which some will never exert the power that they hold. It is not enough to receive the assets needed to exert power – a title, legal authority, a budget, a department, or to become minister of the biggest department, National Health and Welfare, despite its some $23 billion, at the time a quarter of the federal budget. One must occupy power in exercising it; one must take power. Nobody gives it to us, men or women, on a silver platter.

As in all upper levels of decision-making, politicians win some and lose some. However it is not that easy to understand why. We can therefore not stop ourselves from wondering whether we count and how, particularly if we feel set aside from others, which is the case of women. I often told myself how disadvantaged I was in the beginning, because I was not a part of the Canadian social elite. I was often surprised to see important people from the business world, unions, and churches make use of colleagues "who counted." Even if I did not measure up to these standards, I saw nevertheless that some of my interventions "counted" and that "the boss," as we nicknamed Trudeau, seemed to listen to my observations.

In my opinion, in Canada, the majority of federal and provincial ministers who have or seem to have power owe it to the elites of our society. They are chosen and protected by a very small number. They can fast become part of a well-enclosed circle. This power is gained quickly, but can be lost as quickly as a sand castle. In contrast, rare people, and I believe that I was one, derive their power from the grassroots. As much by inclination as by being pushed by Monique Coupal and Roméo LeBlanc, who was already in Cabinet before me, I saw my role as that of a privileged spokesperson for the population subgroups for whom I had mandate. In my position, it meant children, women, senior citizens, native people, ill people, health and social services professionals, and medical researchers, to name a few. I represented them, which is not to say that I did not try to exercise leadership or that I did not show solidarity with the government or that I belonged to lobby groups. Links, first tenuous, then stronger and stronger, developed from encounters, meetings, briefs, and recommendations that were received and discussed. The Canadian Health Act (1984), for example, would never have passed without this extraordinary power base. My other great luck was to have remained in the same department for more than seven years, contrary to the "in vogue" concept where male colleagues liked to change portfolios to expand their contact networks for their eventual leadership candidacy.

At times the two or three women sitting together in Cabinet formed a bloc on questions of criminal law (rape, prostitution, sexual harassment), the loss of status for Native women who married whites, and social policies. I also worked with similar small networks of women in other levels of government, and also within my own department. The greatest advantage, inasmuch as these women had made a feminist analysis, was that we did not have to explain the mysteries of life to each other before each hot issue! My former male colleagues would probably cringe upon learning that certain feats were successful only because of the help of two, three, or four relatively unknown women senior civil servants and that the power, on that day, was female!

PART FIVE

Becoming an Academic

18

A Visiting Professor: Notre Dame and McGill

When I recently read the book of interviews I gave Daniel Raunet in 2015, at the invitation of Les Éditions du Boréal, in a book later published as *Entretiens: Monique Bégin*, I had a pinching in the heart when he started the interview on my life after politics when he said, "You were quite old (approaching fifty) when you left politics and had never been connected to the academic system," suggesting I was a case. If one operates like in the old times when one had a job for life, with promotion and better salary through the decades, then I was a case. In fact, I was a case by a behaviour much ahead of the labour market times! But it is only when reading Daniel's question after the book was published that I realized that this time I might have taken a challenge bigger than I thought going into academia. Basically, I never aimed at developing a career, academic or otherwise; the very concept was foreign to me. At home, once in Canada, I found myself in a small universe almost completely closed on itself, with no outside sources of information – no newspapers, radio, telephone, television, visitors, just books – so I suppose all I knew, as the eldest, was my father's constantly reinvented career.

Between election day on 4 September and my arrival in South Bend, Indiana, on 13 September, life was pretty hectic. Cancelling my Ottawa apartment lease at the Champlain Towers, which I had enjoyed for eight years, and selling what remained of my furniture after my first garage sale (where I felt obliged to offer wine and cheese to visitors, ignorant of the way these things go), packing and moving to my house in Montreal was a first priority. This long week was a back-and-forth between

Ottawa and Montreal. I saw some of my officials in Medical Research and in the department, my political staff, and as much as I could, my friends in Cabinet and caucus: Pierre Bussières, Charles Lapointe, Dennis Dawson, Claude-André Lachance, Lloyd Axworthy, Ed Lumley, and Judy Erola. It was painful and sad, all having been defeated, with the exception of Lloyd Axworthy, re-elected, and Claude-André Lachance and I who had left politics by choice. My sister Marie helped me unpack the Ottawa crates in Montreal while I packed what I would need in South Bend.

Getting from Montreal to South Bend took up almost all of 13 September, as there were no direct flights to that city of some 100,000 in *l'Amérique profonde*, as we say in French. The day after, after I reported to the University Administration, filled out a few forms, and received basic information, the challenge was to get organized in the tiny apartment I had rented in a subdivided mansion on 711 West Washington Street, the historic street where city elites once had their beautiful properties, a few still occupied, many subdivided and now rented to poor tenants. The building where I lived was empty except for two apartments: mine and another on my floor occupied by a nice young banker who commuted every weekend and later committed suicide. The strange odour made me call the police.

And then on Sunday, 16 September, I was initiated into my new life, so to speak, by having to attend mass on campus, before being taken for brunch afterwards to the Emporium, close by, on the St Joseph River, an empty factory warehouse turned into a fashionable restaurant in 1980. I was discovering both South Bend and the University of Notre Dame, with 9,500 students at the time, its main employer. In 1984 South Bend had been living an economic down for the last twenty years. It had lost its three key industries: the Studebaker automobile firm, the Singer Sewing Machine factory, and the Bendix Corporation, maker of avionics, radios, and phonographs. The city had lost 30,000 people and had not yet recovered. When I lived in South Bend, there were close to 1,500 vacant or abandoned houses, as well as abandoned industrial facilities. Blacks were 25 per cent of the population, while people of German origin totalled 17 per cent, those of Polish origin making 10 per cent, followed by smaller percentages of people of other origins. It was said there were more than 100 places of worship, mainly Christian churches and two synagogues, including the first African-American church – the African Methodist Episcopal Church – founded in 1870. I came to know South Bend quite well, as I walked a lot, some areas being a bit dangerous.

The spacious grounds of the university, carefully tended, were magnificent. How can I forget discovering the gorgeous magnolia trees in flower in early spring? And the Grotto of Our Lady of Lourdes, reminding me of Ste Anne-de-Beaupré near Quebec City or St Joseph's Oratory in Montreal ... The new building where the Department of Economics had just moved was very elegant. But the clerical mentality of the institution was a shock to a modern Quebecker. Notre Dame, founded in 1842 by the Holy Cross religious order, was still very old-fashioned, narrow-minded, and Catholic. A few older priests, active or retired professors, pointed out the crime of our Quebec Quiet Revolution – all communists, they told me – that had "killed" the excellent curricula of the classical colleges, to be replaced by secular CEGEPs. Provost Timothy O'Meara, whom I had met on 6 August when I first went to Notre Dame for short meetings, was the first secular provost of the institution. There were still priests in key positions in the power structure: Father Edward Mallory, CSC, for instance, who was associate provost in my time, would become president of the University of Notre Dame less than two years after I left, succeeding the illustrious Father Theodore Hesburgh, CSC, who had been at the helm for thirty-five years. Today's seventeenth president is Rev. John I. Jenkins, CSC, a philosopher and theologian. Notre Dame senior administration also counted nuns of the same religious order; the one I got to know, "Sister John" (Sister John Miriam Jones), was assistant provost. This formal religious environment was quite a surprise to me, in fact quite a shock. It was already very much in decline in Quebec, and clerical institutions had all but disappeared in the sixties with the Quiet Revolution and the socio-cultural "sexual revolution." A noticeable number of priests then left the priesthood. Of the eighteen classmates, out of twenty-three of my final year at the Rigaud Teachers College who entered religious orders and became nuns, one remains today. The others left years ago, married, and had children.

In my first week at the University of Notre Dame, I had already been taken to the Faculty Club for lunch by a professor of history, Vincent de Santis, whose Canadian wife was from Victoria, BC, and had had further invitations from new colleagues in economics: Jennifer Warlick and her husband David Betson, and Linda Hudgins. The half-dozen Canadian students there started contacting me, I gave radio interviews to CBC (Jim Littleton), SRC (Renée Hudon), CBC *Morningside* with Peter Gzowski, and I made a first presentation in Jennifer Warlick's course, "The Economics of Poverty"! I would later do the CBC *National*, with Jason Moscovitz, who came to interview me at Notre Dame! No need to add that I also attended my first football game with the famous "Fighting Irish," without understanding much of what was going on. More, I discovered Chicago, after taking a day train trip with colleague Linda Hudgins, although two hours each way; it would become my great escape once in a while. My office, Room 405, was located in the new elegant Decio Faculty Hall, dedicated to offices for professors of the large College of Arts and Letters, which included the Department of Economics.

I owed my new mandate as a visiting professor to the admiration Father Ted had for Pierre Elliott Trudeau and through Ivan Head, who made that possible. Father Ted, as he was called, invited me for lunch on 16 September, shortly after my arrival. Rev. Theodore M. Hesburgh, CSC, had already done a lot to transform Notre Dame from a respectable undergrad university renowned for its football team into a first-class graduate university with researchers and labs, open to women, of international reputation. I recall learning upon arrival from my colleague next door that Father Ted – forceful, warm, and charismatic – had a CV that consisted of one page of his theological degrees from Rome and dozens of pages listing his 106 honorary doctorates! He had been appointed a member of the Civil Rights Commission by President Eisenhower in 1957 and its chairman in 1969 by President Lyndon Baines Johnson, but Richard Nixon, who could not stand his frequent opposition to his policies, dismissed him in 1972. When I met Father Ted, he had recently completed five years as chair of the Rockefeller Foundation.

Father Ted loved politics, was an ardent Democrat, and had his friend – the former governor of Ohio John J. Gilligan (and his wife

Kathryn), himself also an unapologetic liberal Democrat with a wicked Irish sense of humour – for dinner on campus with me, not far from the famous golden dome Notre Dame Administration building. At the very first such dinner, he asked me what it was like working for Trudeau. How did he function? How often did I meet him? He wanted to know it in detail. At first, I could not even understand what he was after. Then I decided to tell him the way it was. In eight years as Trudeau's minister, I had exactly two appointments with "the boss," as some of us Quebeckers nicknamed him. The first was when I was minister of national revenue and I was accompanied by my taxation deputy minister. We had to inform the prime minister, personally and privately, of some international tax wrongdoing involving foreign royalty. It must have been in 1977. The second time was at my own initiative, when I could not gain P & P (Cabinet Executive Committee) approval for my bill to consolidate our universal health insurance. I went to see him alone. Each of those meetings lasted thirty minutes at most. Father Ted was amazed. He wondered how often I discussed my mandate with him *weekly*! As I explained to Father Ted, Trudeau was a very special prime minister who considered people, including his ministers, as fully responsible adults who, when given a responsibility, discharged it to the best of their ability. And if he had two personal interrelated objectives – patriating the Constitution and passing the Charter of Rights and Freedoms – he relied on and trusted his ministers when it came to each of his ministries. For example, when he appointed me, as I explained to Father Ted and John Gilligan, to Revenue or to Health and Welfare, he never discussed any issue or topic, because, I believe, he would not have known what to tell me his wishes were. We were not on his radar screen. Father Ted was a very special university president and social justice advocate whom I cherished.

It was understood that I would teach a new mandatory course to the 117 seniors in economics for the second semester, January to May, while responding in an ad hoc manner to all invitations of collaboration from other colleagues. My mandate for this course from Father Ted was "to give them, future American economic elites, a social conscience"! On 6 December "to provide me with an important milestone in my new academic career," as he wrote to me shortly later, the Gilbert F. Schaefer

Chair in Arts and Letters was inaugurated with great pomp – mass, most elegant cocktail and dinner, speech, photos – and I was invested as its first distinguished professor. Five other endowed chairs were inaugurated that day – a very wealthy university.

As I had a large class, I would be given a teaching assistant, a brand new experience for me. Mine was a tall African American from Newark, NJ, Tyrone Ferdnance, a wonderful young man in his thirties from whom I learned a lot about another America completely absent from Notre Dame, except for a few more than the twelve black students needed to get the special federal grant. Ferdnance was completing his doctoral thesis on the Italian neo-Marxist theorist and elected politician Antonio Gramsci, quite a daring topic at this still actively Catholic university. As there was no way my assistant could order or obtain the reference books he needed, starting with Gramsci work, I bought them for him while visiting Montreal. Every summer, Tyrone taught in Nigeria. While writing these memoirs, I discovered that he obtained his PhD in economics, became a beloved university professor, and died in 2014 at sixty while teaching at Hampton University, VA.

Slowly and by bits and pieces I learned from Tyrone and Linda L. Hudgins, assistant professor of economics in the office opposite mine, how an academic institution functioned. Linda was horrified when she saw my three-page CV. I felt as if I was worth nothing: why was every speech I had given as a politician not listed? I couldn't believe it. But I was learning this new strange universe, and when I left Notre Dame on 20 May 1985 my new CV had sixteen pages. Then Dean Michael J. Loux wanted my syllabus by mid-October. What did "syllabus" mean? My colleague explained to me that being a university professor was the job closest to being self-employed. My "syllabus" belonged to me exclusively. Nobody could say a word about my teaching methodology or my publications. An unwritten rule recognized that a professor could undertake the equivalent of a day off per week for paid consultations without having to ask permission. Thinking it over, I can see she was expressing in a succinct and pragmatic way the extreme individualism and remarkable autonomy characteristic of academic life.

There were daily requests to participate in academic life. In the second semester, my classes were twice a week. But, upon arrival in

September, I started participating weekly in four seminars/workshops: the Kellogg Institute seminars on Central and South America (being later appointed to its board for some five years), the "Labour Workshop," the "Development," and the "Public Policy" workshops as well. The new Center for Social Concerns had me as a panellist on the famine in Africa. I also gave a few presentations off campus. It was the year Geraldine Ferraro was the first female vice presidential candidate representing a major American political party, the Democrats, and I was invited to speak to the NOW Women of South Bend, and to female students and women's groups. We watched the election night on 6 November at the home of my friendly colleagues Dominique Parent and David Ruccio, horrified at Reagan's victory. During the weekend of 3 November, I was in Vancouver as the keynote speaker at the Canadian Gerontology Association.

The Kellogg Institute for International Studies was only two years old, under the leadership of the Argentinian political scientist Guillermo O'Donnell, its first academic director. At the time, the interests of the network of colleagues participating focused on the democratization of countries of Central and South America. Research papers were written and discussed on community movements opposing dictatorships, military governments, wars, rebellions, torture, emerging new leadership, and, of necessity, poverty, survival, and development. Today the institute also works on "economic development in Africa through innovative research and community engagement." The intellectual atmosphere was open and interdisciplinary, not loaded with academic jargon, just honest research on the development of democratization of these countries. I came to know and befriend remarkable colleagues of different departments as well as discover visiting committed scholars from Latin America. Names of Notre Dame academics that come back to my memory include Denis Goulet (economics and policy studies), Eve (artist) and Mitchell Lifton (Department of Communications), Claude Pomerleau, CSC (international relations), Peter Walshe (an Oxford-educated passionate political science professor, South-African-born anti-apartheid activist fighting for total divestment by Notre Dame Board of Trustees of their important stock holdings in apartheid South Africa, which I supported). In the mid-eighties, the violence in Latin America

was terrible and hard to remember today. In a 2011 paper published
on the web, Brian E. Loveman, the committed political scientist, expert
on Latin America, captured those times: "Long-term military governments, with changing leadership in most cases, controlled eleven Latin
American nations for significant periods from 1964 to 1990: Ecuador,
1963–1966 and 1972–1978; Guatemala, 1963–1985 (with an interlude
from 1966–1969); Brazil, 1964–1985; Bolivia, 1964–1970 and 1971–
1982; Argentina, 1966–1973 and 1976–1983; Peru, 1968–1980; Pana-
ma, 1968–1989; Honduras, 1963–1966 and 1972–1982; Chile, 1973–
1990; and Uruguay, 1973–1984. In El Salvador the military dominated
government from 1948 until 1984, but the last 'episode' was from 1979
to 1984." But what I recall most vividly were the presentations and discussions about the situation in Nicaragua, a country not even listed in
Loveman's list. In 1978–79 the Sandinista National Liberation Front (a
rightist aggregate of counter-revolutionary groups financially helped by
both Russia and the United States) ousted the dictatorship of Somoza,
then made efforts to govern from 1979 until 1990 while it was engaged
in war with the contras. My friend from our days in sociology at Université de Montréal in the 1950s, the Brazilian Raymundo de Andrade,
was teaching at the University of Ottawa, so I forwarded to him many
original papers from the center. He told me they became a precious
source of knowledge for his courses. These case studies of Latin America
from the Kellogg Institute opened up new research paths and better understanding "from within" of the uncertainties, hazards, and vagaries
of the changing times in that part of the world.

As soon as I returned to South Bend from the Christmas holidays,
Ivan Illich, then a visiting professor at Penn State University, had me,
Barbara Duden (medical historian and feminist from University of Han-
nover), and John L. McKnight (Northwestern University, author of *The
Careless Society*) as guest speakers for two days in his seminars on
health and health care in today's world. (I had first met him at our 1979
Couchiching Conference.) We were all challenging the unlimited medicalization of life. This was an unforgettable experience for me, because
of both Ivan Illich's personality and critical mind, and my encounter
with the singular and perceptive approach to one's body by Barbara
Duden. Although they were also different, Ivan Illich reminded me of

Fernand Cadieux: both were serious and original thinkers, sharing extreme sensitivity about others and the state of the world, yet enjoying every moment of life.

Back in South Bend, in February, at my initiative, students and my TA and I met at the Federal Building to observe and ask questions of Indiana Republican Senator Dan Quayle during the budget hearings discussions. None of us suspected that a little more than three years later, as George H.W. Bush's running mate, Quayle would become the US vice president. (I had not found him of any interest during my class visit.)

While at Notre Dame I was the guest of Purdue University at West Lafayette, Smith College in Northampton, Indiana University in Bloomington, and Franklin College in Indianapolis. I was asked to address Canadian medicare, the Foreign Investment Review Agency, the welfare state, the status of women, women and poverty, family issues, and more. At the Mennonite Biblical Seminary in Elkhart, I recall discussing issues of peace and justice. Being invited as guest speaker in the classes of Prof. Theodore (Ted) Marmor at Yale University, in political economy, on 24 April was a fascinating opportunity to exchange in person with one of the most articulate American academics on the modern welfare state, with special emphasis on health and pension issues, and an expert on comparison of our Canadian "medicare" and the American Medicare, Medicaid, and health-care delivery. Later, on 29 May, I would give the keynote address to the Association for the Care of Children's Health, in Boston, speaking at their request on "Strategies for Change within the Canadian Health Care System."

I had given interviews to local media on the way, as well as to some Canadian ones. I had started in September with Peter Gzowski for *Morningside* and, faithful to his word, he had me on the air again before I left South Bend to hear how it had been!

That year at the University of Notre Dame, quite a risk at all levels, turned out to be a most positive experience for me. In moving to another country, our giant neighbour the United States, I had to cut my links to active politics, and I found myself alone in front of new challenges, redefining myself and my active life. Through these months I received the gift of new friendships, some for life, and learned a lot about the world and about America. It is hard to conclude if I got to know more about academic life or about America. The first thing I had done before leaving Montreal was to buy the newly published *Les Américains* by Léo Sauvage, the former critic, author, and foreign correspondent for *Le Figaro*. I saw poverty, abandoned factories, and the deep divide between blacks and white Americans. I also discovered Chicago, two hours by train from South Bend, my special escape for a day when I could afford it. I even had the pleasant surprise of Canadian friends meeting me in Chicago on four weekends, the first being my gang of young former Québécois MPs. If I loved Notre Dame in its clerical dimension and its conservative or social-justice-minded faculty, daily life in South Bend was financially difficult, lonely, and depressing. It was financially difficult because of all the travelling expenses to and from Canada a few times a year and having to rent an apartment. No expenses were covered by the university. A Canadian accountant friend had told me not to worry, because those expenses were tax deductible, and all I had to do was to keep all receipts for travel, moving, and renting. But Revenue Canada considers university contracts as "regular employment"! Because of his mistake, I had to re-mortgage my house in Montreal that year in order to pay my income tax. On a positive note, I had the renewed pleasure of returning to Notre Dame as a member of the Kellogg Institute for International Studies Advisory Board over the following five years.

Dr Stefan Kertezs, a professor emeritus of economics, from Hungary, with whom I had lunch or dinner once a week, convinced me to write a book on our health care and its 1979–84 crisis, as a public policy dossier. Despite my hesitations, I started a year later, able to give a small summer research contract to one of "my" Canadian students of South Bend, Cam Sylvester, who became an instructor of political science at Capilano University, BC, and with whom I am still in regular contact. Dr Kertezs started mentoring me about a future academic career, but I did not quite integrate his wise advice. I was not ready, I suppose. To go from politics to academic life turned out to be quite a challenge for me. With the academic year over and the exams all corrected, I came back home to Montreal by car with two old friends. I was able to spend the month of July in France, first in Angers, visiting Dominique Parent and her family (my new younger friend I met at Notre Dame), then travelling through Brittany with the Tétreaults (Canadian friends from my student time in Paris and the long summer in the south of France and Italy in 1962), and finally piloting Monique Coupal, her husband and daughter, and his Belgian family, in Paris.

I felt secure, as a job was awaiting me for one more year as visiting professor in sociology at McGill University. This was due to my former role of minister for the Medical Research Council and my working relationships and friendships I developed, starting with the deans of medicine of Canada and their researchers. Dr Sam Freedman had been a McGill dean of medicine. We owe gratitude to him and his research teammate, Dr Phil Gold, for major breakthroughs in cancer research. When I announced my departure from politics in July 1984, he was vice principal of McGill. As I said earlier in these memoirs, he contacted me immediately to offer me that one-year contract. In the mid-eighties Canadian universities could no longer advertise tenure-track positions as a result of the economic situation. I accepted his offer with gratitude. So in September 1985 I walked through those prestigious grounds on Sherbrooke Street West, the bastion of English elites, to my new small office in the Stephen Leacock Building. I was not given a teaching workload, the idea being that I would accept invitations here and there as they came. The director of the Department of Sociology did not seem to know what to do with me, although he invited me in November to make a presentation to his class. The Department of Social Work had been the very first to invite me to address two different classes in a huge auditorium, so unwelcoming to both students and professors. The day after, a renowned political scientist, Dr James Mallory, had me lead a graduate seminar on the Constitution. Later, back in his department, I had to explain to 200 undergraduates how Cabinet worked, then answered questions for one hour. I came to know Dr Mallory rather well, discovering and appreciating academic conceptual developments. At the same time, I could see examples of misinterpretations when theoreticians without inside practice develop grand theories. A small Women's Studies Program was starting, and I saw them a lot, participating as best I could. I went back often to social work courses, a dynamic and community-rooted program open to "groupwork" more than to the traditional "casework."

The first week of November took me to Queen's University as their
Michener Visitorship guest that year. Besides having a private dinner
with the chancellor, Agnes Benedickson, the former governor general
Roland Michener, Professor John Meisel, and a few others prior to the
evening public presentation I had agreed to deliver, I made presentations
mornings, afternoons, and evenings at their request. In all, I presented
in the Departments of Sociology, Law, Medicine, the School of Public
Administration, Nursing, Political Science, Women's Studies, and even
the Royal Military College! A true "ministerial" marathon. At around
that time I renewed links with a particular sociology course at University
of Montreal as well as with Concordia's School of Community Affairs.
On almost every Thursday, I joined a small discussion group for dinner
at the home of my former sociology professor, Hubert Guindon. We were
six or seven, the others mostly from Concordia, and each was invited to
present a text recently written, which the group would discuss. That intellectual camaraderie helped me write my book on our Canadian medicare. In McGill, professors and researchers in medicine also started
inviting me to discuss health policy with their students and residents.

At the same time, a former sociology student just ahead of me at the
University of Montreal, Yvan Corbeil, founder and president for some
twenty years of the CROP polling company, invited me for lunch. He
wanted me to join his business and take over as CEO. It was very flattering and I needed a job in six months, although I never mentioned it.
But I could not see myself going into business, recruiting customers and
patrons. CROP was doing excellent work, but I was starting to feel comfortable in the academic world. So I thanked Yvan but did not take up
his offer. Later that year, Claude Forget, a teenage friend from NDG,
lawyer and economist, former Quebec health and social affairs assistant
deputy minister for Claude Castonguay, Liberal minister of health under
Bourassa, just before my time in the same federal office, invited me to
join SECOR, then Canada's largest independent strategic management
consulting firm, where he was an associate. Again, I could not project
myself contributing in such a business milieu, recruiting new clients. I
had already agreed to join the board of directors of McGill-Queen's
University Press, a very different type of business and role for me. We
were meeting alternately in Kingston and in Montreal, and I much en-

joyed addressing the challenges and objectives of that publishing company and working with their CEO, Philip Cercone.

I had accepted the invitation to join the Americas Society, based in New York, with a mission "to foster an understanding of the contemporary political, social and economic issues confronting Latin America, the Caribbean, and Canada, and to increase public awareness and appreciation of the diverse cultural heritage of the Americas and the importance of the inter-American relationship." I attended my first three-day conference with the society in New York in December. I would come back to their meetings for a number of years, meeting with its vice president, author and journalist Lansing Lamont, when we were both in Ottawa. All I recall of my first meeting is that Geraldine Ferraro was the keynote speaker at the opening banquet. Later, in December, at the McCord Museum, was the book launch for the second volume of the memoirs of Paul Martin Sr, which I would not have missed; I knew he had made history for Canadians more than once.

In February 1986 I spent most of the Study Week going back to South Bend and, from there, by car with a local good friend to Kalamazoo, an hour-and-a-half trip. I loved the name of that Michigan city. It was through the Canadian Studies Program that I had landed at Western Michigan University. Upon arrival I did an interview at the WKZO radio station before giving a first presentation, "The Feminization of Poverty," then an evening class, "Women and Western Culture," concluding with a public lecture next evening, "The Canadian and American Health Care Systems Compared."

Back at McGill, life went on with constant invitations to meet individual students on their research projects and individual professors, or to give class presentations. In attending meetings of the Sociology Department, I observed the process of interviewing and hiring professors. At long last I had rediscovered my private life, my garden, my Montreal lifestyle, and it suited me very well. I saw friends, and we went to restaurants, museums, plays, and concerts. In my home, again I started to receive people from my past life and my new one. I spent a week in Paris at Easter. But I still had to find a job for September 1986, at the latest.

Back when I was minister of national health and welfare, a large group of professors and administrators asked me to become a candidate for university president at Concordia. By some miracle, nobody in Ottawa or elsewhere ever heard of it. I had campaigned on weekends in Montreal, and at times even on weekday evenings. Was it in 1982? In 1983? I had to keep it so secret that I cannot find the exact time of this adventure, having not even written it with a code in my agendas! Despite the fact that I had given it my best, listening and learning about the institution, its problems and possible objectives, I was defeated by the man from within. A few years after, while I was at McGill, the request repeated itself at the beginning of January 1986, this time from groups of the UQÀM. I submitted my application. Helped by an impressive and fascinating core group wanting change, I was guided through meetings with professors, students, senior administrators, and union leaders. On 7 April the scenario repeated itself as I was defeated by the man from within, Claude Corbo. I had understood. So when Dr George Connell, a respected force of change in the post-secondary sector as president of University of Toronto, phoned me in 1989, attempting to convince me that I should submit my candidacy to succeed him – a great honour, as far as I was concerned – I thanked him for this vote of confidence but told him that it was a "No."

It is obvious to me now that I had no idea of what becoming a university president was all about. (And I had not yet read Jill Ker Conway, whom I had met and admired, first as vice president of the University of Toronto, then at thirty-nine the successful first woman president of the upscale young women's college, Smith College, from 1975 to 1985, and author in 2001 of *A Woman's Education: The Road from Coorain Leads to Smith College.*) My idea of leadership in higher education bore no relationship to the reality of the day. A president had to find donors for buildings, labs, research, and state-of-the-art equipment; defend his territory with the provincial government; be seen everywhere ... and lead his institution with all the new problems of the day, violence against women and racism being up front. All of these heavy responsibilities within an extraordinary internal bureaucratic structure that looks as if it is from the Middle Ages, no offence to history. Some Canadian university presidents have done pretty well, but it was not a job for me. Not at all.

My other great defeat came at about the same time, after I saw an advertisement for an opening for full professor, in a tenure-track position, in the Department of Political Science at the University of Montreal, to teach the federal political system, federal policies, and so on. I contacted nobody there – my first mistake, as I still had some well-recognized friends in the Faculty of Social Sciences – and I was so anxious to get an academic job, in fact that job, that I did not inquire beforehand while I was still very far from knowing the process and had no idea of who was who in that department. It was a dream: teaching what I knew best, at my alma mater, and remaining at home in Montreal. I was interviewed for two hours by half a dozen professors. Stéphane Dion was one of them – I knew his father, Léon Dion, whom I respected and liked – and three others, including the chair, being leaders of known separatist networks. Having never been particularly partisan as a politician, and my brothers and sisters being separatists, I had no problems and felt completely at ease. A week later a two-line letter: "Vous n'avez pas la compétence voulue" (You do not have the required competency). I never received any feedback. I was seriously hurt. I never mentioned this episode to anyone.

At the end of that same week, a friend I had not seen recently, Monique Lortie-Lussier, professor of psychology and co-founder of the Women's Studies Department at the University of Ottawa, phoned me out of the blue, insisting that I submit my candidacy immediately, with the required CV and so on, as it was the deadline for the search for the first holder of the joint chair in Women's Studies at Ottawa-Carleton. I answered her in the negative, not particularly interested, but above all wanting to stay in Montreal after fifteen, twenty years of having been home just in passing. She insisted, and I finally agreed to submit in my candidacy and the relevant documents for consideration, for the sake of our friendship. I faxed them next morning after, which was the deadline.

At both Notre Dame and McGill I had developed a very general idea of the process of interviewing candidates for academic positions. So I prepared a public presentation in French for University of Ottawa on "the feminization of poverty" and one in English for Carleton University on "women and political power." There were six or seven candidates, each interviewed separately. Then came a luncheon with me and the dozen or so professors of women's studies of both universities, as well as the vice rector responsible for the administration of the new chair, Dr Susan Mann Trofimenkoff, at the U of O Faculty Club. During the meal, the vice rector started asking me what I would like to teach. I had no idea, answering her back, "What are your objectives? What do you need?" She kept repeating her question and me my inquiries. Puzzled that an employer did not know what she needed, I finally said, in order to get back to my meal, thinking of my previous ministerial mandate, "Well, I could teach Women and Health, and Women and Social Policy." The whole group loved it! I later learned that I had been selected when, on 23 April, the vice rector phoned me at home to offer me the job. It would be for at least one year, possibly two or three, depending on the how the market affected the value of the trust fund. It was not a regular tenure-track position. Once again, I would do Montreal-Ottawa-Montreal by bus every weekend for more years, having also to sublet a modest small place to live in Ottawa, as my expenses were not reimbursed.

Before starting that new job and having left McGill, my academic year 1985–86 finished in a completely non-academic, quasi-exotic way, thanks to the French CBC/SRC. At the time it had a highly rated early evening television show entitled *Avis de recherche*, co-hosted by Aline Desjardins and Gaston L'Heureux. On the basis of recommendations from the public, unknown to the guest, a personality was chosen who would be onstage for the five days of a given week. It always started the same way: the newspapers published a class picture with the head of the "victim" circled, and everybody else who was in that school picture was invited to the program as participant on the stage or in the studio audience. It always ended up on Fridays with a surprise appearance of the victim's family and loved one! So a producer informed me that I would be the subject. Since there was not much live television anymore, the show was taped during the first week of August, and scheduled for broadcast in the fall! That was when our public television was very well equipped and had big budgets. Every evening was one surprise after another totally unexpected for the victim! For example, as I do not drive, and as my riding Liberal Association wanted to collect money to buy me a car as a gift when I left politics (!), how can I ever forget my past Liberal Association president arriving on the stage in a red big car!

Also during that summer, as my book in French on the Canada Health Act (1984) as a public policy case had been completed and accepted by Les Éditions Boréal, I had to retype the manuscript (we did not have computers!) with the changes decided by my editor at Boréal, Daniel Latouche, a professor of political science at McGill and a staunch separatist, particularly unpleasant and rude to me, ending my first two years of "life after politics."

19

Four Years in Women's Studies
(Unearthing Women's Health)

Logistics was my first new challenge. Working at 50:50 at each of my new universities, having to sub-rent a small apartment downtown, Ottawa and Carleton being far from each other – the first one downtown and the second one in the southwest of town – and me not driving, I did not have the means to travel by cab and had to take the bus. There was no expenses budget associated with the salary, which was much lower than my ministerial one but double my previous academic years at $20,000. Because of the distance, my most exhausting time was returning home downtown past 9 p.m. from Carleton University, after having taught evening courses. Once home, it was impossible to go to bed until the adrenaline level had decreased! In the fall of 1986 I was invited to present in classes of other professors (law, political science, history, etc.), meet my new program's colleagues, and participate weekly in the seminars of Jill Vickers at Carleton. My own regular course schedule would start in January 1987.

Shortly after my time at McGill, to my surprise I was appointed to its Board of Governors and started attending its monthly meetings, discovering yet another level of academic and administrative worries and new problems for institutions of higher learning. In this case, the separatist PQ government denied McGill the same grants that other Quebec universities received. I discovered that sitting on the McGill Board of Governors, was a coveted, prestigious appointment for Quebec French or English big business names.

For my first semester in women's studies, Mondays and Tuesdays were at Carleton, while Wednesdays and Thursdays were at the University of Ottawa, Fridays being often in Montreal. Back home, besides working on my book and seeing friends and former political colleagues, I was working with the McGill Interfaculty Committee on Women's Studies. On some weekends I stayed in Ottawa for special events, workshops, and conferences, like the Institute for Research on Public Policy's Canada-UK Colloquium on comparative Social Policy Process in October 1986.

A bizarre incident ended that first semester. One Friday morning in Montreal, just before Christmas, David Johnston, the McGill principal (and future governor general of Canada), and Hugh Halward, a successful businessman in the construction industry, philanthropist, and president of the McGill Board of Governors, asked me to be in the principal's office at 9:30 a.m. They silently presented me with a letter to read, that they had signed, informing me that McGill was granting me an honorary doctorate. I stayed silent, as this is not the usual way to receive such information. They then asked me to send them a letter refusing the honour, as it would represent a conflict of interest for me as a McGill governor. I was amazed and thinking fast. They added that it was McGill's policy not to give honorary doctorates to board members but had forgotten that rule until after the letter had been written. I finally told them that I understood, would write them a letter refusing the honour offered, but not for a possible conflict of interest, as there was none in my mind. I was not even reimbursed my expenses for getting to the meetings, which were unpaid. I said my refusal of the honour would be based on the appearance of impropriety or something of the sort. I concluded that top managers could act strangely. To this day I still do not understand why they did not simply destroy that letter, which they had never sent me anyway and of which I knew nothing! In 1991, having left that board when I became the dean of health sciences at the University of Ottawa, McGill granted me an honorary doctorate, then my eighth one ... in science. (I had received two honorary doctorates while a parliamentarian and five while in the chair of Women's Studies.) "My" old principal, David Johnston, and the newly appointed chancellor, Gretta Chambers, honoured me with great elegance at that convocation.

January was approaching and I was going to teach in women's studies. Some academic friends had explained to me the key role played by the

Royal Commission on the Status of Women (1967–70) in leading the development of academic feminist studies in Canada through our research contracts to young professors who would later develop a feminist body of knowledge. The first two Canadian university feminist courses were offered in 1970, by the historian Natalie Zemon Davis at the University of Toronto, and at Concordia jointly by sociologist Greta Nemiroff and philosopher Prudence Allen in 1976. At the University of Sherbrooke, historian Micheline Dumont was giving her first feminist course, while historian Deborah Graham had created one called "Women and Society" in 1971. At the University of Ottawa, Marie-Laure Girou-Swiderski, a French literature specialist, would give her first feminist course in 1978.

During the last days of the Pierre Trudeau government, Judy Erola, minister of the status of women (and minister of consumer and corporate affairs), obtained Cabinet approval to create five chairs in women's studies, one for each region of the country, through a $1 million trust fund established for each university selected. The idea originated from Margaret Fulton, president of Mount St Vincent University in Halifax. Despite Pauline Jewett having been the first and only woman university president in Canada in 1974, by 1978, when first appointed, Margaret Fulton was again the only female university president. Judy Erola had liked the idea very much and had her memo to Cabinet discussed at the infamous (in my view) Super Cabinet Committee of Social Development. All ministers agreed to the proposal, including our committee chair, Jean Chrétien. But it was put aside for consideration at the next "Auction Day," as there was no money. Judy, determined, wise, and pragmatic as usual, "found" the $5 million needed through an obscure unused fund in Consumer and Corporate Affairs, her main department. So the proposal had to be approved at the committee level. Although I was in Cabinet when Judy Erola presented her proposal for the five chairs and had it approved, I never followed what happened later in our academic world. I had not even noticed which universities had been selected from the applications received. I assumed that the University of Toronto would have received the Ontario chair, or perhaps York University. So I was surprised when Monique Lussier reached me in Montreal, begging me to send in my candidacy for the Ottawa-Carleton Universities chair. The two Ottawa universities had been smart enough to have won the Ontario chair by having proposed a joint, bilingual, program.

When I started working in that joint chair in September 1986, I saw with surprise how well women's studies had evolved as an academic field of knowledge, teaching, and research. I still recall meeting very early a particularly interesting and pleasant new colleague from Carleton, Fran Klodawsky, who introduced herself as a feminist geography and environmental studies professor. Despite my feminist past and natural curiosity, I was dumbstruck. A feminist geographer? What was the relationship? In very simple and clear terms she started giving me a few examples relating women's interests to public municipal spaces and their organization, and so on. Fascinated, I got it at once and still follow from afar what she publishes by herself or with Caroline Andrew's shared interest and commitment.

In the early eighties, Marxist thinking had influenced the research and teaching of some feminist academics, including in my new working milieu. In any event, with the passing of time, more and more different schools of thought marked feminist theoretical developments: radical feminism, radical libertarian feminism, radical cultural feminism, liberal feminism, socialist feminism, ecofeminism. With difficulty, I tried to figure out from within what they were. As I started being invited by both Canadian and American Women's Studies Programs, I witnessed how divided academic feminism was; so were feminist community movements. I regretted how each school of thought often despised the others. In my observation of social change dynamics, I had come to believe that social change results from bringing about basic convergence of views from different, even divergent approaches, and moving on from there. I believed in a "rainbow" joint approach. The Royal Commission on the Status of Women and I were defined as "reform" or liberal feminists, obviously viewed with contempt by some.

All this being said, now my first task was to develop syllabi not for one but for three courses: Women and Health, Women and Social Policies, and Women and Political Power, some in French, some in English, and some in both official languages! Not so easy because of the paucity of publications on each topic, in either French or English. My biggest challenge was the issue of "women and their health." To confess, despite my critique of the over-medicalization of life observed in my years at the helm of Health and Welfare as well as of the Medical Research Council, at the time I had never doubted that science – hard science, including medicine – was neutral and objective. I would be in for a few surprises.

I had left National Health and Welfare two years ago, but in my seven plus years there, having done hundreds and hundreds of speeches, interviews, media panels, and talk radio with listeners, I had never heard "women's health" discussed except twice, shortly before leaving politics. One of these times had been a large class at Glendon College in Toronto where I was presenting, accompanied by a younger female civil servant, Jessica Hill, who had particularly impressed me. The speaking notes she had prepared for me were developed around the concept of *women's life-cycle*, a revelation. I had registered the concept but never yet explored it.

When I started immersing myself in women's health, initially all by myself, looking at it from lay women's perspective, not from medical experts or nurses, I slowly discovered a new universe with some excitement. I would develop courses on women and their health during the four years in women's studies, but went on later with courses to nursing students, discussion groups, speeches, and conferences on this topic for my seven years as dean of health sciences, until the end of 1997. I continued, however, to be involved in one way or another in women's health, a topic I still follow. My discovery of women's health as a field of learning and research came, as often it does, by accident. I have always been gifted in finding "the" book or document, outside of the fads of the day, just like that, going around a bookstore or a library. It happened all my life, still does, as if my intuition was operating full time without my knowledge, bringing upfront what my deepest memory kept away from my conscious mind. It applies to every field of knowledge: literature, history, biographies, cookbooks, spirituality, and more. This is how, developing my views and my syllabi about women's health, I discovered five remarkable American authors, whom I never had a chance to meet, all in the physical sciences whom no one around me knew.

A general medical practitioner, Dr Ruth Bleier was a renowned neurophysiologist with a postdoctoral fellowship from Johns Hopkins in neuroanatomy. Her books provided insight into the controversial issues of biological determinism and the origins of gender differences. Dr Anne Fausto-Sterling, twenty years her junior, after graduating in zoology, had obtained her PhD in developmental genetics. Her work exposes the flawed premise of the nature-versus-nurture debate. She believed that both sex and gender are in part social constructs. An American anthropologist and primatologist, Dr Sarah Blaffer Hrdy, also of a younger generation, was also making major contributions to evolutionary psychology and sociobiology. She was considered one of the most radical thinkers of the day. Her research was on the "maternal instinct," which is innate but also learned. She had questioned the book by feminist French public intellectual Elisabeth Badinter, *L'Amour en plus* (1980), in which she stated that maternal instinct was a pure social construct. This was too simplistic a view for Sarah Hrdy. Dr Ruth Hubbard, of an older generation, a Harvard biologist, was the first woman to hold a tenured professorship in biology. She was a first and prominent critic of science and medicine, particularly of gene research, on the ground that women had been excluded from research questions and as research subjects. Finally, my other inspiration had been Dr Sue V. Rosser, of the younger generation, a PhD in zoology. Professor of anthropology, she taught women's studies as well as history, technology, and society at the Georgia Institute of Technology. Among other issues, she documented the "science glass ceiling" for academic women scientists, women inventors and the "gender gap in patenting," women and new technology, always suggesting pragmatic approaches to overcome women's inequality.

However, before discovering these experts, my first surprise had been to learn that the militant dimension of the second wave of feminism, its very first women's liberation expression, its most active and its most radical, in parallel to the grand underground theories being developed in the sixties, had been that of the "women's health movement," completely unknown to me or my feminist friends of the time. The Canadian male health sociologists and economists who were, I was also discovering, great critics of the biomedical model, had never noted that the historical *Our Bodies, Ourselves*, first published by the Boston Women's

Health Book Collective in 1971, then republished in a commercial for-
mat, followed by several editions, rapidly translated for France, Japan,
Italy, Denmark, the Netherlands, Greece, Sweden, Spain, and Latin
America, had preceded Ivan Illich's *The Medical Nemesis* of 1975 by
four years and was no less subversive than his work. Why would a
group of eleven "ordinary" young women of the hippie socio-cultural
revolution decide to research and write a book on their own sexual lives
and their health issues, wanting to challenge not just the young men in
their lives but also the medical establishment to change and improve
the health care that women receive? If there were no problems, ten years
later, in the mid-eighties in Canada, why would three of the five first
chairs in women's studies have chosen women's health as the thrust of
their academic work without consulting each other? I am referring to
psychiatrist Susan Penfold at UBC, sociologist Maria De Koninck at
Laval, and myself at Carleton and Ottawa Universities.

Quite early after starting in women's studies, I subscribed to the
Canadian *Healthsharing* magazine, launched in Toronto in 1971. It was
but one manifestation of the Canadian women's health movement, new
to me and still largely unknown and unacknowledged. The *Canadian
Woman Studies / Les Cahiers de la femme* opened the world of community feminist action and initiatives to academic feminists. In 2004 it
reflected on forty-five years of the Canadian women's health movement:

> From these principles came activities, programs, and services. One
> of the earliest was *Side-effects*, a play and popular education cam-
> paign about women and pharmaceuticals that made a remarkable
> cross-country tour in the early 1980s (Tudiver and Hall). Other
> examples included the formation of home birth and midwifery
> coalitions, the launching of the still-published *A Friend Indeed*
> newsletter on women and menopause, women-centered tobacco
> programs, the Montreal Health Press, environmental action groups,
> women and AIDS activities, endometriosis and breast cancer ac-
> tion groups, the disability rights organization DAWN, feminist
> counselling programs, women's shelters, traditional healing study
> groups, *Healthsharing* magazine, sexual assault support and ac-
> tion groups, anti-racism work, and community-based women's

services such as Le Regroupement des centres de santé des femmes du Québec, Winnipeg's Women's Health Clinic or the Immigrant Women's Health Centre in Toronto to name a few. These organizations, programs, and services were characterized by innovation and social action.

The Canadian Women's Health Network would finally be set up in 1993, under the leadership of strong individuals like Madeline Boscoe, Sue Sherwin, Sharon Batt, Janet Currie, and others. But "women's health" remained circumscribed by community activist circles.

Analysis of women's health issues – not necessarily their diseases but the way the whole medical ideology and system considered and treated them – having started outside the bio-medical world, took quite some time to be of interest to government departments, and even longer into the cursus of nursing or medicine.

Students in my first third- or fourth-year undergraduate courses were from arts, social sciences, even business administration, and I came from sociology. Our Faculties of Medicine were not following at all. However, while I was in the joint chair of women's studies, at first unknown to me and to everyone one around in the women's health movement, the Ontario Medical Association (OMA) set up a Committee on Women's Health Issues for medical education. On the basis of recommendations of that committee report, the OMA adopted the US Public Health Service definition of what constituted the field of women's health. This is the conceptual framework for defining women's health I adopted for my own work once I discovered the article published in September 1989 by the *Ontario Medical Review*:

- Diseases or conditions *unique* to women or some subgroup of women.
- Diseases or conditions *more prevalent* in women or some subgroup of women.
- Diseases or conditions *more serious* among women or some subgroup of women.
- Diseases or conditions for which *the risk factors are different* for women or some subgroup of women.

- Diseases or conditions for which *the interventions are different* for women or some subgroup of women.

This is very much a biomedical definition of women's health based on gender comparisons using medical points of reference. However, it offered rigour and concepts that were easy to grasp for non-medical audiences, including the women's health movement. The 1989 OMA Committee had also said, "The human experience of being a woman in society, the natural history and epidemiology of illness in women and the relationships between them must be isolated and highlighted for attention and careful study" – a long-time and major challenge for medicine and medical faculties, even nursing schools and programs.

Although not a historian, I had noticed that both in the United States and around me – for example at the University of Ottawa – Departments, Schools, or Faculties of Psychology had already started exploring women's psychological health. Let me then add the following to the previous conceptual framework. Besides the notions of the over- and under-medicalization of women's health, a third feminist concept had to be understood, in particular when it comes to women's mental health: that of "women as deviant." If mental health as accepted by therapists was articulated around the traditional sex roles between males and females as the norm – and the corresponding stereotyped behaviours, then a female who is a Type A personality, who has drive, loves power, is aggressive, etc., becomes a "deviant" to the stereotype and might be labelled as having psychological disorders.

I exchanged a great deal with the other chairs in women's studies, then all involved with undergraduate education leading to a bachelor of arts. The five chairs had been granted as follows: Dalhousie (Nova Scotia), Laval (Quebec), jointly Ottawa-Carleton Universities (Ontario), jointly Universities of Manitoba-Winnipeg (Manitoba), and finally Simon Fraser (BC). In that era, the second half of the eighties, I enjoyed one of the longest tenures in that position, followed by Maria De Koninck, who was in the Laval chair for four years but started when I was already in my third year. For example, when I visited Simon Fraser University in Vancouver, where the chair had been named the Ruth Wynn Woodward

Chair, its first incumbent had been a psychiatrist, Dr Susan Penfold, who held the position from September 1985 to June 1986. The next academic year, the incumbent was Rosemary Brown, the former provincial NDP politician, whom I met with pleasure. From September 1988 to June 1989, the incumbent was a writer and literary critic, Daphne Marlatt. Then, corresponding to my last year in the Ottawa-Carleton chair, I met the fourth Simon Fraser incumbent, the economist Marjorie Cohen, whose work I still follow, still seeing her with pleasure once in a while. The Laval University chair was created only in September 1988, and I networked with and learned a lot from Maria De Koninck, its first incumbent, who held the position for four years in a row. A sociologist like myself, Maria then continued the same kind of work when attached to the Faculty of Medicine, and I met her again during my involvement from 2005 regarding the academic development of the social determinants of health in which she was also working. She was followed in the Laval chair by Huguette Dagenais. The joint Universities of Manitoba and of Winnipeg chair was created in 1987 and was called the Margaret Laurence Chair. Its first incumbent was Keith Louise Fulton, a professor of English from the University of Winnipeg, from 1987 to 1992. The focus of her research and teaching was on writings by women.

All our regional chairs went through difficult economic times starting in 1990, depending on how much local money their universities could or could not raise to complement the original $1 million federal endowment and how the latter had been invested. Their management permitted quite a lot of flexibility. Some chairs remained empty for a year or were attributed for a few months only, depending on the financial markets. In Ottawa, Greta Hoffman Nemiroff, who had co-thought the first feminist university course in Canada, succeeded me in the joint chair only in 1991 up to sometime in 1996.

Besides my regular teaching workload and the chair committee meetings, I rapidly joined the Canadian Research Institute for the Advancement of Women (CRIAW/ICREF), co-founded by Carleton professors Naomi Griffiths (history) and Jill Vickers (political science) and fifteen other women and men in 1976, in the wake of the first 1975 International Women's Year. Naomi Griffiths, now "my dean" in women's

studies at Carleton, was that same academic who had insisted on seeing
me in 1977 when I was minister of national revenue, to correct my department's rigid interpretation of the rules and had first rejected CRIAW's
request for "charitable organization" status. CRIAW was, and remains,
a national "research/action" institute of feminist research and community action, a publishing house, also involved in feminist networking
development and organizing a then important annual conference.

I was elected to the board and found CRIAW's approach open-minded,
rigorous in research, and involved in community action-research. At the
time of their creation, their objectives were to promote the advancement
of women through feminist and woman-centred research; to encourage
exchanges between female academics, women's groups, workers and
activists; to disseminate research results through publications; and to
sponsor and assist research of interest to and by women in Canada. It
was the only women's organization in Canada focused exclusively on
nurturing rigorous feminist research and making it accessible. Its leadership was fascinating, and I much enjoyed working with "my" first
board chair, Linda Christiansen-Ruffman, a sociologist from Halifax St
Mary's University, or later with Christine St Peter, chair of women's
studies at the University of Victoria, or Marilyn Assheton-Smith, from
Education at the University of Alberta. The 1987 CRIAW Annual General
Meeting was in Winnipeg, followed by the 1988 one in Quebec City.
The CRIAW Annual Conference of 9–13 November 1989 took place in
Yellowknife in the Northwest Territories with a remarkable attendance
and great enthusiasm. From the Universities of Carleton and of Ottawa
were several professors (Cécile Coderre and Linda Cardinal, for exam-
ple), even the vice rector (academic) Susan Mann, a feminist, directly
responsible for the joint chair. There we also met Ethel Blondin, the first
Aboriginal (a Dene) woman just elected as an MP to the Canadian
Parliament, for the Western Arctic riding. She would later become a
Cabinet minister under both Prime Ministers Chrétien and Martin. The
November 1990 CRIAW Annual Conference took place in Charlotte-
town and did not face any particular challenges.

But at the CRIAW Board we also went through very difficult times,
just avoiding serious violence, not just protests, from feminist activist
groups, particularly at the 1992 Toronto Annual General Meeting,

when I was still on the board, but had become a dean. We had decided that the subject of our conference would be "Making the Links: Anti-Racism and Feminism." The issues at stake were a sense of class oppression, gender and sexual identity, as well as racism. Challenging questions were about lives of women of colour, Aboriginal women, immigrant women, working-class women, women with disabilities, lesbians, and other marginalized women. White Western feminists were labelled ethnocentric. Those strong and new reactions and attacks had to do with the perceived lack of involvement of CRIAW and similar groups with recent networks of women of colour, new immigrants, or groups of lesbians, and their sense of exclusion from the mainstream. For the protesters, we were just bourgeois feminists, liberal feminists. Inclusiveness and diversity would be addressed by CRIAW in each of the following years.

At the time, papers from CRIAW Conferences were published in *Atlantis* and/or in *Resources for Feminist Research*. I published some there, as well as in the *Canadian Woman Studies / Les Cahiers de la femme*, first published in 1976. The other Canadian feminist magazine was a quarterly called *Herizons*, based in Winnipeg. A regional newspaper originally in 1979, it became a magazine in 1983, and a national magazine by 1985 in both scope and content. It is now published four times a year. It is the voice of the women's movement, not of academic feminism. Issues are often thematic, drawing on feminist writers from all spheres. Issues could be covering, as past examples: the environment, popular culture, legal cases affecting women, a woman singer, and so on.

At the 1987 CRIAW conference, where I had been invited as keynote speaker to open the conference, I entitled my presentation, later published by McGill-Queen's University Press, "Redesigning Health Care for Women." At the time, almost all segments of our society worshipped the bio-medical model of health care and its many breakthroughs. In those years, Canadians sought more access to more medical care. Only very slowly and somewhat tardily did the Canadian public begin to question the authoritarian mode of interaction between medical-care providers and patients, the over-specialization and extreme fragmentation of the system, and, above all, the ever increasing medicalization of life. People were very surprised, almost aggressively so, when confronted with the evidence that more medical care does not increase the general health of the population. I submitted that those who had been mistreated the most had been women and the elderly. These groups suffered not only from various diseases but also from malaises and problems of body readjustment that medicine had not considered interesting. While the elderly experienced health problems because of the aging process, throughout their lives women would meet many problems associated with reproductive functions. Such problems had been reduced to diseases, badly diagnosed, and too often badly treated. Good health went beyond a strictly medical definition and was best expressed by the concept of well-being. Using that language at the time was that of a trailblazer, as I was to discover some twenty years later, when a member of the WHO International Commission on Social Determinants of Health.

I invited the women participants to a process of demystification of health care and therapy by demanding information and learning how the system worked in order to make informed choices. To realize that we, the patients, empower physicians and medical experts with our blind faith in science and technology as neutral, "pure," objective visions of progress in the second half of the twentieth century. Calling for a pragmatic approach in our questioning, I reviewed two examples of the times. The first one was the 1980 pioneer work of the Canadian Institute of Child Health in which they surveyed 567 hospitals to assess their maternity care, reassessing them in 1985 to determine if there had been a decrease in dependency upon obstetrical technology, fewer unnecessary or risky routine hospital practices and procedures: perineal shaving, enemas or suppositories, intravenous therapy, electronic fetal heart monitoring, episiotomies, and so on. My second reference was the *Ontario Task Force Report on Midwifery*, led by Mary Eberts, then just released, another example of possible de-medicalization of a life event – giving birth. Empowering women to discuss their health, to control it, and to make decisions about it was one of my objectives. I also wanted us to see that health care was a microcosm of society. All the clichés of patriarchy, sexism, abusive capitalism – each of these diseases of society – were also to be found in our medical care systems. Medicine was and still is practised within an extremely authoritarian, hierarchical, impersonal, and distant organization. It is over-specialized and hence very fragmented in its application and is most alienating for the patient. In a nutshell, my interest was in empowering women's well-being, in this case vis-à-vis a key social institution, that of medicine. Under one form or another, this would be my research, my teaching, and my public speaking, especially in these four years of women's studies.

Somehow life as an academic integrated in a regular university program was as busy and exciting as when I was a Cabinet member. The difference was that there was no travel budget, no secretary, no support staff. There were more and more invitations to be the keynote speaker at a public presentation of one kind or another, generally unpaid, not all related to occupying the chair in women's studies but also on health care or social policies. It may appear as if I was living two parallel lives. The first as that of the chair in women's studies, and the other as a former political personality. In fact, I lived these four years as a unified block of time of learning, teaching, sharing my observations, and listening to others, in whatever role I was being cast by circumstances.

For example, here is what 1987 looked like: As a starting point, I picked the privileged lunch with author Alice Munro at the University of Ottawa, arranged by a friendly colleague of English literature, David Staines, who knew her and my admiration for her. I had just convinced my Ottawa book club to read and discuss *The Progress of Love,* which she autographed for me. To think that, in 2013, she would receive the Nobel Prize in Literature, to my great joy! It was my second meal shared with a Nobel Prize winner, after some good food shared with Roger Guillemin and medical research friends when he passed through Montreal, after being awarded the 1977 Nobel Prize for Medicine for his work on neurohormones! In the following days, weeks, and months beside my courses, I participated in regular half-day sessions of the Science Council Committee on Genetic Predispositions, of which I had become a member. There is no way now to find out how I ended up on that fascinating committee, but logic would point to a request by Dr Charles Scriver, the McGill geneticist befriended when I was the minister of the medical research council. This was also the year I started supervising my first master's thesis at Carleton, that of Rose Mary Murphy, a nurse who was now taking women's studies. Her interest was to define and analyze the "caring vs curing" philosophy in nursing. It turned out to be a most satisfactory experience. In March I participated in a day-long conference for the tenth anniversary of the very worthy Canadian Institute of Child Health, with nurse Shirley Post at the helm, who had already led in establishing the Children's Hospital of Eastern Ontario. On 1 April I presented "Psychologie différentielle des sexes" in Professor Monique Lussier's course in psychology. And at the end of the month, I spent more four days in South Bend, at the board meeting of the Kellogg Institute for International Studies. Upon return, I chaired the jury meeting for the Jean-Paul Pagé Award, a Quebec journalism contest in mental health. I played that role for four years. Mid-May were two days at Kingston with the Ontario University Status of Women officers. May was surprising: to my repeated bewilderment I received not one but two honorary doctorates, one from Dalhousie University in Halifax, and another from Queen's University in Kingston. I would receive more over the years and will always feel thankful for the recognition but with a sense that it was a case of mistaken identity. Then, the first week of June, I had the good fortune of being a participant in the WHO Twenty-First Council for International Organizations of Medical Sciences conference in Amsterdam. CIOMS is an international – at the time, rather limited to the Western world – non-governmental organization established jointly by WHO and UNESCO in 1949. The conference was on bioethics. I had been asked to chair the plenary session as well as a workshop. I presented a text that was later published. I much enjoyed the participants in that long week of exchange of ideas, during which we were also invited to the Muziektheater and to the Concertgebouw, an exceptional treat. I slowly continued to have a voice on important health issues. As I remained connected to the world of health and to a lesser extent to that of social policies through repeated invitations, although no longer institutionally attached to either, I had to make a choice. Without professional help, I could no longer keep myself informed of these two huge spheres of public policy which used to form my department as a minister. I then decided to focus on the health system and related policy issues in a public but nonpartisan way.

The 1987 fall session started during the very first days of September with three days in Quebec City with "my" former commissioner of the

Royal Commission on the Status of Women (1967–70), Professor Jeanne Lapointe, and the Groupe de recherche multidisciplinaire féministe. On 1 October 1987, leaving Ottawa at 3 p.m., after having taught my fourth year course at the University of Ottawa from 10 a.m. to 1 p.m., I took a private plane sent by Trent University, arrived in Peterborough for a bite at suppertime, and was the public speaker on "Redesigning Health Care for Women." The day after was spent at Trent University, meeting professors and giving a few more informal presentations before leaving for the Toronto airport and flying back home to Montreal. Or I would be participating in a conference such as the 29–31 October International Forum on New Reproductive Technology at Concordia University in Montreal. In 6–8 November of that year, the first panel of the five chairs in women's studies was on the agenda of the CRIAW annual conference, in Winnipeg. From there, late on the Sunday, I flew to Vancouver with Rosemary Brown, staying for the night at her home. The Monday was spent meeting with the Simon Fraser University administration, animating a two-hour seminar, followed by recording a one-hour program for Educational TV, then the Vancouver Airport, landing in Ottawa around 11 p.m. The week after, I spent 18–21 November in New York, at the Americas Society Annual Meeting, starting with an evening of private discussion, with Jake Epp, my successor as minister of national health and welfare under Brian Mulroney, also in attendance. Finally, after my teaching was over for that semester, I spent 12–17 December at a meeting on social policy at the Organisation for Economic Co-operation and Development in Paris.

The year 1988 would look as exotic and as busy, again including two more honorary doctorates, the first from the Laurentian University in Sudbury in early June, followed a few days later by one from the University of Toronto. The latter was particularly special for me, as I was honoured with two giants of health care achievements: Justice Emmett Hall and Dr Fraser Mustard. We were treated royally by Chancellor John Aird and President George Connell.

One special project in which I invested much time through these months, discussing and writing, was a long piece in *Daedalus: Journal of the Academy of Arts and Sciences*. Its editor, Stephen Graubard, had put together a working group of Canadians who would discuss the possible structure and themes of the project, with a view to later writing chapters to become part of *In Search of Canada,* first published in 1988 as a special issue of *Daedalus,* then as a book in 1989. Graubard was assisted by Jill Conway, who had recently completed her ten years as president of Smith College and whom I admired and had met when presenting there while at Notre Dame. I knew half of the Canadians invited to participate: Lloyd Axworthy, Gérard Pelletier, Léon Dion, Don Macdonald, Margaret Catley-Carlson, Fraser Mustard, and Bob Evans. Other authors included William Kilbourn, Kenneth Hare, Robert Harney, David Flaherty, Eleanor Cook, Alan Artibise, and John Conway. In my contribution, "Debates and Silences: Reflections of a Politician," I explored two "debates" and two "silences" in our public life in comparison to our American neighbour. My debates were about the changing status of women, as well as on the drawing up of a foreign policy on our own terms, while our silences were religion and politics on the one hand, and the concentration of economic power on the other – two unexpected companions.

The first months of 1989 – the second semester of the 1988–89 academic year – started in Phoenix, as a speaker and participant in the Canadian College of Health Service Executives conference at the end of January. My good friend and former Cabinet colleague Judy Erola had also been invited as the new president of Pharmaceutical Manufacturers Association of Canada (now Canada's Research-Based Pharmaceutical Companies – Rx&D), the voice of the pharmaceutical industry. Also there was Dr Denise Leclerc-Chevalier, still with National Health and Welfare and in charge of the Canadian Blood Committee I had created at the request of the provinces. I had the pleasure of introducing them to each other, and we spent a formidable three days of professional exchange and of visits: the Arizona desert, the sensational and luxury Art Deco Biltmore Hotel ("the jewel of the desert"), Scottsdale, designed in 1929 by Frank Lloyd Wright. The new trio of friends would make several trips together through the years, up to the death of Denise Leclerc in her eighties in the fall of 2010.

Of all the meetings and presentations through these six months, one in particular impressed me deeply: a mid-May feminist symposium in Banff, "Women's Mental Health." Some of the views expressed were troubling and quite controversial among participants, such as passionate presentations on the prostitute rights movement aiming at protecting prostitutes from public designations of deviance and from legal and social control. The movement was not only seeking to make prostitution acceptable but also to celebrate it. To celebrate prostitutes as feminists, having chosen their occupation freely, was hard for me to understand and to accept.

The academic year finished with a Winnipeg speech to the Manitoba Association of Registered Nurses, one more Science Council regular meeting, a CRIAW/ICREF meeting in Ottawa, and a Toronto Conference at the provincial Women's Directorate.

1989–90 was to be my last year in women's studies. The academic year started with a home exchange on 29 August: friend and colleague Cécile Coderre and her husband Daniel Mockle both had a sabbatical to be spent in Montreal, so they took my house on rue St François d'Assise, and I stayed at their Hull townhouse on rue des Narcisses in the "Jardins du Château" compound. I benefitted from the generous offer of Rector D'Iorio's chief of staff, Jacques Lussier, a neighbour, who gave me a ride in the morning and at the end of the day.

The first semester was similar to previous experience in teaching, director of master's theses, the wonderful CRIAW conference in Yellowknife previously mentioned, and the speeches related to my getting one more honorary doctorate, this time in Edmonton at the University of Alberta. However, I had started a longer-term research project, with the help of a fine assistant, Denise Belisle: establishing a bilingual annotated bibliography on *Women and Aging, Canada, 1975–89*, which was published at the end of the year. The project was based at the University of Ottawa. We worked on it almost daily.

At the end of November I was saddened by the passing away of Jean-Claude Malépart, due to cancer, at fifty, a provincial MLA who became a federal Liberal MP in 1979 for the Montreal-Sainte-Marie riding in southeastern Montreal, re-elected in 1980, 1984, and 1988. A blue-collar worker at MacDonald Tobacco, he was a natural populist, in the best sense of the word, a leader who wanted reforms against poverty, for seniors, for a universal health-care system. A fighter when needed, he was a pragmatist pushing as much as feasible the art of the possible.

Close to Montreal municipal politics, he knew the players very well, especially Lucien Saulnier. I often consulted him while in politics and could count on his judgment, political intuition, and support. Bishop Jean-Claude Turcotte of Montreal celebrated the funeral mass, where I was asked to give a eulogy. Recently, in October 2016, having to tape media interviews in the Hochelaga neighbourhood on Ontario Street East in Montreal, I had the shock and pleasure of discovering that the large building across the street from where I was standing was called Le Centre Jean-Claude Malépart, a local sport, culture, and leisure community centre recognizing what Malépart was all about.

My last semester in women's studies included a third-year under-graduate course, "Women and Health," in the University of Ottawa School of Nursing, in addition to the fourth-year "Women and Cana-dian Politics" at Carleton. On 8 March, International Women's Day, I chaired the biggest conference I had ever organized with my research assistant, Denise Belisle, at the request of many. Our intent was to some-how present and discuss the issue of "older women in society." Colle-giality being what it is, Denise and I listened to the students and their professors, in fact to those who pushed us to change the focus, ending up with a conference on "Women and Their Sexualities." The large Uni-versity of Ottawa auditorium was filled with parents, the general public, and students. We had a panel of female students forcefully expressing a variety of views on sexuality. The objective was to encompass the whole spectrum of gender and sexuality. Terms such as *LGBT* were still unknown on campuses and elsewhere. I recall the mother of one of our students, who was taking women's studies classes herself, making a pas-sionate recommendation to be voted on by the whole assembly, that all parents send their teenage girls and boys to workshops where they would be exposed to homosexuality, bisexuality, and all forms of sex, in order "to free these youth from the overbearing and unjust cultural imposition of heterosexuality." I was thinking of Margaret Mead's work and was at a loss for words ... Finally all that I or someone else was able to do was to rule against any vote further to that panel.

I would also meet the nursing students in my office every Thursday afternoon, and those of Carleton on Tuesdays. Ad hoc presentations in colleague classes continued in health administration, *droit civil* or common law at the University of Ottawa, and in psychology and/or in the social policy seminar at Carleton. I was the keynote speaker at the University of New Brunswick Nursing School in Fredericton, and in Winnipeg at the Conference of Canadian Obstetrics, Gynecology, and Neonatal Nurses. And wearing different hats, I presented, chaired a panel, was a panellist, and attended for the first time, with my friend Micheline Dumont as my guide, the Learned Societies in Victoria, BC, at the very end of May 1990.

However, my life had already changed course. Out of the blue, on 31 January of that same year, the University of Ottawa president, Dr Antoine D'Iorio, a biochemist and physiologist who had co-discovered an enzyme linked to metabolism and whom I had known through the Medical Research Council while minister of national health and welfare, invited me for lunch at his office. He simply announced to me that the schools and programs that were not integrated into the medical curriculum were taken out of the Faculty of Medicine to become a faculty of their own: the Faculty of Health Sciences. Assistant Vice Rector (academic) Denis Carrier had the mandate to set up the new faculty and he, as rector/president, wanted me as dean. He asked me to submit my candidacy at once for the position to be opened. After listening and learning a little more about the idea, I thanked him but said that I would not apply, despite his insistence, explaining my past experiences. By then I knew enough to be certain that "the guy from within" would get the job, also remembering how not having completed my doctorate would become a block. In addition, despite my one current course to nursing students, I knew nobody in that future faculty.

Life went on as usual until the beginning of April, when I learned that "my candidacy had been received" and that I would be interviewed with the other candidates around mid-April! It became difficult to juggle everything on my agenda while trying to learn something of that new faculty's objectives, programs, professors, and students. There were, I believe, half a dozen candidates. But there was no way of learning about the faculty! No past documents, no current documents. A friend and neighbour of my women's studies colleague Cécile Coderre, Jean Harvey, a young professor of human kinetics, agreed to meet me, giving me a crash course on who was who and what was new faculty was all about.

I would have needed many, many more hours of briefing! My interview took place on Thursday, 19 April. The Selection Committee was probably chaired by Denis Carrier. I remember that the chair of nursing, Denise Alcock, and of human kinetics, Daniel Soucy, were on the selection committee, as well as other people. One of the first questions, from Daniel Soucy, was why I was not seated straight on my chair! Luckily he did not want to know why I had scoliosis! At the end of the month I learned that I had been selected as the dean of health sciences.

I had to cancel my agenda for the first ten days of May, having been sent to Banff for the annual Senior University Administrators Course, organized and given there by the Centre for Higher Education, Research, and Development of the University of Manitoba. The University of Ottawa vice rector (finances), Dr John Cowan, was much involved in that initiative. I enormously enjoyed the challenges of all the workshops, as well as the professors and the other students from universities all across the country in positions of deans and administrators. I always liked and admired the talent of John Cowan, who was bright, modern, and a reformer in a pragmatic and often original way. I benefitted from the informal conversations in Banff but did not come back with a clear idea of how university organization charts and procedures really operated!

At the time, women's studies at University of Ottawa seemed to me much more convivial than its Carleton counterpart, possibly because we occupied a former private house, an old bourgeois Heritage home next to Tabaret (the high administration), right in the middle of the campus and downtown. My office was the third floor attic, quiet. Colleagues from other faculties teaching in women's studies often came by, as well as our students. On the second floor, we often had lunches, meetings, and dinners in a warm and friendly atmosphere. The program secretary, Margot Santos, was at the centre of the action. Colleagues Monique Lussier (psychology), Cécile Coderre (sociology), Denise Angers (history), and Caroline Andrew (political sciences and coordinator of the Women's Studies Program) were mentors and good friends.

At Carleton we had small, cold, and impersonal offices in the twenty-three-floor Dunton Tower, which were not conducive to the same camaraderie. The atmosphere and the institutional culture of the two campuses were also quite different. Created in 1848 by the Oblate Fathers, the University of Ottawa granted the charter of pontifical university in 1889 and remained a clerical university until 1965. It received a mandate of bilingualism from Ontario in 1974. It was traditional but enjoyed the life of being right downtown. Somehow Carleton University still had a 1968 turbulent student body. Much younger, it took off as a secular institution of higher learning, while returning Second World War veterans needed to obtain degrees and reinsert themselves in the labour market. Carleton then offered evening courses in a philosophy of accessibility.

In all honesty and in lieu of conclusion about these four years as the first joint chair in women's studies, Ottawa-Carleton, with undergraduate classes of third or fourth year, and twenty-five to forty female students (except for the Ottawa courses on social policies attended by a few male students, which made for great discussions), I had a disappointment. It was as if my action had shrunk to the point of being insignificant. I once spoke of it privately with Caroline Andrew, the University of Ottawa program coordinator, always so wise, a subtle and bright political scientist. I told her how, in active politics as a minister, I lost some battles, but when I won one, the results affected the lives of thousands if not millions of Canadians for the better. Now, as a professor, I did not even know if my teaching had an impact on students. She made me go from the quantitative to the qualitative, explaining to me that a professor, an idea, a course, a reasoning could touch the life of one or two students for life. It is true, and I have verified it directly at least twice. Dr Nancy Hansen, now director of the interdisciplinary master's program in disability studies at the University of Manitoba, was my student in the evening courses of Carleton. We came home together by the same bus, past 9 p.m., she for the Glebe, me for downtown. One of the brightest students I ever had, she had a serious physical disability from birth, and I still see her getting on the bus helped by her two crutches and with the greatest difficulty. She had to work to pay for her graduate studies, which she did mainly at Stats Canada. She obtained her PhD from the University of Glasgow and did her post-doc research there as well. Nancy and I always remained in touch. Another former student at

Carleton also comes to mind. In 2001, as I was the first Distinguished Visitor in Women's Studies at the University of Windsor, the program had planned an evening public lecture where hundreds of people came, women especially. To my total surprise, I suddenly recognized the woman introducing me: Joyce Zuk, also in the same course at Carleton! A popular municipal councillor, much involved in community affairs, she is the executive director of Family Services Windsor-Essex!

20

Dean of the New Faculty of Health Sciences

My new mid-1990 deanship started with a grand celebration. Monique Coupal and Judy Erola organized a sumptuous garden party with all our friends, for two of us becoming deans at the same time: Denise Leclerc-Chevalier in pharmacy at the University of Montreal, and I in health sciences at the University of Ottawa. Denise had been the super-competent secretary of the intergovernmental Canadian Blood Committee when I was the minister of national health and welfare; we had been to China together in 1982, and that official trip had sealed our friendship. Dozens and dozens of friends came. Monique Coupal and Henri Vandermeulen had a vast, lovely garden in Rockcliffe. A large tent had been set up with tables and chairs around between flowers, shrubs, and trees. The date chosen was 14 June; Denise had already started on 1 June, and I was officially going to start on 1 August. In the few pictures I still have, I recognize friends from all moments of my life, starting with the NDG Girl Guides! There were Mireille and Fernand Fontaine, Raymundo de Andrade, Robin Boys, Esther and Kalmen Kaplansky, Dolorès Vigneault, Gérald Bouchard, Bernard Daudier and Françoise Borel, Laurie Erola and Peter Channen, Nicole Belisle, Nicole Bisnaire, David Staines, Ann and Ivan Head, Jean-Jacques and Maureen Blais, and others.

To become the dean of a faculty, having never been a regular member of any faculty, having never been a tenure-track university professor anywhere else, in other words, having never seen what a dean does, I found the challenge huge. My beginnings as a dean, and my whole seven years' tenure in that role, would have been impossible without the assistance of Jeannette Giroux, my visionary and talented chief administrative officer, in fact my chief of staff, as we would say on the Hill, formally from central budgeting, who had won the appointment through a selection committee. A very efficient and senior academic, Vice Rector Denis Carrier, had been charged with setting up the new faculty structure on top of his full-time responsibilities. I met him at once on my first day in this new mandate, a first of many more encounters in his office downtown, after 5 p.m., him quiet at his desk, surrounded by files and papers, with only a tiny desk office lamp on. The day after, 2 August, I met Jeannette Giroux for the first time at my new office. We discussed budgetary matters and reviewed invitations, and I had to meet a first student, from Nursing, who had insisted on seeing me.

In the following days, between closing my offices in Carleton and University of Ottawa Women's Studies, moving home from Montreal to Ottawa, where I had rented a small house while putting my beloved first house in Montreal up for sale (I would have to pay the mortgage for twenty-six months before selling in a down market), I started learning the faculty. The University of Ottawa could not bear the "Ts and Ts," those professors who commuted from Montreal from Tuesday to Thursday, some 3,000 persons it was said. Even if I wanted to continue what I had done since 1967, doing my full five weekdays in Ottawa, it would not have been accepted for a dean. Weekends also carried meetings, convocations, special conferences, VIP visitors, and other instances where I should be available.

On 13 August I attended my first academic Senate meeting, a piece of governance I never really understood. It was followed by a couturier taking my measurements for my dean's ceremonial academic gown. I felt as though I was back in medieval times. Then one afternoon, after laughing and discovering each other better, Jeannette Giroux and I visited furniture stores to implement our first serious decision: finding a quality, affordable chesterfield or sofa for my office, both for my visitors and for me, for a rapid nap at the end of the day before evening duties!

No need to add that I did not know, when I started, what it would be like to turn into a dean! I had assumed that the organization chart of a university, using different words, would be a classical traditional pyramidal one. I had forgotten that universities were *sui generis* institutions going back a long time, as my friend Claude-André Lachance would say. Going back, in fact, to the Middle Ages: University of Bologna (1088) and Oxford (1096). More later to close this chapter.

The first fact that hit me was how bureaucratic universities were. Someone of my new faculty secretariat popped up in my new office with two wastepaper baskets. I refused the second one, not needing it. She insisted: "Deans have the right to two wastepaper baskets!" When I was the joint chair in women's studies, I recall making my colleagues of University of Ottawa laugh at my description of the written justification I had had to produce at Carleton University to get a second roll of Scotch tape. That was worse than the government bureaucracy. My academic bureaucratic epiphany happened around the need for toilets of our small francophone programs, occupational therapy and physiotherapy. As there was not enough space for them in Guindon Hall, where medicine was and some of the health sciences, additional space had been provided by two or three temporary prefabricated modular buildings erected in the vast parking lot of the School of Medicine. Even though they had electricity, there was no water, hence no washrooms, in programs with mainly female students and professors. Some were pregnant and it was a good walk to the main building, particularly horrible in winter or other bad weather. After a few weeks in office, with winter in mind, Jeannette Giroux started pressing me to move on with a request to the *haute administration* – meaning the University Executive Committee: the rector, vice rectors, university secretary (Jean-Michel Beillard), the legal advisor – which met once a week. (I learned years later that because my modest request included a financial dimension, it had to go through the Joint Executive Committee of the Senate and the Board of Governors! For toilets?) So, still very ministerial, I repeated to Jeannette that I would be happy to sign the request as soon as it was ready. She presented me with an official form, explaining that I had to personally write the request, justify it, and sign it. I suffered a good two hours, going back to the United Nations Charter of Human Rights, incapable of finding how to justify something so trivial and so basic. Must

I add that fitting plumbing into portable classrooms in the parking lot proved impossible, and that problem is what started our five-year battle for adequate space at Guindon Hall.

As far as I know, health sciences was the only faculty spread over the two campuses, and still is. Our new faculty was made of two older large bilingual schools and four small recent francophone programs. The large School of Human Kinetics still occupies the relatively modern Montpetit Hall on the main campus in downtown Ottawa. Also down-town were the two new graduate programs in audiology and speech therapy, lodged in a former small private apartment building on King Edward Avenue, then the eastward limit of the main campus. At quite a distance, in Alta Vista, were offices of the dean of health sciences, the School of Nursing, and the two small programs of physiotherapy and occupational therapy occupying offices spread through Guindon Hall on Smyth Road (and in their parking lot). Guindon Hall was part of the larger medical campus including the General Hospital, the Chil-dren's Hospital of Eastern Ontario, and the Rehabilitation Building. So it was not surprising that a "space file" came up again and again in dis-cussion with Dr John Seely, the dean of medicine appointed at the same time as I, with whom I worked for the five years of his mandate. (I then worked with his successor, Dr Peter Walker, a very different personality type.) Three months after my arrival, we had an important meeting with Seely and other parties involved, the first of many. Our chief adminis-trative officer, Jeannette Giroux, worked miracles at all levels of the ad-ministration to get more new space for us at Smyth Road, including a decent dean's office. New top floors were built as a vertical extension to the Roger Guindon Hall as well as the redesign of our offices, and those of the Departments of Nursing, Physiotherapy, and Occupational Therapy. Audiology and Speech Therapy were then able to join us on Smyth Road. To arrive at these results took the longest time, and the dean's office and others were ready to move in only on 3 August 1995!

Did I have academic objectives when I started my deanship? No, not specifically. As I had said to the Selection Committee, I felt that our so-ciety was becoming far too "medicalized," budget-wise as well as in ideology, at the expense of other "well-being" fields of learning and practice, such as the disciplines taught in health sciences. In fact, all had happened so fast for me that I had everything to learn about what a faculty, and my faculty, were all about. I had started at the same time as a new rector (president), Dr Marcel Hamelin (a historian, who had been dean of arts for sixteen years), and a new vice rector academic, Dr Bernard Philogène (an entomologist, former sciences dean), while I knew the vice rector of finance, Dr John Cowan (a physiologist who was also expert in labour relations), from my April week as a Senior University Administrators Course student in Banff.

So I wanted to learn what a dean was in the university structure as well as within one's faculty. Where and how would I learn it? In retrospect, I should have been sent to the SUAC courses in Banff *after* my first months as a dean, not before. No one around me had figured out what was obvious to me: having never been a member of a faculty, of any faculty, at any level; two years as visiting professor in two countries; four years in women's studies in two universities at the same time, reporting only and directly to one vice rector academic who would leave the University of Ottawa shortly after I started as a dean – I had no idea of who was who and how it functioned. As I learned after a few years, one additional handicap in my case was that there were only two faculties of health sciences in Canada at the time, meaning everything other than medicine: ours and the Faculty of Health Professions at Dalhousie. All other deans networked through both provincial and national associations of their type of faculties. It was only late in my mandate that I met the Halifax "other dean," Dr Lynn McIntyre. An open-minded younger physician, assertive, a feminist, graduate of medicine from the University of Toronto in 1980, with an additional degree in community health and epidemiology, she had become dean at Dalhousie in 1992 and would be reappointed until 2005. At the same time, she had tenure and taught at the Dalhousie School of Health Services Administration. Afterward, she moved to the University of Calgary, from which she has just retired (more or less!) as a professor emerita. Our situations were not comparable, and we did not develop joint projects or learn from each other.

The monthly deans meeting, chaired by the vice rector academic; the Faculty Executive Committee; the Faculty Council; the Advisory Board of Medicine, the District Health Council and its special task force of

the time (instances to which I belonged ex officio); the CPEF, as franco-
phone staff around me always called it, meaning the sacrosanct Faculty
Teaching Personnel Committee (in no particular order: sabbaticals, contract renewals, promotions, etc.); the School of Graduate Studies; the
University Academic Planning Committee; convocations; the University
Strategic Planning Committee times two; the Inter-Departmental Committee of Gerontology (Social Work, Sociology, Health Sciences); the
Hospitals/Universities Committee; the two main hospital boards; the
Ontario Premier's Council on Health, Well-being, and Social Justice
(member) and its Children and Youth Project (chair), and more, became
fixtures on my agendas. But what had been an easy governance appren-
ticeship, that of joining the Cabinet as a minister of the Crown, turned
into a most deterring enterprise when applied to becoming dean of a
faculty. I never mentioned it to anyone, but I considered resigning on
two or three occasions in my first six months. I had found everything
terribly piecemeal and could not figure out how it was connected and
where it was going. What saved me were my ten days sick in bed at
Christmas, fighting one bug or another. Upon my return, I started seeing
things differently.

What also helped me was to finally get a great secretary, in fact an
executive assistant, confident, with a pleasant personality, with good
communications skills, initiative, and judgment. She was also impervious to stress, another big plus in that new faculty. I will never forget
Julie Perron, whom I met a few times after she left us at the beginning
of 1995 for a better paid and far less bureaucratic job as the executive
assistant of the Canadian Medical Association's CEO, Bill Tholl, who
had worked on the Canada Health Act in my time at Health and Welfare Canada! After the holidays, our chief administrative officer, my
"chief of staff," Jeannette Giroux, was back from her three weeks in
Rome in December 1990, where she had been invited by the Grey Nuns
to attend the canonization ceremonies of Sister Marguerite d'Youville
by Pope John Paul II at the Vatican. There had been friction between
the two of us before her departure for Europe. She was finding it impossible to work while professors constantly barged into her office with
all kinds of problems and requests, without an appointment. Our work-

load was heavy, and the faculty was going nowhere. She made it clear that she wanted me to set up an agenda and establish the rules of the game. I could not agree more, but I did not quite know what to do. So when Julie Perron started organizing my agenda, scheduling regular meetings for all committees that made up the governance structure of a faculty, human resources were channelled where they belonged. After Julie's departure, one of our office secretaries, Lise Theodoris, helped me on an *ad hoc* basis while still also doing her own work until another super pearl of an executive assistant, Marie Cousineau, replaced Julie Perron on 1 May 1996.

We had a first brainstorming session of the Faculty Executive Committee towards the end of October, three months after my appointment. The aim was to work together and figure out common objectives. Then a true first faculty retreat took place a year later, outside our premises, at La Sapinière (Val-David, Quebec), on 18, 19, and 20 June 1991, completed by another one day in mid-September. It had been well organized, the surroundings were pleasant, relaxed, and peaceful, the food was excellent, and nobody could easily disappear elsewhere! Our team of nine was perfect for everyone to fully participate. Around Jeannette Giroux and me were the formal leaders of health sciences – our Faculty Executive Committee – Annette O'Connor (vice dean research), Léo Deschênes (faculty secretary), Denise Alcock (nursing), Daniel Soucy (human kinetics), Louis Tremblay (physiotherapy), Claire-Jehane Dubouloz (occupational therapy), and Andrée Durieux-Smith (audiology and speech therapy). A wonderful photo in my personal albums shows our agenda handwritten on large sheets of paper on the walls, in French or in English, the way we spontaneously functioned:

1 Bilan de ce qu'on est
   a Identités individuelles
   b Interdisciplinarité
   c Complémentarités
   d Différences et ressemblances
2 Cohésion facultaire
3 Plan quinquennal

    a Who will be ...
    b Who will ...
    c Who shall ...

4 Courses Development
    a Undergraduate
    b Graduate

5 Research Faculty interests
    a Collaboration
    b Focus

6 Active search of research $$$

7 To give ourselves a common, clear definition of what we are other than Medicine, one's difference

8 Develop connections
    a Research: consortium, etc.
    b Education
    c Other resources

9 What's our model of Health?

10 Quelle est la position de notre Faculté?
    a La formation professionnelle
    b L'éducation générale
    c Les prérequis de base, etc. etc.

11 Notre identité corporative? Notre marque de fabrique?

Nothing pretentious or particularly sophisticated, but it worked. That kind of retreat was repeated with the same players at the same Laurentian Inn a year later. The faculty retreats that followed, when budgets had been cut drastically, were organized for daytime meetings only at a good hotel in Aylmer, Quebec. We were nurturing the internal leadership of the faculty through these executive committee working sessions. I also made a point of inviting more faculty, enlarging it, depending on circumstances, for some celebrations at my home. As to creating *esprit de corps* among the support staff, we gave it a try as of my second year as a dean, at Halloween, on 31 October 1991. I was hand-in-glove with Jeannette Giroux on her plans to invite the faculty support staff to come to work in costumes, without telling anyone, in order to surprise the dean. What they did not know was that Jeannette and I were going to do the same, disguised in clown costumes, wigs, made up faces, and everything. That was a riot! We even entered the office of the dean of medicine when he was having a staff meeting, and he never recognized me! Then we went to the main campus and visited the rector. They had never seen anything like that, but it worked. We did the same one more year, but that time Jeannette and I were disguised as prisoners with our employee number on our uniform.

Speaking of the faculty academic expansion, following my appointment as dean, we had already been approached seriously and had meetings about a school of pharmacy and, from another group, a school of dietetics, both with some possible professors, a perceived market niche, and potential students. After a few months of discussions, these two distinct projects went dead. Having been a strong supporter of both projects, it was a disappointment. (Today, my former faculty has a school of nutrition sciences, unique in Ontario, granting an honours baccalaureate in nutrition sciences.) So when Ontario called for proposals for a school of midwifery, I had had occasion to know the Ottawa-Hull practising midwives, their organization, the location of their birthing centres, etc., and our nursing expertise (the name of Dr Marie Chamberlain comes to mind), so we started developing a proposal. I knew the time was ripe. In fact, officially recognized midwifery education had been due for quite some time. More women and families wanted a de-medicalized, natural health approach to birthing. The *Ontario Task Force Report on Midwifery*, led by Mary Eberts, had been released in 1987, but in the early 1990s midwifery still had no legal status in Ontario or elsewhere in Canada. We developed a core group of partners, including the Grace Hospital and local midwives, and I convinced Rector Hamelin to endorse our candidacy officially and lobby the provincial government, a dossier he strongly promoted at Queen's Park. In 1993, when the results were announced, we had arrived second in the province, having lost to another campus. Budget and cost differentials probably played a role against us. This sequence of events and these historical facts have been completely erased from documents and publications on the web about the history and development of midwifery in Ontario. Not a word about what we went through: the dates, the competition, and the results. Covering up history: why? The only web postings repeat that, to become a midwife, one must graduate from the four-year Ontario Midwifery Education Program, offered by Ryerson University, Laurentian University, or McMaster University! What kind of power struggle behind the scenes led to a change in the original choice and decision in favour of granting to three universities a monopoly on teaching midwifery?

My penultimate attempt to enlarge the competencies that our faculty could offer came from the Canadian Memorial Chiropractic College (CMCC) in Toronto, a unique initiative established in 1945. At the present time, the undergraduate program at CMCC is a second-entry honours baccalaureate degree program, offered to qualified candidates who have completed a minimum of three years of university-level study prior to admission. This four-year undergraduate program leads to a Doctor of Chiropractic degree. While minister of national health and welfare, I had observed how people with back pain, for example, chose a chiropractor for a solution in much larger numbers than they would look for a physiotherapist. Physiotherapists always put down the chiros as non-scientific charlatans. I had no strong views in favour or against. The college contacted me, wanting to join a university. We met, had discussions, and I started testing the waters. Physiotherapy became extraordinarily upset and we could not even discuss the topic calmly. To avoid a major crisis, I then had to explain the situation to the college and tell them we would not be able to proceed.

As to our own competencies, as early as 1992 I supported nursing in the graduate development of an MSc (nursing). There was already a master's program in human kinetics. A few years later, we went through the development and approval of the diploma in primary health care for nurse practitioners as a post–master's degree option on a full-time or part-time basis. Also in nursing, at one point, La Cité collégiale, an Ottawa community college, and our faculty started discussing a kind of integration, or rather rationalization of our two nursing programs. They were recognized for their clinical teaching and we were better on the theoretical side of nursing. In June 1995 we had the first of many meetings with Andrée Lortie (then president of La Cité collégiale) and her competent and enterprising director of nursing, Linda Assad-Butcher. In addition to mutual benefits in rationalizing our courses, it would help them prepare nurses with the now required entry level to practise: the baccalaureate in nursing science, an additional challenge for La Cité collégiale. Dr Francis (Frank) Reardon, professor of physiology and research scientist in human kinetics, one of those great colleagues we could always count on, who became vice dean academic after my time, retiring in 2009, led the final negotiations, and there is now a collaborative program (four years) between our faculty and La Cité Collégiale granting to students of both institutions a BSc (nursing). This was the way to the future, and I am quite pleased with the results.

As to challenges of our own established courses, issues related to teaching reached me by the back door, so to speak, via human relations/ labour relations (professors' misbehaviour), special equipment needs, and so-called service courses from medicine.

In the School of Human Kinetics, quite early on, I received complaints from individual female students about serious sexual misconduct by some male professors. I had never dealt with that topic or with unions in my previous lives. These complaints ended up as APUO grievances. When appointed at Health Sciences, I learned that deans were "management" and were not members of the Association of Professors of the University of Ottawa (APUO), and I rapidly introduced myself to the union management. When confronted with my first problematic cases, Jeannette Giroux immediately gave me the good advice "to document, document, document," which I started doing at once with no noise. In fact, the few serious dossiers involving the APUO during my tenure were cases from the School of Human Kinetics. It had a professorial body of some thirty to thirty-five, almost all male, including some natural "troublemakers." Two characters come to mind, one older man who would not act as a team member, real deadwood, refusing his course workload, his behaviour leading in 1996 to a union grievance; the other, a bright young aggressive professor who spent his time arguing about everything, confronting me and my office at all the time, accusing me of this or that, and of course quite arrogant, also calling for a grievance. Before the Board of Governors later appointed me professor emerita, he blocked the faculty recommendation for it to the board, so I became the rector's personal recommendation! Yet, in parallel, I also recall a remarkable teacher in that same school, not only revered but loved by all students, generations after generations of learners: Dr Jacques Grenier, an exceptional professor of outdoor education courses. He became a victim of the infamous "publish or perish" regarding his promotion, sabbatical, and so on. To conclude on the grievances tabled, despite my having documented each case over years, cautious about every rule, having explained and exchanged repeatedly with all those involved up to the university top management, the latter managed to lose each one of these cases, including the ones on sexual misconduct by professors.

I worked with two directors of human kinetics during my time as a dean: Dr Daniel Soucy, followed by Dr Roger Gauthier. They too were involved in these conflictual human relations between them and between others of the school. At one point, in January 1995, Daniel Soucy "disappeared" in Singapore – was it where he went during his sabbatical? I never saw him again! I found the situation rather destabilizing. "Cherchez la femme," I was told, but what could I do? In 1998, in publications online I found that, for example, Daniel Soucy was with the Division of Policy and Management Studies of the National Institute of Education at Nanyang Technological University in Singapore ... So I appointed Dr Roger Gauthier to replace him as director. Towards the end of my mandate, at the convincing suggestion of Professor Jean Harvey, I did everything to hire a new, professional director of that school which otherwise had some excellent researchers and professors. He was Denis Prud'homme, MD, at Laval and not ready to move. I never met him, but he finally joined our School of Human Kinetics as its director in 2001 and became dean of health sciences from 2002 to 2012. (He is now the associate vice president research and the scientific director at the Montfort Hospital in Ottawa.) In 2003 Dr Prud'homme set up a "generic" baccalaureate called the baccalaureate of health sciences with more than a hundred new students every year. It had been my dream, as I could see the need for future occupations of trained health sciences generalists capable of interdisciplinary work. Our vice rector academic, Dr Philogène, rejected my project straightaway, as I "could not demonstrate future employment opportunities" for these potential graduates.

Unexpectedly losing a great professor to death was a very sad experience we lived through in October 1991: Dr Anne Lang-Étienne, a fifty-nine-year-old vivacious and smiling colleague with a fierce determination who had set up the Program of Occupational Therapy and had been its first director. I was still discovering her extraordinary leadership after a little more than a year in my job. Dr Rachel Thibault, another exceptional professor in that program, wrote about Anne in 2002 when giving the Muriel Driver Memorial Lecture at the Canadian Association of Occupational Therapists:

> Who else, in the sixties and seventies, spoke of meaning, maturation, and justice as core elements of occupational therapy? Who else would discern the flaws of the then dominant medical model and propose changes? Only a visionary, an early-day dissident ... Anne was marginal, to the end. Her ideals for the profession seemed unconventional when she formulated them, and they still remain on the fringe of current occupational therapy practice. For Anne, the occupational therapist's core goal was to heal through meaning. Without meaning, there is no motivation. Without motivation, there is no engagement. Without engagement, there is no lasting healing.

Another dossier, quite exotic for me as a new dean, was that of the need for a regular supply of cadavers for nursing and physiotherapy students, to learn and practise internal human anatomy especially. Over the centuries, in the history of anatomy, obtaining corpses had always been a big problem. In the last fifty years, donated bodies were the main sources of corpses for practice. But we were informed by Medicine that we were receiving fewer and fewer corpses. (I would not be surprised that this change coincided with recent preference in the population for cremation following death.) There are now only a few dozen North American universities that still train their health-care students using dead bodies. It is usually in their first year of undergraduate studies that students in medicine, nursing, dentistry, and biology, but also students in nutrition, psychology, physical therapy, and pharmacy become involved in the knowledge of anatomy. When confronted with the problem of the supply of corpses, it was believed that practice with artificial anatomical parts/specimens would be less satisfactory than learning from the "true" human body. But what choice did we have? So my involvement had to do with finding new money to purchase mannequins for lack of free cadavers, and convincing our professors to accept and make the best of a new reality. On another file, that of the "Medicine Animal Committee," all that I recall is the important sum of money we were made to pay to them – some of our teaching might have included dissection of animals, but I doubt it. However, I do recall discussions of a new challenge from public opinion and activists: the ethical issue of experimenting on animals as always unacceptable because it causes suffering.

If the Department of Human Kinetics did not require cadavers for their learning, which I can't recall, they did need costly practice equipment. When I became dean, some twenty-five years ago, the behaviour and dress code of students and young people still retained a certain strictness. But I was in for a shock one day when I made an unannounced visit to some classes of "human movement" or whatever, and found young female students in their bras, and both sexes in panties or shorts, in a relatively small exercise room. I was, I admit, flabbergasted, still too European about what a university was supposed to teach. In fact, I should have known better. After all, Montpetit Hall had an Olympic-size swimming pool with a diving tower, not for leisure but for teaching. It had a gymnasium and the first version of today's fitness centres. The equipment was much more basic than now, but it was still an important part of teaching and training our students. And a huge expenditure for our faculty budget at the worst possible time. A portable metabolic system, electrical muscle stimulator, lumbar motion monitor, foot pressure measuring system, platform motion monitoring, and range of motion testing system (lower and upper body) are just a few of these essential gadgets! It was difficult to demonstrate their critical importance to the academic and financial senior administrators. It had to be updated and it had to be replaced when damaged or worn out. It became a big item when universities were seriously cut in my time.

Service courses were yet another eye-opener for me. Anatomy and physiology had always been taught to our students by professors in the Faculty of Medicine. Quite early in my mandate, a tragic physiotherapy student suicide shocked us deeply. Nobody had seen it coming. The young man had finished high school with the highest marks in a small Ontario francophone community and had registered in physiotherapy. He could no longer get the same great marks and had a serious depression. Not connected to this case, I started receiving complaints from first-year students in our two programs regarding the service courses in medicine that they were failing almost systematically. It became serious and I rapidly set up a small task force: Dr Charles Cotton, a great old timer and professor of anatomy in our School of Human Kinetics, and Dr Heather L. Davis, physiologist, a younger career scientist and professor in physiotherapy. They interviewed students, discussed with the Faculty of Medicine, trying to find out what exactly was going on. They then reported to me with a most extraordinary story. Our students were instructed by Medicine to sit along three walls, separate from the medical students, not to ask questions, not to mingle, and so on. In addition, the fact most students of ours had finished francophone high schools led some medical professors to consider them less well educated ... We requested a structural change, at whatever cost, stating that we would give anatomy and physiology courses to our students ourselves. Impossible; it had to be given by people with a doctorate in the subject! This requirement was easy to meet for us with Charles Cotton and Heather Davis. But it all had to go to the highest echelons of the university to finally be approved. And from then on, our students registered marks following the usual bell curves!

An anecdote, this time related to my first convocation at the National Arts Centre as a dean, calling the Nursing students to the podium to receive their diploma, also gives an idea of misogyny at the time. One particular student by the name of Béatrice Mullington had received every possible prize offered for excellence in Nursing Sciences. Curious, I inquired about her from Dr Marian McGee, a senior previous nursing dean with a PhD from Johns Hopkins whom I had befriended. At her suggestion, I invited Béatrice for lunch. The story I learned was hard to believe. A young French family physician, having obtained her doctorate in medicine (with thesis, on a topic of genetics) at the Université d'Angers, she had married an Ottawa journalist then in France and moved to Canada. As she loved medicine and research, once settled here, she met the vice dean (francophone affairs) of our Faculty of

Medicine, inquiring as to what she should do regarding her medical degree in order to be able to practise here, whatever it would take in terms of courses. She was even ready to redo the full curriculum, for she loved medicine! The vice dean told her in no uncertain terms that she would never be accepted into the faculty and that, anyway, the place of a woman was in nursing ... Four years before my arrival as dean, she registered in nursing and had just graduated. The problem was that she could still not find employment and, to my benefit, she agreed in the meantime to do some research and writing for my numerous speaking invitations to discuss women's health. We became friends for life. She was never able to practise medicine again but finally used her medical knowledge as a regulator at the Canadian Patented Medicine Prices Review Board.

I was able to get back to teaching myself and developed a new course for nursing students, not mandatory (as I would have preferred), on women and health. What I appreciated was its unusual outreach. In addition to the class in front of me were a dozen "sites," in fact hospitals across the province, where working nurses now needing a baccalaureate in nursing were given time off by their employers to take our courses. Through an unsophisticated audio system they could hear the course, having received the material for discussion from me ahead of time, but were not seen and could not see us. For them to participate, I had to interrupt my teaching at intervals, slowly calling each station and giving them time for questions. I felt like a train station master! The logistics ahead of the class entailed quite some additional work. My chief of staff Jeannette Giroux reminded me recently of end-of-year faculty parties – which I don't recall at all – where each of us in responsibility, from the dean downward, was copied and mocked by other staff or professors. Mocking the dean was someone imitating my French accent in English calling all the small towns of Ontario: "Sudbury: are you there? Do you hear me? It's your dean ..."

This established, I had not forgotten nor abandoned women's health!

Just after my four years in women's studies, in 1991, parliamentary action brought the paucity of knowledge and of research in women's health to the forefront of public opinion. Further to survivors of breast cancer lobbying parliamentarians, a House of Commons Special Subcommittee was set up, thanks to three female MPs: Barbara Greene (PC), Mary Clancy (Liberal), and Dawn Black (NPD). Medicine was put on the front burner through the public hearings of all key medical research players summoned to testify and answer MPs' questions: the MRC, the National Cancer Institute of Canada, Health Canada, PMAC regrouping the pharmaceuticals, further to having tabled their individual presentations. They had to identify the money allocated specifically for breast cancer research and related medical issues, such as the Meme breast implants used after a mastectomy or for cosmetic reasons, very much in the media at the time. Then two young women came as witnesses: Pat Kelly, from Burlington, Ontario, and Sharon Batt, from Montreal, both charismatic breast cancer survivors from the survivors network. When the subcommittee report was released eight months later, all the media focused on one single fact: breast cancer was only getting 3 per cent of the Canadian medical research budget! Even taking into consideration basic research which might be of a more general nature, this figure still reflected the medical research priorities of the time. The 1992 report also recommended that women be admitted to participate in clinical research trials, a first and important breakthrough for women's health. I recall, while being the joint chair in Women's Studies, having been told by University of Ottawa medical colleagues that women's participation in clinical trials "skewed research results due to their special plumbing system."

In November 1993, in the wake of this House of Commons report, Health Canada (by then deprived of its welfare component) and others – the Medical Research Council, the National Cancer Institute of Canada, the Avon/Flame Foundation, and the Canadian Breast Cancer Foundation – regrouped to form the Canadian Breast Cancer Research Initiative (CBCRI/ICRCI). A $30 million fund for the first five years, then $50 million for the next five years was voted on and approved, being funded through each partner. This was the very first Canadian health research institution bringing together clinical research, basic research, cancer agencies, Health Canada, the business world, and lay breast cancer survivors in a partnership. I had the honour and most rewarding experience of chairing this initiative, as a volunteer, from 1995 to 1999. With the open-minded and supportive attitude of the two women at the top of the Canadian Cancer Society/National Cancer Institute at the time, Dorothy Lamont and Maaike Asselbergs, we concluded our search for an executive director by unanimously selecting Dr Marilyn Schneider, a PhD from Columbia University (1983) ... in medieval art, with a prized thesis: "The Sculptures of the North Gallery of the Cloister of Saint-Trophime at Arles"! A breast cancer survivor herself, although that had nothing to do with our selection, she became the pillar of the CBCRI in no time. A humanist with solid judgment, excellent in human relations, Marilyn loved, understood, and was able to make scientific research projects accessible to the general public, hence forcefully promoting the CBCRI and its funding needs. Marilyn Schneider was with the initiative, first as executive director, then as research program director, until she retired in 2005. A few years ago, I did go to Arles and visited the remarkable fifth-century Romanesque Saint Trophime Cloisters ...

I particularly appreciated working in such an unusual milieu of multi-faceted expertise and knowledge, including how unique it was to listen to survivors. It was also very painful to suddenly lose one of them. It happened twice in my mandate when two survivors, young and full of life, were suddenly faced with a recurrence, this time fatal. They are still in my memory: Ninon Bourque from Ottawa, forty-two, who died in October 1997, and a wonderful mother from Sri Lanka whom I helped with her immigration papers, but whose name escapes me, whom we lost shortly after.

It was also very special to follow some of the greatest scientific minds of our country questioning, arguing, suggesting research paths. It reconnected me with pleasure to my more than seven years as minister of the Medical Research Council of Canada. At the CBCRI I was benefitting from and discovering a newer generation of Canadian medical researchers, enjoying as much as I had twenty years before at the MRC, their sense of purpose and the excitement of discovery through their work. One of these researchers, Dr Victor Ling, a biochemist and a fine and modest leader, had discovered, in 1974, P-glycoprotein, a protein that enables cancer cells to resist many drugs and helps protect brain cells from toxic substances. In the 1990s he was with the BC Cancer Agency and had already been recognized by many prestigious awards. Three years later, Dr Tak Mak, from Toronto, also a biochemist and a biophysicist, joined our work to beat breast cancer. In 1983 he had discovered T-cell receptors, a vital element of the immune system. He has since won almost every international prestigious medical research prize except the Nobel. One is humbled by such an environment. And by the fatality of breast cancer.

It would be towards the end of my mandate there, in 1998–99, that I slightly influenced the sacred principle that all medical research had to be "investigator initiated research," which I recognized is critical in research. We then created an additional modest research stream of "targeted research," following public priorities, meaning patients' priorities. We were also able to open up and legitimize interdisciplinary research, which at the time was so narrowly defined that biology talking with microbiology and immunology was considered the ultimate interdisciplinary approach! Our 1998–2003 CBCRI Strategic Plan was finally formally adopted while reiterating the sacrosanct peer review system. I was offered a second five-year mandate to chair the CBCRI but refused for personal reasons, breast cancer being for me at that time a very emotional issue, a fact I kept privy.

In the 1990s, outside of this Canadian Breast Cancer Research Initiative, the medical world, starting with our Faculties of Medicine, were not in women's health at all. We owe our gratitude to Dr May Cohen, a top academic physician and the associate dean of Health Services at McMaster University, for creation of the first Faculty of Medicine Women's Health Office in 1991, challenging our other seventeen Canadian medical schools to do the same. Dr Cohen, a great friend, had been inspired to set up this office by the work of a group of women physicians in the OMA, working in the late 1980s on wife abuse. In time, this McMaster office led to the Women's Health Inter-School Curriculum Committee for Ontario Medical Schools. Dr Cohen was at long last inducted into our Canadian Medical Hall of Fame in 2016. Another pioneer had been Dr Ruth Wilson, professor of family medicine at Queen's University, who created, also in the 1990s, Canada's very first courses on women's health for medical students. I followed and somehow got involved in these developments, because I was made a member of our University Advisory Board of Medicine, sat on the strategic meetings with universities and hospitals to set up the MRC's successor – the thirteen

Canadian Institutes for Health Research – and was regularly invited across the country as a speaker on women's health and medicine, and also I suppose, as the perennial old minister of health of Canada.

In the summer of 1996 five centres of excellence for women's health, funded by Health Canada and respectively located in Vancouver, Winnipeg, Toronto, Montreal, and Halifax, were announced by the federal government. Each centre received approximately $2 million over six years to conduct policy-based research, fostering multidisciplinary collaboration with a view to introduce "gender" into health research. The centres consisted of provincial, regional, and national partnerships, each with its own research focus on making the health system more responsive to the health needs of women. I am afraid that after a number of years of activities, these centres closed or were absorbed into the new National Collaborating Centres funded by Health Canada. It is certainly the case of the Atlantic Centre, which closed in 2013 after sixteen years of operation.

In 1999, for the first time in our history, not one but two women physicians would be appointed deans of medicine. The very first one was Dr Noni MacDonald, with whom I had often exchanged with pleasure on children's health issues during her eighteen years at University of Ottawa, who was appointed dean of medicine at Dalhousie University in Halifax. Shortly after, Dr Carol Herbert was appointed dean of the Schulich School of Medicine and Dentistry, at Western University, in London, Ontario.

As of 1995, on the national scene, academic women involved in women's health teaching and research in the country were very busy pressing and making sure that there would be an Institute of Gender and Health amongst the thirteen future Canadian Institutes for Health Research, replacing "my" old Medical Research Council of Canada as of June 2000. They campaigned repeatedly to make sure one such institute would exist. The institutes would be accountable to Parliament through the minister of health of Canada. Finally, in late 2000, Dr Miriam Stewart, a PhD in nursing, University of Alberta, was appointed the inaugural scientific director of the Institute of Gender and Health, an excellent appointment. At around the same time, quite a behind-the-scenes undertaking developed among women all over the country interested in defining research in women's health and a list of priorities. Yes, the various lists often had thirty-five priorities and, yes, I knew the problem first-hand! Still, it is fundamental to note the importance of a holistic approach to women's lives and, consequently, to their health conditions, problems, and treatment.

Should we still be speaking of women's health if it is an accepted and legitimate issue of public policies and of political agendas? Yes, we should. Women's health has started to be accepted – at least at the rhetorical level and at times through ad hoc programs such as the five 1996 federal centres of excellence for women's health, or through a university chair here or there – and constantly forgotten, or worse, kept at the margin of our institutions. On the basis of first-hand observation, I can attest to how much education is needed just to move data collection and research from considering the variable "sex" as fully accounting for women's health, when what should be applied is a "gender-based analysis," because what affects health is not just the biological and genetic endowment but all the other societal and environmental determinants of health.

This established, a dean can do some teaching, almost on the side, with the first job being to run a faculty. That means individual and collective human relations of every kind all the time, and it means administration and budgets. To develop a new faculty in times of economic downturn, suddenly facing major budgetary cuts, is not to be recommended to anyone. Yet it is what happened to me.

Although it was not on the map when I started on 1 August 1990, a new Ontario premier, Bob Rae, had taken office in October 1990. No one around me at the time wondered if the serious recession that the new young premier inherited would affect education. The Peterson Liberal government had forecast a small surplus earlier in the year, but our economy had worsened, leading to an Ontario deficit of $700 million at the time of the provincial election. It only became worse with the years, continuing until late in 1993. By then, the Ontario NDP government had introduced the "Social Contract," affecting all public sector unions and requiring wage cuts. That forced faculty associations to negotiate 5 per cent wage cuts. Higher education also suffered from a per capita decrease in its provincial funding.

Ontario universities are funded through an allocation model developed in 1967, often modified by bits and pieces, making the funding formula complicated and opaque. However, the formula that distributed operating grants still somehow reflected the number of students enrolled, assigning "basic income units" (BIUS), which were and still are supposed to reflect the relative costs of teaching and research. For example, in my time as a dean it meant that for the year 1992, while the Faculty of Medicine counted 1,206 professors and 931 students (including the "post-docs"), it received an operating budget of $20 million and a research budget of $29 million. For that same year 1992, my Faculty of Health Sciences had 374 professors and 1,572 students, and it received an operating budget of $9 million and a research budget of $3 million. So what about the underpinning concept of the importance of enrolment? And what about cost equity?

What that really meant, for the University of Ottawa under Gilles Patry as president (2001–08), for example, was that the importance given to enrolment in the funding formula resulted in going from some 28,000 to 40,000 students, allowing the university to make a surplus, but lacking the physical capacities to teach so many new "clients," as we were no longer speaking of "students."

At University of Ottawa the real budgetary crunch came in 1995 for our faculties. By the way, deans were never consulted on their budgets or other university budgets. The Health Sciences Faculty owes its budgetary survival and visionary renewal to Jeannette Giroux and to the fact that our smaller programs were funded by special allotments for the Ontario francophone population. Fully mastering the faculties' financial systems, and ours in particular, Jeannette was able to fight all attempts from the vice rector finance, Carol Workman, and her key assistant to make us give away the important portion of recurrent funds. Giroux knew that our recurrent funds were our safety valve that made rapid financial adjustments possible in time of crisis. She was always quietly ahead of the times.

We still had to cut in our faculty expenditures. It was done through modernizing our operations. The first change she brought in was to equip us all with a voice-mail system. In 1995, it did not exist in the university. We still recall the morning when I was in a meeting and the rector phoned me, and he was answered by a message with my voice asking him to leave his name and phone number. Marcel Hamelin was so shocked that he phoned Jeannette Giroux's office at once, asking what that impertinence was all about. She explained to him this new modern tool was now mandatory in all our offices because of "his" budgetary cuts. We had a good laugh after. It had to be explained to secretaries and to professors when to use it and how, so that now they could create some uninterrupted productive working time for themselves. We had to review all aspects of our functioning in the office, as support staff costs were expenditures under our control to some extent. We agreed not to dismiss employees in the process. So jobs that had been left vacant and were awaiting action due to relocation of employees who had already left for other positions were simply cancelled. In fact we went from some fifty positions to thirty-five. We had to dismiss only one information technician who was not really productive. With my enthusiastic support, Jeannette quietly went forward with more rationalization through the faculty. She hired Régis Foré, a senior informatics expert, to develop a small team, to prepare the budget required, to organize the training not just of support staff but more challenging of all professors, having equipped everyone in the faculty with a computer, in another big first. Once these changes were approved by the senior administration, the rector and his vice rector finance wanted the whole university to do likewise under Giroux's leadership, but she wisely refused.

We also used these cuts to restructure our faculty academic entities. I had never liked the power imbalance, real or perceived, between the two old and well-developed Schools of Nursing and that of Human Kinetics, and the small programs. I negotiated with the latter the possibility of regrouping, yet keeping completely independent identities and functioning. It was accepted without a crisis, and we created the School of Rehabilitation Sciences made up of Departments of Physiotherapy, Occupational Therapy, Audiology, and Speech Therapy. In the process, we managed to save a few more administrative positions.

◆ ❋ ◆

At one point in my life as a dean, the drama of contaminated blood suddenly reappeared. HIV/AIDS had been one of the most critical and worrisome dossiers of my department during the last two years of my mandate. Although I was worried by the tone the Krever Commission had set, further to its creation by Kim Campbell in her last month in office in October 1993, I knew that Health Canada, minister and staff, had acted immediately, setting up a National Task Force on AIDS in August 1983 with the best Canadian medical scientists. They were kept well informed and were at all times deeply committed to public health. But the fact-finding mission of the Krever Commission had rapidly become vitiated by the toxic system of identifying culprits launched and fed by the Canadian Hemophilia Society (CHS). It was natural and laudable that the CHS would want to speak in the name of victims and to bring to the public's attention the plight of one group amongst others of innocent victims of an intergovernmental health system tragedy. It was something else to accuse certain individuals constantly and from the start, instead of trying to analyze the situation critically and propose avenues of solution.

Suddenly, on 15 December 1995, I was interviewed in my office by one of the commission's lawyers, Leslie Paine, in the presence of Counsel Linda Wall, of the Department of Justice, who was acting as my defence lawyer (under General Counsel Donald J. Rennie). The Department of Justice was interested only in the reputation of the Justice Department, its current minister, and the Crown. To my memory, nothing was taped, and I have no idea how this interrogation was used.

However, a week later, on 21 December, the same day the commission had officially completed its public hearings, its senior counsel, Marlys Edwardh, delivered on a confidential basis forty-five notices advising various parties "named" by her "that the Commissioner may make findings that may amount to misconduct against the recipient" and that the latter would have the right to respond. I was one of the "named" parties. Early in January I received a five-page letter from the general counsel of the federal Department of Justice explaining that a charge of "misconduct" had a criminal connotation and would attract a criminal charge. To a lay person with no legal training, the whole thing was very scary. The attorney general of Canada later petitioned the Federal Court to get an order quashing and setting aside the notices directed to eighteen of us associated with the federal government. I had no say in any part of that process. I was familiar with royal commissions; this was a big game and a most unusual situation.

And again the waiting game continued, for some five months. One morning, on 31 May 1996, I read in the *Globe & Mail* that the Krever Commission had just tabled with the Federal Court two new lists separating the forty-five notices to individuals "whose actions and inactions may be blameworthy." Their counsel added that the lists were not definitive. I was on the new list of persons not to be named by Krever. "It's not a change ... it's not a compromise" added Krever's senior counsel, Marlys Edwardh. The waiting game again.

Another month went by. I then received a copy of a judgment by Justice Jean Richard, of the Federal Court of Canada, dated 27 June. He had accepted Krever's new lists and confirmed that none of the federal and provincial ministers, deputy ministers, and assistant deputy ministers (and a handful of other senior federal officials) would be "named." In other words, I was "free." More precisely, two federal ex-ministers (Jake Epp and I) and the thirteen federal most senior officials of my former department previously "named," deputy ministers and assistant deputy ministers, were suddenly "free." So were thirty-two provincial ministers. So were the fourteen people from the Canadian Red Cross who had also received notices. In other words, everyone "at the top" in government or at the Red Cross who had received notices, except the two less senior officials of my former department on the list (Dr Denise Leclerc-Chevalier and Dr John Furesz), as well as a McGill professor, chair of Canada's National Task Force on AIDS, appointed by me and serving as a volunteer (Dr Norbert Gilmore), was "free." But these last three persons associated with National Health and Welfare were not "free" and could be "named" in adverse findings of facts.

I could not believe it. At the same time I was relieved of a personal nightmare, but profoundly shocked at the injustice of the decision. I inquired around me to try to fully understand what was going on. The Department of Justice, of course, was very pleased with the judgment. I kept submitting that it was wrong and unfair to give a blanket exoneration to all senior individuals while keeping the less senior ones open to accusations. I mentioned my unease to our minister of justice at the time, Allan Rock, when I met him informally, and asked at least twice to see him. I never heard a word from him or his office. My misgivings interested nobody.

July went by. Nothing was happening. I felt more and more uncomfortable. During my holidays I kept thinking of the situation. Upon my return in early August, I made up my mind. I would write a letter to Justice Krever, whatever the personal consequences to me. Without an appointment, I took the train to Montreal on the Friday and went to consult Professor Margaret Somerville, the McGill University ethicist, with my draft letter to Justice Krever. She helped me clarify my thinking and we agreed on an action plan. The letter, with copy to the minister of justice, was hand delivered on the Monday morning (19 August 1996). As there was no national news at that time in mid-summer, my letter made all the Canadian media, and the rest, as they say, is history.

Why did I write that letter? On the one hand, if I was shocked that ministers were now "automatically" exempted of any eventual blame, I was even more shocked that deputy ministers and assistant deputy ministers – the most senior bureaucrats and the "bosses" of the civil servants, senior bureaucrats who, by the way, were paid much more than ministers – were exempted from any responsibility. I had written, "If you have to lay the blame, I consider it my duty to take my share of the responsibility. The notion of 'ministerial responsibility' is the cornerstone of our executive government. Justice is offended if people at the top of government in bureaucratic structures are not held responsible for their actions, but employees at less senior levels of the hierarchy are. Moreover, public ethics requires that those at the top be accountable."

Years later, in 2001, I had to engage a lawyer, as I was again interrogated on the contaminated blood dossier, this time by the RCMP. Nothing came out of the interviews, but those moments have been quite stressful.

All through these years, as well as when I was in Cabinet, I had looked for definitions of ministerial responsibility and accountability, to no avail. If there were any in the Privy Council Office, they were not known or available to us ministers. In 1996, thanks to a friend, I did obtain a photocopy of part (fifty-six pages only!) of a thicker PCO document, which did not offer a clear, applicable definition of ministerial responsibility, except to say, "The way in which ministers fulfill their responsibilities and are called to account for the exercise of their statutory authority is subject to practice and convention." Or this: "The essential principles of accountability are, therefore, that power flows from the Crown and is exercised by ministers who are responsible to Parliament." When such a basic ethical concept as ministerial responsibility remains undefined, it is not surprising that the credible Auditor General Denis Desautels, in his 2000 annual report to Parliament, saw himself forced to request a clarification of the concept. As far as I know, his recommendation was not implemented.

Without looking for it, I kept a public profile through my deanship, criss-crossing the country for keynote speeches, participation in conferences and workshops, and media interviews – often on women's health or the Canada Health Act, or on women and politics. In my first two years as a dean, I gave two dozen such professional and academic keynote addresses, in addition to half a dozen others in community public settings. Two were particularly special for me. I was invited by Carleton University to give the 1991 Florence Bird Lecture, which I entitled "Women in Health Sciences: Points of Resistance to Change." A few months later, McGill University asked me to present the prestigious 1991 Osler Lecture at their Faculty of Medicine, where I was bold enough to call my lecture "'Inside-Out Men': Women in Medicine," having borrowed my title from Galen, a follower of Hippocrates in ancient Greece.

Another, more personal memory was the conference at St Francis Xavier University, in Antigonish, on 4–6 July 1996, celebrating Allan J. MacEachen on the occasion of his retirement from the Senate of Canada. I had been asked to give a testimony of his public life. Friends and former and current politicians were there, and the occasion was full of joy. It was one of the very last occasions when I would spend time with Gérard Pelletier and Jacques Hébert, two cultural national leaders, both looking in great shape. (I would sadly attend Gérard Pelletier's funeral at St Léon-de-Westmount in Montreal a year later, on 27

June 1997.) Then, in that same summer 1996, one major undertaking was the 8–10 August US-Canada Forum on Women's Health organized by Minister of Health David Dingwall, just appointed to the portfolio, and Secretary of Health and Human Services Donna Shalala, an impressive personality, appointed by Bill Clinton, here in Ottawa. I was asked to cover "The Impact of the Health System on Women's Health in the 21st Century." These proceedings, like many others, have been published.

In 1992 I received the Canadian Public Service Award and the Fellowship Award of the Ryerson Polytechnic Institute, not yet a university. I was also the recipient of three honorary doctorates, from McGill in 1991, McMaster in 1993, and York 1995. In November 1996 I was made a Fellow of the Royal Society of Canada, introduced by my historian friend Micheline Dumont, another very special recognition.

In mid-term dean's mandate, I would enjoy a higher public profile, not of my making but thanks to two special unexpected mandates. First, I was appointed commissioner (and acting VP) of the Independent Commission on Population and Quality of Life, attending my first meeting in Paris on 21–23 April 1993. Two weeks later, with Marcel Hamelin's enthusiastic approval, I was made full-time co-chair of Ontario's Royal Commission on Learning, at Bob Rae's request. These experiences will be covered in the last chapter of these memoirs.

In 1997, the end of my mandate as a dean was approaching with just six months left. Life went on as usual, and we had more discussions about budgetary matters! Conferences took me to Saskatoon, Toronto, Calgary, and Halifax, with a last major keynote address in Vancouver on the history of nursing, under the auspices of the Canadian Association for the History of Nursing. My talk was entitled "Into the Third Millennium: A Slimmer, Integrated, Patient-Centred and Better Canadian Health Care." Twenty years later, it still is only a dream.

Far too early to assess if I had enjoyed these seven years as a dean. One thing was certain: the previous six years, those between politics and the deanship, when I recycled as an academic after politics, I had remained an individual, sharing in a local community of colleagues and students, but I had felt an individual. When I became a dean, I had become "institutional" again with the corresponding feeling of *une chape de plomb* on my shoulders, like wearing a heavy new uniform. I gave it my best, but a change was called for.

At the end of my mandate as dean of health sciences, University of Ottawa feminist women academic leaders now in positions of authority had a party at Dr Sanda Rodger's home for "The Girls," as Jean Chrétien had once called Judy Erola and me in Cabinet the day of Bertha Wilson's appointment as the first female justice of the Supreme Court in Canada. Besides a beautiful *objet d'art* received from the group, a modern glass bowl, was the funniest good wishes card signed by all: a woman doing a one-handed handstand on the back of a chair, body and legs straight up towards the ceiling, her face smiling lightly. It is in one of my cookbooks, and I still laugh when I open the page on it. At that party were Carole Workman, the only female vice rector (finance), who had taken all of us through the terribly difficult 1990s of serious economic budget cuts of Ontario universities; and three new deans of faculty, another first: Sanda Rodger (common law), Caroline Andrew (social sciences) and Denise Alcock (my successor in health sciences). Times were, slowly, changing! Also present were Ruby Heap, historian who would become associate vice president (research); Martha Jackman, full law professor in social rights, poverty, and health-care accountability, in whose class I had often presented; Meryn Stuart, an exceptional nursing history research leader; Marian McGee, a former dean of nursing when the discipline was a separate faculty at University of Ottawa; a mentor and a friend, Nadia Mikhael, MD, a passionate and committed professor, chair of pathology, and assistant dean of medical education; and Cécile Coderre, a sociologist quite a bit younger than I and my mentor in women's studies. To answer Nadia Mikhael's search on how women could break through the glass ceiling, I had given her Betty Harragan's almost 400-page pocketbook published in 1989, *Games Mother Never Taught You: Corporate Gamesmanship for Women*, which I had just discovered. At a more modest level, in my School of Human Kinetics of only two women professors in 1990, Drs Denise Allard and Hélène Dallaire, there were now eight female professors all with doctorates benefitting from Hélène Dallaire energetic leadership!

Just before the party with "the Girls," I had received the vice rector academic, Bernard Philogène, and his wife Hélène for dinner at my home, to honour Bernard at the end of his seven-year mandate of vice rector, as well as of three colleague deans: Dr John Seely in medicine, Henry Edwards in social sciences and spouse Frances, and David Staines in arts, as well as my friend Judy Erola. Bernard Philogène, an entomologist expert in plant–insect interactions, was born in Mauritius, of parents from l'Île de la Réunion, and he had emigrated to Canada at age twenty-one, completing his science studies at University of Montreal, McGill, and Wisconsin. How often did I have to control my quick wit and not suggest to him to apply his science to our university management! A researcher before all, I never perceived him playing institutional politics; he followed the trend, definitely an honest traditionalist with a French rigid conservative official approach. What I regret to this day, for example, is when he refused to support my request to hire Ginette Lemire Rodger as a professor after she had completed her PhD in nursing at University of Calgary in 1995, one of the very few doctorate nurses in Canada. As chair of the Canadian Nurses Association during the years leading to the passage of the Canada Health Act (1984), Ginette Rodger's leadership had been key in Cabinet approval of the legislation and then its unanimous passage in the House of Commons, she and the CNA having helped convince the Canadian public. I wanted her very much as a professor in nursing and to succeed me as dean, both for her leadership and her vision of how our Department of Nursing, and the whole faculty, could develop. Ginette Rodger was then in her prime, but all Vice Rector Philogène kept repeating was that she did not have enough publications! Of course, she couldn't. She then became the chief nursing executive at the Ottawa Hospital.

I was tired and looking to refuel, needed a sabbatical, not knowing that I could have obtained a two-year paid administrative leave. So, at sixty-two, I decided to take an early retirement from the university, flew to Bari, Italy, and joined friends for the summer, resting first at the beach in Metapunto, then visiting Italy from south to north!

21

Visiting Professor in Health Administration:
Insolent Thoughts about Universities

Preparing future hospital administrators did not happen immediately, as I had not planned anything for my future. After thirteen years as an academic, without any sabbatical, I needed a break, taking things a little more relaxed and feeling free! Shortly after having completed my seven years as a dean and after declining Rector Marcel Hamelin's request to stay a few more years in that position, I found myself involved in two unique official trips to Africa, always as a volunteer: to Tanzania in September 1997, after my Italian holidays, and to Senegal in December. A third such official trip would take me to Jamaica in June 1998. These travels stemmed from my past role as a member of the Independent Commission on Population and Quality of Life, which will be covered in the next chapter.

So the story that needs to be told in this chapter covers approximately twelve more years of "public life," from early retirement from the university in the summer of 1997 to joining the School of Management as a visiting professor in the Master's in Health Administration Program, teaching my first course there on 12 January 1999, and finally retiring "for real" and emptying my Desmarais building office on 30 December 2010, after having retired once more in June 2004 but having come back!

Back in September 1997 my agenda kept me quite busy, honouring earlier commitments, especially as chair of the Canadian Breast Cancer Research Initiative (CBCRI) in Toronto, and as a consequence my participation on the NCIC Board of Directors, its Grants Panel (the Canadian Cancer Society research arm), 1999. I had given myself a general objective to connect, if invited, as a volunteer on established or newer initiatives in local and provincial health care. I did not move on that but kept the idea dormant at the back of my mind. And then the phone started ringing. Over the next few years I got involved in more projects but I also started being invited to join boards as a member or as a chair. I joined the Atkinson Foundation workshops, the OISE/UofT Advisory Board (following my Ontario Royal Commission on Education), accepted the chair of the Radiation Safety Institute of Canada and became a board member of the Clinical Research Institute of Montreal and of the University of Ottawa Heart Institute. I joined the Canadian Population Health Initiative (a part of the Canadian Institute for Health Information, created in 1999) as a council member, under Dr Cameron Mustard as chair, with colleagues such as Drs Clyde Hertzman, Richard Lessard, Cory Neudorf, Charlyn Black, Catherine Donovan, Gerry Predy, and Michael Wolfson; also members were Ian Potter (ADM in Health Canada) and Judith Maxwell. Every one of these colleagues was a hero of public health and population health. At the invitation of Denis Desautels, then auditor general of Canada, I agreed to join his Panel of Senior Advisors from 1999 to 2004 and enjoyed it tremendously. Reviewing dates and mandates, I saw that I served on each such board or ongoing initiative for roughly between four and six years.

One of these involvements remains dear to my heart: that of having participated as a steering committee member on the "Dialogue on Health Reform," convened by the Atkinson Foundation on the eve of the new millennium and chaired by Terrence Sullivan, assisted by Patricia Baranek. The initiative had stemmed from the total inaction of the federal and provincial governments on health reform. The National Forum on Health (1994–97), set up by Prime Minister Jean Chrétien (and chaired by him), had released a remarkable report and set of recommendations after three years of work, but nothing had moved. They had focused on four key issues: "(1) the determinants of health; (2) evidence-based decision making; (3) values that should guide health system renewal and policy development; and (4) ethical dilemmas and the identification of strategies to improve the efficiency of the health care system and to put resources where they have the greatest potential to improve the health of Canadians," as synthetized in *Canada's Health*

Care System: Its Funding and Organization (1994), the book edited by Anne Crichton immediately after the report's release. That was the Canada following Finance Minister Paul Martin's historical 27 February 1995 $25 billion budgetary cuts in transfers to the provinces, federal employment (45,000 jobs), and federal programs. Provinces had to follow: hospitals were closed, nurses and other health workers lost their jobs, and "restructuring" was the provincial health-care buzzword but it had more to do with physical buildings and not at all with rethinking delivery of services or with governance. Our steering committee offered rich, imaginative, and grounded exchanges between experts: Michael Decter, Colleen Flood, Vivek Goel, Peter Coyte, Doris Grinspun, Steven Lewis, Jim Laclean, Tom Noseworthy, and Greg Stoddard. With the financial support of the Atkinson Foundation, we commissioned papers on issues of strategic importance. A clearly written small book by Sullivan and Baranek, released in 2002 at the end of our work, *First Do No Harm: Making Sense of Canadian Health Reform,* is one of a few more special initiatives pointing to avenues for reforming our health-care system still valid today.

Our health-care system was definitely in the news. In November 2002 Roy Romanow released his final report: *Building on Values: The Future of Health Care in Canada.* I considered the Romanow exercise in value-definition to be as honest and valid as it can be, the state of the art. It was also the first time that a truly national debate on medicare had taken place after my years in office. The innovative consultative model adopted by the Romanow Commission made it probably the Canadian royal commission with the most important public consultations record ever. In comparison, Senator Michael Kirby's Senate report, *The Health of Canadians: The Federal Role,* released a month earlier, in October, recommended, as one possibility, experimentation with private specialty hospitals or clinics. The reasoning was always tempting; however the reality is that such an approach within a public delivery system skims the creams from the market, leaving the heavier and most onerous cases to the state, not to mention the cases experiencing complications in post-private treatment. It was also a way of introducing an element of competition in the system, another fascinating idea for some. But is competition at that level even feasible with a single payer?

So in the new millennium we became the usual suspects (Michael Decter, Colleen Flood, me, and, in this case, Henry Friesen, Maureen Quigley, Duncan Sinclair, and Carolyn Tuohy) involved in initiatives pushing governments towards action on serious reforms of our health-care system. We formed a Task Force on Health Policy, set up by the IRRP under the chairmanship of Michael Decter. The idea was to alert public opinion, following the Romanow and Kirby inquiries into the future of health care tabled in 2002, but before the announcement of the February 2003 Health Care Renewal Accord and its financial transfer to the provinces – $36.8 billion – to ensure that it would not be more money thrown away without accountability. Our task force called on first ministers to commit themselves to "major, systemic reform" of the health-care system, and not just refunding, when they met in early February 2003 to consider the recommendations of the Senate committee and the report of the Romanow Commission. Our six-page "Letters to the First Ministers," sent on 23 January 2003, suggested new approaches to guarantee that reforms would be a major part of a unique new deal between the federal and provincial governments.

At another level and for the only time in my life, at the pressing request of Dr Antoine Noujaim, a PhD in bionucleonics who had just left the Faculty of Pharmacy and Pharmaceutical Sciences at the University of Alberta to launch his own R & D entrepreneurial business, and someone I trusted, I joined the Board of AltaRex, his creation, at the end of May 1998, resigning some three years later. AltaRex was registered both in Edmonton and in Boston. Our offices were located in Waltham, Massachusetts, some twenty-five minutes from the Boston Airport. I enjoyed my time there at first, learning a completely different universe. However, once the company started clinical trials, and with some change in personnel, I was left with unanswered questions and simply resigned.

January 1998 started with a bang with the infamous, beautiful, and dangerous ten days of "the" ice storm. I was without electricity for hours at a time – heating, stove, fridge, freezer, washers, television, radio, and all music sources – but at least I enjoyed a large fireplace and had lots of wood logs. So I was able to have friends for meals, sleeping over, and even partying! In our European family traditions, my Belgian mother and Italian-converted father always celebrated *"les Rois,"* the Epiphany or Three Kings Day on 6 January. That year was no different: candles were everywhere (it was the total lack of electricity day), friends (with the ice storm all over Quebec, there was no way for my family to come from Montreal). There was a *"galette des Rois,"* an outstanding pithivier pastry (pre-ordered by chance!). My oldest friend, whom I had known since becoming a Girl Guide at eleven, Mireille Fontaine, drew the little traditional porcelain charm in it, hence becoming the queen for the evening!

On 8 February my friend Claude-André Lachance gave a superb party in his dream house up in the mountains in Aylmer, bordering on Gatineau Park, to celebrate my having been made an officer of the Order of Canada. My former ministerial front bench seat mate and old friend, Roméo LeBlanc, now the governor general, had granted me this completely unanticipated honour four days before. I had asked Monique Coupal to accompany me at the Rideau Hall ceremony, and to be surrounded by old friends at that party was a bonus!

Ten days later I would spend two weeks in India, from 18 February to 3 March, my second trip to that fascinating country, as a participant in seminars and as a speaker. Upon arrival in Delhi, I made a two-day trip by train to Jaipur for a glimpse of the enchanting Rajasthan capital city. Back by train to Delhi, I then flew to Bombay. A driver awaited me upon arrival, taking me quite a distance from the city to the Tata Institute for Social Sciences campus on a large estate. I was the guest of their National Workshop on Women's Occupational and Reproductive Health. Even though my spartan student room on campus, surrounded at all times by innumerable tiny monkeys, and the basic meals in the student cafeteria were disconcerting, the discussions themselves were quite enriching. But I never saw Mumbai, to my chagrin.

Then I took the plane to New Delhi, being nicely received for a drink by our high commissioner to India, Peter Walker and his wife, who were packing and returning to Canada, their mandate completed. It was the end of the afternoon, and I saw my first flight of countless green parakeets, all leaving the premises together suddenly for another point. The day after, I was warmly welcomed as a guest visiting professor at the Centre for Women's Development Studies. I was lodged in the India International Centre, where some of the seminars would also take place, in the Lodi Gardens. It turned out to be a daily renewed delight with the gardens architectural works of the fifteenth century, tombs and mosques, a lake, the various palms and the pink flowers trees, not to forget the numerous green parakeets flying over, alone or regrouped and in a hurry!

The Centre for Women's Development Studies was founded in 1980 by Dr Vina Mazumdar, an Oxford graduate political scientist, social activist, and feminist, the two of us having met as members of the Independent Commission on Population and Quality of Life (1993–95). We had also shared the experience of having animated similar national government commissions of inquiry on the status of women, in my case the RCSW (1967–70), in hers, the Committee on the Status of Women in India (1971–74), just after ours. We had become good friends and I admired Vina *Di*, always draped in her beautiful silk, the warm, quiet, persistent, convincing social reformer fighting for simple justice for women. And for all. She died in 2013, at age eighty-seven.

Besides workshops and seminars with the researchers and professors of the centre, I had been asked to give the 1998 J.P. Naik Memorial Lecture, which they published. My colleagues of the moment had been told that I had a "double take as to politics." Not surprisingly, I had been asked to discuss "women and politics." I had been encouraged by a concept developed by Scandinavian feminists that I discovered after having left politics through publications of Drude Dahlerup, a Danish political scientist, so I titled my presentation "Towards a Critical Mass: Women in Politics." This concept was based on her extensive empirical data on what changed when there was a critical mass of women in Parliament, a critical mass corresponding to women having won 30–33 per cent of the seats. The changes observed were about the reaction of women to politics; the performance and efficiency of women politicians; the political culture (norms and social conventions, etc.); the political discourse (women as a subject had entered the political arena); and change in policy, as the political agenda started to include issues of interests to women. For me, a theoretical discussion of patriarchy was most oppressive, equivalent to a millstone around the neck; I knew it had to be tackled, but it always remained theoretical. Patriarchy meant going to the historical and cultural roots of the notions of power, authority, hierarchy, and social control under all its forms, embodied in immovable institutions over centuries. An important discussion, one going to the roots of a pernicious, thousands-of-years-old state of affairs, painful for women to explore. That was when I started paying attention to more rooted, applied approaches to social change. My stay at this centre was most valuable. My new colleagues and I exchanged on practical approaches to increase the presence of women in Parliaments: quotas, "reserved seats" for women, legislated parity between men and women in elected Assemblies, in Cabinets, in Senates, not to forget the Indian Constitutional Amendment, the Women's Reservation Bill 1996, which during each election put aside one-third of the seats for women, at every level of government. One feels humbled when faced with the weight of culture. Of all the too-short visits I was lucky enough to make around the world, windows bringing in fresh air from elsewhere, this stay in India remains as a great gift!

My other predilection, "women's health," was always around somehow! Later that same year, in the fall of 1998, Dr Michael Shannon, director of the Laboratory Centre for Disease Control – that almost secret if not mysterious Health and Welfare Canada building at Tunney's Pasture, not far from the Brooke Claxton one – asked me to set up a team and to undertake a project on priorities for women's health "surveillance." Health surveillance had been established to prevent and control the spread of infectious diseases. By then it was expanding into chronic diseases, risk factors associated with diseases, injuries, and non-chronic events such as abortion or pregnancy. Surveillance is the ongoing monitoring and reporting of trends. In 1998 the LCDC had undertaken an environmental scan including "gaps analysis." As chair, I was most fortunate in identifying and recruiting seven exceptional women health professionals, and we rapidly became a great team. They were PhDs, three were MDs, and there was a professor of nursing, a psychiatrist, a neurologist, professors of community medicine, of epidemiology, a clinical epidemiologist, and a sociologist! They were from Memorial, McMaster, Dalhousie, UBC, University of Manitoba, University of Toronto, Université de Montréal, and me, from University of Ottawa: Sharon Buehler, May Cohen, Pat Kaufert, Arminee Kazanjian, Heather Maclean, Donna Stewart, and Bilkis Vissandjee.

We divided our work into two tasks. The first was to describe the characteristics of the women's health surveillance system we believed was needed and to provide concrete examples of health issues and how they would be handled in such a system. The second was to identify what data were available, what analytic model would be most appropriate, which partners would be needed, and what plan of action would allow the LCDC to move in the recommended direction most rapidly and effectively. We undertook national consultations with experts, researchers, and frontline workers. Such a range of participants sometimes leads to counterproductive polarization along researcher-practitioner, social-medical, or other axes. This was not what we encountered: the diversity on these occasions resulted in lively debate, a positive atmosphere, and a remarkable convergence in thinking. As described in our final report, a consensus developed around the need for a paradigm shift in surveillance if it was to have a significant impact on the health of women. There was also considerable agreement on how to ensure that the priorities for surveillance remain responsive to changing needs. On 15 August 1999 we presented our 102-page report to Dr Shannon, a plan of action in nine recommendations to the Laboratory Centre for Diseases Control. It had been more than a year of work.

Our report was published in 1999 and accepted, and its implementation along the lines suggested started moving inside Health Canada, then was transferred in 2004 to the new Public Health Agency – the responsibility of the competent Marie DesMeules – attached to Health Canada. In parallel there were learned articles on the topic in medical journals, a major joint report in 2003 by the Canadian Institute for Health Information on women's health surveilliance, and so on. For me personally, in addition to discovering disease surveillance – another aspect of health services, a fascinating experience for a sociologist – and of having made new friends for life, this research contract had been a blessed transition from my seven years as a dean of health sciences to finally coming out of my too early retirement and agreeing to become visiting professor at the master's program in health administration at the School of Management of University of Ottawa (renamed the Telfer School of Management in 2007).

Before going back to teaching again, this time in health administration, around 1999–2000, I had more time for myself and for connecting with friends in other health initiatives. One of them was Janet Hatcher Roberts, then CEO for the Canadian Society for International Health (CSIH), whose office on 1 Nicholas Street was close to mine at University of Ottawa. I had known her father, Donald Hatcher, who had become a much respected and committed dean of medicine at Dalhousie shortly before I became minister of the Medical Research Council. This was the time of bad cuts in that field. He was also there when my repeated efforts to re-establish positive budgets for the MRC were successful! Janet's responsibility at the CSIH was, and still is, to "envision a world where Canada and the broader international health community fully embrace their obligations to reduce global health inequities and increase social justice by effectively using available knowledge." Health projects such as hospital construction in Africa and other CIDA initiatives were familiar to me through my role as minister, but despite my annual WHO health minister meetings, international health, global health, were new to me.

I bonded easily and rapidly with Janet Roberts, much younger than me, who was opening new horizons for me. She was also giving the course on international health and development at our Faculty of Medicine. In addition, she was co-directing the WHO Collaborating Centre for Knowledge Translation, Technology Assessment for Health Equity with Peter Tugwell, with whom I would later work. Some of CSIH early work in Ukraine with CIDA funding and the work in Croatia with World Bank funds, contracts that Janet had won for the society, built on the ground-breaking work in Canada in health promotion and determinants of health. Many of her consultants had worked at Health Canada in the team of Ron Draper during my ministerial time. Other projects like her society's Chile project involved academic nursing leaders like Annette O'Connor, my assistant dean for research. Still co-directing the

WHO Collaborating Centre for Knowledge Translation, I would meet her again, in 2017, through her collaboration with UpStream, the Canadian movement pushing for a social determinants of health priority in public policy and practice.

Some approaches had been made by the School of Management dean and former colleague, Jean-Louis Malouin, and by Professor Doug Angus as early as May 1998 inviting me to join their master's program in health administration, the public administration orphan of that business school. I joined for the fall of 1998 as visiting professor, co-teaching my first course in January 1999 with Doug Angus up until the next fall only, being committed to an old dream: a several-weeks-long stay in Lourmarin, in Provence, with Judy Erola, Denise Leclerc, and Dolorès Vigneault, from the end of September on. It would be only in January 2000 that I would truly join the School of Management through the master's program in health administration on a "soft" timetable: I was there daily (when in town), had an office, participated in all meetings related to the program, but was given a lighter course workload, supervised individual student "directed readings" as well as theses, and became a "full" member of the team. The salary was also "soft" but it was appreciated. I developed my own syllabus and course material for the mandatory course HAH 6260 – Health Services Organization and Policy. I was back to teaching evenings, finishing at 10 p.m. to accommodate, on top of our regular full-time students, health-care practitioners in need of a graduate degree.

Our MHA program aimed at preparing responsible professionals to assume management and leadership positions in the ever-changing health service system in Canada or internationally. The program was very structured with only compulsory courses. In all my years there, each new cohort admitted in late August for the new fall term would be in classes or residency for an uninterrupted eighteen months, including courses in the evenings, on Saturdays, and in the summer! Today, the University of Ottawa MHA is clearly structured around an Intensive Program structure lasting sixteen months, for newcomers to this field, usually recently graduated from universities, and a Professional Program structure built over twenty-eight months for individuals already working in the health-care system. In my years there, this professional program did not exist and as we always had some individuals wanting to study for the master's, we adapted a program for each of them according to what was feasible. I do not recall courses on weekends, but yes, we taught all summer long, and taught some courses in the evenings. The former regular (now called Intensive) Program had the same structure: eight MBA courses with the business students and fifteen MHA courses. Then they had to succeed in their four- (six?) month residency including a field project, a bit like a thesis. From the start, our students had access to and were guided by select professors and executives in residence such as Michel Lalonde or George Langill, to help them clarify their interests and future objective as a health care administrator. In 2000–10 we partnered with some seventy-five renowned health organizations, especially local and regional. We experimented with institutions located elsewhere in Canada, but the supervision of a few of our candidates became a huge problem. No need to add that it was impossible for our students to be in even part-time paid employment during their MAH Program.

Our students were super motivated. We had around twenty to twenty-four newcomers per year in the uninterrupted eighteen-month program plus two or three professionals coming on evenings or day courses to upgrade their knowledge and status. But at first our students were not a group, as they came from different Canadian universities, the School of Management not offering a baccalaureate in health administration. So a first objective was to create an esprit de corps and a collegial atmosphere for frank exchanges. My only surprise was when we started receiving Chinese students who would return to their country. What I taught did not lend itself to exams made of quizzes or multiple questions, or other mechanistic tests; I always gave a choice of topics to be written as essays, personal reflections on a topic. My Chinese students panicked and could not function, until I realized that they were prisoners of an established culture of giving "the only right answer." What is the way you want me to answer, Madam Professor? I did not change my exams but tried to explain the idea behind my approaches. Not evident.

Later, shocked by the complete ignorance of our students and future managers of our thirteen health-care systems on what was going on elsewhere in health care, starting with the American scene, the program adopted my recommendation of an additional compulsory course, ADM 6496H – International Perspectives on Health Systems. I developed it and gave it myself for a while (using the new PowerPoint computer program to create wonderful slides that I loved to do, as no handbook existed yet on the topic). I then passed on my syllabus and documents to the experienced friend Michel Bilodeau when I became too busy with new international commitments.

When I joined that more-than-fifty-year-old master's in health administration at University of Ottawa, the program was in a somewhat bad shape. Its faculty was old in age and tenure. One important older professor, a troublemaker, a physician, had just left. Another professor totally refused to speak to anyone else and to participate, his door closed at all times. A director had had to take a leave of absence for health reasons. The atmosphere within our relatively small academic team had not improved when Professor Angus's term as a director came to an end in June 2001. Early in 2000 Michel Lalonde, a former graduate of the program (in 1972), joined our team as executive-in-residence. A positive, dynamic, experienced administrator who had practised "team learning" – his stewardship "being in service to, rather than in control of the people around you," having turned around the Hawkesbury General Hospital as a "learning organization" when he was its CEO – and I, the minister facing all the attacks on our medicare, became a pair towards reviving the spirit of our program. A "whole system" thinker, he was a pleasure to work with. Students adored him, for he was a role model if there is one of what they aspired to become. Like me, he did not want a management position in the program.

As the faculty needed to recruit a new MHA program director, Dean Micheàl Kelly (2000–10) set up a small committee made of Michel Lalonde and me and chaired by Vice-Dean Georges Hénault. We had two or three candidates, no more, one being the colleague who would not speak to anyone else. Another one was a complete newcomer to the School of Management, a former professor from Carleton University Sprott School of Business: Wojtek Michalowski, MSc, PhD (Central School of Planning and Statistics, Warsaw). Bright, open, committed to orient the program towards more innovative research, he shared with us how he would like to apply his systems analysis to health-care systems. The committee sensed a breath of fresh air! And he was not at all connected to, even aware of, the recent troublesome years of our program. We selected him, and our recommendation was approved at once. He was our director from 2001 to 2004.

Under his leadership, we started slowly hiring a newer generation of health management professors. Our first new recruit was Marie-Pascale Pommey, MD, now a public health specialist and researcher at University of Montreal, also currently director of their master's program in health systems management. Through the following years we were joined by others listed here in no particular order: Samia Chreim (PhD, HEC-Montréal), Jonathan Patrick (PhD, UBC), Mirou Jaana (PhD, University of Iowa), Craig Kuziemsky (PhD, University of Victoria), who is now the director of the master program in science health systems (Wojtek's baby), or Kevin Brand (ScD, Harvard), who is the current director of the MHA Program. I much enjoyed exchanging with them and learning.

Through his mandate as a director, Wojtek started developing the idea of a parallel research-based master's program in health systems. I encouraged him from the start. Then at the end of his mandate as director, besides continuing teaching our students as the professor of health informatics, Wojtek invested his time and efforts in getting off that research-based master's the ground, convincing the Dean's Office and getting start-up funding, setting up corresponding labs and recruiting its first students. He was appointed its director in 2008, the official new entity name being master of science in health systems program. From memory, assisting him from the start was Szymon Wilk, today adjunct professor. In 2004, to succeed Wojtek in the old MHA Program, Doug Angus had come back for a few years as director, but he was not the same; it was as if all was now about power and control, not listening to us his colleagues and peers. It could not last and didn't. Around 2007–08, Michel Lalonde agreed to take over, to everyone's general satisfaction. Most unfortunately, he resigned when he learned in December 2008 that his old cancer had returned. He died in February 2010. In September 2010 Brian Malcolmson, who had just joined the MHA program in May as executive-in-residence, assumed the position of MHA director. As for Wojtek Michalowski, he is now vice-dean (research) at the Telfer School of Management. He teaches undergraduate, graduate, and postgraduate courses and is theses supervisor. He is also the principal investigator of an NSERC-funded research program. The research aims at making clinical practice guidelines applicable for patients with multiple diseases and developing clinical decision support systems for cross-platform applications.

During those years at Telfer, besides teaching and fulfilling the other duties of a professor, I continued to honour my previous commitments, while my mandate as chair of the Radiation Safety Institute came to an end, and I thought it was time for someone else to take over. I kept travelling, often to Toronto, but it felt less all over the map.

One very special and totally unexpected such trip was a week in London, England, in early May 2000, where Judy Erola and I had been invited as speakers at a "Women in Sciences" conference. This particular event was part of an initiative by Debra Davies, our councillor of public affairs at the Canadian High Commission in London, who had set up a successful series of "Women Crossing Borders" conferences, an intersectoral meeting of women in high office in different fields of activities. Our friend and former colleague Lloyd Axworthy, then minister of foreign affairs, sponsored our trip. There were dozens of interesting women participating. I recall the environmentalist Elizabeth Dowdeswell, now Ontario lieutenant-governor, as well as the British feminist psychoanalyst Susie Orbach, known for her famous first book *Fat Is a Feminist Issue*. Having myself created the first academic courses on women's health in Canada outside of medicine – which had nothing on women's health for years – Orbach's presentation fascinated me.

At one point in 2002, under the leadership of André Potworowski in Telfer, where he was associate director, research and development, Centre for Research in Biopharmaceuticals and Biotechnology, a research team was set up to do a feasibility study of clinical trials, also including Dr George Wells, professor of epidemiology and community medicine at the university, my former colleague Minister Judy Erola and me. We obtained a financial contribution from the federal Department of Industry, Trade and Commerce, and one from Health Canada. As a business proposal, in Canada, clinical trials represented economic activity of between $800 million and $1 billion, with some thirteen stakeholders involved, at the centre of which are patients. This was the section of our research that Judy Erola and I chose to focus on. Besides patients, large pharmas, biotech companies, clinical research organizations, private research clinics, hospitals and university faculties are the places where clinical trials take place. And that includes research nurses, investigators, and ethics research boards, the last too often considered the bottleneck to progress. The research project on clinical trials was business oriented at first, and Judy and I convinced our group that it was also and primarily a business involving patients. We designed our research section and interviewed patients, expecting to spend about a half-hour with each patient, but instead taking half a day to a full day. As usual in good research, we had samples from a variety of sources, and respondents were very pleased to be involved and to have had a voice at long last. So our report on patients was integrated into the whole feasibility study report, including recommendations, from 2002 to 2005. The feasibility study report was entitled *Accelerating Access for Patients to Best Medicine*.

My second retirement came at the end of my last class of the course HAH-6266 (title forgotten) on 1 April 2004, when the students and the professors celebrated me – and it had nothing to do with April Fools' Day! In fact I had started saying that I was going to retire for good in the upcoming summer. I had loved teaching. It had been a great group of students, truly motivated, but suddenly my heart was no longer in it. So pictures were taken and I was presented with a gift. Of course, I had to correct the exams and so on. I continued giving class presentations on invitation in the faculty, not just in the MHA, and participate to seminars all through April, May, June, and July of that year.

It is also in the same months that I started participating in the intensive meetings of an advisory panel to a very special royal commission: the so-called Arar Commission. On 5 February 2004, Prime Minister Paul Martin Jr established the Commission of Inquiry into the Actions of Canadian Officials in Relation to Maher Arar, appointing Justice Dennis O'Connor as its commissioner. He in turn set up an advisory committee to give him advice directly and in a non-judicial set-up from national security and intelligence experts on, say, anti-terrorism legislation – some academics, a retired deputy RCMP commissioner – and myself, as a public policy practitioner, all of us speaking from outside government. Everything was top secret – each of us had been cleared after passing the highest level of security screening and had been designated "Persons Permanently Bound to Secrecy" – but as Justice O'Connor thanked us publicly, here is the Advisory Committee membership: Alphonse Breau, Kent Roach, Martin Rudner, Reg Whitaker, and me. We worked several days in a row, reading documents on our own, discussing specific topics in meetings, meeting with officials as directed, all through April to the end of August 2004. Then the readings (lots!) and meetings resumed in 2005, and I participated in all until September, as I went then to India for a previous academic commitment. My agenda does not show any other Arar Advisory Committee activity for the fall of 2005. In 2006, as of the beginning of April, we reviewed draft chapters of the report. Justice Dennis O'Connor presented his report to the Governor-General-in-Council – the new prime minister being Stephen Harper – on 18 September 2006.

A few months after joining Justice Dennis O'Connor's Advisory Committee, another rare ad hoc opportunity, of a completely different nature, presented itself: to give "Gender and Social Policies" workshops for female lawmakers in Vietnam, in their country, over a week. There would be eighty participants, of which twenty-five to thirty were members of the Committee of Social Affairs, thirty others were as MPs of the national Parliament and Office of the National Assembly, and twenty-five to thirty were members of people's councils of major cities and provinces. The vice minister of home affairs, Dr Nguyen Trong Dieu, also presented and participated, the objective being the acquisition of tools for a critical look at current or upcoming legislation and policies around gender social issues. It rapidly became obvious to me that the topics to be covered also required Judy Erola's expertise, both as a former minister of the status of women and as the past president of the Pharmaceutical Manufacturers Association of Canada (PMAC) for eleven years. Our workshop was one of many others stemming from a decade-long CIDA development project, managed at the top by Marc

Lalonde's law firm in Montreal, who approved the additional expenditure of having Judy part of this workshop. The project director was Michael McCabe, resident director of CIDA Policy Implementation Assistance Project (PIAP) office in Hanoi.

As I had resigned from the University of Ottawa for the second time, I had the summer to research and develop PowerPoint slides in English, mine and new ones from the texts Judy Erola sent me from her summer camp on Lake Panache near Sudbury. All our presentations had to be transmitted to Vietnam as soon as they were ready, for translation into Vietnamese. Women's health and medicine, breast cancer survivors action, pensions and women, women and drugs, maternity leave, violence against women, and women and aging were a few topics covered. Judy and I left on 15 August, returning to Canada on 28 August. We had a chance to see Ho Chi Minh City (the former Saigon) where we landed and met Mike McCabe and our fantastic young translator, Ms Nguyen Thi Xuan Hoa, and Hanoi further to the workshop. The conference itself and its workshops took place in a nondescript modern small industrial town, Phan Rang, the capital of Ninh Thuân Province on the South Central Coast of the country. All participants were lodged some kilometres from town, on the seaside, the Vietnamese in one resort (better food) and we, the guests, at the quiet and fine Den Gion Ninh Chu Resort (better accommodation in low motels-hotels). Judy and I swam every morning at six in the warm turquoise China Sea, before getting in the van that commuted between meeting places. We knew the other resort had the best food as the Vietnam vice-president, Mrs Truong Thi My Hoa, and Mrs Nguyen Thi Hoai Thu, chair of Social Affairs of the National Assembly, gave a delicious banquet to welcome everyone at their resort, with Cham dancers (we were in Cham country and visited their magnificent thirteenth-century Poklongarai towers). Once in a while I look through a thick photo album of all the people we met and the sites we were able to visit (too rapidly) on our own after the workshop.

Sometime just before this Vietnam project, the last time I had been in Halifax, at dinner with friends Liz and Brian Crocker, after they had heard of my plans to soon retire for good, they immediately exclaimed, "And what are your retirement projects?" I just said that I had none, had never thought of that, having a thousand dreams of books to read, music to discover, trips to make. Where? How? Why? I had no such plans. They concluded that my retirement would be wasted. I was flabbergasted. And then, as if by magic, when I went back home in Ottawa, a close Montreal friend from my youth phoned with a proposal one could not refuse. We would go to Florence for the fall months, until Christmas, rent a modest apartment, register in a good school teaching Italian, and enjoy Italian daily life. No sooner said than done. Chantal Perrault's daughter had married an Italian and they, with two children, lived in Pistoia, some forty to fifty kilometres from Florence. She wanted to communicate with them to the maximum and had taken a year of evening courses at the Dante Institute of Montreal. My motivation: an old personal challenge and a feeling of guilt – my birth in Rome; my parents speaking Italian at home when they did not want us to understand; the fact that after three hours of studying with my mom the night before, I got such high marks in Italian at the French baccalaureate that I was exempted from the oral exam (which I would have failed miserably); ... and my Italo-Canadian riding of St Leonard, where I understood nothing of the conversations (they were Calabrese and Sicilians). So Chantal was put in a higher class than I was, re-starting as a beginner with international young students in an excellent and relaxed school not far from the Duomo. Those were of the moments in life one never forgets because of their beauty, the discoveries they offered, their friendship, their happiness.

I came back on 10 December and I spent 13–17 ... at Telfer, participating in the master of health administration activities! So much for having retired. Colleagues Michel Lalonde, Wojtek Michalowski, and Doug Angus – the senior administration – wanted me back as visiting professor, again on a relaxed timetable. So in 2005, when in Ottawa, I was at Telfer, still located in the old Vanier building, in a most pleasant community of colleagues, as the MHA and MHSC were not physically separated from the other School of Management colleagues. That is how I got to know and befriend Gilles Paquet, a true public intellectual, stopping in his office a few doors from mine, full of the most numerous sets of books and documents piled up in delicate balance I ever saw! I was very present in all MHA events and gave a few presentations in colleagues' classes. I also continued participating in the Arar Advisory

Committee, different public health groups, the Institut de Recherches cliniques de Montréal Board, and more.

And then, still in 2005, as always in my life, something unexpected happened: I was invited to serve as a commissioner on the International WHO Commission on Social Determinants of Health. The chair, Sir Michael Marmot, phoned me in February, and we had a long conversation. I was immediately enthused by his mandate and his views, and I accepted. It would last until November 2008. More in the last chapter of these memoirs. To conclude on this part of my academic life – 2006, 2007, and 2008 – I was regularly at Telfer, participating in the MHA and in the new MHSc programs, co-supervising master's theses there or PhD theses at the Institute of Population Health, and speaking at the university or elsewhere in the country of the science behind the social determinants of health. I also served an eighteen-month mandate as a mentor for two graduate students at the Trudeau Foundation – remarkable young women, one in medicine and the other in political sciences – a new experience I much appreciated. I was also slowly limiting my academic presence through these years, but attending International WHO Commission meetings and public hearings around the world "full time."

Through these years, to my repeated confusion, I was awarded the great honour of eight more honorary doctorates, adding to the ten already received. This last list reads as follows: Memorial University (2000), Royal Military College of Canada (2001), University of Windsor (2002), University of Ottawa (2003, together with the former Saskatchewan Premier Roy Romanow, doubling the honour and pleasure for me), Simon Fraser (2006), Université de Montréal (2009, together with Sir Michael Marmot), University of Waterloo (2010), and Carleton University (2011). Other distinctions were also bestowed upon me such as the second Distinguished Fellowship, just after Dr John Evans, from the Canadian Academy of Health Sciences in 2008.

And finally, the time came to truly retire, for good, with no return. On 30 December 2010, after having given books to women's studies or our libraries, made boxes, cleared the walls of artwork, and moved all, I left my modern lifeless Desmarais building office, the door half open as usual, and gave back my keys to the secretariat. A few weeks later, on the Tuesday, 15 February 2011, as I mentioned at the start of this

chapter, further to having been invited "for something of a surprise,"
Allan Rock, the university president, and Dean François Julien dedicated a Graduate Students Study Room (Room 4155) of the new Desmarais building, housing the Telfer School of Management, the "Salle
Monique Bégin Room."

◆ ✳ ◆

I never planned this long and varied academic career! I was offered
challenges that I accepted. I would finally spend twenty-five years in
university life after politics. Our universities, the oldest one in North
America being a Canadian one, Laval University in Quebec City, going
back to 1663, our universities are not innovative creations but in direct
filiation to the Sorbonne of Paris (1150 and 1231), the University of
Bologna (1088), Oxford (1096 and 1167), or Heidelberg (1386) and
all the other great universities of the Western world. Of course, we
never think of that past with our students in miniskirts, shorts, too-
short tops or no tops for guys, and leggings in the winter! One description of universities that bears relationship to today, in my opinion,
comes from one of their noted historians, Hastings Rashdall, who
wrote in his 1895 *The Universities of Europe in the Middle Ages*,

> The University, no less than the Roman Church and the feudal
> Hierarchy headed by the Roman Emperor, represents an at-
> tempt to realise in concrete form an ideal of life in one of its as-
> pects ... The institutions which the Middle Age has bequeathed
> to us are of greater and more imperishable value even than its
> Cathedrals ... Their organisation and their traditions, their
> studies and their exercises affected the progress and intellectual
> development of Europe more powerfully, or (perhaps it should
> be said) more exclusively, than any schools in all likelihood will
> ever do again ... Paris and Bologna are the two archetypal – it
> might almost be said the only original universities: Paris sup-
> plied the model for the Universities of Masters, Bologna for the
> Universities of Students.

Under *medieval university*, Wikipedia adds, "Universities were generally structured along three types, depending on who paid the teachers. The first type was in Bologna, where students hired and paid for the teachers. The second type was in Paris, where teachers were paid by the church. Oxford and Cambridge were predominantly supported by the crown and the state." If universities were creatures of monks or other scholastic guilds, they were established formerly by popes, emperors, and kings. These were the roots of these institutions and they have endured through time. Universities are unique creatures.

At commencement ceremonies, or convocations, twice a year, our students are very proud of parading in their longer black gown with ample sleeves, bordered with the colours of their faculty – their toga – with their hood on top of the shoulders and the square academic cap – the mortarboard – all representing the levels of academic achievement: undergraduate, graduate, doctorate. Professors and deans wear a fancier robe version, with an elaborate hood and a velvet large flat bonnet or square cap. We faculty dress in our best regalia in a special room before forming the procession leading the way to the graduation ceremonies. The hood in its original form was the upper part of the cowl worn by the monks and friars of the Middle Ages. I could not believe it at first. This theatre goes back to the medieval times in Europe. Only our institution of the judiciary still also wear special regalia, except that wigs are not worn in Canada but are based on the correct dress for attending the royal court in previous centuries. These court traditions came from the Crown and not from the church. Almost no special clothing remains in parliamentary life. Through history, secret societies continued to wear special costumes for their meetings, but they are more an object of ridicule today. The contemporary business institutions that stemmed from the Industrial Revolution have no such ancient roots and traditions.

When I started as an academic, for my first six years, I felt only minimally attached to my university of the moment. Of course they had my loyalty. Everything changed when I became a dean! From "individual" I became "institutional." I will be the first to admit that I found university power structure, organization, and politics appalling and not that clear to decode at first. And super-bureaucratic! As a new dean, I tried to figure out the organization chart of the University of Ottawa by comparing it mentally with Cabinet and Parliament. Who of the "high administration" was Treasury Board? The minister of finance? And so on. I rapidly jumped to the conclusion that we, the deans, were like the Cabinet ministers of different departments. Fatal error. I realize now that deans are only middle management, not executive management. What I did conclude with healthy cynicism at the time, keeping it to myself, after a few months of regular lunchtime meetings with the vice rector academic, was that we were treated like schoolboys and collectively had no role whatsoever, no importance, and no power. Worse, these monthly deans meetings were even, very early in my mandate, a tool of financial extortion by the top powers when, after a particular meeting, each dean was obliged to immediately move next door, where the rector had a contract ready for signature, by which one had to "give" to the university some of one's salary (8 per cent if I recall), as a charitable donation, year after year. We had absolutely no choice, and I still resent the method. It was completely unacceptable. Deans and their administrative assistants had to meet once a year with the "senior administration" at budget time, but not collectively, rather one by one, all of us waiting our turn on chairs at the door of the meeting room in the Tabaret building ...

On a few occasions, almost spontaneously, as I had learned in politics, I simply quietly bypassed the lines of command, reaching directly to whoever was in the decision-making position for my request x, y, or z.

The governance at the top of our universities with their boards of governors/regents basically representing the outside world of business and other elites and the academic top hierarchy made of learned experts in teaching and research raises a huge problem in today's world. I simply do not understand how the academics become like second-class citizens at that top level of decision-making, when they are the very essence and raison d'être of the institution. This dual, often conflictual locus of ultimate power surely goes back straight to medieval times. It seems we hear more and more of serious unsolved conflictual situations, discharges or sudden resignations of university presidents. It seems to me urgent to rethink universities' current shared model of governance. I was a member of the McGill Board of Governors for almost five years. Granted, I had everything to learn, but what I observed leads me to conclude that key decisions made unanimously had been the object of previous behind-the-scenes one-to-one discussion with a few key play- ers only.

I attended a number of University of Ottawa Senate meetings as a dean, made up of faculty members, deans, student representatives, and other senior administrators. I still don't quite understand what it does and why it exists. However, I realize that the university Senate is a gov- erning body of importance. The definition of the University of Ottawa Senate on the web makes it a supremely key player: "The Senate sets the University's educational policies and is responsible for the sound management of academic issues on campus. For instance, subject to the approval of related expenses by the Board of Governors, the Senate has the power to create and abolish faculties, departments, schools and in- stitutes. In addition, the Senate creates or abolishes academic regulations and programs of studies, sets admission, degree and diploma require- ments, confers certificates, degrees at all levels and, with the approval of the Board of Governors, honorary doctorates."

In fact it is depicted as "the supreme" academic authority for the in- stitution. Above all, I remember how large an attendance it attracted. The sheer number around the table was proof for me that the decisions were made elsewhere and differently. At Senate meetings I had the im- pression of rubber stamping decisions from elsewhere. And I did not understand the links between the Senate, the hierarchical academics top of the institution (its executive committee), and the board of governors.

Impossible not to quote Henry Mintzberg, the McGill guru of man- agement science, and his five types of organizational structures:

- Simple Structure, also called the entrepreneurial organization
- Machine Bureaucracy
- Professional Bureaucracy
- Divisionalized Form
- Adhocracy

The McGill management expert puts universities in the category of
"professional bureaucracy":

> It is the structure hospitals, universities, and accounting firms
> tend most often to favor. Most important, because it relies for its
> operating tasks on trained professionals – skilled people who
> must be given considerable control over their own work – the or-
> ganization surrenders a good deal of its power not only to the
> professionals themselves but also to the associations and institu-
> tions that select and train them in the first place. As a result, the
> structure emerges as very decentralized; power over many deci-
> sions, both operating and strategic, flows all the way down the
> hierarchy to the professionals of the operating core. For them this
> is the most democratic structure of all ... Above the operating
> core we find a unique structure. Since the main standardization
> occurs as a result of training that takes place outside the profes-
> sional bureaucracy, a technostructure is hardly needed. And be-
> cause the professionals work independently, the size of operating
> units can be very large, and so few first-line managers are needed.
> (I work in a business school where 55 professors report directly
> to one dean.) Yet even those few managers, and those above
> them, do little direct supervision; much of their time is spent link-
> ing their units to the broader environment, notably to ensure ad-
> equate financing ... On the other hand, the support staff is
> typically very large in order to back up the high-priced profes-
> sionals. But that staff does a very different kind of work – much
> of it the simple and routine jobs that the professionals shed. As
> a result, parallel hierarchies emerge in the professional bureau-
> cracy – <u>one democratic with bottom-up power for the profession-
> als, a second autocratic with top-down control for the support
> staff.</u> Professional bureaucracy is most effective for organizations
> that find themselves in stable yet complex environments.

This last statement, and the final part I underlined, could correspond
to my observations about university structures. So we have the paradox
of collegiality – the horizontal organizational peers' culture – coupled

with fierce individualism and top-down bureaucratic rules. By the way, a lot could be said to debunk "collegiality," which, because of its informal rules of the game, is often undemocratic and has much to do with the Old Boys network. And then there coexists the kind of institutional culture nurtured by the top academic leadership. For instance, for all my years as dean in the 1990s, an inter-sectoral, interdisciplinary capacity was not only missing but opposed. I am thinking of our committee work trying to develop a program in gerontology, judged dangerous, wishy-washy, and so on. Today, interdisciplinary approaches for academic disciplines are the buzzword, but rethinking governance of interdisciplinarity has not followed. In the same way as it used to be a major roadblock in Cabinet work, interdisciplinary capacity and mechanisms, not just to develop new programs but to solve any kind of complex problematic situations – those Gilles Paquet calls "wicked situations" – do not spontaneously appear. People generally function in closed territories, in vertical silos, not talking with others elsewhere in the system. In public administration – whether it be international or domestic, in universities or in government – what is usually missing is the possibility of crossing sectoral boundaries, of a safe common space to figure out the internal logic that "the Other" is operating from.

Now on a more down-to-earth level, I once asked Dr Lorna Marsden, a sociologist and very successful past president of York University, what was the beginning of the pathway towards a senior administrative academic position. "Department chair" was her immediate answer. Why? "Because you will administer a budget, manage people, and start interfacing with senior administrators. And learn how to read a balance sheet! And if you live in Ontario, also learn about BIUS!" So you are a department chair, or you have just been selected as dean of a faculty. What if you are a woman exercising academic power? One must occupy power in exercising it; one must take power. Nobody gives it to us on a silver platter. This rule applies to both men and women, and it is as valid in universities as it is in politics or in business.

Since I joined the ranks of academics, I have found it even more compelling to call myself a feminist, for knowledge – education and research – as well as the institutions of higher learning are far from being gender-neutral. I am convinced that every discipline taught on our campuses is seriously distorted when it comes to understanding human nature, including, in a very pervasive way, biology, medicine, and sciences. In addition, the milieu and the institutional culture of each discipline and faculty reproduces the machismo of society.

Finally, when co-supervising graduate theses in my last academic years, I observed how, only too often, so-called applied knowledge is at risk of seeing an otherwise rich and important thesis rejected at the last minute. A doctoral student is supposed to present only "pure" new theoretical developments in the final text. This is either super-hypocritical or plain dumb. Lots of our knowledge is of an applied nature and represents knowledge.

And I have not yet said what I think of how women are treated in universities ... When I got the phone call from Rector D'Iorio informing me I had been selected as a dean, in May 1990, I was at a special training session in Banff and he wanted my answer immediately. So I said yes and thanked him, and he informed me that my salary would be such-and-such and my term was seven years. That was it. I never negotiated a thing. Coming from a world where all salaries and pensions were public and the same, it did not cross my mind to enquire. One of the results is that, further to Ontario legislation in the mid-nineties forcing all salaries of $100,000 and over paid from public taxes to be listed annually in the *Globe & Mail* on 31 March, I was in awe to discover that all my male dean colleagues had made the list but not me. I never made it! I sarcastically denounced it in a major public speech. As I was retiring, it was too late for me to receive justice, but Caroline Andrew, appointed dean by then, is still grateful to me: her salary was readjusted at once when I spoke of it publicly and it was raised ... to exactly $100,000! Should I add how unjust, illegal, and unequitable I find the fact that women academics are globally paid, in today's Canada, 30 per cent less than their male counterparts? My last observation is that, for the 106 or so universities in Canada, there should be approximately fifty women university presidents, in addition to half of all the positions of vice presidents or the equivalent, and 50 per cent of all deans.

22

An Ontario Report on Education and
Two International Commissions

I knew that "royal commissions," as we called them in Canada, be they federal or provincial, were usually set up as independent temporary bodies for both research and public discussion of an intractable issue. As stated in the Canadian Encyclopedia, other kinds of public inquiry, task forces, and investigations have also been established under statutory powers of the Inquiries Act passed by Parliament ... in 1858. It could be an economic question, a socio-political one (the B&B Commission), or the recent Truth and Reconciliation Commission (2008–15), a component of the Indian Residential Schools Settlement Agreement, and so on. By definition, their reports make recommendations to governments. My first involvement in one such inquiry, the Royal Commission on the Status of Women in Canada (1967–70), of which I was the executive secretary, was no exception. Just regarding health care and our health-care systems, from the famous Hall Commission (1961–64) which gave us "medicare," through the decades when I was involved in health-care issues, I counted more than two dozen federal and provincial royal commissions of inquiry on that topic alone, one being the Romanow Commission (2001–02)! Their legal existence ceases the day their report is tabled in Parliament. Yet some of these reports have changed Canada, while others did not make it and were shelved.

When in Grade 4 at NDG elementary school in Montreal, I recall as if it were yesterday the sunny afternoon when all students were outside in the schoolyard, invited to sing with Gérard and Alec Pelletier that year's Jeunesse étudiante catholique (JEC) campaign theme: *Les idées changent le monde! Changent le monde!* (Pelletier was the JEC's president that year, and Alec was involved at the JEC Centrale.) That is the power of ideas Rianne Mahon recognizes when she wrote in 2014, "The idea of a pan-Canadian child care policy, based on the principles of universality, was placed on the agenda by the Royal Commission on the Status of Women, which recognised that such a program was required to establish equality of opportunity between the sexes. All mothers needed the kind of support a publicly subsidized child care could offer if they were to become equal to men."

That is what commissions, especially international ones, are all about. I have always believed in the power of ideas. We know that knowledge is power. But how knowledge is disseminated at the level of global governance should tell us more about successful international commissions. In *International Commissions and the Power of Ideas*, originally published in 2005, the editors John English, Andrew Cooper, and Ramesh Thakur (all from the University of Waterloo at the time) give us fifteen most interesting articles stemming from the growth during the 1980s and 1990s of commissions addressing global issues: international commissions. Some are independent, some originate from the United Nations or its institutional family. We remember the Brandt Commission (independent) which reported on the North-South divide (1980); the Palme Commission (1980–82) on Disarmament and Security (independent); or the Brundtland Commission (UN) (1983–87) on the question of development – all milestones. The editors make the point that international commissions "were important in pioneering this way of using groups of prominent individuals to make policy inputs on significant global issues." Members of such commissions are appointed as individuals, not representing their government. They are, hopefully, "idea carriers," retaining the capacity to remain high profile even once a commission report has been tabled. Its chair becomes a champion of "the cause," while the ideas offered can also be embraced by key political figures, gaining the attention of high-level policymakers, networks of NGOs, of scholars, and by the media. Such a champion was Gro Harlem Brundtland, who travelled the world meeting heads of state to promote the idea of "sustainable development" after her commission report had been tabled. No need to add that, for the success of international commissions, "timing matters." That role of international commissions is summed up by Geoffrey Wiseman (Australian National University) in the same book: it is expected that international commissions "produce new ideas, concepts and proposals; gain the attention of high-level policy-makers (at the UN and within governments); acquire enough attention by the media, academics, NGOs and sections of the public; convince significant players in the official policy-making process to become advocates of the commission's conclusions or recommendations; sustain a shelf-life (so that principal concepts and recommendations remain part of the international dialogue on these issues for at least five years)."

I had the privilege of co-chairing one Ontario commission (1993–95) and of being a commissioner of two international commissions: the independent one on Population and Quality of Life (1993–95) and then the WHO Commission on Social Determinants of Health (2005–08).

One day, when I was the joint chair in women's studies (1986–90), a feminist conference to be given by Maria de Lourdes Pintasilgo was advertised at the University of Ottawa and I went. I had never heard of her. The speaker, a chemical engineer by profession, had served as Portugal's minister of social affairs in 1974–75 immediately after the 25 April 1974 historic "Carnation Revolution," which ended the half-century of dictatorship of Salazar and his followers. She was later sworn in as prime minister of Portugal in the caretaker government, with a three-month mandate (!) on 1 August 1979, and later became "consultant to the president of the republic," General Antonio Ramalho Eanes, in 1981–85. At the end of the question period that followed, quite impressed by the speaker's personality and her ideas, I just went and introduced myself, adding spontaneously that I would have loved working with her in politics!

Shortly after I became the dean of health sciences in 1990, she contacted me, informing me that she would chair the Independent Commission on Population and Quality of Life which was being set up, and she asked if I would serve as a commissioner. After understanding her mandate, I accepted with pleasure. I later learned that she had spoken with Pierre Trudeau, whom she knew and admired via the famous Club de Madrid of former democratic heads of states, testing with him if it was a good idea to appoint me to her commission! Then I never heard of it for months and forgot about it.

Three years later, in my dean's office at the University of Ottawa, in early March 1993, first the deputy minister of education, Charles Pascal, whom I knew as a member of Premier Bob Rae's Council on Health, Well-being and Social Justice, telephoned me, followed by Bob Rae himself, asking me to chair a royal commission on education in the province. I was honoured, however I declined repeatedly, as it would be a full-time mandate and I was a full-time dean of a new faculty! (The previous invitation from Maria de Lourdes Pintasilgo to be a member of her international commission would have been a totally different type of time and responsibility commitments.) At one point I thought I should inform the rector, Marcel Hamelin, of this invitation and my refusal, as he would certainly come across Bob Rae in his dealings with Queen's Park. I went down to Tabaret on 27 April, just sharing this with him by courtesy, for his information. To my complete surprise, Marcel Hamelin immediately took it very seriously and concluded that I should accept at once. He would mandate one of my senior professors, with a pleasant personality and academic management experience, to be vice dean *pro tempore* in charge of the faculty. We would remain in contact for unexpected problems through a fax and on weekends, as I would travel back home to Ottawa. So I accepted.

Relieved, on 5 May 1993, Premier Bob Rae then announced the creation of the Royal Commission on Learning "to ensure that Ontario's youth are well-prepared for the challenges of the twenty-first century." I was appointed chair, after having reluctantly agreed to Bob Rae's last-minute request to accept a co-chair, Gerry Caplan – "reluctantly agreed," as I could not forget the catastrophic experience of having accepted and lived with an associate deputy minister in National Health and Welfare, who then systematically undermined her/my deputy minister. Gerry Caplan and I worked together quite well, despite a few mini-dramatic moments. In the following week, we announced to faculty and explained that Dr Charles Cotton, from the Department of Human Kinetics, had agreed to be vice dean and would be supported with pleasure by Jeannette Giroux, our exceptional chief administrator officer, and I asked for everyone's assistance. That was on Monday, 10 May, and the day after I was in Toronto for the rest of that week meeting my new entourage.

All this being nicely organized and explained, something else had suddenly happened in the meantime, unnoticed by my office, as I had always had several conferences to give or outside meetings to attend during whatever full-time job I had. The Independent Commission on Population and Quality of Life had suddenly reappeared on the radar screen. I spent 21–23 April in Paris, at the UNESCO offices, attending my first meeting of the International Independent Commission on Population and Quality of Life, chaired by Maria de Lourdes Pintasilgo, a commission in the wake of Gro Harlem Brundtland's commission, Our Common Future.

Population pressure in its multiple relationships to development, poverty, human rights, the environment, or, as stated in our mandate, "situating population matters within the socio-economic context," clearly called for interdisciplinary knowledge and inter-sectoral work and action. Most of its regular meetings would take place at the UNESCO premises in Paris. I appraised my new colleagues of the technique of public hearings used by our Canadian commissions of inquiries, the added credibility and the buy-in they could bring to our work, and their role and importance, and I convinced this international commission to adopt the idea. Once my domestic Commission on Learning in Ontario started, I saw that I would have to miss several of the international commission public hearings, much to my chagrin.

In Ontario I had no say on who the commissioners would be. Many will recall a first in its membership when Manisha Bharti – a seventeen-year-old St Lawrence High School student, from Cornwall – was appointed. The five of us were virtual strangers to one another when we first met: besides Gerry Caplan and myself and young Manisha were Dr Avis Glaze, superintendent of education with the North York Board, and Monsignor Dennis Murphy, who had been secretary general of the Canadian Conference of Catholic Bishops as well as many other mandates in Catholic education, now a priest of the Diocese of Sault Ste Marie. I did not know the newly appointed minister of education and training, the outspoken MPP for the then Windsor-Riverside riding, David Cooke, who had joined Cabinet in 1990. He first had been the minister of housing and municipal affairs, then government house leader, and finally chair of the management board of Cabinet before becoming the minister of education on 3 February 1993, three months before we were set up as the commission on education!

The deputy minister of education simply informed me that he was appointing one of his ADMs, Dr Jill Hutcheon, a sociologist as I recall, as executive director, but six months later he had replaced her with Raffaella (Raf) Di Cecco, originally from "Training" in the ministry and recently appointed regional director of education for the Central Region. Raf did not have a teaching certificate, but that was not a problem for me. In addition, Charles Pascal, the powerful, innovative, and dynamic DM, wanted us to use or retain the services, as much as possible, of the expert who had expected to be appointed head of the commission: Dr Michael Fullan, from the Ontario Institute for Studies in Education (OISE). A respected academic in the field of education, professor in their Department of Theory and Policy Studies, and future dean of OISE/UT, we found ourselves, as far as I was concerned, in one more unnecessarily rather delicate situation.

Almost from the start I had to understand the complex socio-political situation that had preceded our creation, a piece of it being that Gerry Caplan had been the chief strategist of Bob Rae's electoral victory as premier and would always remain an ardent and actively involved NDP party member. He had his own network in the government, in the NDP, and in the media. On the education front, in January 1992, then Education Minister Tony Silipo had announced a major restructuring initiative for Grades 7–9 in Ontario schools that would prepare children for "an ever-changing world" and take education from an industrial society to a post-industrial world. In September 1992 he had stated that by the next September, Grade 9 courses would no longer be streamed into advanced, general, and basic course levels. In addition, the Grade 9 curriculum would be converted from credit courses to integrated studies in the four core program areas: language; the arts; self and society; and mathematics, sciences, and technology. These reforms, dubbed the three "D's" (de-labelling, de-streaming, de-coursing), strongly criticized by parent groups and business interests, were simply nonsense to me. This messy situation was followed by a Cabinet shuffle, a new Speech from the Throne, and the creation of a Royal Commission on Learning with a very broad mandate to examine the purpose and direction of Ontario's school system! I knew none of that background.

In addition, we faced another extraordinary external constraint. Two weeks into our mandate, Premier Bob Rae announced the Social Contract, as the deficit he had inherited from the David Peterson Liberals in 1993 had become a $12 billion deficit, going on to $16 billion, because of the worsening recession. Premier Rae requested $2 billion in wage cuts within the "broader public sector," begging its unions to work together with the government to implement the cuts. The two largest unions (OPSEU and CUPE) refused, forcing the government to act unilaterally. It meant a forced twelve days of unpaid leave for all civil service workers who made more than $30,000 a year, including ... teachers (!), the infamous "Rae Days"! The Rae government did attain its financial objective and avoided layoffs among the civil servants. But it had become extremely unpopular and Rae lost the support of the unions forever. So we needed to work with teachers to improve and reform the education system while they hated their government, although, of course, many of them had put Bob Rae in power to start with.

If I had become an expert on medicare and health issues, my Rigaud Teachers College diploma and my years of teaching children and teenagers in Montreal were a very long time ago, as was my very first classroom, at age nineteen, of fifty-two little girls of Grade 4, in the very poor Ste-Elizabeth-du-Portugal elementary school in Saint-Henri. In the sixties I had read with passion the 1968 Hall-Dennis Report on Education in Ontario, *Living and Learning: The Report of the Provincial Committee on Aims and Objectives of Education in the Schools of Ontario.* It had been produced by the unique team of Justice Emmett Hall (the same Justice Emmett Hall of medicare) and Lloyd Dennis, a Toronto school teacher, consultant and principal, and principal writer of the report, which opened with these words: "The underlying aim of education is to further man's unending search for truth."

The beginnings of the commission were difficult: we were forming a team and learning to work together, a completely different challenge from that of the 1967 Royal Commission on the Status of Women in Canada. At times, such as when I had joined Cabinet, I felt that human egos had no limitations. We started structuring our staff, which again was a challenge. However, when Raf Di Cecco came onboard, everything changed for the better. I recall our little selection committee of Gerry and myself and one other person from the ministry. When Caplan asked Raf what her theory of management was, she calmly replied with a smile, "Eclectic." That convinced me. Wise, solid, unruffled, whatever the people and the circumstances, demonstrating great judgment and seeing through situations and challenges, she was the most controlled Italo-Canadian I had ever met! I loved working with her, learned a lot, and we became friends for life. We built a small team of eight top-notch and younger experts who were familiar with the latest research work and able to draft our report, chapter by chapter. Names include Nancy Watson, Suzanne Ziegler, Julie Lindhout, and Wane Burnett to list only half of them. We benefitted from a loyal and competent very small secretariat of nine (for such a huge initiative, especially the public hearings) led by Robert Graham. For the French version, we benefitted from the superb work of Francine Watkins, while communications were very professionally handled by Diana Crosbie Communications.

Having identified all these potential obstacles, I have to say that I enjoyed fully and with great satisfaction the twenty months of Ontario's Royal Commission on Learning. We decided to have our public hearings all over the province and quite early in the game. Our public consultations started in the fall of 1993, lasting over twelve weeks in twenty-seven cities across the province. We heard 1,396 groups and individuals: parents, students, teachers, trustees, school administrators, business representatives, and more. We benefitted from extensive media coverage. Commissioners, staff, and volunteers also visited detention centres, jails, homes for pregnant teens, multi-service agencies, and cultural organizations in thirty-six meetings and focus groups. After all, we had to offer ideas for the future education of the more than two million students enrolled in the elementary and secondary schools in Ontario, anglophones and francophones. We heard a distinct sense of unease and uncertainty about the educational system. Accountability, or lack of it, also came up regularly in the presentations.

Gerry Caplan and I made a point of listening to teenagers where they hung out; we ended up sitting on floors in the middle of commercial malls, splitting pizzas with young people who were ready to join us and tell us what they thought of their education. It was most interesting and revealing. They also came to the public hearings. Nobody recommended doing away with Grade 13, but it was from the teenagers' descriptions that I made up my mind that we had to recommend it. I knew it did not exist anywhere else in Canada, was unnecessary, and was costly, especially when these young students told us how boring it was, with not enough to learn in some years. So Grades 9 to 12 simply had to be redesigned and their teaching compacted, so to speak. Those teenagers were also the source of the importance we gave to learning more than just the official languages.

We had neither the time nor the money to travel abroad and exchange on education at an international level, and I do not think we missed it, although it is always an enrichment to see what others are doing and why. Personally, mid-October 1993, as I was in Paris for the second meeting of my Population Commission, the France-Canada Association organized a presentation in the Senate where I would introduce our Royal Commission on Learning. At the formal lunch, their minister of education, François Bayrou (future candidate in the presidential election 2002, 2007, and 2012), promoting private schools in the centre-right government of Édouard Balladur, and appointed at the same time we started our commission, could not have been more arrogant and lightweight, his conversation being on *"ma cabane au Canada"*! I can only hope that other people attending the event gained something out of my talk.

From early on – it was a passion of Gerry Caplan's but also a curiosity and a big question mark for me – we spent time at St Joachim School in the Dufferin-Peel Roman Catholic School Board, where computers were not just the domain of students and teachers in regular classrooms. The school had computers in the classrooms used by the child/youth worker, ESL, and special education and resource teachers. In addition, there were workshops that involved parents. The school was using computers to communicate with students in Kentucky, Louisiana, and Maryland! That school impressed the two of us the most, as we give it as a "success story" in the fourth volume of our report, but more because I never forgot watching these young students communicating by computer with their peers in American states from north to south, following the long annual fall pilgrimage of our monarch butterflies to Michoacán, Mexico!

A revelation for me was the discovery of how the Accelerated School Project developed by the US economist and educator Henry M. Levin was a pedagogical project that could transform education. He established it in 1986 and was, at the time of our commission, director of the National Center for the Accelerated Schools Project at Stanford University. I just loved the concept: all so-called at-risk students – very poor, in remedial programs, in repair programs, Black minorities in big city slums, etc. – instead of being lifted are slowed down even more by the efforts to catch up with what they missed. Levine came up with an idea: "Why not try to accelerate students?" The more the efforts to remediate, the more these cohorts will always lag behind. By accelerating the learning process, they are motivated to give the best of themselves and see themselves not just catching up but eventually at the head of the class. The enriched approach, the one reserved for so-called gifted and talented children, is used here based on the idea that at-risk populations do not exist. What do exist are at-risk situations.

In Ottawa, Gerry and I also spent hours simply sitting without a word at the back of kindergarten and Grade 1 and 2 classes. The way time is experienced in these educational settings in comparison with classes of grown-ups, teenagers, or students had a lot to teach me. In small kids' classrooms, time feels suspended and could appear quite irritating for driven bodies like Gerry and myself. With very young children, we were, of necessity, back in agrarian time, so to speak, where one takes the time needed. Slowly, we will enter the industrial time, linear, busy, and active or activist.

When we started thinking how to frame our analysis and our report and recommendations, I immediately realized that, in comparison with reflecting about medicine and health care, for which critical analytical frameworks had been developed, I had never heard of the equivalent for education as a system. I had no frame of reference. Further to discussion between ourselves and our senior staff, we came up with the idea of offering the students "a curriculum for literacies" (from the French word). The levels of literacy will vary with age groups, but what remains constant is that literacy always focuses on enquiry, expression, and understanding.

What satisfied me enormously is when we came to agree to develop four "engines or levers for change," over and above the more than a hundred recommendations we had slowly developed on the most vital areas of education reform. We then identified critical intervention points in the system, with a view to initiating change within these areas, which could move the system in the direction of reform. These four "engines" (sorry for the mechanistic term) would be:

1 Early childhood education (particularly dear to me because of my past work with Drs Fraser Mustard and Dan Offord)
2 Teacher professionalization and development (almost all Ontario Faculties of Education were not of the level of teaching and research expected in a university)
3 Information technology
4 Community-education alliances

More specifically, our first motor of change read: "By providing better learning opportunities for very young children at three years instead of four, and full time instead of half time – schools can positively affect what comes after."

The very last months of the commission had been difficult. At the beginning of December 1994, after a major leak of a few key recommendations of our report to the media, a nightmare in itself, my co-chair disappeared without explanation, coming back for the report launch on 25–26 January. With our gifted and committed small team, Raf Di Cecco and the researcher-drafters of the report, we were almost alone full time at the commission's offices for the last two months, except for Dennis Murphy. I could always count on his assistance and good ideas. We did not always agree, but he was always there with ways out of the problem of the day. For example, we owe him the innovative interactive CD attached to the report, a first in Canada. In the same way, we owe Gerry Caplan the short version of the four-volume report which benefits from his journalistic talent to present difficult concepts and issues in a friendly and lively way. And the title, *For the*

Love of Learning, was suggested by Manisha Bharti. We jumped at her suggestion and approved the title at once. And I borrowed it in turn for a chapter of these memoirs.

On 26 January 1995, we launched our unanimous 550-page report in four volumes accompanied by an 83-page short version, including an interactive CD-ROM version, presented in a solid box, one set in English and one in French. We had devised 167 recommendations, and I now realize that "my" 1970 Royal Commission on the Status of Women in Canada also had ... 167 recommendations! I am quoted as follows:

> "This is a report that is both idealistic and practical," said co-chair Bégin. "There is no question that, even taking into account the economic situation, we have the capacity to forge a truly excellent, high-quality education system. This is what thousands of Ontarians, parents and students alike, told us they expect. Despite the apparently contradictory demands made of the school system, we sensed a substantial agreement: people want to do what is best for our youngsters. It won't be easy, but it's possible. The only question is whether we have the will to start, and I believe we do."

Early childhood education, the very first recommendation of our report, was killed on the spot by the knee-jerk reaction of Mike Harris, who, five months later, in June 1995, became the Conservative premier of Ontario with his "Common Sense Revolution." At our official launch of *For the Love of Learning*, Mike Harris simply told the media, "It's the dumbest idea I've ever heard! Tiny kids strapped to their desks with their baby bottle!"

Our report was very well received by the population and by the educational milieu in Ontario and in other provinces as well, and it is still considered a valuable reference document.

In June 1995 I quietly met with and was well received by Harris's new minister of education and training, the original and successful businessman John Snobelen, explaining and pleading, but to no avail, as the Harris government wanted to break the teacher unions and, if possible, privatize whatever they could of the educational system. After that and up to November 1999, over close to five years, I accepted every invitation in the province to explain and sell our report *For the Love of Learning*, discussing with professionals, faculties of education (who badly needed serious upgrading and professionalization), community groups, and Franco-Ontarian associations, doing newspaper, radio, and television interviews, participating in town hall meetings organized by the Atkinson Foundation on early childhood education, and so on. I was as much of a champion as I could be, selling ideas rather than attacking the Harris government.

When I started telling the story of this Ontario Royal Commission on Learning, which I co-chaired, I mentioned that I had spent 21–23 April in Paris, at the UNESCO offices, attending my first meeting of the International Independent Commission on Population and Quality of Life (ICPQL), chaired by Maria de Lourdes Pintasilgo, for I was in two commissions at the same time!

So I had been to the first meeting of this international commission, when everyone discovers the other members, tries to understand what goes on, and what the mandate is all about. It was not going to be simple! Although I admired, trusted, and cherished our chair, who became a personal friend, transparency was truly lacking. To start with, the origins of this new independent international commission were never clear to me, although I learned long after that two meetings of international population/family planning leaders and NGOs concerned by the "population explosion" challenge had taken place, one in December 1991 in London, England, and the other in March 1992 at Bellagio, Italy. Our commission was funded by the Rockefeller Foundation, in association with the MacArthur Foundation, the Ford Foundation, the Hewlett Foundation, and the Population Council, all from America. Seven countries, including Canada, also funded the commission's work; I was never made privy to what the Canadian funding contribution had been. The chair was remunerated but not the other commissioners, except for our travel and living expenses at the time of meetings or public hearings.

We understood at that first meeting that we had been set up in the wake of the Brundtland Commission, the World Commission on Environment and Development (1983–87), charged to define "a global agenda for change," an offspring of the United Nations General Assembly but an independent commission. Its famous report, *Our Common Future*, led to the no less successful Rio Conference of 1992, the United Nations Conference on Sustainable Development, under the leadership of Canadian Maurice Strong, who had also been a member of the Bruntdland Commission.

Besides our chair, we were nineteen commissioners in equal numbers of women and men, nine from the North and nine from the South. There was no vice chair or the equivalent, although with the passage of time our chair used me in most official situations as her vice chair during the commission and after at all the international conferences where we were presenting and discussing the report and possible follow-up action. The only name I knew around the table was that of Bernard Kouchner, co-founder of Médecins sans frontières, who had just lost his mandate of health minister of France further to the Socialist Party parliamentary electoral defeat on 28 March 1993; I recall seeing him only once at our meetings, as he had soon become elected to the European Parliament. The only person I knew, however, was Alexander Yakovlev, who had been "exiled" as Soviet ambassador to Canada for ten years (1973–83), becoming a friend of Pierre Trudeau. He is considered the "godfather of glasnost" and the intellectual force behind Mikhail Gorbachev's perestroika. At the time of the Population Commission, he was an academician, chairing the state-owned Ostankino television station for Yeltsin, the first president of the Russian Federation. Exchanging with Yakovlev at meals or coffee was a rare treat.

There were many interesting commissioners. Several were activists back home for different causes. The feminist colleague sociologist from India, Vina Mazumdar, whom I presented earlier in these memoirs when I spent time in New Delhi in 1998, was one. So was Anders Wijkman, then the DG of the Agency for Research Cooperation with Developing

Countries, the Swedish "IDRC" and only other such institution in the world. From the Philippines, Karina Constantino-David, with whom I was asked by Maria Pintasilgo to later structure and write parts of the report, also a sociologist, had been the DM for Social Welfare and Development and was then professor of community development at the University of the Philippines. It was both fun and easy to work with her. Ruth Cardoso, an anthropologist and exceptional human being, was a long-standing personal friend of Maria de Lourdes Pintasilgo. Her husband, Fernando Enrique Cardoso, was then the minister of finance of Brazil, elected its president the year after. Ruth, an academic, spoke beautiful French and English and was a low-key but determined advocate in Brazil for agrarian reform, the legal status of NGOs, and the integration of social programs under the *Bolsa Familia*. The Dutch Jan Pronk, an academic economist who had just retired as a Labour parliamentarian and minister for development cooperation, was involved in refugee and migrant issues, peacekeeping challenges, and sustainable development. In the twenty-first century he would become a UN assistant secretary-general and deputy secretary-general of UNCTAD, a truly committed policy and program individual. I could speak of more colleagues of that commission, but I will end with a word about a formidable politician and personality, a special colleague: General Olusegun Obasanjo, the former commander-in-chief and president of Nigeria who had handed over power to a democratically elected civilian president in October 1979, by then recycled as a farmer. Arriving in his grand African regalia and dress, he actively participated in the meetings of the commission up until mid-1995, when he was arrested, jailed, tortured, and secretly tried, finally freed in June 1998, after the death of the November 1993–98 dictatorship of Sani Abacha. His arrest happened shortly after our commission meeting in Sintra, Portugal, and we never saw him after. In the following democratic elections, Obasanjo would become Nigeria's president for the second time, from 29 May 1999 to 29 May 2007.

Despite a collection of impressive personalities, the problem of that commission, the way I experienced it, was that it was unable to coalesce as a group. Reflecting on the situation today, I would conclude that it was due to the extraordinarily fragmented structure of work adopted by Maria de Lourdes Pintasilgo, splitting responsibilities between different unconnected individuals, including some commissioners, in parallel "silos" or entities, never linked between them, each reporting directly to the chair. She had hired on her own the services of an international bureaucracy under Pierre de Senarclens, which she dropped at one point in 1994. At all times, however, she enjoyed the total loyalty and benefitted from the competence of a tiny nucleus of advisors and support staff that she knew from previous experience.

A potential threat to our very raison d'être from the outside world was the International Conference on Population and Development, coordinated by the United Nations, which took place in Cairo on 5–13 September 1994, and the resulting program of action became the agenda of the UN Population Fund. Some 179 countries adopted a bold new vision for reproductive health and rights for the future. As it was reported on the web, "By placing the causes and effects of rapid population growth in the context of human development and social progress, governments and individuals of all political, religious, and cultural backgrounds could support the recommendations. Although there were ideological and religious differences over issues such as definitions of reproductive health, adolescent sexuality, and abortion, all but a few nations fully endorsed the final program." But publications following the Cairo Conference usually conclude that it was the participation of NGOs that transformed the Cairo Conference. This is also the approach our ICPQL had in mind when it started its work. And it was at such a negative conjuncture that Maria de Lourdes Pintasilgo was at her best as an intellectual and a scientist, a generalist by choice, with a positive mind. She rejoiced that the very technical issues of demographic analyses and assessment of services and methods would have been covered comprehensively. For her, the opening of thinking brought by the Cairo Conference confirmed the value of the broader approach she was interested in pushing forward. She considered that both the Cairo Conference and the "Earth Summit" or Rio de Janeiro 1992 conference on the environment had set the directions she wanted us to explore.

During its existence, from April 1993 to the end of June 1996, we had only six meetings of the commissioners, all at the UNESCO offices in Paris, the fourth one having exceptionally taken place in the chair's country, in Sintra, Portugal – the last meeting with Olu Obasanjo as per my photo album. However, almost in parallel, regional public hearings – the importance of which I had convinced the commission, approved at its second meeting in January 1994 and a first for such an international body – were organized, starting in Harare, Zimbabwe, in December 1993, two months later! In fact its responsibility had been delegated to two commissioners, Olu Obasanjo (Nigeria) and Aminata Traoré (Mali), with the assistance of Leonard Appel's team and the participation of George Zeidenstein, a pillar of our public hearings. If one city was hosting public hearings, the co-chairs were joined by government officials for five or six surrounding countries. In addition to these activities, the Independent Commission on Population and Quality of Life also commissioned sixty-five "studies" from experts at the initiative of the chair and had two meetings of experts: one in Bellagio at the end of September 1993, the second one in Stockholm mid-May 1994. These activities are listed in our report, but I was never told of them.

I watched as many regional hearings videos as I could and read the related documents and testimonies, such as *Who Will Listen to My Voice?*, the report of our ICPQL African public hearings, a ninety-six-page document published in Paris in 1995. The testimonies from Africa were the most disturbing. They naturally reconnected me with my rant against the mid-1970s infatuation of most of our Canadian elites, and others around the Western world with the neo-liberalism" stemming from the monetarist theories. In many industrialized countries, the "safety net" of social security programs was eroded first by unemployment and successive recessions, then by deliberate cuts in programs.

This reduction in the safety net built through the years for citizens was accompanied by a renewed faith in the market forces and the need for competition at all cost. We witnessed free or freer trade, privatization of government operations and other public assets, downsizing of industries, and restructuring of public institutions. Small businesses faced bankruptcy. Jobs were lost by the millions, not just by the thousands. Inflation rates went up. Stagnant, frozen, or declining wages are still a reality. Coupled with the extraordinary developments in information technologies, untamed globalization then became unavoidable, a reality from which only a few benefitted and for which governments and civil societies were not, and are not yet, prepared.

International lending institutions in turn applied the same drastic remedy to developing countries. During the commission's public hearings in Africa, in both Harare (Zimbabwe) and Bamako (Mali), we kept facing ordinary people involved in local community development denouncing the famous Economic Structural Adjustment Policy (ESAP) imposed on their governments by the World Bank and the International Monetary Fund. "You, ESAP, you lied to me that all will be well!" they chanted to us. The general feeling coming from the testimonies heard was that, since independence, most African countries had come a long way in improving the status of their people. Women were still struggling, but the situation was a little comfortable. ESAP eroded all the gains made, and it was women and children who were bearing the strain.

There is no doubt in my mind that there was, in the Western world, government over-regulation, closed economies, protectionist trade policies, resistance to change from organized labour and rigid labour markets, holes and at times abuses in social programs, and ever-growing public deficits. In countries of Africa, Asia, and Latin America, beleaguered economies had to be reformed, corruption and diversion of public funds controlled. But if the remedies prescribed augmented the number of unemployed, of homeless and of *exclus* (excluded) of all sorts in countries of the North, the increased hardships created for large segments of populations in the South by adjustment programs have been, and still are, simply dramatic. For instance, at the time of our commission, Africa had about ten million street children. These street kids could also be found in Asia or in Latin America. Abidjan, Bogota, Manila (or New York, or Milan), or almost any megalopolis, even medium-size cities, were, still are, their home. Besides supplies of food and clean water at the survival level, basic health care and education have been hit the hardest. We could not be farther from the Alma Ata 1978 WHO's call of "Health for All by the Year 2000."

Occasionally, if I was going through Paris or Lisbon, Maria de Lourdes would spend hours with me discussing her philosophy for the report, with which I fully agreed. The challenge was to link the pieces together. In 1995, towards the end, deeply unsatisfied with what she was receiving from the regular staff, she had on her own retained the services of Paul Harrison, a British environmentalist with a PhD from Cambridge in earth sciences and geography, who had recently published *The Third Revolution*. She asked my colleague from Manila, Karina Constantino-David, and me to spend two days in Lisbon, working with Paul Harrison, before going to Sintra for the fourth meeting. I then undertook to write the chapter on health care, "From Medical to Health Care," part of the Part III of our report, entitled "From Vision to Policies." Harrison became the editor-in-chief of our final report.

The writing of our report drafts on such complex topics somehow interrelated was not going to be any easier than the functioning of the commission. Right from the very first meeting of our commission, a large and clear consensus emerged by which we privileged as a pivotal concept "quality of life," not "population (control)." Much later in our work, when trying to list the elements necessary for "quality of life," and the subjectivity of any such list, the commission, at the suggestion of Paul Harrison, came up with the observation that lies at the heart of our chapter 5: the sum total of the legal instruments of the United Nations proclaiming various "rights," if implemented, would give quality of life to the people of the world. We agreed that this international set of instruments was the best tool to give to the concept of quality of life an unquestionable and commonly shared operational meaning.

One recommendation was a very difficult one for China: our opposition to any form of direct or indirect coercion in family planning. Somehow, at the Sintra meeting, I became the one quietly negotiating with our colleague Professor Pu Shan – an economist, once the private secretary to former Chinese Premier Chou En-lai – for his support for the recommendation and for the whole report. Was it because of my modest three weeks in China as Canadian health minister? He had presented very good points regarding what "work" and working activities should mean, enlarging our definition to include service activities, for example. Not dogmatic, he was right, and we adopted his approach. We toned down the text of our recommendation in the final report, taking a pragmatic approach that voluntary family programs were far more effective to promote sustained use of contraceptives and the value of having small families. Since his death, China has instituted the Pu Shan Award, the most prestigious award in world economics.

Of all the recommendations, the ones related to the need for a global tax on financial dealings, a Tobin Tax, to fund our most important recommended programs were both reasonable and feasible. The commission had in mind a mere 0.01 per cent tax on international financial transactions, which would yield $150 billion a year to fund major international priority programs for development and environment. In a completely unanticipated way, this recommendation would haunt me at the launch of the report.

The launching had been fixed: the Commission Chair Maria de Lourdes Pintasilgo would table the report and recommendations in London, England, on 25 and 26 June 1996, then fly to the UN in New York, at a special launch at the Delegates Dining Room at lunch time on 28 June, and, from there, fly to Washington to launch it there at the beginning of July. Just before she left, she asked me to join her for the entire launching ceremonies, and I accepted. We were to meet in a good but not posh hotel in London on 24 June. A professional local PR man introduced himself to me but he was not interested in me at all. Maria finally arrived. I had not yet seen a printed copy of the report, not even a final draft, which I kept asking for, and that made me very nervous. We had a rapid dinner and went to our rooms on different floors. Mine was the usual tiny European one with a teenager's narrow bed, which I can't stand. I started looking through the report and went to bed, having to recuperate from the transatlantic flight. At 3 or 4 a.m. my phone rang; it was Maria, asking me to come to her room at once as she was feeling sick. I put a housecoat on and rushed to find her in her blood. She was very weak, asked me to call a doctor, and told me I had to take over the functions planned, which entailed being at the *Financial Times* television station at 7 a.m. to be interviewed on the report! I arranged with the hotel for a good doctor, phoned her ambassador, dressed, and was at the TV station in time, a complete automaton. Me, at the City, selling a Tobin Tax! I never felt more idiotic. I can't recall the rest of the day. The day after was the big press conference to be chaired by Maria's friend, Baroness Shirley Williams, whom I had received for lunch at 24 Sussex at the request of Prime Minister Trudeau's Office, in December 1974, when she was the new minister of state for prices and consumer protection in Harold Wilson's Labour government. I explained the situation, and she could not have been more gracious, saying she remembered me from Ottawa! She knew every reporter and media person, would act as the MC, and wished me good luck. We were at Regent's Park, at the Overseas Development Institute. It was understood that, after the press conference, I would be introduced at Question Period in the House of Commons. When I got back to my hotel I wished farewell to Maria de Lourdes Pintasilgo, very weak but relieved, taken by ambulance with Ambassador Antonio Costa Lobo, a loyal political old friend of hers, to the airport and back to Lisbon.

On Thursday, 27 June, I was at London Heathrow airport, where I spent hours reorganizing my tickets. I still can't believe my first decision: acting outside my standard norm, I took an airplane ticket to go back home in Ottawa for the night. Then, I rescheduled a ticket from Ottawa to New York for the next morning, in time for the lunch and launch at the UN, which went more or less well, with a small attendance, not surprisingly, as it was a gorgeous Friday and I was not the commission's chair. While still re-orchestrating my travel plans, I made another executive decision further to a phone call to my American colleague, Eleanor Holmes Norton, who completely concurred with me. I asked her to cancel the Washington appearances. It would have been the week of Canada Day (1 July) and of the US Independence Day (4 July). Nobody would have been there.

The good news is that Maria de Lourdes recovered very well, but I would learn that our joint travels were not yet completed! More than a year later, just when I had completed my mandate as dean of health sciences, she invited me to join her for an Eastern and Southern Africa seminar on our *Caring for the Future* report of the ICPQL, at the Faculty of Engineering of UDSM, in Dar-es-Salaam, Tanzania, which I accepted. When I arrived, I was greeted by the two usual friendly suspects, Drago Najman and Leonard Appel, but no Maria Pintasilgo, who was suddenly sick again. As what was becoming usual, from second violin, I was becoming orchestra conductor, while still not mastering our report and recommendations! So I did my best. Things were well organized, with Tanzania's ambassador to the UN, Gertrude Mongela, in the chair, a lively, strong personality. With us were leaders from surrounding participating countries: from memory, Kenya, Uganda, Somalia, and Ethiopia. On the last day there, probably the Sunday, 21 September 1997, my two "assistants" who knew Africa, took me to visit Zanzibar, a special exotic island with a dark slavery past.

A little more than two months later, Maria Pintasilgo invited me to join her again, this time in Dakar, Senegal, for a similar initiative, and this time with her there in person. The opening ceremony for the seminar took place at the University Cheikh Ante Diop, with the rector, Maria de Lourdes Pintasilgo, and Abdou Diouf, the president of Senegal. I was joined in the reserved seats by Kafui Kegba Dzodsi, MP from Togo, Aminata Traoré, of our commission, now minister of culture of Togo, Henriette Diabaté, ex-minister of culture of Ivory Coast whom I had met there as a minister, and a Senegalese sociologist, Fatou Sow, a friend when she was at the University of Ottawa. Our two consultants and friends, Drago Najman and Leonard Appel, were also there. During the seminar sessions, Maria and I were quietly taken away to see another Dakar, spending an afternoon with an old French community worker, Jacques, and the kids in a poor Peuls *bidonville* school in Dakar. Hard to forget and think it does not exist. I was also shocked, of course differently, by a visit to the Gorée Island and its physical remnants of the African slave trade. We were in Dakar from 3 to 8 December 1997.

Six months later, from 10 to 14 June 1998 in Jamaica, was the last of the seminars to which Maria invited me. After the commission I met her privately at her home in Lisbon, also in Paris, and we corresponded by mail until her death in 2004.

What remains unique to the report *Caring for the Future* of the Pintasilgo Commission (ICPQL) is that it offered timetables for action and financial funding through a modest global Tobin Tax. It also clearly stated, against the prevalent business opinion, that globalization and the free market economy new credo, far from being engines of development for the South, had instead exacerbated the gap between the rich and the poor. Thinkers and opinion-makers such as Hazel Henderson, the futurist and iconoclastic economist, have considered our report exceptional and innovative. But as far as I can judge, that report and its ideas never got the international recognition other commissions got in those years. In Canada, it was as if I had never contributed to circulating those important ideas about ensuring the quality of life. In 1998 I was invited to speak about and discuss the ICPQL report at Harvard and in Amsterdam at a European conference, and that was it. Otherwise, in Canada, my public speaking at the time covered more or less the Ontario Royal Commission on Education, the usual "medicare" challenges, and, of course, women's health.

My last international commission could not have been a more different experience. We were in 2005 and I was back as a visiting professor at the master in health administration program at the Telfer School of Management, University of Ottawa, after my unforgettable fall, learning Italian in Florence.

In February, when I was contacted by telephone by Sir Michael Marmot to discuss the possibility of my serving on the still unannounced WHO Commission on Social Determinants of Health, I had no idea who he was. In the course of our conversation, I observed to him that I had never heard of a commission whose mandate was written almost entirely in terms of "action." Usually commissions study, listen to presentations, undertake new research, report, and recommend. That is the end of their lives. I liked the action-oriented philosophy of this endeavour.

Familiar with the 1980 *Black Report*, as well as Margaret Whitehead's 1987 follow-up report, *The Great Divide*, which I used in my courses, I knew a bit about the existence of the Whitehall Studies I and II, which Marmot had led. However, as far back as 1993, in speeches on women's health, I had referred to and discussed the "social determinants" of women's health: gender, poverty, and violence. I knew the words, but I did not know the science behind them, or the research evidence. So I Googled "Sir Michael Marmot" to get to know him and his work. One of the very first texts I accessed was a long interview with him, conducted in March 2002 by Professor Harry Kreisler of the Institute of International Studies at the University of California at Berkeley.

I was fascinated. An internationally known scientist, a physician with impeccable credentials in epidemiology who had been a clinician in a cardiac clinic and a chest clinic — a "British empiricist" as Marmot calls himself — addressing the societal role in health, discussing individual versus societal causation of disease? I could not believe what I was reading. And right then, before I had been confirmed as a commissioner and we had met as a commission and shaken hand with Sir Michael, what surprised me most was his observation that, besides the classical factors leading to pathologies, much had to do with the degree to which people were able to participate fully in society. "We found clear social gradients in people's participation in social networks," he added. That was a very surprising observation, as the first Whitehall study was set up as a rather conventional study of ten years of risk factors for cardiovascular and respiratory disease in male British civil servants. In the 2009 excellent PBS series *Unnatural Causes*, Marmot would later say,

> We have strong evidence that there are two important influences on health in explaining the hierarchy in health. The first is autonomy, control, empowerment ... The second is what I loosely call social participation. It's being able to take your place in society as a fully paid-up member of society, as it were, to benefit from all that society has to offer. Now, in part that's social supports and social networks, but it also functions at a psychological level. It's self-esteem; it's the esteem of others. It's saying that I can benefit from the fruits that society has to offer.

I was thrilled to be confirmed as a commissioner. Later meeting Amartya Sen as a colleague commissioner was another rare privilege. In the same spirit as Marmot, in *Development as Freedom* (1999), he had also come to the same conclusion, having written, "The success of an economy and of a society cannot be separated from the lives that the members of the society are able to lead ... we not only value living well and satisfactorily, but also appreciate having control over our own lives." This would later correspond to the fact that the health status was a matter of social class – evidence hard to accept for Canadians

who like to think that we are deeply "egalitarian" country without social classes! The more power one had, the more healthy one was.

Having by then served on or chaired commissions – international,
national, and provincial – on 13 March 2005, when I landed in Santiago, Chile, for our first meeting (14 to 18), under the sun in a dry 27
degrees, I was excited that something new might be happening. I would
not be disappointed.

The international Commission on Social Determinants of Health had
been set up by the WHO director general, Dr Jong-wook Lee (who
would die suddenly in office on 22 May 2006), who knew Michael
Marmot's research work and truly believed that such an approach was
the way of the future. The commission would be in existence from
March 2005 to the end of August 2008. We were nineteen members,
including the chair. Our meetings would take place in countries that
had expressed the desire and provided the assistance required to host
us. Chronologically, the meetings took place in Chile (Santiago, March
2005), Egypt (Cairo, May 2005), India (New Delhi and Ahmedabad,
September 2005), Islamic Republic of Iran (Teheran, January 2006),
Kenya (Nairobi, June 2006), Brazil (Rio de Janeiro, September 2006),
Switzerland (WHO in Geneva, January 2007), Canada (Vancouver, June
2007), China (Beijing, October 2007), United States (New Orleans,
November 2007), and Japan (Tokyo and Kobe, January 2008). The
meetings usually consisted of a week, a day of which was reserved for
"participant observation" in the field, our group being split and sent to
suburbs, close-by villages, small communities in the mountains, etc. For
example, in India, during the September 2005 monsoon, a local interpreter from Ahmedabad accompanied me to a village to meet and learn
from members of the local newly created women farmers' co-op how it
had changed their lives, when they finally got rid of all the middlemen
who had sold the milk of their one or two cows, and we listened to their
plans for the future. I will never forget that experience. In Iran, where
the field visits had been planned for 17 January 2006, three commissioners, of which I was one, were transported to a mountain village
north of Teheran, where we met the community workers – the *beh-
varzan* – always working in pairs, a man and a woman, based at the

"health house," a successful primary care concept that should be copied everywhere in the world, including in our own country.

Michael Marmot's commissioners included Ricardo Lagos, the president of Chile, Pascal Mocumbi, former prime minister of Mozambique, Giovanni Berlinguer of the European Parliament; academics (the Nobel Prize–winning economist Amartya Sen, Fran Baum, Hoda Rashad, Denny Vagero, Kiyoshi Kurokawa, Yan Guo, and David Satcher); consultants (William H. Foege, former director of the Atlanta Center for Disease Control; Gail Wilensky); current or former ministers of health (Alireza Marandi, Charity Kaluki Ngilu, and myself); community workers (Mirai Chatterjee); and international officials (Anna Tibaijuka, Ndiorio Ndiaye).

We always met the head of state or president and some ministers and/or parliamentarians. So in Tehran, for example, it was the very day of our field visits, at the end of the afternoon, that we were to meet the eminent leader of the Islamic Republic of Iran, Ayatollah Khamenei. Sir Michael asked me to make a short presentation of our work, of which I later received the video … in Farsi! Upon arrival in Iran on 16 January (where we would be for four days), we were formally welcomed by President Ahmadinejad and twenty-one of his ministers. Later that morning we were introduced to Dr Hashemi Rafsanjani, the former president of the country, a smooth and classy operator. (No need to stress that we, the women, wore a long veil around our head at all times, completely covering our hair. And each commissioner was assigned a bodyguard.) Despite these formalities, we had good meetings with the staff of the Ministry of Health and of Social Affairs.

Before or after each meeting of the commission, my colleague Fran Baum, by then a good friend, and I would take three days to extend our visit on our own. In Iran, we discovered Isfahan, one of the most beautiful cities in the world, with a young female public health physician of the ministry, Dr Mehrnoosh Hadadi, whom we had befriended. I managed to visit her later in Baltimore. In Japan, it would be Kyoto; in Rio de Janeiro (1–7 September 2006), three favelas, the biggest one Rocinha (150,000 people), built on a steep hillside overlooking Rio, with a local man guiding us, and then Alemao with a young local physician, Dr Daniel Becker, joined by our colleague Alireza Marandi. These additional three days in Rio, by the way, were the highlights of the only commission meeting we all concluded had been a complete waste of our time. In China, Fran and I first stopped at Xi'an before joining the meeting in Beijing.

At the first meeting in Santiago, not yet knowing each other, we also met quite a number of senior WHO officials – WHO assistant director general Tim Evans, Jeanette Vega, and others. Paul Martin's Canadian minister of state for public health, Carolyn Bennett (who told me she had suggested my name), accompanied by Dr Elinor Wilson, then CEO of the Canadian Public Health Association, and many other people attended that whole first session of our commission. When introduced, Dr Bennett stated, "Finding strategies to improve these social determinants is equally, and in some cases more important than medical care and improving personal health behaviours." We introduced each other rapidly, and Michael Marmot started describing the purpose of our commission and the agenda for the week.

Shortly after, the WHO senior officials took over with thick documents, charts, and briefing books. We no longer existed. It very slowly became clear that these senior officials were in charge, that it would be their report, and that they had defined the commissioners as simply a board of directors with Michael Marmot as chair of the board, a "puppet" board. Without having yet had the time to even share a coffee among ourselves, some of us spontaneously started raising our hands, disrupting the formal presentations, politely asking questions about the objective of these heavy-handed briefings, and so on. No need to say I was one of them, and so was Fran Baum, as well as Stephen Lewis (who attended that first meeting and only one other, as he resigned because of his work as UN special envoy for HIV/AIDS in Africa), as well as a few other commissioners. At one point, pretty discouraged and wondering what was going on, Sir Michael called a coffee break.

I will always recall our Canadian Elinor Wilson, relaxed and laughing, explaining to Michael Marmot, everyone standing around with a coffee or another drink, a cookie or whatnot, that the apparent lack of order that had taken over was perfectly normal in any "group development." She went on, all of us mesmerized, quoting us Tuckman's teamwork theory and its four stages: forming, storming, norming, and

performing. Obviously, none of us had ever heard of it. Michael Marmot
was amazed and wrote down the four words. It completely relaxed the
atmosphere, and when we returned to the table, the tension loosened
somehow. It would take a few more meetings to make it clear to the officials that it was our commission, not theirs, and that the intellectual
leadership was originating with the chair and his research and work team
at the University College in London. (This power struggle of WHO officials' to take ownership of this prestigious commission would take some
time to calm down, and in truth never really died, creating problems behind the scenes for us. But it definitely became "our" commission.)

Back at Santiago, we were able to continue listening to the Geneva
officials but asked them to give us a historical overview of the philosophy on creating health of WHO through the decades. We then received
from a younger official a most interesting history of ideas and successive
philosophies of WHO since its creation in 1948. There have been great
strengths, great drawbacks and constraints, and there were now great
opportunities with Dr Jong-wook Lee at the helm. Although the social
dimensions of health were affirmed in the WHO Constitution of 1948,
these factors were downplayed during the 1950s and the 1960s, the era
of the "disease campaigns." In the 1970s the social determinants re-
emerged under the leadership of Dr Halfdan Mahler with the Health
for All agenda, and everyone interested in health – not health systems
– would remember Alma Ata (1978) and primary health care as the
strategy. Unfortunately, the 1980s can be viewed as the "Lost Decade,"
with a proliferation of strategies played in targeted, isolated silos, primary health care being the first victim. So primary health care as the
point of entry for everyone to any health system became reduced to maternal health or to child health or other limited targets, with UNICEF's
GOBI strategy as the centrepiece (the mnemonic for four essential
measures for the maintenance of child health in developing areas:
growth monitoring, oral rehydration, breast-feeding, and immuniza-
tion). Neo-liberalism took over in the 1990s, leading to a decade of economic reform and globalization, where themes were of efficiency of
bureaucracy and introduction of market economies in the health sector.
The young health economics discipline introduced new ways of mea-

suring resources and health achievements, influencing design of health systems financing and efficiency measures. We witnessed national budgets for health increase as percentage of GDP, while equitable distribution of services decreased.

It is believed that in the 2000s, the broader health and development context had evolved in ways that provided strategic openings for an explicit linkage between health and social development, as well as intersectoral action to address a major rebalancing of resources. At the time of our commission, the global development agenda was increasingly shaped by the Millennium Development Goals (MDGs), which called for coordinated multi-sectoral action. To quote from that paper prepared for us in Santiago, "Without progress in fighting poverty, strengthening food security, improving access to education, supporting women's empowerment and improving living conditions in slums, for example, the health-specific MDGs will not be attained in many low- and middle-income countries. At the same time, without progress in health, countries will fail to reach their MDG targets in other areas." Action in the health-care system was therefore only one of the influences of a population's health. Our commission thought there was a new opportunity to enlarge the problem definition and get to the "causes of the causes." And so on. Unfortunately, my complete electronic copy of that history as received in Santiago that day was destroyed in the cybercrime of which I was victim in March 2015, when absolutely every file, dossier, etc., of mine was encrypted against ransom to be paid in bitcoins. I would have loved to at least been able to identify the young WHO author of this history of ideas.

Later that week, President Ricardo Lagos launched the commission officially, and we were graciously received at the historical Palacio de La Moneda, in Santiago, by our colleague – the president! In fact Lagos would resume his participation in our meetings only at the end of his term in office, beginning of March 2006. At our first meeting, we also owed him a very interesting first field visit. In four small groups, we were taken to different poor suburbs to observe in action the famous Solidario program Lagos had launched, centred around the family, where health, education, socioeconomic needs, etc., were integrated in local programs. I was sent with colleagues Berlinguer, Marandi, and two Canadians (Elinor Wilson and C. Bennett's chief-of-staff) to Pudahuel. The time spent in the kindergarten, with kids from six months to five years of age, was the highlight of that day for me.

We agreed to our chair's proposal to have "knowledge networks" (KNs) set up by academics to explore key fields of necessary action, for our commission was not about studies – there existed plenty of them already – but their translation into action. During that first meeting, Michael Marmot asked me if I could stay one more week in Santiago, attending and making notes for the commissioners about the sixty or so academics invited to discuss how they viewed KNs and how they could contribute to such an approach. I accepted. The idea was to have eight such networks — international research teams, each working on a specific determinant of health. For example, one would be on social exclusion. We could have easily identified a dozen different determinants, but we focused on eight. Jennie Popay, professor of sociology and public health at Lancaster University, whom I rapidly noticed, was in Santiago that second week and would later chair a rich KN on social exclusion, which released a report titled *Understanding and Tackling Social Exclusion* (*A Person Is a Person Because of Other People* – from an African proverb), which I still consider a gem. It discussed country case studies both of situations and of processes of social exclusion as well as good practices in different parts of the world, and it offered recommendations to the commission for us to consider for our own final report.

Our final list comprised eight KNs, in no particular order:

- Early Childhood Development (Dr Clyde Hertzman, UBC)
- Urban Settings
- Employment Conditions
- Women and Gender Equity
- Diseases of Public Heath Importance
- Health Systems (IDRC and their South Africa project)
- Social Exclusion
- Globalization (Dr Ron Labonte, University of Ottawa)

Three networks were funded by and under the direction of Canadians. Only one KN, the one on employment conditions, did not work as planned and we had to replace it with a different team.

In a public conference in Toronto, still early in the commission's life, where Sir Michael was the keynote speaker, Bernice Downey, a community health worker in attendance as part of a support group for the commission set up by Public Health Canada, ran after Michael Marmot on his way to the airport and asked him where Aboriginal Canadians belong would. In what knowledge network? "Social Exclusion," was Marmot's immediate answer. "No way!," was Bernice's polite but firm reply. A very interesting and difficult new chapter of our work had just opened up. Bernice Downey was a nurse of Oji/Cree and Celtic heritage. (She is now Dr Bernice D., a medical anthropologist having earned a PhD in medicine at McMaster, where she is now on faculty, teaching Indigenous health.)

We started receiving very strong negative reactions, in particular from the Canadian First Nations, that they did not belong to the KN entitled Social Exclusion, for the very roots of their contemporary problems had a different and unique historical origin of lands, customs, and culture stolen or killed by European colonization. We were all taken by surprise, the more so because the KN on social exclusion was made up of very sensitive researchers. After discussion, we came to see the Indigenous peoples' viewpoint. The commission then created a special working group of three First Nations representatives with relatively comparable past history in contemporary settings: Canadian, Australian, and New Zealand Aboriginals. Fran Baum and I were the voices in the commission for this initiative, which culminated in an international symposium on the social determinants of Indigenous health in Adelaide, 29–30 April 2007. Canadian Aboriginal groups presented well-documented briefs, one example being that of the Native Women's Association of Canada.

For the duration of the commission and up to the end of 2012, I made as many public presentations on the commission and its approaches, or of the evidence of the social determinants of health at home and across the world, as I could. I spoke across the country at universities, NGOs,

learned societies, professional associations, and government meetings. I
accepted media interviews in the same spirit. I would stress how Canada
would brag that for seven years in a row the United Nations voted us
"the best country in the world in which to live." But did all Canadians
share equally in that great quality of life? No, they didn't. The truth was
that our country was so wealthy, and still is, that it managed to mask
the reality of food banks in our cities, of unacceptable housing, of very
high suicide rates among young Inuit and First Nations. At the time of
the commission, in Canada close to 1.5 million people, largely single
mothers and children, lacked safe and affordable housing, dealt with violence both in their homes and in their neighbourhoods, and faced serious food and nutrition insecurity. Out of 600, more than 100 First
Nations reserves had been, and still are, identified as lacking safe water
supply and sanitation systems, having substandard housing and inadequate community services. In 2005 (and after), several hundred people
from the Kashechewan Cree community near James Bay were evacuated
and temporarily housed throughout Ontario because of unsafe water.
Unfortunately, the people were sent back to their communities without
addressing the issues that created the crises in the first place.

Then and after the report launch, I kept speaking of our biggest challenge in Canada in truly addressing health inequity as being – to borrow
from a famous Canadian, John Kenneth Galbraith – that we had lived
in a "culture of contentment" for a good twenty-five years. It was a culture of contentment where long-term benefits were sacrificed for short-
term comfort, where we hated welfare and other programs for the poor,
and we loved tax cuts and new tax credits. It was relatively easy to feel
generous during the Affluent Society, and the 1960s saw the development of most of our social and health programs. We had leadership that
pushed for the "Just Society" for a while. We haven't heard of values
since. The only success story we have had in the last twenty-five years
is the alleviation of poverty of seniors as of mid-1984. There, public expenditures had made a dent into poverty. And "my" Child Tax Credit,
alive and growing, had helped mothers and children who were counting
every penny.

In general, poverty in Canada, when compared to other countries,
had become almost physically invisible. Horribly rundown neighbour-

hoods have often been gentrified, with their inhabitants being dispersed outside their community of origin. Appearances were misleading. We heard of, and (rarely) saw, small sections of our city streets with prostitutes or homeless persons. We concluded they were few, and they became cases of exception. In today's Canada, nobody believes that poverty is systemic, except eventually in the case of First Nations, but what could we do about it? I generally offered visual examples of the evidence of social determinants of health like this one. A little boy born in my hometown of Montreal had a life expectancy of:

- 79.5 years if born in the West Island or Hampstead,
- 68.6 years if born in Hochelaga-Maisonneuve, and
- 66 years if born in Downtown, Griffintown, etc.

Speaking of social exclusion, our meeting in India, after the official welcoming presentations in New Delhi, took place in Ahmedabad (Gujarat), the city of our colleague Mirai Chatterjee and the head office of her beloved Self-Employed Women's Association, a labour union registered in 1972, hosting our commission meeting. As this unique co-op movement describes itself, "It is an organisation of poor, self-employed women workers. These are women who earn a living through their own labour or small businesses. They do not obtain regular salaried employment with welfare benefits like workers in the organised sector. They are the unprotected labour force of our country. Constituting 93% of the labour force, these are workers of the unorganised sector." They have well over two million members, starting with over a million members in the state of Gujarat but in development in a dozen other states, reaching well over 650,000 members in Madhya Pradesh, for example. The village where I was sent for the field visit was one such women's co-op. We in the West do not give the same meaning to "small businesses." In India, it meant the women selling five coconuts or two dozen eggs in an alley.

At our second meeting, we, former and current ministers of health and other colleagues, figured out that, in order to engage countries – at least a number of them – in endorsing a "social determinants of health" perspective, we needed a few guidelines. I actively participated in these discussions as a result of my political observations of how social change could occur and how power worked. First would be the expression of a political will (signals from the top) at the highest level to apply a social determinants of health approach to reducing health inequities. Then ideally there would be the designation of a (senior) lead minister or VP (not necessarily the health minister) made responsible for the operation. Finally, an intersectoral or, ideally, a "whole-of-government" approach (and mechanism) would be needed, completed by the facilitation of community participation and ownership. At the end of our first year of existence, the following countries had expressed interest, and MOUs along those lines were signed with the following governments: India, Brazil, Iran, the United Kingdom, Sweden, Kenya, and Canada. Compared to other partner countries, in a way Canada's role unfortunately remained very "in house" around the Public Health Agency of Canada (PHAC), probably a result of the January 2006 change of government. We are not, definitively not, "going social determinants of health" anywhere in the country, and it is a pity.

In 2005, shortly after the commission's creation, PHAC, under the leadership of our first chief public health officer, Dr David Butler-Jones, set up a Canadian Reference Group (CRG), chaired by Jim Ball, one of his directors general, a network of some twenty members that met quite regularly. From PHAC the participants were Marie DesMeules, Heather Fraser, and others, together with someone from Health Canada and others across the country, such as Elinor Wilson (CEO of the Canadian Public Health Association), Bernice Downey (National Aboriginal Health Organization), and Margo Greenwood (National Collaborating Centre on Aboriginal Health). The CRG worked closely with our commission's secretariat in Geneva. With a few other countries, it contributes financially: for example, besides covering my travel expenses (commissioners were volunteers), the PHAC supported the work of the two Canadian KNs. I am referring here to Dr Clyde Hertzman and his team working on early childhood development in Vancouver, out of UBC, and to the group based at the Institute of Population Health at University of Ottawa, headed by Dr Ron Labonte and including Ted Shrecker, the KN on globalization and the public's health. A third KN, that on women and gender equity, based in South Africa, was also funded by Canada through IDRC. Canada also supported the Vancouver meeting of the commission, in conjunction with the Nineteenth International Union for Health Promotion and Health Education in June 2007. In Vancouver, we even invited Tony Clement, Harper's minister of health, to join us, which he did for a few hours. With a few other countries, the CRG undertook an analysis of "intersectoral action" and published in 2008 an excellent joint WHO-PHAC report entitled *Health Equity through Intersectoral Action: An Analysis of 18 Country Case Studies.*

The commission's report, presented in Geneva by Sir Michael Marmot to Dr Margaret Chan, director general of WHO, on 28 August 2008, started with a dramatic but evidence-based statement: "Social injustice is killing people on a grand scale." It challenged all countries to achieve health equity within a generation. It called for immediate action to lessen the impact of the structural and social conditions that negatively affect the health of all people. It was our hope that the commission's report might be one of a few international commission reports, like that of the Brundtland Commission on sustainable development (1987), that would have a real impact. At least, officials like Commonwealth ministers were already talking the language of social determinants of health! The report had over 200 recommendations, regrouped into three principles of action:

1 Improve the conditions of daily life – the circumstances in which people are born, grow, live, work and age;

2 Tackle the inequitable distribution of power, money, and resources – the structural drivers of those conditions of daily life – globally, nationally, and locally; and,

3 Measure the problem, evaluate action, expand the knowledge base, develop a workforce that is trained in the social determinants of health, and raise public awareness about the social determinants of health.

What I concluded long after the report had been made public was that, despite the evidence, countries' investments in and through the healthcare sector are *overwhelmingly confined to the provision of curative medicalized health services,* especially hospital services, rather than being channelled to prevention and health promotion. Moreover, when health promotion is incorporated at all, it is generally aimed at changing the behaviour of individuals rather than creating collective, physical, social, and economic environments that support healthy behaviour. In any case, an investment emphasis on new medical interventions tends to increase health inequities, because interventions reach more advantaged groups before, if ever, trickling down. On top of this, as being one of the world's biggest spenders in health care, we have one of the worst records in providing an effective social safety net. Simply continuing to chase new biomedical and technical interventions from the United States will clearly not be good enough. And again, when are we going to have real, working, inter-sectoral government approaches to Canadians' health and well-being?

No society can adopt the social determinants of health as the overarching goal of their government agendas without one more condition for action in addition to evidence-based research. "Going social determinants of health" is far from being a neutral proposal. As Professor Louis Charland, an ethicist, said at the University of Western Ontario, "Without facts, discussing social determinants of health is empty; without values, it is directionless." A discussion of values in societies followed by one on advocacy and the need to create the demand for reorienting health public policies are necessary at this point – values such as solidarity, sharing, fairness, inclusion, caring, or compassion, denouncing as Roy Romanow once wrote in the *Walrus* (June 2006), "unbridled competition [as] the new orthodoxy."

Conclusion

It's June 2014. I'm at the National Gallery of Canada in Ottawa at the Gustave Doré exhibit. Because I love my copy of *Les Fables de la Fontaine*, illustrated by Doré, I would not have missed this event. As I meander through the works of that great nineteenth-century French artist, I stop before reaching the next monumental grey/black painting, which depicts an intricate and action-filled scene. I hesitate to go nearer, as there is a man in a wheelchair studying it up close. With his great mane of white hair, he looks just like John Meisel, the Canadian political scientist and intellectual. And indeed it is him – ninety-one years old, visiting with friends from Kingston! We hug and say hello. Having recently read his *A Life of Learning and Other Pleasures: John Meisel's Tale* – a memoir full of life, irony, joy, and profound analyses, which I greatly enjoyed – I compliment him on it. As he has done before, he repeats that I should start writing my own memoirs at once. More precisely, this time he orders me to do so! I suppose that day I fell for his European charm and replied that I would think about it.

During my thirty years after life in politics, friends and strangers alike had repeatedly asked me to write my autobiography, my memoirs. My answer had always been a forceful *Never! No way!*

I always felt of two minds when it came to memoirs, which I enjoy reading. I remember a clipping from an October 1962 *Time* magazine that survived all my moves from one house to the next, quoting Oscar Wilde's "favourite paradox": "Man is least himself when he talks in his own person; give him a mask and he will tell you the truth." When I told Meisel of my reservations about the self-justification and preening of many memoirs, he agreed: "It is odd that often able and accomplished people feel the need to tell us how good they are. It diminishes them." Six months later, I sent him my first fifty-five pages. He encouraged me to continue. We emailed no more than four or five times since then; four years later, here are my memoirs (not my autobiography).

◆ ✳ ◆

I agreed to run for political office further to having observed, as the civil servant I had become, that being elected and joining Pierre Trudeau's government was a route faster than any other to accelerate the development and adoption of national progressive policies and programs in any domain. I felt at home with "the Just Society" and "participatory democracy." Decades later, I must conclude that elected politics gives an image of yielding much more power than it really has.

Recently I heard current observers of the political scene state that in the past – in Pierre Trudeau's time, for example, when I was there – it was still possible, although not easy, to bring about important policy changes and new programs, new legislation, relatively rapidly. In comparison, the current political scene in Quebec, in other provinces, and in Canada is perceived as one of inaction, deadlock, inertia. Having been there, I want to correct that perception. What has to be understood about governing in Canada is that the key concept is "gradualism": socio-economic change, and change in general, can be achieved, but in small, discrete increments and over time. That's what gave Canadians the Canada Health Act: adopting a small-steps strategy was the only approach possible. I lived the same slow, longer-term schedule for my other successful dossiers and legislation: in old age pensions, finally lifting all seniors above the poverty line, or in modestly starting a devolution of community health services to First Nations.

Contrary to what I have just said, one of my proudest moments as a politician – the creation of the innovative Child Tax Credit (now the Canada Child Benefit) – stemmed from a military coup, so to speak, turning a negative political circumstance into a positive one overnight. From the rejection of my May 1978 memorandum to Cabinet to create a Child Tax Credit, to its official announcement by the minister of finance at the end of August and its legislation approved by the two Houses in December, that revolutionary new social program took less than eight months! But that is not the rule.

Did I love my years of elected political life? Yes, I did, although I will always consider myself an accidental politician. I admired the role and accomplishments of an Allan J. MacEachen, but I could never have become a professional politician. I don't have what it takes. I was always project oriented, not a long-term institutional process player. The Manichean dimension of political life offended me greatly, not just in the House of Commons, but in parliamentary committee work, media coverage, public speaking, and more. What also upset me was the cynicism-as-total-distrust that the entire political process breeds, although I find essential an attitude of doubt or a disposition to incredulity. And I most regret what I saw starting at the end of Pierre Trudeau's government, namely how the use of innovative, instantaneous media communication technologies has turned politics (in its best sense) into a superficial instantaneous game.

I consider myself particularly lucky to have served under Pierre Trudeau as prime minister: because he was a man of values and beliefs that I share, because of his culture and his solid legal expertise, and because he had a sense of our country and its components. The notion of governing, under Pierre Trudeau, did include discussing ideas, ideals, and values. I was lucky to have senior colleagues, and I owe much to them. They were not mentors; if mentorship existed at that time, it was not my experience. I am thinking of pillars of government who appear in the pages of this book, who gave me opportunity after opportunity. My other good fortune was to have been appointed and then reappointed minister of national health and welfare over some seven years, from September 1977 to September 1984 (with a nine-month interruption when the Liberals were in Opposition, leaving me time to pause and reflect). Without asking for it, I inherited a well-established, well-structured, huge department with competent leaders and staff. It did not take me long to figure out that deputy ministers or assistant deputy ministers are, as a rule, generalists, not experts – "spokespersons" for the civil servants responsible for the daily issues and dossiers. (And, yes, I did get impatient with their culture of second-guessing the minister!)

When necessary, I asked the people at the top to bring with them the people on the front lines. Finally, I was surrounded and exceptionally supported by a dynamic, pleasant, and very competent political staff. Unfortunately, they suffered from my quick temper at times. On a personal level, I always nurtured a few clear and important objectives for action, wherever I was.

With the benefit of hindsight, are there dossiers that could have been handled differently? Probably. The Canada Health Act is one case where I might have gone for what both the experts and the supporters of medicare were recommending: doing away with the fee schedule structure to pay physicians and expanding coverage to other health-care practitioners (in addition to physicians). I judged it impossible to take that risk at the time. And it is still a major problem in the optimal functioning of our thirteen provincial health-care systems. One thing is sure: my crusades while in politics – the Child Tax Credit, pension reform, saving medicare – are still key challenges today, both in Canada and far more dramatically in the United States.

I never expected that health, as a huge field of human concern and action, would define the rest of my professional life, even to this day. And would take me to develop the new field of "women's health" outside of medicine. Circumstances offered me knowledge and a unique perspective on, appreciation for, and familiarity with health and health care. Frequent speaking invitations as well as new academic and voluntary commitments, and the fact that I chose early on not to be politically partisan, turned me into a credible voice, saying or writing about what many think but cannot express – an elder's voice, you could say.

However, if my new academic roles after 1984 reinforced my previous public role in health, they were lived very differently. I found it difficult to suddenly find myself completely alone, working as an academic. For the previous twenty-five years, I had worked as part of a team, both out of necessity and by choice. I loved it. In academic life, for the longest time, I felt lonely. I also found the hierarchical structure of universities to be obsolete, their power structure impervious to change, and their institutional culture, macho and sexist. In politics, at least everyone had to be elected! It was when I was teaching full-time, first during my four years in women's studies, then later in the 2000s with my classes of the master of health administration, that I was able to bond with the students in a rewarding way.

◆❋◆

On a more optimistic note, I deeply believe that the most extraordinary revolutions of my times, more precisely of the twentieth century, are those of decolonization and of feminism's second wave, both of which started in the 1960s. In different ways, they each brought to humankind the key ingredients of democracy and civilization: freedom, autonomy, and dignity of the person.

Decolonization, the undoing of colonialism, was not always achieved peacefully – far from it. However, in country after country, on entire continents and subcontinents, it went on. Unfortunately, the historical origins of colonialism are still at the roots of horrible tribal wars in Africa and other parts of the world. In Canada we are still trying to undo the damage of our own colonialism as experienced by Indigenous peoples. I see hope for real progress for the first time in our history, with the recent creation of the new Department of Indigenous Services under Minister Jane Philpott. When turning to the lot of women in Canada and around the world, despite all that remains to be done, people my age have witnessed remarkable progress. When I was first elected, women made up 1.8 per cent of the House of Commons. There are more women MPs today, but they still comprise only 26.3 per cent of the House of Commons, close to fifty years later! As is said in China, where is the other half of the sky? I lived through "equality of opportunity and equity," then through "equality of outcome." Those concepts and metaphors like "breaking through the glass ceiling" do not address the origin of many deeply rooted social problems such as sexual abuses and harassment. Behind each of these "equality objectives," Man stands as the norm. I am not interested in being equal to men. I want the roots of patriarchy to be addressed. As the late Belgian feminist philosopher Françoise Collin wrote, "Equality is a principle of assimilation, not a concept of social transformation."

For me, Nelson Mandela will remain the hero of nurturing democracy. He and the admirable Simone Veil are my two heroes. Writing this

today, I see clearly for the first time that they embody the best of decolonization and of feminism, respectively.

Our past always catches up with us. I have spoken in these memoirs
of how I had the extraordinary good fortune to have first been appointed executive secretary to the Royal Commission on the Status of
Women in Canada, then to lead or be a member of three major commissions of inquiry, chairing the one on education for Ontario (1993–
95) in parallel with participating in the international commission on
Population and Quality of Life, in continuation with the Brundtland
Commission on the environment and development. Finally, from 2005
to the end of 2008, I served under Sir Michael Marmot's leadership on
the International WHO Commission on Social Determinants of Health,
a unique experience.

I should confess that after the WHO report had been tabled, while
talking about it to Canadians and in public speaking in the United
States, I realized I had repeatedly bragged about Canada as the Sweden
of the Americas. I made that claim in good faith, seeing Canada as a
model of social and economic justice and well-being. But as I said when
apologizing publicly in an interview with the *Province* in December
2008, "Well, I made a huge mistake." We revel in thinking of Canada
as a great place to live, a society that is not afraid of offering both universal medicare and a safety net to its people. We see this as our trade-
mark in North America. But how much of it was a myth?

I discovered my error when checking the 2005 OECD report on total
public social expenditure for twenty-nine countries, by percentage of
GDP, for 1980–2001. Canada was the twenty-fourth on the list in welfare spending, followed by Japan, the United States, Mexico, and Korea.
Ahead of Canada were twenty-three European countries (including
Poland, the Czech Republic, Hungary, and the Slovak Republic). For
some reason, I was not familiar with comparative international social
expenditures statistics at the time. To complete that saga, in the spring
of 2017 I received a request from an American economics journal for a
short article on my biggest mistake, a request made to several academics. So I have now apologized both to Canadians and to Americans.

◆ ✳ ◆

My life has been so full of rich experiences, compelling projects, and interesting people. From the age of thirty-six and for the next twelve years of my life, I was as dedicated to politics as can be. I loved those years. I lived them to the fullest, with great satisfaction, being at the heart of a world attained by few men and even fewer women. Then I discovered the multi-faceted life of an academic, also very public and full of challenges and surprises. Quite often, through these decades, in order to survive, I had to resort in my heart of hearts to my metaphor of the solitary traveller in faraway lands, where the locals are strange and the mores incomprehensible.

I have but two regrets. My parents died too young – first, my father in 1964, and then my mother in 1967. I would have loved to have had them with me when I was first elected as a member of Parliament in 1972. When Mom died, I was finally earning the first decent salary of my life, and would have taken her on trips to Europe. My other great regret is not having had the money to do the eight years of the Quebec classical college full-time, as my friends from elementary school did. To this day, I long for the integrated intellectual knowledge this institutional system would have given me. Still, it has been a life of adventure from the beginning, and I have been so fortunate!

Acknowledgments

My last chapter started with the story of how I owe to John Meisel, in June 2014, the push to embark on this project. I never regretted it. Still, it never crossed my mind that writing one's memoirs would be such a long, uninterrupted, full-time, and demanding task. I have always enjoyed writing. I love writing!

With already some 135 pages typewritten, in French of course, one morning at the end of March 2016, I lost all my computer files through criminal encryption. And yes, I had not regularly saved my files. Overwhelmed by this setback and ready to quit, friends Charlotte Gray, Edith Cody-Rice, and Judith Erola challenged me to just get up and start all over again. After having my computer cleaned of the criminal encryption, I went back to the keyboard. But I wrote in English this time, as I no longer felt creative in French, as if I was repeating myself again and again. (Pre-encryption, I had in parallel to my memoirs agreed to be interviewed about my public life for a series published in French by Boréal, Montreal: *Entretiens, Monique Bégin*, by Daniel Raunet, released in October 2016.)

Another unanticipated shock was that my famous elephantine memory went on holiday. But with practice, many recollections resurfaced, at times almost on command! Memory can definitely be challenged, with surprising successes. The writing of these memoirs has not followed the traditional path of teams of researchers backing up the development of the chapters, even writing them with the author. Only while a Cabinet minister did I work with others on speeches, documents, press releases, and more. I much enjoyed working in teams, but not when it comes to

writing for myself, like these memoirs, a solitary adventure of discovery.
I simply worked with my old agendas! I do have an archival holding (*un
fonds d'archives*) at Library and Archives Canada in Gatineau about my
ministerial years but did not feel a need to go and consult it. For no particular reason, I had kept my desk and pocket daily agendas since 1960,
neatly organized in boxes in my locker. They moved with me from one
home to the next, yet I never consulted them. The older ones, when a
student in Paris, are tiny French notebooks for a purse. At one point, in
my prime, they turned into the large daily desk agendas from the
Economist, with beautiful red leather covers and my name engraved in
gold, and the corresponding small thin black leather ones. From there,
the quality dropped as they turned into lifeless, anonymous, cheap business agendas. All of them offered only names of people to meet or places
to go – when they did! They were supplemented by my four dozen photo
albums, faithfully annotated, including photos from my earliest days in
Rome and Paris, recovered from France after the war. Here and there,
photos reminded me of ministerial trips to Indigenous communities, political barbecues, or official trips abroad. As expected, I first went to consult and print some past Hansard pages at the welcoming Law Library
of University of Ottawa. Once having figured out the types of parliamentary documents I was after – House and Senate debates, committee
records, budgetary estimates – I corresponded by email with the Reference desk of the Library of Parliament, receiving rapid, courteous, and
very professional assistance from Michaël Dumais, Josée Gagnon, Chris-
tianne Gareau, and Louise Ouimet through the years. Very special thanks
go to them.

My other thanks go first to my old friends when we were university
students in Montreal who read my first chapters in French, a practice I
discontinued later: Monique Coupal, Renée Dandurand, Raymundo de
Andrade, Micheline Dumont, Mireille and Fernand Fontaine, Rodrigue
Johnson, and Chantal Perrault.

I owe many specific recollections and clarifications of events to
friends and former colleagues going back to politics and the civil service,
whom I meet regularly as members of the Round Table lunches, referred
to in the *Ottawa Citizen* as "the most exclusive club in Ottawa," whose

chairs in my years included Gordon Robertson, Arthur Kroeger, Si (James) Taylor, and Maureen O'Neil. I have named some in the memoirs and I want to thank them here. I have also mentioned past collaborators: MPs and ministers of my days, my political staff, and officials to whom I owe a lot. We will see if their names can stay in the various chapters or transferred to these acknowledgements.

Reviewing my years in academic life and my community engagement on boards and committees, I owe a lot of memories to Linda Assad-Butcher, Raf Di Cecco, Jeannette Giroux, Louis Maheu, Frank Reardon, Marilyn Schneider, as well as Thérèse and Robert Sévigny.

Thank you, Naomi Griffiths, always the historian, for having recommended from the start that I never forget giving the temper of the time! Very special thanks go to Charlotte Gray, Edith Cody-Rice, my former Cabinet colleague Judith Erola, and Caroline Andrew, "my literary team," honest but non-judgmental, always there for encouragement and decoding the art of writing for me. That is when I first heard the word, and importance of, "a grabber" – the French *incipits* – of a first sentence, a first chapter, and so on! One of my best critics and early fans was my much younger multilingual friend from Hamburg, Catherine Vandermeulen. She observed at once when I switched to writing in English that she almost preferred it as my story was more direct, more punchy!

Finally, Anne Louise Mahoney appeared in my life in early spring 2017, further to learning from "my literary team" of my Gallicisms, syntax, and more challenges when thinking in French and writing in English. I was shocked. Had I suspected the problem, I would have faced the issue head on from the start. A professional editor and a pleasant collaborator, Anne Louise Mahoney copy-edited the first three chapters and three others, and I thank her for that last-minute special collaboration.

Last but not least, it is my pleasure to thank Philip Cercone from my heart as well as his McGill-Queen's University Press team! Chronologically, I had the pleasure of dealing with managing editor Ryan Van Huijstee, Filomena Falocco and Jacqui Davis of marketing, editorial assistant Joanne Pisano, Kathleen Fraser, associate managing editor, Judy Dunlop, who developed a great index, and others who will take this manuscript to life and then to the outside world! Finally, this story could not be read, let alone appreciated, without the thoughtful, professional, and elegant copy editing of Ian MacKenzie. Thanks also to the three anonymous reviewers for their insightful feedback and suggestions. I owe them a lot. I particularly enjoyed the team spirit and empathic attitude of each one I got to interact with on the challenging task of turning my typewritten pages into a good book.

Index

The abbreviation MB refers to Monique Bégin; NHW refers to National Health and Welfare; PET refers to Pierre Elliott Trudeau.

guage courses, 149; mandate letters, 255; MB on gender of, 341–5; media discussions, 340; meeting preparation, 339–40; ministerial responsibility, 414–15; parliamentary secretaries, 129; PET's view as responsible adults, 163, 337, 353; rank of power of, 344; silos approach, 169, 339; social elites, 344–5; super committees, 168–9, 338; training for role, 148, 149; women's issues, 345. *See also* assistant deputy ministers (ADMs); deputy ministers (DMs)

monetarist policies and neo-liberalism: about, 185–6, 461–2; free markets, 472–3, 480; global impacts, 198, 461–2, 472–3, 476, 480; impact on MRC, 178; impact on NHW, 198–9; MB's resistance to, 247–8; PET's economic policies, 136–7; welfare state dismantling, 185–6, 476

Montreal University Women's Club, 54

Morin, Albanie, 88, 97, 102–3, 123, 149

Morrison, Alex, 166, 167(t), 283–7, 294

MRC. *See* Medical Research Council (MRC) (NHW)

Mulroney, Brian: Canada Health Act support, 274; devolution of Aboriginal health services, 230; election (1984), 323–4, 329; ending of universality of social programs (1989), 201–2; health transfer policy framework (1989), 230; Indigenous health professionals, 232; Meech Lake Accord, 313–14; omnibus bills, 202; opposition leader, 266; palliative care, 288; pay equity, 72; on PET's political appointments (1984), 319; Thérèse-Casgrain Award, 209

National Action Committee on the Status of Women (NAC), 75

National Collaborating Centres (Health Canada), 408

National Council of Welfare, 202, 323

National Council of Women, 71

National Forum on Health (1994–97), 420–1

National Health and Welfare (NHW), Minister (1977–79, 1980–84): acting prime minister (1984), 328; appointment and reappointments, 163–4, 246, 296, 303, 317, 326; block funding (1977), 164, 235–6; budgets, 164–5, 191–2; cabinet super committees, 168–9, 338; Carleton Affair (McDonald Commission), 183–4; devolution of powers for Aboriginal health, 216–17, 230–1, 247; DMs and ADMs, 165, 167–70, 167(t), 240–4; election (1979), 241–4; election (1980), 246, 303; EPF funding, 186; GAI support, 182–3; MB's housing, 349–50; MB's meeting with PET, 353; MB's reflections on, 296–300, 483–4; MB's speech on social policy myths, 189–90; media coverage, 164, 182–4; monetarist policies (neo-liberalism), 185–6, 198; nursing officer, 165; opposition critic (1979), 244–6; parliamentary secretaries, 296; payments as mailed cheques, 194; payments as tax credits, 194; PET's support for, 255, 266–7, 270–1; Quebec referendum, 305; research and planning, 187, 193, 198, 202; staff reductions, 191–2; universality debates, 184–6, 189, 193, 198–202, 262. *See also* Saint-Léonard-Anjou (Montreal) riding, MB as MP

National Health and Welfare (NHW), structure: about, 165–7, 167(t); ADMs, 167(t); corporate services, 167(t); fitness and amateur sport, 166, 167(t); intergovernmental and international affairs, 167(t); policy, planning, and information, 167(t). *See also* Health Protection (NHW); Health Services and Promotion (NHW); Income Security (NHW); Medical Research Council (MRC) (NHW); Medical Services (NHW) (for Aboriginal health); Social Services (NHW)

National Health Research and Development Program, 282–3. *See also* Health Services and Promotion (NHW)

National Indian Brotherhood (NIB), 220–1

National Revenue, Minister (1976–77): appointment, 141–3, 145–6; cabinet retreats, 147–8; charitable organiza-